The World, the Text, and the Critic

The World,

the Text,

and the Critic

Edward W. Said

Harvard University Press
Cambridge, Massachusetts

Library of Congress Cataloging in Publication Data
Said, Edward W.
  The world, the text, and the critic.
  Includes bibliographical references and index.
  1. Criticism.   2. Literature—History and criticism.   I. Title.
PN85.S27   1983   801'.95   82-11969
ISBN 0-674-96186-2 (cloth)
ISBN 0-674-96187-0 (paper)

Acknowledgments

DURING the twelve years when the contents of this book were taking shape, numerous friends and colleagues gave me the benefit of their interest. Others provided me with occasion to present my ideas in public. I am grateful to the following for their encouragement: Murray Krieger, Eugenio Donato, Hayden White, Richard Poirier, Ronald Paulson, Albert Hourani, William Spanos, Angus Fletcher, and Michael Wood. To Stanley Fish I have a long-standing debt, professional and personal. I must also record that it was Arthur Szathmary, Professor of Philosophy at Princeton University, who taught me the essentials of critical thinking; he has the affectionate gratitude of a former undergraduate student.

Some of the material in this book was first presented as lectures at various universities. I am honored to mention my particular obligation to Joseph Frank and the Christian Gauss Seminar at Princeton, Alan Roper and the Clark Memorial Library Lecture at UCLA, Richard Poirier and the Marius Bewley Lecture at Rutgers University. Earlier versions of some essays were published by these organizations and journals, to whom I express my appreciation: *Boundary 2, Bulletin of the Midwest MLA*, Columbia University Press, *Contemporary Literature, Critical Inquiry, Daedalus, Eighteenth-Century Studies*, Harvard English Studies, *Novel, Raritan Review*, and Undena Publications. The essays have all been revised to some degree for this book.

Completion of the manuscript was made possible by a generous fellowship from the National Endowment of the Humanities and a sabbatical leave from Columbia University. Eric Burns helped me a great deal in the preparation of the manuscript. To the admirable

Maud Wilcox of Harvard University Press I must express the gratitude of an author much indulged and much forgiven. And to Joyce Backman of the Press, who edited my first book, I am indebted for her wit, intelligence, and superb editorial skills.

E.W.S.

New York

June 1982

Contents

Introduction:
Secular Criticism

LITERARY criticism is practiced today in four major forms. One is the practical criticism to be found in book reviewing and literary journalism. Second is academic literary history, which is a descendant of such nineteenth-century specialties as classical scholarship, philology, and cultural history. Third is literary appreciation and interpretation, principally academic but, unlike the other two, not confined to professionals and regularly appearing authors. Appreciation is what is taught and performed by teachers of literature in the university and its beneficiaries in a literal sense are all those millions of people who have learned in a classroom how to read a poem, how to enjoy the complexity of a metaphysical conceit, how to think of literature and figurative language as having characteristics that are unique and not reducible to a simple moral or political message. And the fourth form is literary theory, a relatively new subject. It appeared as an eye-catching topic for academic and popular discussion in the United States later than it did in Europe: people like Walter Benjamin and the young Georg Lukacs, for instance, did their theoretical work in the early years of this century, and they wrote in a known, if not universally uncontested, idiom. American literary theory, despite the pioneering studies of Kenneth Burke well before World War Two, came of age only in the 1970s, and that because of an observably deliberate attention to prior European models (structuralism, semiotics, deconstruction).

The essays collected in this book derive from all four forms, even if the realms of journalistic book reviewing and classroom literary appreciation are not directly represented. But the fact is that my activities during the twelve years (1969–1981) when these essays were

1

written involved me in all four varieties of literary critical practice. That of course is an ordinary enough thing, and true of most literary critics today. But if what in this volume I call criticism or critical consciousness has any contribution to make, it is in the attempt to go beyond the four forms as defined above. And this effort (if not its success) characterizes the critical work undertaken in these essays over and above the occasions and the conventions to which they are indebted.

Now the prevailing situation of criticism is such that the four forms represent in each instance specialization (although literary theory is a bit eccentric) and a very precise division of intellectual labor. Moreover, it is supposed that literature and the humanities exist generally within the culture ("our" culture, as it is sometimes known), that the culture is ennobled and validated by them, and yet that in the version of culture inculcated by professional humanists and literary critics, the approved practice of high culture is marginal to the serious political concerns of society.

This has given rise to a cult of professional expertise whose effect in general is pernicious. For the intellectual class, expertise has usually been a service rendered, and sold, to the central authority of society. This is the *trahison des clercs* of which Julien Benda spoke in the 1920s. Expertise in foreign affairs, for example, has usually meant legitimization of the conduct of foreign policy and, what is more to the point, a sustained investment in revalidating the role of experts in foreign affairs.[1] The same sort of thing is true of literary critics and professional humanists, except that their expertise is based upon noninterference in what Vico grandly calls the world of nations but which prosaically might just as well be called "the world." We tell our students and our general constituency that we defend the classics, the virtues of a liberal education, and the precious pleasures of literature even as we also show ourselves to be silent (perhaps incompetent) about the historical and social world in which all these things take place.

The degree to which the cultural realm and its expertise are institutionally divorced from their real connections with power was wonderfully illustrated for me by an exchange with an old college friend who worked in the Department of Defense for a period during the Vietnam war. The bombings were in full course then, and I was naively trying to understand the kind of person who could order daily B-52 strikes over a distant Asian country in the name of the American interest in defending freedom and stopping communism. "You know," my friend said, "the Secretary is a complex human being: he doesn't fit the picture you may have formed of the cold-blooded imperialist murderer. The last time I was in his office I noticed Durrell's *Alexandria Quartet* on his desk." He paused meaningfully, as if to let Durrell's presence on that desk work its awful power alone. The further implication of my friend's story was that no one who read and presumably appreciated a novel could be the cold-blooded butcher one might suppose him to have been.[2] Many years later this whole implausible anecdote (I do not remember my response to the complex conjunction of Durrell with the ordering of bombing in the sixties) strikes me as typical of what actually obtains: humanists and intellectuals accept the idea that you can read classy fiction as well as kill and maim because the cultural world is available for that particular sort of camouflaging, and because cultural types are not supposed to interfere in matters for which the social system has not certified them. What the anecdote illustrates is the approved separation of high-level bureaucrat from the reader of novels of questionable worth and definite status.

During the late 1960s, however, literary theory presented itself with new claims. The intellectual origins of literary theory in Europe were, I think it is accurate to say, insurrectionary. The traditional university, the hegemony of determinism and positivism, the reification of ideological bourgeois "humanism," the rigid barriers between academic specialties: it was powerful responses to all these that linked together such influential progenitors of today's literary theorist as Saussure, Lukacs, Bataille, Lévi-Strauss, Freud, Nietzsche, and Marx. Theory proposed itself as a synthesis overriding the petty fiefdoms within the world of intellectual production, and it was manifestly to be hoped as a result that all the domains of human activity could be seen, and lived, as a unity.

And yet something happened, perhaps inevitably. From being a bold interventionary movement across lines of specialization, American literary theory of the late seventies had retreated into the labyrinth of "textuality," dragging along with it the most recent apostles of European revolutionary textuality—Derrida and Foucault—whose trans-Atlantic canonization and domestication they themselves seemed sadly enough to be encouraging. It is not too much to say that American or even European literary theory now explicitly accepts the principle of noninterference, and that its peculiar mode of appropriating its subject matter (to use Althusser's formula) is *not* to appropriate anything that is worldly, circumstantial, or socially contaminated. "Textuality" is the somewhat mystical and disinfected subject matter of literary theory.

Textuality has therefore become the exact antithesis and displacement of what might be called history. Textuality is considered to take place, yes, but by the same token it does not take place anywhere or anytime in particular. It is produced, but by no one and at no time. It can be read and interpreted, although reading and interpreting are routinely understood to occur in the form of misreading and misinterpreting. The list of examples could be extended indefinitely, but the point would remain the same. As it is practiced in the American academy today, literary theory has for the most part isolated textuality from the circumstances, the events, the physical senses that made it possible and render it intelligible as the result of human work.

Even if we accept (as in the main I do) the arguments put forward by Hayden White—that there is no way to get past texts in order to apprehend "real" history directly[3]—it is still possible to say that such a claim need not also eliminate interest in the events and the circumstances entailed by and expressed in the texts themselves. Those events and circumstances are textual too (nearly all of Conrad's tales and novels present us with a situation—say a group of friends sitting on a ship's deck listening to a story—giving rise to the narrative that forms the text), and much that goes on in texts alludes to them, *affiliates* itself directly to them. My position is that texts are worldly, to some degree they are events, and, even when they appear to deny it, they are nevertheless a part of the social world, human life, and of course the historical moments in which they are located and interpreted.

Literary theory, whether of the Left or of the Right, has turned its back on these things. This can be considered, I think, the triumph of the ethic of professionalism. But it is no accident that the emergence of so narrowly defined a philosophy of pure textuality and critical noninterference has coincided with the ascendancy of Reaganism, or for that matter with a new cold war, increased militarism and defense spending, and a massive turn to the right on matters touching the economy, social services, and organized labor.[4] In having given up the world entirely for the aporias and unthinkable paradoxes of a text, contemporary criticism has retreated from its constituency, the citizens of modern society, who have been left to the hands of "free" market forces, multinational corporations, the manipulations of consumer appetites. A precious jargon has grown up, and its formidable complexities obscure the social realities that, strange though it may seem, encourage a scholarship of "modes of excellence" very far from daily life in the age of declining American power.

Criticism can no longer cooperate in or pretend to ignore this enterprise. It is not practicing criticism either to validate the status quo or to join up with a priestly caste of acolytes and dogmatic metaphysicians. Each essay in this book affirms the connection between texts and the existential actualities of human life, politics, societies, and events. The realities of power and authority—as well as the resistances offered by men, women, and social movements to institutions, authorities, and orthodoxies—are the realities that make texts possible, that deliver them to their readers, that solicit the attention of critics. I propose that these realities are what should be taken account of by criticism and the critical consciousness.

It should be evident by now that this sort of criticism can only be practiced outside and beyond the consensus ruling the art today in the four accepted forms I mentioned earlier. Yet if this is the function of criticism at the present time, to be between the dominant culture and the totalizing forms of critical systems, then there is some comfort in recalling that this has also been the destiny of critical consciousness in the recent past.

NO reader of Erich Auerbach's *Mimesis*, one of the most admired and influential books of literary criticism ever written, has failed to be impressed by the circumstances of the book's actual writing. These are referred to almost casually by Auerbach in the last lines of his epilogue, which stands as a very brief methodological explanation for what is after all a monumental work of literary intelligence. In remarking that for so ambitious a study as "the representation of reality in Western Literature" he could not deal with everything that had been written in and about Western literature, Auerbach then adds:

> I may also mention that the book was written during the war and at Istanbul, where the libraries are not equipped for European studies. International communications were impeded; I had to dispense with almost all periodicals, with almost all the more recent investigations, and in some cases with reliable critical editions of my texts. Hence it is possible and even probable that I overlooked things which I ought to have considered and that I occasionally assert something that modern research has disproved or modified . . . On the other hand, it is quite possible that the book owes its existence to just this lack of a rich and specialized library. If it had been possible for me to acquaint myself

with all the work that has been done on so many subjects, I
might never have reached the point of writing.[5]

The drama of this little bit of modesty is considerable, in part because
Auerbach's quiet tone conceals much of the pain of his exile. He was
a Jewish refugee from Nazi Europe, and he was also a European
scholar in the old tradition of German Romance scholarship. Yet now
in Istanbul he was hopelessly out of touch with the literary, cultural,
and political bases of that formidable tradition. In writing *Mimesis*,
he implies to us in a later work, he was not merely practicing his profession despite adversity: he was performing an act of cultural, even
civilizational, survival of the highest importance. What he had risked
was not only the possibility of appearing in his writing to be superficial, out of date, wrong, and ridiculously ambitious (who in his right
mind would take on as a project so vast a subject as Western literature
in its entirety?). He had also risked, on the other hand, the possibility
of *not* writing and thus falling victim to the concrete dangers of exile:
the loss of texts, traditions, continuities that make up the very web of
a culture. And in so losing the authentic presence of the culture, as
symbolized materially by libraries, research institutes, other books
and scholars, the exiled European would become an exorbitantly dis-
oriented outcast from sense, nation, and milieu.

That Auerbach should choose to mention Istanbul as the place of
his exile adds yet another dose of drama to the actual fact of *Mimesis*.
To any European trained principally, as Auerbach was, in medieval
and renaissance Roman literatures, Istanbul does not simply connote
a place outside Europe. Istanbul represents the terrible Turk, as well
as Islam, the scourge of Christendom, the great Oriental apostasy in-
carnate. Throughout the classical period of European culture Turkey
was the Orient, Islam its most redoubtable and aggressive representative.[6] This was not all, though. The Orient and Islam also stood for
the ultimate alienation from and opposition to Europe, the European
tradition of Christian Latinity, as well as to the putative authority of
ecclesia, humanistic learning, and cultural community. For centuries
Turkey and Islam hung over Europe like a gigantic composite monster, seeming to threaten Europe with destruction. To have been an
exile in Istanbul at that time of fascism in Europe was a deeply res-
onating and intense form of exile from Europe.

Yet Auerbach explicitly makes the point that it was precisely his
distance from home—in all senses of that word—that made possible
the superb undertaking of *Mimesis*. How did exile become converted

from a challenge or a risk, or even from an active impingement on his European selfhood, into a positive mission, whose success would be a cultural act of great importance?

The answer to this question is to be found in Auerbach's autumnal essay "Philologie der Weltliteratur." The major part of the essay elaborates on the notion first explicitly announced in *Mimesis,* but already recognizable in Auerbach's early interest in Vico, that philological work deals with humanity at large and transcends national boundaries. As he says, "our philological home is the earth: it can no longer be the nation." His essay makes clear, however, that his earthly home is European culture. But then, as if remembering the period of his extra-European exile in the Orient, he adds: "The most priceless and indispensable part of a philologist's heritage is still his own nation's culture and heritage. Only when he is first separated from this heritage, however, and then transcends it does it become truly effective."[7] In order to stress the salutary value of separation from home, Auerbach cites a passage from Hugo of St. Victor's *Didascalicon:*

> It is, therefore, a great source of virtue for the practiced mind to learn, bit by bit, first to change about in visible and transitory things, so that afterwards it may be able to leave them behind altogether. The man who finds his homeland sweet is still a tender beginner; he to whom every soil is as his native one is already strong; but he is perfect to whom the entire world is as a foreign land [the Latin text is more explicit here—*perfectus vero cui mundus totus exilium est*].

This is all that Auerbach quotes from Hugo; the rest of the passage continues along the same lines.

> The tender soul has fixed his love on one spot in the world; the strong man has extended his love to all places; the perfect man has extinguished his. From boyhood I have dwelt on foreign soil, and I know with what grief sometimes the mind takes leave of the narrow hearth of a peasant's hut, and I know, too, how frankly it afterwards disdains marble firesides and panelled halls.[8]

Auerbach associates Hugo's exilic credo with the notions of *paupertas* and *terra aliena,* even though in his essay's final words he maintains that the ascetic code of willed homelessness is "a good way also for one who wishes to earn a proper love for the world." At this point, then, Auerbach's epilogue to *Mimesis* suddenly becomes clear: "it is quite possible that the book owes its existence to just this lack of a rich and specialized library." In other words, the book owed its existence to the very fact of Oriental, non-Occidental exile and homelessness. And if this is so, then *Mimesis* itself is not, as it has so frequently been taken to be, only a massive reaffirmation of the Western cultural tradition, but also a work built upon a critically important alienation from it, a work whose conditions and circumstances of existence are not immediately derived from the culture it describes with such extraordinary insight and brilliance but built rather on an agonizing distance from it. Auerbach says as much when he tells us in an earlier section of *Mimesis* that, had he tried to do a thorough scholarly job in the traditional fashion, he could never have written the book: the culture itself, with its authoritative and authorizing agencies, would have prevented so audacious a one-man task. Hence the executive value of exile, which Auerbach was able to turn into effective use.

Let us look again at the notion of place, the notion by which during a period of displacement someone like Auerbach in Istanbul could feel himself to be out of place, exiled, alienated. The readiest account of place might define it as the nation, and certainly in the exaggerated boundary drawn between Europe and the Orient—a boundary with a long and often unfortunate tradition in European thought[9]—the idea of the nation, of a national-cultural community as a sovereign entity and place set against other places, has its fullest realization. But this idea of place does not cover the nuances, principally of reassurance, fitness, belonging, association, and community, entailed in the phrase *at home* or *in place*. In this book I shall use the word *culture* to suggest an environment, process, and hegemony in which individuals (in their private circumstances) and their works are embedded, as well as overseen at the top by a superstructure and at the base by a whole series of methodological attitudes. It is in culture that we can seek out the range of meanings and ideas conveyed by the phrases *belonging to* or *in a* place, being *at home in a place*.

The idea of culture of course is a vast one. As a systematic body of social and political as well as historical significance, "culture" is similarly vast; one index of it is the Kroeber-Kluckhohn thesaurus on meanings of the word "culture" in social science.[10] I shall avoid the details of these proliferating meanings, however, and go straight to what I think can best serve my purposes here. In the first place, culture is used to designate not merely something to which one belongs but something that one possesses and, along with that proprietary process, culture also designates a boundary by which the concepts of what is extrinsic or intrinsic to the culture come into forceful play. These things are not controversial: most people employing *culture* would assent to them, as Auerbach does in the epilogue when he speaks of being in Istanbul, away from his habitual cultural environment, within its research materials and familiar environment.

But, in the second place, there is a more interesting dimension to this idea of culture as possessing possession. And that is the power of culture by virtue of its elevated or superior position to authorize, to dominate, to legitimate, demote, interdict, and validate: in short, the power of culture to be an agent of, and perhaps the main agency for, powerful differentiation within its domain and beyond it too. It is this idea that is evident in French Orientalism, for example, as distinguished from English Orientalism, and this in turn plays a major role in the work of Ernest Renan, Louis Massignon, and Raymond Schwab, major scholars whose work is assessed in the last part of this book.

When Auerbach speaks of not being able to write such a book as *Mimesis* had he remained in Europe, he refers precisely to that grid of research techniques and ethics by which the prevailing culture imposes on the individual scholar its canons of how literary scholarship is to be conducted. Yet even this sort of imposition is a minor aspect of culture's power to dominate and authorize work. What is more important in culture is that it is a system of values *saturating* downward almost everything within its purview; yet, paradoxically, culture dominates from above without at the same time being available to everything and everyone it dominates. In fact, in our age of media-produced attitudes, the ideological insistence of a culture drawing attention to itself as superior has given way to a culture whose canons and standards are invisible to the degree that they are "natural," "objective," and "real."

Historically one supposes that culture has always involved hierarchies; it has separated the elite from the popular, the best from the less than best, and so forth. It has also made certain styles and modes of thought prevail over others. But its tendency has always been to move downward from the height of power and privilege in order to diffuse, disseminate, and expand itself in the widest possible range. In its beneficent form this is the culture of which Matthew Arnold speaks in *Culture and Anarchy* as stimulating in its adherents a powerful zeal:

The great men of culture are those who have had a passion for
diffusing, for making prevail, for carrying from one end of society to the other, the best knowledge, the best ideas of their
time; who have laboured to divest knowledge of all that was
harsh, uncouth, difficult, abstract, professional, exclusive; to hu-
manise it, to make it efficient outside the clique of the cultivated
and learned, yet still remaining the *best* knowledge and thought
of the time [Arnold's definition of culture of course] and a true
source, therefore, of sweetness and light.[11]

The question raised by Arnold's passion for culture here is the relationship between culture and society. He argues that society is the
actual, material base over which culture tries, through the great men
of culture, to extend its sway. The optimum relationship between
culture and society then is *correspondence*, the former covering the
latter. What is too often overlooked by Arnold's readers is that he
views this ambition of culture to reign over society as essentially
combative: "the best that is known and thought" must contend with
competing ideologies, philosophies, dogmas, notions, and values, and
it is Arnold's insight that what is at stake in society is not merely the
cultivation of individuals, or the development of a class of finely tuned
sensibilities, or the renaissance of interest in the classics, but rather
the assertively achieved and *won* hegemony of an identifiable set of
ideas, which Arnold honorifically calls culture, over all other ideas in
society.

Yet it is still pertinent to ask Arnold where this struggle for
hegemony takes place. If we say "in society" we will approach the answer, I think, but we will still have to specify *where* in society. In
other words, Arnold's attention is to society defined grossly as, let us
say, a nation—England, France, Germany—but more interestingly
he seems also to be viewing society as a process and perhaps also an
entity capable of being guided, controlled, even taken over. What Arnold always understood is that to be able to set a force or a system of
ideas called "culture" over society is to have understood that the
stakes played for are an identification of society with culture, and
consequently the acquisition of a very formidable power. It is no accident that in his conclusion to *Culture and Anarchy* Arnold resolutely
identifies a triumphant culture with the State, insofar as culture is
man's best self and the State its realization in material reality. Thus
the power of culture is potentially nothing less than the power of the
State: Arnold is unambiguous on this point. He tells first of his unqualified opposition to such things as strikes and demonstrations, no

matter how noble the cause, and then goes on to prove that such "anarchy" as strikes and demonstrations challenge the authority of the State, which is what morally, politically, and aesthetically they are:

> Because a State in which law is authoritative and sovereign, a firm and settled course of public order, is requisite if man is to bring to maturity anything precious and lasting now, or to found anything precious and lasting for the future.
> Thus in our eyes, the very framework and exterior order of the State, whoever may administer the State, is sacred; and culture is the most resolute enemy of anarchy, because of the great hopes and designs for the State which culture teaches us to nourish.[12]

The interdependence in Arnold's mind between culture, the sustained suzerainty of culture over society (anything precious and lasting), and the framework and quasi-theological exterior order of the State is perfectly clear. And it signifies a coincidence of power, which Arnold's entire rhetoric and thought constantly elaborates. To be for and in culture is to be in and for a State in a compellingly loyal way. With this assimilation of culture to the authority and exterior framework of the State go as well such things as assurance, confidence, the majority sense, the entire matrix of meanings we associate with "home," belonging and community. Outside this range of meanings—for it is the outside that partially defines the inside in this case—stand anarchy, the culturally disfranchised, those elements opposed to culture and State: the homeless, in short.

It is not my intention here to discuss in detail the profoundly important implications of Arnold's concluding remarks on culture. But it is worth insisting on at least a few of those implications in a broader setting than Arnold's. Even as an ideal for Arnold, culture must be seen as much for what it is not and for what it triumphs over when it is consecrated by the State as for what it positively is. This means that culture is a system of discriminations and evaluations—perhaps mainly aesthetic, as Lionel Trilling has said, but no less forceful and tyrannical for that[13]—for a particular class in the State able to identify with it; and it also means that culture is a system of exclusions legislated from above but enacted throughout its polity, by which such things as anarchy, disorder, irrationality, inferiority, bad taste, and immorality are identified, then deposited outside the culture and kept there by the power of the State and its institutions. For if it is true that culture is, on the one hand, a positive doctrine of the best

that is thought and known, it is also on the other a differentially negative doctrine of all that is not best. If with Michel Foucault we have
learned to see culture as an institutionalized process by which what is
considered appropriate to it is kept appropriate, we have also seen
Foucault demonstrating how certain alterities, certain Others, have
been kept silent, outside or—in the case of his study of penal discipline and sexual repression—domesticated for use inside the culture.

Even if we wish to contest Foucault's findings about the exclusions
by classical European culture of what it constituted as insane or irrational, and even if we are not convinced that the culture's paradoxical
encouragement and repression of sexuality has been as generalized as
he believes, we cannot fail to be convinced that the dialectic of self-
fortification and self-confirmation by which culture achieves its hegemony over society and the State is based on a constantly practiced
differentiation of itself from what it believes to be not itself. And this
differentiation is frequently performed by setting the valorized culture over the Other. This is by no means a metaphysical point, as two
nineteenth-century English examples will demonstrate quickly. Both
are related to the point I made earlier about Auerbach, that culture
often has to do with an aggressive sense of nation, home, community,
and belonging. First there is Macaulay's famous Minute of 1835 on
Indian education:

> I have no knowledge of either Sanskrit or Arabic. But I have
> done what I could to form a correct estimate of their value. I
> have read translations of the most celebrated Arabic and
> Sanskrit works. I have conversed, both here and at home, with
> men distinguished by their proficiency in the Eastern tongues. I
> am quite ready to take the oriental learning at the valuation of
> the orientalists themselves. I have never found one among them
> who could deny that a single shelf of a good European library
> was worth the whole native literature of India and Arabia. The
> intrinsic superiority of the Western literature is indeed fully ad-
> mitted by those members of the committee who support the ori-
> ental plan of education . . . It is, I believe, no exaggeration to say
> that all the historical information which has been collected in the
> Sanskrit language is less valuable than what may be found in the
> paltry abridgements used at preparatory schools in England. In
> every branch of physical or moral philosophy, the relative posi-
> tion of the two nations is nearly the same.[14]

This is no mere expression of an opinion. Neither can it be dismissed, as in his *Grammatology* Derrida has dismissed Lévi-Strauss,

as a textual instance of ethnocentrism. For it is that and more. Macaulay's was an ethnocentric opinion with ascertainable results. He was speaking from a position of power where he could translate his opinions into the decision to make an entire subcontinent of natives submit to studying in a language not their own. This in fact is what happened. In turn this validated the culture to itself by providing a precedent, and a case, by which superiority and power are lodged both in a rhetoric of belonging, or being "at home," so to speak, and in a rhetoric of administration: the two become interchangeable.

A second instance also concerns India. With admirable perspicacity Eric Stokes has studied the importance of utilitarian philosophy to British rule in India. What is striking in Stokes's *The English Utilitarians and India* is how a relatively small body of thinkers—among them Bentham, of course, and both Mills—were able to argue and implement a philosophic doctrine for India's governance, a doctrine in some respects bearing an unmistakable resemblance to Arnold's and Macaulay's views of European culture as superior to all others. John Stuart Mill among the India House Utilitarians has today a higher cultural status, so much so that his views on liberty and representative government have for generations passed as the advanced liberal cultural statement on these matters. Yet of Mill, Stokes has this to say: "In his essay *On Liberty* John Stuart Mill had carefully stated that its doctrines were only meant to apply to those countries which were sufficiently advanced in civilization to be capable of settling their affairs by rational discussion. He was faithful to his father in holding to the belief that India could still be governed only despotically. But although he himself refused to apply the teachings of *Liberty* or *Representative Government* to India, a few Radical Liberals and a growing body of educated Indians made no such limitations."[15] A quick glance at the last chapter of *Representative Government*—to say nothing of the passage in the third volume of *Dissertations and Discussions* where he speaks of the absence of rights for barbarians—makes absolutely clear Mill's view that what he has to say about the matter cannot really apply to India, mainly because in his culture's judgment India's civilization has not attained the requisite degree of development.

The entire history of nineteenth-century European thought is filled with such discriminations as these, made between what is fitting for us and what is fitting for them, the former designated as inside, in place, common, belonging, in a word *above*, the latter, who are designated as outside, excluded, aberrant, inferior, in a word *below.* From these distinctions, which were given their hegemony by the culture, no one could be free, not even Marx—as a reading of his articles on India and the Orient will immediately reveal.[16] The large cultural-national designation of European culture as the privileged norm carried with it a formidable battery of other distinctions between ours and theirs, between proper and improper, European and non-European, higher and lower: they are to be found everywhere in such subjects and quasi-subjects as linguistics, history, race theory, philosophy, anthropology, and even biology. But my main reason for mentioning them here is to suggest how in the transmission and persistence of a culture there is a continual process of reinforcement, by which the hegemonic culture will add to itself the prerogatives given it by its sense of national identity, its power as an implement, ally, or branch of the state, its rightness, its exterior forms and assertions of itself: and most important, by its vindicated power as a victor over everything not itself.

There is no reason to doubt that all cultures operate in this way or to doubt that on the whole they tend to be successful in enforcing their hegemony. They do this in different ways, obviously, and I think it is true that some tend to be more efficient than others, particularly when it comes to certain kinds of police activities. But this is a topic for comparative anthropologists and not one about which broad generalizations should be risked here. I am interested, however, in noting that if culture exerts the kinds of pressure I have mentioned, and if it creates the environment and the community that allows people to feel they belong, then it must be true that resistance to the culture has always been present. Often that resistance takes the form of outright hostility for religious, social, or political reasons (one aspect of this is well described by Eric Hobsbawm in *Primitive Rebels*). Often it has come from individuals or groups declared out of bounds or inferior by the culture (here of course the range is vast, from the ritual scapegoat to the lonely prophet, from the social pariah to the visionary artist, from the working class to the alienated intellectual). But there is some very compelling truth to Julien Benda's contention that in one way or the other it has often been the intellectual, the *clerc*, who has stood for values, ideas, and activities that transcend and deliberately interfere with the collective weight imposed by the nation-state and the national culture.

Certainly what Benda says about intellectuals (who, in ways specific to the intellectual vocation itself, are responsible for defiance) resonates harmoniously with the personality of Socrates as it emerges in Plato's *Dialogues,* or with Voltaire's opposition to the Church, or more recently with Gramsci's notion of the organic intellectual allied with an emergent class against ruling-class hegemony. Even Arnold speaks of "aliens" in *Culture and Anarchy,* "persons who are mainly led, not by their class spirit, but by a general humane spirit," which he connects directly with ideal culture and not, it would appear, with that culture he was later to identify with the State. Benda is surely wrong, on the other hand, to ascribe so much social power to the solitary intellectual whose authority, according to Benda, comes from his individual voice and from his opposition to organized collective passions. Yet if we allow that it has been the historical fate of such collective sentiments as "my country right or wrong" and "we are whites and therefore belong to a higher race than blacks" and "European or Islamic or Hindu culture is superior to all others" to coarsen and brutalize the individual, then it is probably true that an isolated individual consciousness, going against the surrounding environment as well as allied to contesting classes, movements, and values, is an isolated voice out of place but very much *of* that place, standing consciously against the prevailing orthodoxy and very much for a professedly universal or humane set of values, which has provided significant local resistance to the hegemony of one culture. It is also the case, both Benda and Gramsci agree, that intellectuals are eminently useful in making hegemony work. For Benda this of course is the *trahison des clercs* in its essence; their unseemly participation in the perfection of political passions is what he thinks is dispiritingly the very essence of their contemporary mass sellout. For Gramsci's more complex mind, individual intellectuals like Croce were to be studied (perhaps even envied) for making their ideas seem as if they were expressions of a collective will.

All this, then, shows us the individual consciousness placed at a sensitive nodal point, and it is this consciousness at that critical point which this book attempts to explore in the form of what I call *criticism.* On the one hand, the individual mind registers and is very much aware of the collective whole, context, or situation in which it finds itself. On the other hand, precisely because of this awareness—a worldly self-situating, a sensitive response to the dominant culture—that the individual consciousness is not naturally and easily a mere child of the culture, but a historical and social actor in it. And because of that perspective, which introduces circumstance and distinction where there had only been conformity and belonging, there is distance, or what we might also call criticism. A knowledge of history, a recognition of the importance of social circumstance, an analytical capacity for making distinctions: these trouble the quasi-religious authority of being comfortably at home among one's people, supported by known powers and acceptable values, protected against the outside world.

But to repeat: the critical consciousness is a part of its actual social world and of the literal body that the consciousness inhabits, not by any means an escape from either one or the other. Although as I characterized him, Auerbach was away from Europe, his work is steeped in the reality of Europe, just as the specific circumstances of his exile enabled a concrete critical recovery of Europe. We have in Auerbach an instance both of filiation with his natal culture and, because of exile, *affiliation* with it through critical consciousness and scholarly work. We must look more closely now at the cooperation between filiation and affiliation that is located at the heart of critical consciousness.

RELATIONSHIPS of filiation and affiliation are plentiful in modern cultural history. One very strong three-part pattern, for example, originates in a large group of late nineteenth- and early twentieth-century writers, in which the failure of the generative impulse—the failure of the capacity to produce or generate children—is portrayed in such a way as to stand for a general condition afflicting society and culture together, to say nothing of individual men and women. *Ulysses* and *The Waste Land* are two especially well-known instances, but there is similar evidence to be found in *Death in Venice* or *The Way of All Flesh, Jude the Obscure, À la recherche du temps perdu*, Mallarmé's and Hopkins' poetry, much of Wilde's writing, and *Nostromo*. If we add to this list the immensely authoritative weight of Freud's psychoanalytic theory, a significant and influential aspect of which posits the potentially murderous outcome of bearing children, we will have the unmistakable impression that few things are as problematic and as universally fraught as what we might have supposed to be the mere natural continuity between one generation and the next. Even in a great work that belongs intellectually and politically to another universe of discourse—Lukacs' *History and Class Consciousness*—there is much the same thesis being advanced about the difficulties and ultimately the impossibility of natural filiation: for, Lukacs says, reification is the alienation of men from what they have produced, and it is the starkly uncompromising severity of his vision that he means by this all the products of human labor, children included, which are so completely separated from each other, atomized, and hence frozen into the category of ontological objects as to make even natural relationships virtually impossible.

Childless couples, orphaned children, aborted childbirths, and unregenerately celibate men and women populate the world of high modernism with remarkable insistence, all of them suggesting the difficulties of filiation.[17] But no less important in my opinion is the second part of the pattern, which is immediately consequent upon the first, the pressure to produce new and different ways of conceiving human relationships. For if biological reproduction is either too difficult or too unpleasant, is there some other way by which men and women can create social bonds between each other that would substitute for those ties that connect members of the same family across generations?

A typical answer is provided by T. S. Eliot during the period right after the appearance of *The Waste Land.* His model now is Lancelot Andrewes, a man whose prose and devotional style seem to Eliot to have transcended the personal manner of even so fervent and effective a Christian preacher as Donne. In the shift from Donne to Andrewes, which I believe underlies the shift in Eliot's sensibility from the world-view of *Prufrock, Gerontion,* and *The Waste Land* to the conversion poetry of *Ash Wednesday* and the *Ariel Poems,* we have Eliot saying something like the following: the aridity, wastefulness, and sterility of modern life make filiation an unreasonable alternative at least, an unattainable one at most. One cannot think about continuity in biological terms, a proposition that may have had urgent corroboration in the recent failure of Eliot's first marriage but to which Eliot's mind gave a far wider application.[18] The only other alternatives seemed to be provided by institutions, associations, and communities whose social existence was not in fact guaranteed by biology, but by affiliation. Thus according to Eliot Lancelot Andrewes conveys in his writing the enfolding presence of the English church, "something representative of the finest spirit of England of the time [and] . . . a masterpiece of ecclesiastical statesmanship." With Hooker, then, Andrewes invoked an authority beyond simple Protestantism. Both men were

on terms of equality with their Continental antagonists and [were able] to elevate their Church above the position of a local

heretical sect. They were fathers of a national Church and they
were Europeans. Compare a sermon of Andrewes with a sermon
by another earlier master, Latimer. It is not merely that Andrewes knew Greek, or that Latimer was addressing a far less
cultivated public, or that the sermons of Andrewes are peppered
with allusion and quotation. It is rather that Latimer, the
preacher of Henry VIII and Edward VI, is merely a Protestant;
but the voice of Andrewes is the voice of a man who has a
formed visible Church behind him, who speaks with the old authority and the new culture.[19]

Eliot's reference to Hooker and Andrewes is figurative, but it is
meant with a quite literal force, just as that second "merely" (Latimer is merely a Protestant) is an assertion by Eliot of "the old authority and the new culture." If the English church is not in a direct
line of filiation stemming from the Roman church, it is nevertheless
something more than a mere local heresy, more than a mere protesting orphan. Why? Because Andrewes and others like him to whose
antecedent authority Eliot has now subscribed were able to harness
the old paternal authority to an insurgent Protestant and national
culture, thereby creating a new institution based not on direct genealogical descent but on what we may call, barbarously, *horizontal affiliation*. According to Eliot, Andrewes' language does not simply
express the anguished distance from an originating but now unrecov-
erable father that a protesting orphan might feel; on the contrary, it
converts that language into the expression of an emerging affiliative
corporation—the English church—which commands the respect and
the attention of its adherents.

In Eliot's poetry much the same change occurs. The speakers of
Prufrock and *Gerontion* as well as the characters of *The Waste Land*
directly express the plight of orphanhood and alienation, whereas the
personae of *Ash Wednesday* and *Four Quartets* speak the common
language of other communicants within the English church. For Eliot
the church stands in for the lost family mourned throughout his earlier poetry. And of course the shift is publicly completed in *After
Strange Gods* whose almost belligerent announcement of a credo of
royalism, classicism, and catholicism form a set of affiliations
achieved by Eliot outside the filial (republican, romantic, protestant)
pattern given him by the facts of his American (and outlandish)
birth.

The turn from filiation to affiliation is to be found elsewhere in the
culture and embodies what Georg Simmel calls the modern cultural

process by which life "incessantly generates forms for itself," forms that, once they appear, "demand a validity which transcends the moment, and is emancipated from the pulse of life. For this reason, life is always in a latent opposition to the form."[20] One thinks of Yeats going from the blandishments of "the honey of generation" to the Presences who are "self-born mockers of man's enterprise," which he set down in *A Vision* according to a spacious affiliative order he invented for himself and his work. Or, as Ian Watt has said about Conrad's contemporaries, writers like Lawrence, Joyce, and Pound, who present us with "the breaking of ties with family, home, class, country, and traditional beliefs as necessary stages in the achievement of spiritual and intellectual freedom": these writers "then invite us to share the larger transcendental [affiliative] or private systems of order and value which they have adopted and invented."[21] In his best work Conrad shows us the futility of such private systems of order and value (say the utopian world created by Charles and Amelia Gould in *Nostromo*), but no less than his contemporaries he too took on in his own life (as did Eliot and Henry James) the adopted identity of an emigré-turned-English-gentleman. On the other side of the spectrum we find Lukacs suggesting that only class consciousness, itself an insurrectionary form of an attempt at affiliation, could possibly break through the antinomies and atomizations of reified existence in the modern capitalist world-order.

What I am describing is the transition from a failed idea or possibility of filiation to a kind of compensatory order that, whether it is a party, an institution, a culture, a set of beliefs, or even a world-vision, provides men and women with a new form of relationship, which I have been calling affiliation but which is also a new system. Now whether we look at this new affiliative mode of relationship as it is to be found among conservative writers like Eliot or among progressive writers like Lukacs and, in his own special way, Freud, we will find the deliberately explicit goal of using that new order to reinstate vestiges of the kind of authority associated in the past with filiative order. This, finally, is the third part of the pattern. Freud's psychoanalytic guild and Lukacs' notion of the vanguard party are no less providers of what we might call a restored authority. The new hierarchy or, if it is less a hierarchy than a community, the new community is greater than the individual adherent or member, just as the father is greater by virtue of seniority than the sons and daughters; the ideas, the values, and the systematic totalizing world-view validated by the new affiliative order are all bearers of authority too, with the result that something resembling a cultural system is established. Thus if a filial relationship was held together by natural bonds and natural forms of authority—involving obedience, fear, love, respect, and instinctual conflict—the new affiliative relationship changes these bonds into what seem to be transpersonal forms—such as guild consciousness, consensus, collegiality, professional respect, class, and the hegemony of a dominant culture. The filiative scheme belongs to the realms of nature and of "life," whereas affiliation belongs exclusively to culture and society.

It is worth saying incidentally that what an estimable group of literary artists have adumbrated in the passage from filiation to affiliation parallels similar observations by sociologists and records corresponding developments in the structure of knowledge. Tönnies' notion of the shift from *Gemeinschaft* to *Gesellschaft* can easily be reconciled with the idea of filiation replaced by affiliation. Similarly, I believe, the increased dependence of the modern scholar upon the small, specialized guild of people in his or her field (as indeed the very idea of a field itself), and the notion within fields that the originating human subject is of less importance than transhuman rules and theories, accompany the transformation of naturally filiative into systematically affiliative relationships. The loss of the subject, as it has commonly been referred to, is in various ways the loss as well of the procreative, generational urge authorizing filiative relationships.

The three-part pattern I have been describing—and with it the processes of filiation and affiliation as they have been depicted—can be considered an instance of the passage from nature to culture, as well as an instance of how affiliation can easily become a system of thought no less orthodox and dominant than culture itself. What I want abruptly to talk about at this juncture are the effects of this pattern as they have affected the study of literature today, at a considerable remove from the early years of our century. The structure of literary knowledge derived from the academy is heavily imprinted with the three-part pattern I have illustrated here. This imprinting has occurred in ways that are impressive so far as critical thought (according to my notion of what it ought to be) is concerned. Let me pass directly now to concrete examples.

Ever since Eliot, and after him Richards and Leavis, there has been an almost unanimously held view that it is the duty of humanistic scholars in our culture to devote themselves to the study of the great monuments of literature. Why? So that they may be passed on to younger students, who in turn become members, by affiliation and formation, of the company of educated individuals. Thus we find the university experience more or less officially consecrating the pact between a canon of works, a band of initiate instructors, a group of younger affiliates; in a socially validated manner all this reproduces the filiative discipline supposedly transcended by the educational process. This has almost always been the case historically within what might be called the cloistral world of the traditional Western, and certainly of the Eastern, university. But we are now, I think, in a period of world history when for the first time the compensatory affiliative relationships interpreted during the academic course of study in the Western university actually exclude more than they include. I mean quite simply that, for the first time in modern history, the whole imposing edifice of humanistic knowledge resting on the classics of European letters, and with it the scholarly discipline inculcated formally into students in Western universities through the forms familiar to us all, represents only a fraction of the real human relationships and interactions now taking place in the world. Certainly Auerbach was among the last great representatives of those who believed that European culture could be viewed coherently and importantly as unquestionably central to human history. There are abundant reasons for Auerbach's view being no longer tenable, not the least of which is the diminishing acquiescence and deference accorded to what has been called the Natopolitan world long dominating peripheral regions like Africa, Asia, and Latin America. New cultures, new societies, and emerging visions of social, political, and aesthetic order now lay claim to the humanist's attention, with an insistence that cannot long be denied.

But for perfectly understandable reasons they are denied. When our students are taught such things as "the humanities" they are almost always taught that these classic texts embody, express, represent what is best in our, that is, the only, tradition. Moreover they are taught that such fields as the humanities and such subfields as "literature" exist in a relatively neutral political element, that they are to be appreciated and venerated, that they define the limits of what is acceptable, appropriate, and legitimate so far as culture is concerned. In other words, the affiliative order so presented surreptitiously duplicates the closed and tightly knit family structure that secures generational hierarchical relationships to one another. Affiliation then becomes in effect a literal form of *re-presentation*, by which what is ours is good, and therefore deserves incorporation and inclusion in our programs of humanistic study, and what is not ours in this ultimately provincial sense is simply left out. And out of this representation come the systems from Northrop Frye's to Foucault's, which claim the power to show how things work, once and for all, totally and predictively. It should go without saying that this new affiliative structure and its systems of thought more or less directly reproduce the skeleton of family authority supposedly left behind when the family was left behind. The curricular structures holding European literature departments make that perfectly obvious: the great texts, as well as the great teachers and the great theories, have an authority that compels respectful attention not so much by virtue of their content but because they are either old or they have power, they have been handed on in time or seem to have no time, and they have traditionally been revered, as priests, scientists, or efficient bureaucrats have taught.

It may seem odd, but it is true, that in such matters as culture and scholarship I am often in reasonable sympathy with conservative attitudes, and what I might object to in what I have been describing does not have much to do with the activity of conserving the past, or with reading great literature, or with doing serious and perhaps even utterly conservative scholarship as such. I have no great problem with those things. What I am criticizing is two particular assumptions. There is first the almost unconsciously held ideological assumption that the Eurocentric model for the humanities actually represents a natural and proper subject matter for the humanistic scholar. Its authority comes not only from the orthodox canon of literary monuments handed down through the generations, but also from the way this continuity reproduces the filial continuity of the chain of biological procreation. What we then have is a substitution of one sort of order for another, in the process of which everything that is nonhumanistic and nonliterary and non-European is deposited outside the structure. If we consider for a minute that most of the world today is non-European, that transactions within what the UNESCO/McBride Report calls the world information order is therefore not literary, and that the social sciences and the media (to name only two modes of cultural production in ascendancy today over the classically defined humanities) dominate the diffusion of knowledge in ways that are scarcely imaginable to the traditional humanistic scholar, then we will have some idea of how ostrichlike and retrograde assertions about Eurocentric humanities really are. The process of representation, by which filiation is reproduced in the affiliative structure and made to stand for what belongs to us (as we in turn belong to the family of our languages and traditions), reinforces the known at the expense of the knowable.

Second is the assumption that the principal relationships in the study of literature—those I have identified as based on representation—ought to obliterate the traces of other relationships within literary structures that are based principally upon acquisition and appropriation. This is the great lesson of Raymond Williams' *The Country and the City.* His extraordinarily illuminating discussion there of the seventeenth-century English country-house poems does not concentrate on what those poems represent, but on what they *are* as the result of contested social and political relationships. Descriptions of the rural mansion, for example, do not at bottom entrail only what is to be admired by way of harmony, repose, and beauty; they should also entail for the modern reader what in fact has been excluded from the poems, the labor that created the mansions, the social processes of which they are the culmination, the dispossessions and theft they actually signified. Although he does not come out and say it, Williams' book is a remarkable attempt at a dislodgement of the very ethos of system, which has reified relationships and stripped them of their social density. What he tries to put in its place is the great dialectic of acquisition and representation, by which even realism—as it is manifest in Jane Austen's novels—has gained its durable status as the result of contests involving money and power. Williams teaches us to read in a different way and to remember that for every poem or novel in the canon there is a social fact being requisitioned for the page, a human life engaged, a class suppressed or elevated—none of which can be accounted for in the framework rigidly maintained by the processes of representation and affiliation doing above-ground work for the conservation of filiation. And for every critical system grinding on there are events, heterogeneous and unorthodox social configurations, human beings and texts disputing the possibility of a sovereign methodology of system.

Everything I have said is an extrapolation from the verbal echo we hear between the words "filiation" and "affiliation." In a certain sense, what I have been trying to show is that, as it has developed through the art and critical theories produced in complex ways by modernism, filiation gives birth to affiliation. Affiliation becomes a form of representing the filiative processes to be found in nature, although affiliation takes validated nonbiological social and cultural forms. Two alternatives propose themselves for the contemporary critic. One is organic complicity with the pattern I have described.

The critic enables, indeed transacts, the transfer of legitimacy from filiation to affiliation; literally a midwife, the critic encourages reverence for the humanities and for the dominant culture served by those humanities. This keeps relationships within the narrow circle of what is natural, appropriate, and valid for "us," and thereafter excludes the nonliterary, the non-European, and above all the political dimension in which all literature, all texts, can be found. It also gives rise to a critical system or theory whose temptation for the critic is that it resolves all the problems that culture gives rise to. As John Fekete has said, this "expresses the modern disaffection for reality, but progressively incorporates and assimilates it within the categories of prevailing social (and cultural) rationality. This endows it with a double appeal, and the expanding scope of the theory, corresponding to the expanding mode of the production and reproduction of social life, gives it authority as a major ideology."[22]

The second alternative is for the critic to recognize the difference between instinctual filiation and social affiliation, and to show how affiliation sometimes reproduces filiation, sometimes makes its own forms. Immediately, then, most of the political and social world becomes available for critical and secular scrutiny, as in *Mimesis* Auerbach does not simply admire the Europe he has lost through exile but sees it anew as a composite social and historical enterprise, made and remade unceasingly by men and women in society. This secular critical consciousness can also examine those forms of writing affiliated with literature but excluded from consideration with literature as a result of the ideological capture of the literary text within the humanistic curriculum as it now stands. My analysis of recent literary theory in this book focuses on these themes in detail, especially in the way critical systems—even of the most sophisticated kind—can succumb to the inherently representative and reproductive relationship between a dominant culture and the domains it rules.

WHAT does it mean to have a critical consciousness if, as I have been trying to suggest, the intellectual's situation is a worldly one and yet, by virtue of that worldliness itself, the intellectual's social identity should involve something more than strengthening those aspects of the culture that require mere affirmation and orthodox compliancy from its members?

The whole of this book is an attempt to answer this question. My position, again, is that the contemporary critical consciousness stands between the temptations represented by two formidable and related powers engaging critical attention. One is the culture to which critics are bound filiatively (by birth, nationality, profession); the other is a method or system acquired affiliatively (by social and political conviction, economic and historical circumstances, voluntary effort and willed deliberation). Both of these powers exert pressures that have been building toward the contemporary situation for long periods of time: my interest in eighteenth-century figures like Vico and Swift, for example, is premised on their knowledge that their era also made claims on them culturally and systematically, and it was their whole enterprise therefore to resist these pressures in everything they did, albeit of course, that they were worldly writers and materially bound to their time.

As it is now practiced and as I treat it, criticism is an academic thing, located for the most part far away from the questions that trouble the reader of a daily newspaper. Up to a certain point this is as it should be. But we have reached the stage at which specialization and professionalization, allied with cultural dogma, barely sublimated ethnocentrism and nationalism, as well as a surprisingly insistent quasi-religious quietism, have transported the professional and academic critic of literature—the most focused and intensely trained interpreter of texts produced by the culture—into another world altogether. In that relatively untroubled and secluded world there seems to be no contact with the world of events and societies, which modern history, intellectuals, and critics have in fact built. Instead, contemporary criticism is an institution for publicly affirming the values of our, that is, European, dominant elite culture, and for privately setting loose the unrestrained interpretation of a universe defined in advance as the endless misreading of a misinterpretation. The result has been the regulated, not to say calculated, irrelevance of criticism, except as an adornment to what the powers of modern industrial society transact: the hegemony of militarism and a new cold war, the depoliticization of the citizenry, the overall compliance of the intellectual class to which critics belong. The situation I attempt to characterize in modern criticism (not excluding "Left" criticism) has occurred in parallel with the ascendancy of Reaganism. The role of the Left, neither repressed nor organized, has been important for its complaisance.

I do not wish to be misunderstood as saying that the flight into method and system on the part of critics who wish to avoid the ideology of humanism is altogether a bad thing. Far from it. Yet the dan-

gers of method and system are worth noting. Insofar as they become
sovereign and as their practitioners lose touch with the resistance and
the heterogeneity of civil society, they risk becoming wall-to-wall
discourses, blithely predetermining what they discuss, heedlessly
converting everything into evidence for the efficacy of the method,
carelessly ignoring the circumstances out of which all theory, system,
and method ultimately derive.

Criticism in short is always situated; it is skeptical, secular, reflec-
tively open to its own failings. This is by no means to say that it is
value-free. Quite the contrary, for the inevitable trajectory of critical
consciousness is to arrive at some acute sense of what political, social,
and human values are entailed in the reading, production, and transmission of every text. To stand between culture and system is therefore to stand *close to*—closeness itself having a particular value for
me—a concrete reality about which political, moral, and social judge-
ments have to be made and, if not only made, then exposed and demystified. If, as we have recently been told by Stanley Fish, every act
of interpretation is made possible and given force by an interpretive
community, then we must go a great deal further in showing what
situation, what historical and social configuration, what political interests are concretely entailed by the very existence of interpretive
communities.[23] This is an especially important task when these communities have evolved camouflaging jargons.

I hope it will not seem a self-serving thing to say that all of what I
mean by criticism and critical consciousness is directly reflected not
only in the subjects of these essays but in the essay form itself. For if
I am to be taken seriously as saying that secular criticism deals with
local and worldly situations, and that it is constitutively opposed to
the production of massive, hermetic systems, then it must follow that
the essay—a comparatively short, investigative, radically skeptical
form—is the principal way in which to write criticism. Certain
themes, naturally enough, recur in the essays that make up this book.
Given a relatively wide selection of topics, the book's unity, however,
is also a unity of attitude and of concern. With two exceptions, all of
the essays collected here were written during the period immediately
following the completion of my book *Beginnings: Intention and
Method*, which argued the practical and theoretical necessity of a
reasoned point of departure for any intellectual and creative job of
work, given that we exist in secular history, in the "always-already"
begun realm of continuously human effort. Thus each essay presupposes that book. Yet it is more important to point out that (again with

two exceptions) all of these essays were written as I was working on three books dealing with the history of relations between East and West: *Orientalism* (1978), *The Question of Palestine* (1979), and *Covering Islam* (1981), books whose historical and social setting is political and cultural in the most urgent way. On matters having to do with the relationship between scholarship and politics, between a specific situation and the interpretation and the production of a text, between textuality itself and social reality, the connection of some essays here to those three books will be evident enough.

The essays collected here are arranged in three interlinked ways. First I look at the worldly and secular world in which texts take place and in which certain writers (Swift, Hopkins, Conrad, Fanon) are exemplary for their attention to the detail of everyday existence defined as situation, event, and the organization of power. For the critic, the challenge of this secular world is that it is not reducible to an explanatory or originating theory, much less to a collection of cultural generalities. There are instead a small number of perhaps unexpected characteristics of worldliness that play a role in making sense of textual experience, among them filiation and affiliation, the body and the senses of sight and hearing, repetition, and the sheer heterogeneity of detail. Next I turn to the peculiar problems of contemporary critical theory as it either confronts or ignores issues raised for the study of texts (and textuality) by the secular world. Finally, I treat the problem of what happens when the culture attempts to understand, dominate, or recapture another, less powerful one.

A word is in order about the special role played by Swift in this book. There are two essays on him, both of them stressing the resistances he offers to the modern critical theorist (resistance being a matter of central relevance to my argument in this book). The reasons for this are not only that Swift cannot easily be assimilated to current ideas about "writers," "the text," or "the heroic author," but that his work is at once occasional, powerful, and—from the point of view of systematic textual practice—incoherent. To read Swift seriously is to try to apprehend a series of events in all their messy force, not to admire and then calmly to decode a string of high monuments. In addition, his own social role was that of the critic involved with, but never possessing, power: alert, forceful, undogmatic, ironic, unafraid of orthodoxies and dogmas, respectful of settled uncoercive community, anarchic in his sense of the range of alternatives to the status quo. Yet he was tragically compromised by this time and his worldly circumstances, a fact alluded to by E. P. Thompson and

Perry Anderson in their dispute over his real (progressive or reactionary) political commitments. For me he represents the critical consciousness in a raw form, a large-scale model of the dilemmas facing the contemporary critical consciousness that has tended to be too cloistered and too attracted to easy systematizing. He stands so far outside the world of contemporary critical discourse as to serve as one of its best critics, methodologically unarmed though he may have been. In its energy and unparalleled verbal wit, its restlessness, its agitational and unacademic designs on its political and social context, Swift's writing supplies modern criticism with what it has sorely needed since Arnold covered critical writing with the mantle of cultural authority and reactionary political quietism.

It is an undoubted exaggeration to say, on the other hand, that these essays make absolutely clear what my critical position—only implied by *Orientalism* and my other recent books—really is. To some this may seem like a failing of rigor, honesty, or energy. To others it may imply some radical uncertainty on my part as to what I do stand for, especially given the fact that I have been accused by colleagues of intemperate and even unseemly polemicism. To still others—and this concerns me more—it may seem that I am an undeclared Marxist, afraid of losing respectability and concerned by the contradictions entailed by the label "Marxist."

Without wishing to answer all the questions raised by these matters, I would like my views to be as clear as possible. On the question of government and foreign policy that particularly involve me, nothing more should be added here than what is said in the last four essays in this book. But on the important matter of a critical position, its relationship to Marxism, liberalism, even anarchism, it needs to be said that criticism modified in advance by labels like "Marxism" or "liberalism" is, in my view, an oxymoron. The history of thought, to say nothing of political movements, is extravagantly illustrative of how the dictum "solidarity before criticism" means the end of criticism. I take criticism so seriously as to believe that, even in the very midst of a battle in which one is unmistakably on one side against another, there should be criticism, because there must be critical consciousness if there are to be issues, problems, values, even lives to be fought for. Right now in American cultural history, "Marxism" is principally an academic, not a political, commitment. It risks becoming an academic subspeciality. As corollaries of this unfortunate truth there are also such things to be mentioned as the absence of an important socialist party (along the lines of the various European par-

ties), the marginalized discourse of "Left" writing, the seeming inca-
pacity of professional groups (scholarly, academic, regional) to organize effective Left coalitions with political-action groups. The net effect of "doing" Marxist criticism or writing at the present time is of
course to declare political preference, but it is also to put oneself outside a great deal of things going on in the world, so to speak, and in
other kinds of criticism.

Perhaps a simpler way of expressing all this is to say that I have
been more influenced by Marxists than by Marxism or any other *ism.*
If the arguments going on within twentieth-century Marxism have
had any meaning, it is this: as much as any discourse, Marxism is in
need of systematic decoding, demystifying, rigorous clarification.
Here the work of non-Marxist radicals (Chomsky's, say, or I. F.
Stone's) is valuable, especially if the doctrinal walls keeping out non-
members have not been put up to begin with. The same is true of
criticism deriving from a profoundly conservative outlook, Auerbach's own, for example; at its best, this work also teaches us how to
be critical, rather than how to be good members of a school. The positive uses of affiliation are many after all, which is not to say that authoritarianism and orthodoxy are any less dangerous.

Were I to use one word consistently along with *criticism* (not as a
modification but as an emphatic) it would be *oppositional.* If criticism is reducible neither to a doctrine nor to a political position on a
particular question, and if it is to be in the world and self-aware simultaneously, then its identity is its difference from other cultural activities and from systems of thought or of method. In its suspicion of
totalizing concepts, in its discontent with reified objects, in its impa-
tience with guilds, special interests, imperialized fiefdoms, and orthodox habits of mind, criticism is most itself and, if the paradox can be
tolerated, most unlike itself at the moment it starts turning into organized dogma. "Ironic" is not a bad word to use along with "oppositional." For in the main—and here I shall be explicit—criticism must
think of itself as life-enhancing and constitutively opposed to every
form of tyranny, domination, and abuse; its social goals are noncoercive knowledge produced in the interests of human freedom. If we
agree with Raymond Williams, "that however dominant a social system may be, the very meaning of its domination involves a limitation
or selection of the activities it covers, so that by definition it cannot
exhaust all social experience, which therefore always potentially contains space for alternative acts and alternative intentions which are
not yet articulated as a social institution or even project,"[24] then criti-

cism belongs in that potential space inside civil society, acting on behalf of those alternative acts and alternative intentions whose advancement is a fundamental human and intellectual obligation.

There is a danger that the fascination of what's difficult—criticism being one of the forms of difficulty—might take the joy out of one's heart. But there is every reason to suppose that the critic who is tired of management and the day's war is, like Yeats's narrator, quite capable at least of finding the stable, pulling out the bolt, and setting creative energies free. Normally, however, the critic can but entertain, without fully expressing, the hope. This is a poignant irony, to be recalled for the benefit of people who maintain that criticism is art, and who forget that, the moment anything acquires the status of a cultural idol or a commodity, it ceases to be interesting. That at bottom is a *critical* attitude, just as doing criticism and maintaining a critical position are critical aspects of the intellectual's life.

1

The World, the Text,
and the Critic

SINCE he deserted the concert stage in 1964, the Canadian pianist Glenn Gould has confined his work to records, television, and radio. There is some disagreement among critics as to whether Gould is always, or only sometimes, a convincing interpreter of one or another piano piece, but there is no doubt that each of his performances now is at least special. One example of how Gould has been operating recently is suited for discussion here. In 1970 he issued a record of his performance of Beethoven's Fifth Symphony in the Liszt piano transcription. Quite aside from the surprise one felt at Gould's eccentric choice of the piece (which seemed more peculiar than usual even for the arch-eccentric Gould, whose controversial performances had formerly been associated either with classical or contemporary music), there were a number of oddities about this particular release. Liszt's Beethoven transcription was not only of the nineteenth century but of its most egregious aspect, pianistically speaking: not content with transforming the concert experience into a feast for the virtuoso's self-exhibition, it also raided the literature of other instruments, making of their music a flamboyant occasion for the pianist's skill. Most transcriptions tend on the whole to sound thick or muddy, since frequently the piano is attempting to copy the texture of an orchestral sound. Liszt's Fifth Symphony was less offensive than most transcriptions, mainly because it was so brilliantly reduced for the piano, but even at its most clear the sound was an unusual one for Gould to be producing. His sound previously had been the clearest and most unadorned of all pianists', which was why he had the uncanny ability to turn Bach's counterpoint almost into a visual experience. The Liszt transcription, in short, was an entirely different idiom, and yet Gould was very successful in it. He sounded as Lisztian now as he had sounded Bachian in the past.

Nor was this all. Accompanying the main disc was another one, a longish, informal interview between Gould and, as I recall, a record company executive. Gould told his interlocutor that one reason for his escape from "live" performance was that he had developed a bad performing habit, a kind of stylistic exaggeration. On his tours of the Soviet Union, for example, he would notice that the large halls in which he was performing caused him to distort the phrases in a Bach partita—here he demonstrated by playing the distorted phrases—so that he could more effectively "catch" and address his listeners in the third balcony. He then played the same phrases to illustrate how much more correctly, and less seductively, he was performing music when no audience was actually present.

It may seem a little heavy-handed to draw out the little ironies from this situation—transcription, interview, and illustrated performance styles all included. But it serves my main point: any occasion involving the aesthetic or literary document and experience, on the one hand, and the critic's role and his or her "worldliness," on the other, cannot be a simple one. Indeed Gould's strategy is something of a parody of all the directions we might take in trying to get at what occurs between the world and the aesthetic or textual object. Here was a pianist who had once represented the ascetic performer in the service of music, transformed now into unashamed virtuoso, whose principal aesthetic position is supposed to be little better than that of a musical whore. And this from a man who markets his record as a "first" and then adds to it, not more music, but the kind of attention-getting immediacy gained in a personal interview. And finally all this is fixed on a mechanically repeatable object, which controls the most obvious signs of immediacy (Gould's voice, the peacock style of the Liszt transcription, the brash informality of an interview packed along with a disembodied performance) beneath a dumb, anonymous, and disposable disc of black plastic.

If one thinks about Gould and his record, parallels will emerge with the circumstances of written performance. First of all, there is the reproducible material existence of a text, which in the most recent phases of Walter Benjamin's age of mechanical reproduction has multiplied and remultiplied so much as to exceed almost any imaginable limits. Both a recording and a printed object, however, are subject to certain legal, political, economic, and social constraints, so far as their sustained production and distribution are concerned; but why and how they are distributed are different matters. The main thing is that a written text of the sort we care about is originally the result of some immediate contact between author and medium. Thereafter it can be reproduced for the benefit of the world and according to conditions set by and in the world; however much the author demurs at the publicity he or she receives, once the text goes into more than one copy the author's work is in the world and beyond authorial control.

Second, a written and musical performance are both instances of style, in the simplest and least honorific sense of that very complex phenomenon. Once again I shall arbitrarily exclude a whole series of interesting complexities in order to insist on style as, from the standpoint of producer and receiver, the recognizable, repeatable, preservable sign of an author who reckons with an audience. Even if the audience is as restricted as oneself and as wide as the whole world, the author's style is partially a phenomenon of repetition and reception. But what makes style receivable as the signature of its author's manner is a collection of features variously called idiolect, voice, or irreducible individuality. The paradox is that something as impersonal as a text, or a record, can nevertheless deliver an imprint or a trace of something as lively, immediate, and transitory as a "voice." Glenn Gould's interview simply makes brutally explicit the frequent implicit need for reception or recognition that a text carries even in its most pristine, enshrined forms. A common form of this need is the staged (or recorded) convention of a talking voice addressing someone at a particular time and in a specific place. Considered as I have been considering it, then, style neutralizes the worldlessness, the silent, seemingly uncircumstanced existence of a solitary text. It is not only that any text, if it is not immediately destroyed, is a network of often colliding forces, but also that a text in its actually *being* a text is a being in the world; it therefore addresses anyone who reads, as Gould does throughout the very same record that is supposed to represent both his withdrawal from the world and his "new" silent style of playing without a live audience.

To be sure, texts do not speak in the ordinary sense of the word. Yet any simple diametric opposition asserted on the one hand between speech, bound by situation and reference, and on the other hand the text as an interception or suspension of speech's worldliness is, I think, misleading and largely simplified. Here is how Paul Ricoeur puts this opposition, which he says he has set up only for the sake of analytic clarification:

In speech the function of reference is linked to the role of the *sit-uation of discourse* within the exchange of language itself: in ex-changing speech, the speakers are present to each other, but also to the circumstantial setting of discourse, not only the perceptual surroundings, but also the cultural background known by both speakers. It is in relation to this situation that discourse is fully meaningful: the reference to reality is in the last analysis refer-ence to that reality which can be pointed out "around," so to speak, the instance of discourse itself. Language . . . and in gen-eral all the ostensive indicators of language serve to anchor dis-course in the circumstantial reality which surrounds the instance of discourse. Thus, in living speech, the *ideal* meaning of what one says bends towards a *real* reference, namely to that "about which" one speaks . . .

    This is no longer the case when a text takes the place of speech . . . A text . . . is not without reference; it will be precisely the task of reading, as interpretation, to actualize the reference. At least, in this suspension wherein reference is deferred, in the sense that it is postponed, a text is somehow "in the air," outside of the world or without a world; by means of this obliteration of all relation to the world, every text is free to enter into relation with all the other texts which come to take the place of the cir-cumstantial reality shown by living speech.[1]

According to Ricoeur, speech and circumstantial reality exist in a state of presence, whereas writing and texts exist in a state of suspen-sion—that is, outside circumstantial reality—until they are "actual-ized" and made present by the reader-critic. Ricoeur makes it seem as if the text and circumstantial reality, or what I shall call *worldliness*, play a game of musical chairs, one intercepting and replacing the other according to fairly crude signals. But this game takes place in the interpreter's head, a locale presumably without worldliness or circumstantiality. The critic-interpreter has his position reduced to that of a central bourse on whose floor occurs the transaction by which the text is shown to be meaning x while saying y. And as for what Ricoeur calls "deferred reference," what becomes of it during the interpretation? Quite simply, on the basis of a model of direct ex-change, it comes back, made whole and actual by the critic's reading.

    The principal difficulty with all this is that without sufficient argu-ment Ricoeur assumes circumstantial reality to be symmetrically and exclusively the property of speech, or the speech situation, or what writers would have wanted to say had they not instead chosen to write. My contention is that worldliness does not come and go; nor is it here and there in the apologetic and soupy way by which we often designate history, a euphemism in such cases for the impossibly vague notion that all things take place in time. Moreover, critics are not merely the alchemical translators of texts into circumstantial reality or worldliness; for they too are subject to and producers of circumstances, which are felt regardless of whatever objectivity the critic's methods possess. The point is that texts have ways of existing that even in their most rarefied form are always enmeshed in circumstance, time, place, and society—in short, they are in the world, and hence worldly.[2] Whether a text is preserved or put aside for a period, whether it is on a library shelf or not, whether it is considered dangerous or not: these matters have to do with a text's being in the world, which is a more complicated matter than the private process of reading. The same implications are undoubtedly true of critics in their capacities as readers and writers in the world.

If my use of Gould's recording of the Beethoven Fifth Symphony serves any really useful purpose, it is to provide an instance of a quasi-textual object whose ways of engaging the world are both numerous and complicated, more complicated than Ricoeur's demarcation drawn between text and speech. These are the engagements I have been calling worldliness. But my principal concern here is not with an aesthetic object in general, but with the text in particular. Most critics will subscribe to the notion that every literary text is in some way burdened with its occasion, with the plain empirical realities from which it emerged. Pressed too far, such a notion earns the justified criticism of a stylistician like Michael Riffaterre, who, in "The Self-Sufficient Text," calls any reduction of a text to its circumstances a fallacy, biographical, genetic, psychological, or analogic.[3] Most critics would probably go along with Riffaterre in saying, yes, let's make sure that the text does not disappear under the weight of these fallacies. But, and here I speak mainly for myself, they are not entirely satisfied with the idea of a self-sufficient text. Is the alternative to the various fallacies *only* a hermetic textual cosmos, one whose significant dimension of meaning is, as Riffaterre says, a wholly inward or intellectual one? Is there no way of dealing with a text and its worldly circumstances fairly? No way to grapple with the problems of literary language except by cutting them off from the more plainly urgent ones of everyday, worldly language?

I have found a way of starting to deal with these questions in an unexpected place, which is perhaps why I shall now seem to digress. Consider the relatively unfamiliar field of medieval Arabic linguistic speculation. Many contemporary critics are interested in speculation about language in Europe, that is, in that special combination of theoretical imagination and empirical observation characterizing romantic philology, the rise of linguistics in the early nineteenth century, and the whole rich phenomenon of what Michel Foucault has called the discovery of language. Yet during the eleventh century in Andalusia, there existed a remarkably sophisticated and unexpectedly prophetic school of Islamic philosophic grammarians, whose polemics anticipate twentieth-century debates between structuralists and generative grammarians, between descriptivists and behaviorists. Nor is this all. One small group of these Andalusian linguists directed its energies against tendencies amongst rival linguists to turn the question of meaning in language into esoteric and allegorical exercises. Among the group were three linguists and theoretical grammarians, Ibn Hazm, Ibn Jinni, and Ibn Mada' al-Qurtobi, all of whom worked in Cordoba during the eleventh century, all belonging to the Zahirite school, all antagonists of the Batinist school. Batinists held that meaning in language is concealed within the words; meaning is therefore available only as the result of an inward-tending exegesis. The Zahirites—their name derives from the Arabic word for clear, apparent, and phenomenal; *Batin* connotes internal—argued that words had only a surface meaning, one that was anchored to a particular usage, circumstance, historical and religious situation.

The two opponents trace their origins back to readings of the sacred text, the Koran, and how that unique event—for, unlike the Bible, the Koran is an event—is to be read, understood, transmitted, and taught by later generations of believers. The Cordovan Zahirites attacked the excesses of the Batinists, arguing that the very profession of grammar (in Arabic *nahu*) was an invitation to spinning out private meanings in an otherwise divinely pronounced, and hence unchangeably stable, text. According to Ibn Mada' it was absurd even to associate grammar with a logic of understanding, since as a science grammar assumed, and often went so far as to create by retrospection, ideas about the use and meaning of words that implied a hidden level beneath words, available only to initiates.[4] Once you resort to such a level, anything becomes permissible by way of interpretation: there can be no strict meaning, no control over what words in fact say, no responsibility toward the words. The Zahirite effort was to restore by rationalization a system of reading a text in which attention was focused on the phenomenal words themselves, in what might be considered their once-and-for-all sense uttered for and during a specific occasion, not on hidden meanings they might later be supposed to contain. The Cordovan Zahirites in particular went very far in trying to provide a reading system that placed the tightest possible control over the reader and his circumstances. They did this principally by means of a theory of what a text is.

It is not necessary to describe this theory in detail. It is useful, however, to indicate how the controversy itself grew out of a sacred text whose authority derived from its being the uncreated word of God, directly and unilaterally transmitted to a Messenger at a particular moment in time. In contrast, texts within the Judeo-Christian tradition, at whose center is Revelation, cannot be reduced to a specific moment of divine intervention as a result of which the Word of God entered the world; rather the Word enters human history continually, during and as a part of that history. So a very important place is given to what Roger Arnaldez calls "human factors" in the reception, transmission, and understanding of such a text.[5] Since the Koran is the result of a unique event, the literal "descent" into worldliness of a text, as well as its language and form, are then to be viewed as stable and complete. Moreover, the language of the text is Arabic, which therefore becomes a privileged language, and its vessel is the Prophet (or Messenger), Mohammed, similarly privileged. Such a text can be regarded as having an absolutely defined origin and consequently cannot be referred back to any particular interpreter or interpretation, although this is clearly what the Batinites tried to do (perhaps, it has been suggested, under the influence of Judeo-Christian exegetical techniques).

In his study of Ibn Hazm, Arnaldez puts his description of the Koran in the following terms: the Koran speaks of historical events, yet is not itself historical. It repeats past events, which it condenses and particularizes, yet is not itself an actually lived experience; it ruptures the human continuity of life, yet God does not enter temporality by a sustained or concerted act. The Koran evokes the memory of actions whose content repeats itself eternally in ways identical with itself, as warnings, orders, imperatives, punishments, rewards.[6] In short, the Zahirite position adopts a view of the Koran that is absolutely circumstantial without at the same time making that worldliness dominate the actual sense of the text: all this is the ultimate avoidance of vulgar determinism in the Zahirite position.

Hence Ibn Hazm's linguistic theory is based upon an analysis of the imperative mode, since according to this the Koran at its most radical verbal level is a text controlled by two paradigmatic imperatives, *iqra* (read or recite) and *qul* (tell).[7] Since those imperatives obviously control the circumstantial and historical appearance of the Koran (and its uniqueness as an event), and since they must also control uses (that is, readings) of the text thereafter, Ibn Hazm connects his analysis of the imperative mode with a juridical notion of *hadd,* a word meaning both a logico-grammatical definition and a limit. What transpires in the imperative mode, between the injunctions to read and write, is the delivery of an utterance (*khabar* in Arabic, translated by Arnaldez as *énoncé*), which is the verbal realization of a signifying intention, or *niyah.* Now the signifying intention is synonymous not with a psychological intention but exclusively with a verbal intention, itself something highly worldly—it takes place exclusively in the world, it is occasional and circumstantial in both a very precise and a wholly pertinent way. To signify is only to use language, and to use language is to do so according to certain lexical and syntactic rules, by which language is in and of the world; the Zahirite sees language as being regulated by real usage, and neither by abstract prescription nor by speculative freedom. Above all, language stands between man and a vast indefiniteness: if the world is a gigantic system of correspondences between words and objects, then it is verbal form—language in actual grammatical use—that allows us to isolate the denominated objects from among these massively ordered correspondences. Thus, as Arnaldez puts it, fidelity to such "true" aspects of language is an ascesis of the imagination.[8] A word has a strict meaning understood as an imperative, and with that meaning there also goes a strictly ordained series of resemblances (correspondences) to other words and meanings, which, strictly speaking, play around the first word. Thus figurative language (as it occurs even in the Koran), otherwise elusive and at the mercy of the virtuosic interpreter, is part of the actual structure of language, and part therefore of the collectivity of language users.

What Ibn Hazm does, Arnaldez reminds us, is to view language as possessing two seemingly antithetical characteristics: that of a divinely ordained institution, unchanging, immutable, logical, rational, intelligible; and that of an instrument existing as pure contingency, as an institution signifying meanings anchored in specific utterances. It is exactly because the Zahirites see language in this double perspective that they reject reading techniques that reduce words and their meanings back to radicals from which (in Arabic at least) they may be seen grammatically to derive. Each utterance is its own occasion and as such is firmly anchored in the worldly context in which it is applied. And because the Koran, which is the paradigmatic case of divine-and-human language, is a text that incorporates speaking and writing, reading and telling, Zahirite interpretation itself accepts as inevitable not the separation between speech and writing, not the disjunction between a text and its circumstantiality, but rather their necessary interplay. It is the interplay, the constitutive interaction, that makes possible this severe Zahirite notion of meaning.

I have very quickly summarized an enormously complex theory, for which I cannot claim any particular influence in Western European literature since the Renaissance, and perhaps not even in Arabic literature since the Middle Ages. But what ought to strike us forcibly about the whole theory is that it represents a considerably articulated thesis for dealing with a text as significant form, in which—and I put this as carefully as I can—worldliness, circumstantiality, the text's status as an event having sensuous particularity as well as historical contingency, are considered as being incorporated in the text, an infrangible part of its capacity for conveying and producing meaning. This means that a text has a specific situation, placing restraints upon the interpreter and his interpretation not because the situation is hidden within the text as a mystery, but rather because the situation exists at the same level of surface particularity as the textual object itself. There are many ways for conveying such a situation, but what I want to draw particular attention to here is an ambition (which the Zahirites have to an intense degree) on the part of readers and writers to grasp texts as objects whose interpretation—by virtue of the exactness of their situation in the world—*has already commenced* and are objects already constrained by, and constraining, their interpretation. Such texts can thereafter be construed as having need at most of complementary, as opposed to supplementary, readings.

NOW I want to discuss some of the ways by which texts impose constraints upon their interpretation or, to put it metaphorically, the way the closeness of the world's body to the text's body forces readers to take both into consideration. Recent critical theory has placed undue emphasis on the limitlessness of interpretation. It is argued that, since all reading is misreading, no one reading is better than any other, and hence all readings, potentially infinite in number, are in the final analysis equally misinterpretations. A part of this has been derived from a conception of the text as existing within a hermetic, Alexandrian textual universe, which has no connection with actuality. This is a view I do not agree with, not simply because texts in fact are in the world but also because as texts they place themselves—one of their functions as texts is to place themselves—and indeed are themselves, by soliciting the world's attention. Moreover, their manner of doing this is to place restraints upon what can be done with them interpretively.

Modern literary history gives us a number of examples of writers whose text seems self-consciously to incorporate the explicit circumstances of its concretely imagined, and even described, situation. One type of author—I shall be discussing three instances, Gerard Manley Hopkins, Oscar Wilde, and Joseph Conrad—deliberately conceives the text as supported by a discursive situation involving speaker and audience; the designed interplay between speech and reception, between verbality and textuality, *is* the text's situation, its placing of itself in the world.

The three authors I mentioned did their major work between 1875 and 1915. The subject matter of their writing varies so widely among them that similarities have to be looked for elsewhere. Let me begin with a journal entry by Hopkins:

> The winter was called severe. There were three spells of frost with skating, the third beginning on Feb. 9. No snow to speak of till that day. Some days before Feb. 7 I saw catkins hanging. On the 9th there was snow but not lying on the heads of the blades. As we went down a field near Caesar's Camp I noticed it before me *squalentem*, coat below coat, sketched in intersecting edges bearing 'idiom,' all down the slope:—I have no other word yet for that which takes the eye or mind in a bold hand or effective sketching or in marked features or again in graphic writing, which not being beauty nor true inscape yet gives interest and makes ugliness even better than meaninglessness.[9]

Hopkins' earliest writing attempts in this way to render scenes from nature as exactly as possible. Yet he is never a passive transcriber since for him "this world then is word, expression, news of God."[10] Every phenomenon in nature, he wrote in the sonnet "As Kingfishers Catch Fire," *tells* itself in the world as a sort of lexical unit: "Each mortal thing does one thing and the same:/ Deals out that being indoors each one dwells;/ Selves—goes itself; *myself* it speaks and spells,/ Crying *What I do is me: for that I came*."[11] So in the notebook entry Hopkins' observation of nature is dynamic. He sees in the frost an intention to speak or mean, its layered coats *taking* one's attention because of the idiom it bears toward meaning or expression. The writer is as much a respondent as he is a describer. Similarly the reader is a full participant in the production of meaning, being obliged as a mortal thing to act, to produce some sense that even though ugly is still better than meaninglessness.

This dialectic of production is everywhere present in Hopkins' work. Writing is telling; nature is telling; reading is telling. He wrote to Robert Bridges on May 21, 1878, that in order to do a certain poem justice "you must not slovenly read it with the eyes but with your ears, as if the paper were declaiming it at you . . . Stress is the life of it."[12] Seven years later he specified more strictly that "poetry is the darling child of speech, of lips and spoken utterance: it must be spoken; *till it is spoken it is not performed*, it does not perform, it is not itself. Sprung rhythm gives back to poetry its true soul and self. As poetry is emphatically speech, speech purged of dross like gold in the furnace, so it must have emphatically the essential elements of speech."[13] So close is the identification in Hopkins' mind among world, word, and the utterance, the three coming alive together as a moment of performance, that he envisages little need for criticial intervention. It is the written text that provides the immediate circumstantial reality for the poem's "play" (the word is Hopkins'). So far from being a document associated with other lifeless, worldless texts, Hopkins' own text was for him his child; when he destroyed his poems he spoke of the slaughter of the innocents, and everywhere he speaks of writing as the exercise of his male gift. At the moment of greatest desolation in his career, in the poem entitled simply "To R. B." the urgency of his feeling of poetic aridity is expressed biologically. When he comes to describe finally what it is he now writes, he says:

> O then if in my lagging lines you miss
> The roll, the rise, the carol, the creation,
> My winter world, that scarcely breathes that bliss
> Now, yields you, with some sighs, our explanation.[14]

Because his text has lost its ability to incorporate the stress of creation, and because it is no longer performance but what in another poem he calls "dead letters," he now can only write an explanation, which is lifeless speech "bending towards a real reference."

It was said of Oscar Wilde by one of his contemporaries that everything he spoke sounded as if it were enclosed in quotation marks. This is no less true of everything he wrote, for such was the

consequence of having a pose, which Wilde defined as "a formal recognition of the importance of treating life from a definite reasoned
standpoint."[15] Or as Algernon retorts to Jack's accusation that "you
always want to argue about things" in *The Importance of Being
Earnest:* "That's exactly what things were originally made for."[16] Always ready with a quotable comment, Wilde filled his manuscripts
with epigrams on every conceivable subject. What he wrote was intended either for more comment or for quotation or, most important,
for tracing back to him. There are obvious social reasons for some of
this egoism, which he made no attempt to conceal in his quip "To
love oneself is the beginning of a life-long romance," but they do not
exhaust the speaking in Wilde's style. Having forsworn action, life,
and nature for their incompleteness and diffusion, Wilde took as his
province a theoretical, ideal world in which, as he told Alfred
Douglas in *De Profundis*, conversation was the basis of all human relations.[17] Since conflict inhibited conversation as Wilde understood it
from the Platonic dialogue, the mode of interchange was to be by
epigram. This epigram, in Northrop Frye's terminology, is Wilde's
radical of presentation: a compact utterance capable of the utmost
range of subject matter, the greatest authority, and the least equivo-
cation as to its author. When he invaded other forms of art, Wilde
converted them into longer epigrams. As he said of drama: "I took the
drama, the most objective form known to art, and made it as personal
a mode of expression as the lyric or the sonnet, at the same time that I
widened its range and enriched its characterization." No wonder he
could say: "I summed up all systems in a phrase, and all existence in
an epigram.[18]

  De Profundis records the destruction of the utopia whose individualism and unselfish selfishness Wilde had adumbrated in *The Soul of
Man Under Socialism*. From a free world to a prison and a circle of
suffering: how is the change accomplished? Wilde's conception of
freedom was to be found in *The Importance of Being Earnest*, where
conflicting characters turn out to be brothers after all just because
they say they are. What is written down (for example, the army lists
consulted by Jack) merely confirms what all along has been capri-
ciously, though elegantly, said. This transformation, from opponent
into brother, is what Wilde had in mind in connecting the intensification of personality with its multiplication. When the communication between men no longer possesses the freedom of conversation,
when it is confined to the merely legal liability of print, which is not
ingeniously quotable but, because it has been signed, is now crimin-

ally actionable, the utopia crumbles. As he reconsidered his life in *De Profundis* Wilde's imagination was transfixed by the effects of one text upon his life. But he uses it to show how in going from speech to print, which in a sense all of his other more fortunate texts had managed somehow to avoid by virtue of their epigrammatic individuality, he had been ruined. Wilde's lament in what follows is that a text has too much, not too little, circumstantial reality. Hence, with Wildean paradox, its vulnerability:

> You send me a very nice poem, of the undergaduate school of verse, for my approval: I reply by a letter of fantastic literary conceits . . . Look at the history of that letter! It passes from you into the hands of a loathsome companion: from him to a gang of blackmailers: copies of it are sent about London to my friends, and to the manager of the theatre where my work is being performed: every construction but the right one is put on it: Society is thrilled with the absurd rumours that I have had to pay a huge sum of money for having written an infamous letter to you: this forms the basis of your father's worst attack: I produce the original letter myself in Court to show what it really is: it is denounced by your father's counsel as a revolting and insidious attempt to corrupt Innocence: ultimately it forms part of a criminal charge: the Crown takes it up: the Judge sums up on it with little learning and much morality: I go to prison for it at last. That is the result of writing you a charming letter.[19]

For in a world described by George Eliot as a "huge whispering gallery," the effects of writing can be grave indeed: "As the stone which has been kicked by generations of clowns may come by curious little links of effect under the eyes of a scholar, through whose labours it may at last fix the date of invasions and unlock religions, so a bit of ink and paper which has long been an innocent wrapping or stop-gap may at last be laid open under the one pair of eyes which have knowledge enough to turn it into the opening of a catastrophe."[20] If Dr. Casaubon's caution has any purpose at all, it is by rigid secrecy and an endlessly postponing scriptive will to forestall the opening of a catastrophe. Yet he cannot succeed since Eliot is at pains to show that even Casaubon's tremendously nursed *Key* is a text, and therefore in the world. Unlike Wilde's, Casaubon's disgrace is posthumous, but their implication in a sort of worldly textuality takes place for the same reason, which is their commitment to what Eliot calls an "embroiled medium."

Lastly, consider Conrad. Elsewhere in this book I shall be describ-

ing the extraordinary presentational mode of his narratives, how each
of them dramatizes, motivates, and circumstances the occasion of its
telling, how all of Conrad's work is really made out of secondary, reported speech, and how the interplay between appeals to the eye and
the ear in his work is highly organized and subtle, and is that work's
meaning. The Conradian encounter is not simply between a man and
his destiny embodied in a moment of extremity, but just as persistently, the encounter between speaker and hearer. Marlow is
Conrad's chief invention for this encounter, a man who is haunted by
the knowledge that a person such as Kurtz or Jim "existed for me,
and after all it is only through me that he exists for you."[21] The chain
of humanity—"we exist only in so far as we hang together"—is the
transmission of actual speech, and existence, from one mouth and
then from one eye to another. Every text that Conrad wrote presents
itself as unfinished and still in the making. "And besides, the last
word is not said,—probably shall never be said. Are not our lives too
short for that full utterance which through all our stammerings is of
course our only and abiding intention?"[22] Texts convey the stammerings that never ever achieve that full utterance, the statement of
wholly satisfactory presence, which remains distant, attenuated
somewhat by a grand gesture like Jim's self-sacrifice. Yet even though
the gesture closes off a text circumstantially, in no way does it empty
it of its actual urgency.

   This is a good time to remark that the Western novelistic tradition
is full of examples of texts insisting not only upon their circumstantial reality but also upon their status as *already* fulfilling a function, a
reference, or a meaning in the world. Cervantes and Cide Hamete
come immediately to mind. More impressive is Richardson playing
the role of "mere" editor for *Clarissa*, simply placing those letters in
successive order after they have done what they have done, arranging
to fill the text with printer's devices, reader's aids, analytic contents,
retrospective meditations, commentary, so that a collection of letters
grows to fill the world and occupy all space, to become a circumstance as large and as engrossing as the reader's very understanding.
Surely the novelistic imagination has always included this unwillingness to cede control over the text in the world, or to release it from the
discursive and human obligations of all human presence; hence the
desire (almost a principal action of many novels) to turn the text
back, if not directly into speech, then at least into circumstantial, as
opposed to meditative, duration.

   No novelist, however, can be quite as explicit about circumstances as Marx is in *The Eighteenth Brumaire of Louis Bonaparte.* To my mind no work is as brilliant and as compelling in the exactness with which circumstances (the German word is *Umstände*) are shown to have made the nephew possible, not as an innovator, but as a farcical repetition of the great uncle. What Marx attacks are the atextual theses that history is made up of free events and that history is guided by superior individuals.[23] By inserting Louis Bonaparte in a whole intricate system of repetitions, by which first Hegel, then the ancient Romans, the 1789 revolutionaries, Napoleon I, the bourgeois interpreters, and finally the fiascos of 1848–1851 are all seen in a pseudo-analogical order of descending worth, increasing derivativeness, and deceptively harmless masquerading, Marx effectively textualizes the random appearance of a new Caesar. Here we have the case of a text itself providing a world-historical situation with circumstances otherwise hidden in the deception of a *roi des drôles.* What is ironic— and in need of the analysis I shall be giving in subsequent parts of this book—is how a text, by being a text, by insisting upon and employing all the devices of textuality, preeminent among them *repetition,* historicizes and problematizes all the fugitive significance that has chosen Louis Bonaparte as its representative.

There is another aspect to what I have just been saying. In producing texts with either a firm claim on or an explicit will to worldliness, these writers and genres have valorized speech, making it the tentacle by which an otherwise silent text ties itself to the world of discourse. By the valorization of speech I mean that the discursive, circumstantially dense interchange of speaker facing hearer is made to stand—sometimes misleadingly—for a democratic equality and copresence in actuality between speaker and hearer. Not only is the discursive relation far from equal in actuality, but the text's attempt to dissemble by seeming to be open democratically to anyone who might read it is also an act of bad faith. (Incidentally, one of the strengths of Zahirite theory is that it dispels the illusion that a surface reading, which is the Zahirite ambition, is anything but difficult.) Texts of such a length as *Tom Jones* aim to occupy leisure time of a quality not available to just anyone. Moreover, all texts essentially dislodge other texts or, more frequently, take the place of something else. As Nietzsche had the perspicacity to see, texts are fudamentally facts of power, not of democratic exchange.[24] They compel attention away from the world even as their beginning intention as texts, coupled with the inherent authoritarianism of the authorial authority (the repetition in this phrase is a deliberate emphasis on the tautology

within all texts, since all texts are in some way self-confirmatory),
makes for sustained power.

Yet in the genealogy of texts there is a first text, a sacred prototype,
a scripture, which readers always approach through the text before
them, either as petitioning suppliants or as initiates amongst many in a
sacred chorus supporting the central patriarchal text. Northrop
Frye's theory of literature makes it apparent that the displacing
power in all texts finally derives from the displacing power of the
Bible, whose centrality, potency, and dominating anteriority inform
all Western literature. The same is no less true, in the different modes
I discussed earlier, of the Koran. Both in the Judeo-Christian and in
the Islamic traditions these hierarchies repose upon a solidly divine,
or quasi-divine, language, a language whose uniqueness, however, is
that it is theologically and humanly circumstantial.

We often forget that modern Western philology, which begins in
the early nineteenth century, undertook to revise commonly accepted
ideas about language and its divine origins. That revision tried first to
determine which was the first language and then, failing in that ambition, proceeded to reduce language to specific circumstances: language groups, historical and racial theories, geographical and anthro-
pological theses. A particularly interesting example of how such
investigations went is Ernest Renan's career as a philologist; that was
his real profession, not that of the boring sage. His first serious work
was his 1848 analysis of Semitic languages, revised and published in
1855 as *Histoire générale et système comparé des langues sémitiques.*
Without this study the *Vie de Jésus* could not have been written. The
accomplishment of the *Histoire générale* was scientifically to describe the inferiority of Semitic languages, principally Hebrew, Ara-
maic, and Arabic, the medium of three purportedly sacred texts that
had been spoken or at least informed by God—the Torah, the Koran,
and, later, the derivative Gospels. Thus in the *Vie de Jésus* Renan
would be able to insinuate that the so-called sacred texts, delivered by
Moses, Jesus, or Mohammed, could not have anything divine in them
if the very medium of their supposed divinity, as well as the body of
their message to and in the world, was made up of such comparatively poor worldly stuff. Renan argued that, even if these texts were
prior to all others in the West, they held no theologically dominant
position.

Renan first reduced texts from objects of divine intervention in the
world's business to objects of historical materiality. God as author-
authority had little value after Renan's philological and textual revi-

sionism. Yet in dispensing with divine authority Renan put philological power in its place. What comes to replace divine authority is the textual authority of the philological critic who has the skill to separate Semitic languages from the languages of Indo-European culture. Not only did Renan kill off the extratextual validity of the great Semitic sacred texts; he confined them as objects of European study to a scholarly field thereafter to be known as Oriental.[25] The Orientalist is a Renan or a Gobineau, Renan's contemporary quoted here and there in the 1855 edition of the *Histoire générale*, for whom the old hierarchy of sacred Semitic texts has been destroyed as if by an act of parricide; the passing of divine authority enables the appearance of European ethnocentrism, by which the methods and the discourse of Western scholarship confine inferior non-European cultures to a position of subordination. Oriental texts come to inhabit a realm without development or power, one that exactly corresponds to the position of a colony for European texts and culture. All this takes place at the same time that the great European colonial empires in the east are beginning or, in some cases, flourishing.

I have introduced this brief account of the twin origin of the Higher Criticism and of Orientalism as a European scholarly discipline in order to be able to speak about the fallacy of imagining the life of texts as being pleasantly ideal and without force or conflict and, conversely, the fallacy of imagining the discursive relations in actual speech to be, as Ricoeur would have it, a relation of equality between hearer and speaker.

Texts incorporate discourse, sometimes violently. There are other ways, too. Michel Foucault's archeological analyses of systems of discourse are premised on the thesis, adumbrated by Marx and Engels in *The German Ideology*, that "in every society the production of discourse is at once controlled, selected, organized and redistributed according to a certain number of procedures, whose role is to avert its powers and dangers, to cope with chance events, to evade its ponderous, awesome materiality." Discourse in this passage means what is written and spoken. Foucault's contention is that the fact of writing itself is a systematic conversion of the power relationship between controller and controlled into "mere" written words—but writing is a way of disguising the awesome materiality of so tightly controlled and managed a production. Foucault continues:

In a society such as our own we all know the rules of *exclusion*. The most obvious and familiar of these concerns what is *prohib-*

ited. We know perfectly well that we are not free to say just anything. We have three types of prohibition, covering objects, ritual with its surrounding circumstances, and the privileged or
exclusive right to speak of a particular subject; these prohibitions
interrelate, reinforce and complement each other, forming a
complex web, continually subject to modification. I will note
simply that the areas where this web is most tightly woven
today, where the danger spots are most numerous, are those
dealing with politics and sexuality . . . In appearance, speech
may well be of little account, but the prohibitions surrounding it
soon reveal its links with desire and power . . . Speech is no mere
verbalization of conflicts and systems of domination . . . it is the
very object of man's conflicts.[26]

Despite Ricoeur's simplified idealization, and far from being a type
of conversation between equals, the discursive situation is more
usually like the unequal relation between colonizer and colonized,
oppressor and oppressed. Some of the great modernists, Proust and
Joyce prominent among them, had an acute understanding of this
asymmetry; their representations of the discursive situation always
show it in this power-political light. Words and texts are so much of
the world that their effectiveness, in some cases even their use, are
matters having to do with ownership, authority, power, and the imposition of force. A formative moment in Stephen Dedalus' rebellious
consciousness occurs as he converses with the English dean of studies:

What is that beauty which the artist struggles to express from
lumps of earth, said Stephen coldly.
    The little word seemed to have turned a rapier point of his
sensitiveness against this courteous and vigilant foe. He felt with
a smart of dejection that the man to whom he was speaking was a
countryman of Ben Jonson. He thought:—The language in
which we are speaking is his before it is mine. How different are
the words *home, Christ, ale, master,* on his lips and on mine! I
cannot speak or write these words without unrest of spirit. His
language, so familiar and so foreign, will always be for me an acquired speech. I have not made or accepted its words. My voice
holds them at bay. My soul frets in the shadow of his language.[27]

Joyce's work is a recapitulation of those political and racial separa-
tions, exclusions, prohibitions instituted ethnocentrically by the as-
cendant European culture throughout the nineteenth century. The
situation of discourse, Stephen Dedalus knows, hardly puts equals

face to face. Rather, discourse often puts one interlocutor above another or, as Frantz Fanon brilliantly described the extreme to which
it could be taken in *The Wretched of the Earth*, discourse reenacts
the geography of the colonial city:

> The zone where the natives live is not complementary to the
> zone inhabited by the settlers. The two zones are opposed, but
> not in the service of a higher unity. Obedient to the rules of pure
> Aristotelian logic, they both follow the principle of reciprocal
> exclusivity. No concilation is possible, for of the two terms, one
> is superfluous. The settlers' town is a strongly-built town, all
> made of stone and steel. It is a brightly-lit town; the streets are
> covered with asphalt, and the garbage-cans swallow all the leav-
> ings, unseen, unknown and hardly thought about. The settler's
> feet are never visible, except perhaps in the sea; but there you're
> never close enough to see them. His feet are protected by strong
> shoes although the streets of his town are clean and even, with no
> holes or stones. The settler's town is a well-fed town, an easy-
> going town; its belly is always full of good things. The settler's
> town is a town of white people, of foreigners.
>
> The town belonging to the colonized people, or at least the
> native town, the negro village, the medina, the reservation, is a
> place of ill fame, peopled by men of evil repute. They are born
> there, it matters little where or how; they die there, it matters
> not where, nor how. It is a world without spaciousness; men live
> there on top of each other, and their huts are built on top of the
> other. The native town is a hungry town, starved of bread, of
> meat, of shoes, of coal, of light. The native town is a crouching
> village, a town on its knees, a town wallowing in the mire. It is a
> town of niggers and dirty arabs. The look that the native turns
> on the settler's town is a look of lust, a look of envy; it expresses
> his dreams of possession—all manner of possession: to set at the
> settler's table, to sleep in the settler's bed, with his wife if possi-
> ble. The colonized man is an envious man. And this the settler
> knows very well; when their glances meet he ascertains bitterly,
> always on the defensive "They want to take our place." It is true,
> for there is no native who does not dream at least once a day of
> setting himself up in the settler's place.[28]

No wonder that the Fanonist solution to such discourse is violence.

Such examples make untenable the opposition between texts and the
world, or between texts and speech. Too many exceptions, too many
historical, ideological, and formal circumstances, implicate the text in
actuality, even if a text may also be considered a silent printed object

with its own unheard melodies. The concert of forces by which a text is engendered and maintained as a fact not of mute ideality but of *production* dispels the symmetry of even rhetorical oppositions. Moreover, the textual utopia envisioned each in his own way by T. S. Eliot and Northrop Frye, whose nightmarish converse is Borges' library, is at complete odds with form in texts. My thesis is that any centrist, exclusivist conception of the text, or for that matter of the discursive situation as defined by Ricoeur, ignores the self-confirming will to power from which many texts can spring. The minimalist impulse in Beckett's work is, I think, a counterversion of this will, a way of refusing the opportunity offered to him by modernist writing.

B UT where in all this is the critic and criticism? Scholarship, commentary, exegesis, *explication de texte*, history of ideas, rhetorical or semiological analyses: all these are modes of pertinence and of disciplined attention to the textual matter usually presented to the critic as already at hand. I shall concentrate now on the essay, which is the traditional form by which criticism has expressed itself. The central problematic of the essay as a form is its *place*, by which I mean a series of three ways the essay has of being the form critics take, and locate themselves in, to do their work. Place therefore involves relations, affiliations, the critics fashion with the texts and audiences they address; it also involves the dynamic taking place of a critic's own text as it is produced.

The first mode of affiliation is the essay's relation to the text or occasion it attempts to approach. How does it come to the text of its choice? How does it enter that text? What is the concluding definition of its relation to the text and the occasion it has dealt with? The second mode of affiliation is the essay's intention (and the intention, presumed or perhaps created by the essay, that its audience has) for attempting an approach. Is the critical essay an attempt to identify or to identify with the text of its choice? Does it stand between the text and the reader, or to one side of one of them? How great or how little is the ironic disparity between its essential formal incompleteness (because after all it is an essay) and the formal completion of the text it treats? The third mode of affiliation concerns the essay as a zone in which certain kinds of occurrences happen as an aspect of the essay's production. What is the essay's consciousness of its marginality to the text it discusses? What is the method by which the essay permits history a role during the making of its own history, that is, as the essay moves from beginning to development to conclusion? What is the quality of the essay's speech, toward, away from, into the *actuality*, the arena of nontextual historical vitality and presence that is taking place simultaneously with the essay itself? Finally, is the essay a text, an intervention between texts, an intensification of the notion of textuality, or a dispersion of language away from a contingent page to occasions, tendencies, currents, or movements in and for history?

A just response to these questions is a realization of how unfamiliar they are in the general discussion of contemporary literary criticism. It is not that the problems of criticism are undiscussed, but rather that criticism is considered essentially as defined once and for all by its secondariness, by its temporal misfortune in having come after the texts and occasions it is supposed to be treating. Just as it is all too often true that texts are thought of as monolithic objects of the past to which criticism despondently appends itself in the present, then the very conception of criticism symbolizes being outdated, being dated from the past rather than by the present. Everything I tried earlier to say about a text—its dialectic of engagement in time and the senses, the paradoxes in a text by which discourse is shown to be immutable and yet contingent, as fraught and politically intransigent as the struggle between dominant and dominated—all this was an implicit rejection of the secondary role usually assigned to criticism. For if we assume instead that texts make up what Foucault calls archival facts, the archive being defined as the text's social discursive presence in the world, then criticism too is another aspect of that present. In other words, rather than being defined by the silent past, commanded by it to speak in the present, criticism, no less than any text, is the present in the course of its articulation, its struggles for definition.

We must not forget that the critic cannot speak without the mediation of writing, that ambivalent *pharmakon* so suggestively portrayed by Derrida as the constituted milieu where the oppositions are opposed: this is where the interplay occurs that brings the oppositions into direct contact with each other, that overturns oppositions and transforms one pole into another, soul and body, good and evil, inside and outside, memory and oblivion, speech and writing.[29] In particular the critic is committed to the essay, whose metaphysics were sketched by Lukacs in the first chapter of his *Die Seele und die Formen*. There Lukacs said that by virtue of its form the essay allows, and indeed is, the coincidence of inchoate soul with exigent material form. Essays are concerned with the relations between things, with values and concepts, in fine, with significance. Whereas poetry deals in images, the essay is the abandonment of images; this abandonment the essay ideally shares with Platonism and mysticism. If, Lukacs continues, the various forms of literature are compared with sunlight refracted in a prism, then the essay is ultraviolet light. What the essay expresses is a yearning for conceptuality and intellectuality, as well as a resolution to the ultimate questions of life. (Throughout his analysis Lukacs refers to Socrates as the typical essayistic figure, always talking of immediate mundane matters while at the same time through his life there sounds the purest, the most profound, and the most concealed yearning—*Die tiefste, die verborgenste Sehnsucht ertönt aus diesem Leben.*)[30]

Thus the essay's mode is ironic, which means first that the form is patently insufficient in its intellectuality with regard to living experience and, second, that the very form of the essay, its being an essay, is an ironic destiny with regard to the great questions of life. In its arbitrariness and irrelevance to the questions he debates, Socrates' death perfectly symbolizes essayistic destiny, which is the absence of a real tragic destiny. Thus, unlike tragedy, there is no internal conclusion to an essay, for only something outside it can interrupt or end it, as Socrates' death is decreed offstage and abruptly ends his life of questioning. Form fills the function in an essay that images do in poetry: form is the reality of the essay, and form gives the essayist a voice with which to ask questions of life, even if that form must always make use of art—a book, a painting, a piece of music—as what seems to be the purely occasional subject matter of its investigations.

Lukacs' analysis of the essay has it in common with Wilde that criticism in general is rarely what it seems, not least in its form. Criticism adopts the mode of commentary on and evaluation of art; yet in reality criticism matters more as a necessarily incomplete and preparatory process toward judgment and evaluation. What the critical essay does is *to begin* to create the values by which art is judged. I said earlier that a major inhibition on critics is that their function as critics is often dated and circumscribed for them by the past, that is, by an already created work of art or a discrete occasion. Lukacs acknowledges the inhibition, but he shows how in fact critics appropriate for themselves the function of starting to make values for the work they are judging. Wilde said it more flamboyantly: criticism "treats the work of art as a starting point for a new creation."[31] Lukacs put it more cautiously: "the essayist is a pure instance of the precursor."[32]

I prefer the latter description, for as Lukacs develops it the critic's position is a vulnerable one because he or she prepares for a great aesthetic revolution whose result, ironically enough, will render criticism marginal. Later, this very idea will be converted by Lukacs into a description of the overthrow of reification by class consciousness, which in turn will make class itself a marginal thing.[33] Yet what I wish to emphasize here is that critics create not only the values by which art is judged and understood, but they embody in writing those processes and actual conditions in the *present* by means of which art and writing bear significance. This means what R. P. Blackmur, following Hopkins, called the bringing of literature to performance. More explicitly, the critic is responsible to a degree for articulating those voices dominated, displaced, or silenced by the textuality of texts. Texts are a system of forces institutionalized by the reigning culture at some human cost to its various components.[34] For texts after all are not an ideal cosmos of ideally equal monuments. Looking at the Grecian urn Keats *sees* graceful figures adorning its exterior, and also he actualizes in language (and perhaps nowhere else) the little town "emptied of this folk, this pious morn." The critic's attitude to some extent is sensitive in a similar way; it should in addition and more often be frankly inventive, in the traditional rhetorical sense of *inventio* so fruitfully employed by Vico, which means finding and exposing things that otherwise lie hidden beneath piety, heedlessness, or routine.

Most of all, criticism is worldly and in the world so long as it opposes monocentrism, a concept I understand as working in conjunction with ethnocentrism, which licenses a culture to cloak itself in the particular authority of certain values over others. Even for Arnold, this comes about as the result of a contest that gives culture a dominion that almost always hides its dark side: in this respect *Culture and Anarchy* and *The Birth of Tragedy* are not very far apart.

2
Swift's Tory Anarchy

SWIFT'S work is a persisting miracle of how much commentary an author's writing can accommodate and still remain problematic. The efforts on his behalf have been mainly restorative, since few major authors in English have presented themselves so resolutely in a long series of occasional pieces that defy easy classification. One way of checking this intransigence is to note how much more certainly we can use the adjective "Swiftian" than we can identify, locate, and see "Swift." The latter seems often to be little more than an adjunct to the former, even as "Swift" somehow energetically covers thirteen volumes of prose, three of poetry, seven of correspondence, and innumerable pages of strange jottings. Thus Swift is restored by editors to a definitive text, by biographers to a chronology of events from birth in 1667 to death in 1745, by psychological critics to a set of characteristics, by historians to an age, by literary critics to a genre, a technique, a rhetoric, a tradition, and by moralists to the norms he is said to have defended. His identity has been very much in the shadow of claims made on his work, and if this is always true with major authors it doesn't, in Swift's case, make it seem any less of what Norman O. Brown has called a housebreaking and domestication of the tiger of English literature.

Yet despite their differences each of these restorations, consciously or not, is also taking Swift as a *resistance* to the order in which he will come to be placed. In no author do the regulations of order and the challenging anarchy of dispersion cohabit with such integrity. R. P. Blackmur's remark that "true anarchy of spirit should always show (or always *has* showed) a tory flavor"[1] is, I think, best applied to Swift. His work can be approached and characterized as the highly dramatic encounter between the anarchy of resistance to the written page and the abiding tory order of the page. This is the most literally basic form of encounter: it is capable of great multiplication, going from the difference between waste and conservation, absence and presence, obscenity and decorum, to the negative and positive dimensions of language, imagination, unity, and identity. The life of such an encounter is, so to speak, the active content of Swift's mind as we are able to grasp it in its essential resistance to any fixed boundaries. Nevertheless, the limits of that mind's play seem to have been set by the exclusion of everything but highly specialized and obsessive work—I am recalling Swift's own reference to his conjured spirit. So constant an experience of force and pressure warrants Yeats's granting to Swift the discovery of the intellect's madness.

The tension between an individual author, as an irreducible existence, and the tory institutions of literature to which the writing contributes is, of course, an implicit one, always to be taken into account by the critic. This tension is exploited, rather than tolerated, by critical methods whose bias stresses the anterior privileges of the writer's experience to his finished product. Whether as phenomenology, *Lebensphilosophie,* or psychoanalysis, such methods investigate dimensions of privacy, what we may call literal pretexts, whose mastery of the text is asserted either from within (see Ortega's essay *Pidiendo un Goethe desde dentro*), from all sides (Jean-Pierre Richard's *L'Univers imaginaire de Mallarmé*), or from without (Bernard Meyer's *Joseph Conrad: A Psychoanalytic Biography*). What results is an often impressive totality and the achievement of an intimate partnership between critic and writer, in which each in a sense is part of the other.

A number of important preconditions inform these critical enterprises. The texts examined are problematic in every way except *as texts.* That is, the critic is concerned with interpretations of a text, but not with asking if the text is a text or with ascertaining the discursive conditions by which a so-called text may, or may not, have become a text. Clearly, for example, a work like Swift's "Some Considerations upon the Consequences Hoped and Feared from the Death of the Queen" (1714) does not occupy the same place in the canon as *Gulliver's Travels* (1726); yet in any integral account of Swift's oeuvre it would be very hard to say what place the *Travels* ought to stand in without considering its relation to "Some Considerations." Is one work more of a text than the other? The uncomplicated facts of either completion or publication cannot so easily determine whether one piece of writing is a text and another not. Furthermore, the tautology text-pretext-text is not questioned because the pretext is shown to inhabit the text on a different spiritual, temporal, or spatial level (anterior, more profound, interior); the critic's job therefore is to assemble pretext to text in a new order of simultaneity that eradicates the differences between them—so long as one has a transcendant principle of convertibility at hand that transforms the differences. Without such a principle the pretext would remain extrinsic, and hence useless. Finally, there is an assumption made about a space common to text, pretext, and criticism, in which important hidden things become visible, in which nothing crucial is lost, and in which whatever merits saying can be said and connected. It is not accidental that these methods are best suited to romantic and postromantic authors for whom all writing is an apparently imperfect metaphor of consciousness and writing as mirrors of each other's topographies. The debt to criticism has become evident, since it is criticism that lines things up in this way.

Studied in this manner, writing is also a form of temporal duration. Literary language in particular contains its intention and, during the reader's efforts, acquires its varied significations by virtue of its temporality: this is a commonplace of interpretation. No matter how severe the interruptions, the continuity of serial movement must always be established even if the direction of that movement is ultimately circular. Georges Poulet's *Les Métamorphoses du cercle* demonstrates the figure with formidable insistence. At its best, then, the restorative method is extraordinarily absorptive and catholic; at its worst it can become reductive and exclusive. What underlies the critic's project of restoration is an attitude that resembles acquisitiveness, for one cannot restore what one does not possess. And what can be possessed is only what is believed previously to be *there.*

It is against this ideological premise of fundamental appropriation that Swift's work militates.[2] With a few exceptions, most of his writing was precisely occasional: it was stimulated by a specific occasion and planned in some way to change it. This is as explicitly true of *A Tale of a Tub* (1704) as it is of *The Conduct of the Allies* (1711), *The Examiner* (1711), and *The Drapier's Letters* (1724). Moreover, the publication and subsequent dissemination of most of his individual pieces, including *Gulliver's Travels*, occupied his attention in many ways as event, not as art in our sense of the word or as craftsmanship for its own sake. What the manic narrator of *A Tale of a Tub* admits, that what he says is true only for the moment, is a comic foreshadowing of what was literally to be true of Swift's later writing. *The Conduct of the Allies* and *The Public Spirit of the Whigs* (1714) take place, as it were, in their actual dispersion on the streets of London; their efficacy as instruments of urgent Tory policy during the Harley–St. John regime is essentially in the fact that they got to as many people as possible, as quickly as possible, and as unerringly as possible. Distribution and skillful rhetoric are aspects of each other and of an event they aim to promote. Once enacted, they become historical events that have taken place; if they remain at all, they do so as shadowy traces that adumbrate an occasion, monuments of a specific time whose original power has been exhausted.

Swift himself seems to have been haunted by the impermanence of events, a concern that accounts not only for his life-long interest in conversation (a speaking event) but for his solicitude for history, for correct language, for his stubborn distrust of everything that could not be verified by direct experience. Dr. Johnson's portrait of Pope, writing letters with a jealous eye cocked at their future publication, is nicely balanced by the malicious anecdote in his *Life of Swift* in which the Dean reflects with an old man's disbelief on the genius of a youth that had produced *A Tale of a Tub*, a unique event. Indeed most apocryphal stories about Swift, whether told by Mrs. Pilkington, Johnson, or Nichols, have a curious discontinuity to them. In the same narrative, one version of Swift contradicts another: so Mrs. Pilkington tells stories of Swift's gratuitous nastiness alongside those in which he is the kindest of men. Certainly these stories belong to Swift, but they waver in their fidelity to Swift, the once dynamically alive and complex man, and to another being disjunctive with him, the mythic figure who later looms so impressively in Yeats's poetry, Joyce's fiction, or Beckett's entire oeuvre. The lapse between what Swift actually said or did and what could be said about him is exactly the gap that exists between words spoken specifically for an occasion and words recorded in writing whose situation has fallen away from it. The difference is between strict, and sometimes even unpleasant, events and a permissive aftermath that beseeches interpretation and reconstruction. Not surprisingly, *A Tale of a Tub* and *Gulliver's Travels* are at once Swift's best-known "texts" and, concomitantly, those whose intention is most general, most textually bound, and those that have welcomed the most critical attention. They are also works most amenable to generic and technical classification.

Yet, judged by most of his other works, these possessions of the library and of the critic seem like accidents intended by Swift to dramatize the fact that he was really a writer of paraliterature who used literary institutions when it suited him, or during moments of enforced idleness. Swift's purposely ingenuous letters to friends in England about Gulliver, the various guides and keys to *A Tale of a Tub* cleverly incorporated into later versions of the work, such oddities as Smedley's *Gulliveriana*—all these are comic appendages to writing that has already indicted itself for being an appendage to reality. What distinguishes the most literary of Swift's writings from his numerous political and religious tracts is that the latter are embedded as events in a complex of events in the world, whereas the former are comic or literary or textual because they are not events at all; on the contrary the *Tale* is explicitly written to forestall an event and to distract serious attention. In *The Stoic Comedians* Hugh Kenner brilliantly discusses the *Tale* as a book that parodies the sheer bookishness of books. And whatever else it is, *Gulliver's Travels* is a work that uses the historical preterite as a self-conscious literary barrier between the reader and the pseudo-present tense in which most of Gulliver's exploits are narrated. We are then forced to take seriously Swift's discovery that words and objects in the world are not simply interchangeable, since words extend away from objects into an entirely verbal world of their own. If words and objects ever coincide, it is because at certain propitious times both converge into what the prevailing polity can readily identify as an event, which does not necessarily involve exchange or communication. Yet the contrast between an event and writing as a substitute for an event is an important working opposition in Swift.

In addition, Swift seems to have been very sensitive to the differences between writing and speaking. Each activity—and this notion is entirely apt for the severity of his thought—can take two forms, which we may call correct on the one hand and debased on the other. Correct speaking is conversation, defined in "Hints towards an Essay on Conversation" (1710–1712) as being more readily achieved than any idea, because incapable of refinement into mere ideality:

> Most Things, pursued by Men for the Happiness of publick or private Life, our Wit or Folly have so refined, that they seldom subsist but in Idea; a true Friend, a good Marriage, a perfect Form of Government, with some others, require so many Ingredients, so good in their several Kinds, and so much Niceness in mixing them, that for some thousands of Years Men have despaired of reducing their Schemes to Perfection: But in Conversation, it is, or might be otherwise; for here we are only to avoid

a Multitude of Errors, which, although a Matter of some Difficulty, may be in every Man's Power, for Want of which it re-
maineth as meer an Idea as the other. Therefore it seemeth to
me, that the truest Way to understand Conversation, is to know
the Faults and Errors to which it is subject, and from thence,
every Man to form Maxims to himself whereby it may be regulated.[3]

One reason for this assertion is of course the necessary physical presence of at least two people, and all of Swift's subsequent hints are designed to preserve the presence to each other of the conversants. The
rules of conversation are made subordinate to that presence, which
ought to prevail and in whose interest the subject, mode, and style of
exchange must serve. Even in his description of a good sermon,
Swift's concern is to make the fact of speaking and listening into an
event with duration, and this can only happen if the prior facts of
presence are respected. There is, however, one obvious handicap to
conversation. For once said in a conversation, words are lost forever,
except perhaps as pleasant memory. Now "debased" conversation, of
which *The Polite Conversation* (1738) is the prime example, is
speaking without respect to presence. A social occasion is only license
for speaking: that turns speaking into the formalism of modish cliché,
which really needs nothing specific either to set it going or to keep it
going. The rationale of *The Polite Conversation*, as set forth in its
introduction, is that polite talk really speaks itself. It can be learned
by heart, it is always applicable, it is finite and closed, and its rules
are intrinsic to it, that is, not really subordinated to the presence of
speaker or listener: hence, the "success" of Wagstaff's years of transcription. Above all, debased conversation is economical and capable
of preservation since it works on the all *and* nothing principle: it
never means anything and it always means the same thing—polite
conversation, an absolute constant, language using people.

    Swift's views on conversation remain relatively unchanged
throughout his life, even if we consider such works as *The Journal to
Stella*, his birthday poems to Stella, the Anglo-Latin games, the Cas-
tilian experiments, and the Scriblerus Club enterprises as variations
on the theme of conversation. Or if not variations, then the closest
Swift ever came to demonstrating the peripheries at which conversation shades subtly into writing. What needs to be remarked here is
that Swift's writing itself was a far less integral activity than speaking; and that, I believe, is something Swift understood about his own
work and more universally about writing in general. Formulas like

"the plain style," affixed by Johnson to Swift's writing, and "proper words in proper places" (Swift's own catch-all) do little service to the fineness of his writing. Correct writing for him did not merely conform to reality. It was reality; better still, it was an event necessitated by other events, and leading to still other events. The best writing, such as *The Conduct of the Allies*, was a matter of exquisite timing and placing. Conversely, debased writing was a matter of bad timing and bad placing.

The consequences of this notion of writing, which appears to be a simple one, are of immense importance—and not only for Swift but for his reader. Consider, first of all, how relative good writing is to its time and place. Retrospectively, good writing has happened, like the past. Its force is lost to the later present of the historian or the critic; ironically again, the writer himself is no less cut off from that force. To Swift the "simple" truth meant a great deal: it meant that (as the work he did in Letcombe shortly after the Tory demise so poignantly testifies) his time and place as a writer of worth had happened and had passed. From being a good writer he had changed into a writer of confused reminiscence, then of projections.

Roland Barthes' distinction between *écrivant* (someone who writes about subjects that exist and who is a transactor of events and ideas) and *écrivain* (someone whose subject is, if not nonexistent, then merely writing itself) applies respectively to Swift's work in 1710–1714 and the periods before and after it. Here are two passages, taken first from *A Tale of a Tub* and then from "Memoirs, Relating to That Change which happened in the Queen's Ministry in the Year 1710" (written in 1714). Both are statements about why the work is being undertaken, although in the first passage Swift uses a mask and in the second his own voice. What is strikingly true of both passages is that the same stratagem is used—the present work is a diversion produced by an *écrivain*—with the same consequences: the style is roundabout, as if to conceal the fact that the real subject is the act of writing itself. The author, for various reasons, does not feel justified in honestly standing at the center of what he says. In the *Tale* digression is a technique; in the "Memoirs" digression has almost become Swift's way of life away from the center of things. As we shall see, it was not until his old age that Swift could allow himself to grow confidently into the subject of his writing.

The Wits of the present Age being so very numerous and penetrating, it seems the Grandees of Church and State begin to fall under horrible Apprehensions, lest these Gentlemen, during the intervals of a long Peace, should find leisure to pick Holes in the weak sides of Religion and Government. To prevent which, there has been much Thought employ'd of late upon certain Projects for taking off the Force, and Edge of those formidable Enquirers, from canvasing and reasoning upon such delicate Points. They have at length fixed upon one, which will require some Time as well as Cost, to perfect. Meanwhile the Danger hourly increasing, by new Levies of Wits all appointed (as there is Reason to fear) with Pen, Ink, and Paper which may at an hours Warning be drawn out into Pamphlets, and other Offensive Weapons, ready for immediate Execution: It was judged of absolute necessity, that some present Expedient be thought on, till the main Design can be brought to Maturity. To this End, at a Grand Committee, some Days ago, this important Discovery was made by a certain curious and refined Observer; That Seamen have a Custom when they meet a Whale, to fling him out an empty Tub, by way of Amusement, to divert him from laying violent Hands upon the Ship. This Parable was immediately mythologiz'd: The Whale was interpreted to be Hobbes's Leviathan, which tosses and plays with all other Schemes of Religion and Government, whereof a great many are hollow, and dry and empty, and noisy, and wooden, and given to Rotation. This is the Leviathan from whence the terrible Wits of our Age are said to borrow their Weapons. The Ship in danger, is easily understood to be its old Antitype the Commonwealth. But, how to analyze the Tub, was a matter of difficulty; when after long Enquiry and Debate, the literal Meaning was preserved: And it was decreed, that in order to prevent these Leviathans from tossing and sporting with the Commonwealth, (which of itself is too apt to fluctuate) they should be diverted from that Game by a Tale of a Tub. And my Genius being conceived to lye not unhappily that way, I had the Honor done me to be engaged in the Performance. (*Prose Works*, I, 24–25)

Having continued, for near the space of four years, in a good degree of confidence with the ministry then in being, though not with so much power as was believed, or at least given out, by my friends as well as my enemies, especially the latter, in both houses of parliament: And this having happened during a very busy period of negotiations abroad, and management or intrigue at home, I thought it might probably, some years hence, when the present scene shall have given place to many new ones that will arise, be an entertainment to those who will have any personal regard for me or my memory, to set down some particularities which fell under my knowledge and observation, while I was supposed, whether truly or no, to have part in the secret of affairs. (*Prose Works*, VIII, 107)

For Swift, and for the critic, the distinctions between the two passages are only secondarily literary ones. They are primarily linguistic and ontological—and I use the word hesitantly. The writing's status in the world has changed with the status of political and historical reality. In the *Tale*, Swift imitates diversion, whereas in the later piece his work really has become a diversion. Each work, however, is produced by an *écrivain*, albeit for different reasons. Held rigidly to a regime that, Swift thought, his efforts entered into and partnered, his writing maintained a position of supremacy over all other writing between 1710 and 1714. The Tory policy Swift supported and wrote about was policy in the world of actuality: here he was an *écrivant*. The Whig opposition was projection, mere scribbling. This was always the basis of his strategy. After 1714 Swift occupied no place except as outsider to the Whigs' monolithic machine. He had become the scribbler and projector he once impersonated (in *A Tale of a Tub*) and attacked (in *The Examiner* and elsewhere).

Recent works of historical research (J. H. Plumb's *The Origins of Political Stability: England, 1675–1725*, Peter Dickson's *The Financial Revolution*, or Isaac Kramnick's *Bolingbroke and His Circle*) vindicate Swift's sense of loss. In many ways England changed after 1714, but chiefly in that political authority was no longer vested in personalities but rather in the impersonal machinery of bureaucracy, devised and perfected by Walpole. The change was England's version of the changes in the structure of European society at the end of the seventeenth century, changes studied by Franz Borkenau, Lucien Goldmann, and Bernard Groethuysen. Events were no longer linked directly to individuals. The solid values of blood and land were transformed into the shifting values of currency, a perpetual national debt, and city mercantilism. The Tory aristocracy of merit, which for Swift embodied the English people at their best, was dislodged from power by a Whig oligarchy of special interests. If previously Swift had seen his pamphlets as events that existed in a state of homology, or as coevals, with political reality, after 1714 he saw that both he and his writings repeatedly demonstrated the intractable *opposition* between language and actuality, two versions of inauthenticity cut off from what he called nostalgically "life in the common forms."

This is why the role of Irish patriot suited him so eminently: it was a role full of the infuriating contradictions between the pen and the polity. Perfect in itself, the written language of Irish protestation exacerbated the discontinuity between the intolerability of what was (Ireland) and the improbability of what could be (English colonialist plans for it). Wood's halfpence, for instance, was just the wrong Swift could attack in *The Drapier's Letters*, mainly by taking the scheme as a scheme and, in those brilliant fancies where squires went shopping with carriages full of debased coin trailing after them, projecting the project in its own element—imagination.[4] An imaginative event and, by extension, writing that involved imaginative projections comically displaced real events; thus Swift's mind remained faithful to the presence of events, if only by mocking merely verbal fictions of reality, like Wood's scheme, with alternative fictions.

What I have so rapidly summarized requires much further exposition and demonstration. If this outline has any value, however, it is to have situated Swift's work at the axes of the basic oppositions and discontinuities that make the work's total accessibility to the twentieth century so limited. We are challenged therefore by an oeuvre that exists recalcitrantly as a negative judgment passed on itself for not having succeeded as an event, which would have meant its extinction and dispersion in time past. To Swift, history supported itself adequately without need of interpretation, so long as language (as his public letter to Harley on the maintenance of the English language tries to prove) was synonymous with political power. Too proud to believe that his writing merely served the Tory power, Swift saw his pamphlets retrospectively as part of the regime, events in its history; yet the obsessive way in which, very early and very late in his career, he recognized the inherent dangers of language loosed from political power and social reality suggests that he felt himself in need of assurances that his control over language was strong. He realized ultimately that only he could assure himself by periodically exposing the abuses to which language far too easily lent itself. The symmetry, for instance, between Swift's dismissal of the muse in "Occasioned by Sir William Temple's Late Illness and Recovery" (1693) and his attack, forty years later, on the blasts of "poetick Fire" (in "On Poetry: A Rapsody," 1733) is striking. The following passages show first the muse dismissed in anticipation of the poet's espousal of reality, and then poetry debased by the loss of a real subject. What intervenes between the two poems is a period during which Swift was only a poet incidentally, 1710–1714. Those four years, in the context of his entire life's work, are the gap over which writing,

interpretation, and memory—all verbal and all imperfect—put down
a cloud of words:

> To thee I owe that fatal bend of mind,
> Still to unhappy restless thoughts inclin'd;
> To thee, what oft I vainly strive to hide,
> That scorn of fools, by fools mistook for pride;
> From thee whatever virtue takes its rise,
> Grows a misfortune, or becomes a vice;
> Such were the rules to be poetically great,
> "Stoop not to int'rest, flattery, or deceit;
> "Nor with hir'd thoughts be thy devotion paid;
> "Learn to disdain their mercenary aid;
> "Be this thy sure defence, they brazen wall,
> "Know no base action, at no guilt turn pale;
> "And since unhappy distance thus denies
> "T'expose thy soul, clad in this poor disguise;
> "Since thy few ill-presented graces seem
> "To breed contempt where thou hast hop'd esteem."—
> Madness like this no fancy ever seiz'd,
> Still to be cheated, never to be pleas'd;
> Since one false beam of joy on sickly minds
> Is all the poor content delusion finds.—
> There thy enchantment broke, and from this hour
> I here renounce thy visionary pow'r;
> And since thy essence on my breath depends
> Thus, with a puff the whole delusion ends.
> (*Poetical Works*, 41–42)

> How shall a new Attempter learn
> Of different Spirits to discern,
> And how distinguish, which is which,
> The Poet's Vein, or scribling Itch?
> Then hear an old experienc'd Sinner
> Instructing thus a young Beginner.
> "Consult yourself, and if you find
> A powerful Impulse urge your Mind,
> Impartial judge within your Breast
> What Subject you can manage best;
> Whether your Genius most inclines
> To Satire, Praise, or hum'rous Lines;
> To Elegies in mournful Tone,
> Or Prologue sent from Hand unknown.
> Then rising with Aurora's Light,
> The Muse invok'd, sit down to write;

Blot out, correct, insert, refine,
Enlarge, diminish, interline;
Be mindful, when Invention fails,
To scratch your Head, and bite your Nails."
(*Poetical Works*, 571–572)

The rhyme of "sinner" and "beginner" is eloquent, for it ties the habitual practitioner to the novice with inevitable firmness. Both are writers, *écrivains*, for whom the practice of poetry is an exercise in trying vainly to insert literary composition into the real world. A muse dismissed and, with a sense of savage inferiority, writing installed alongside reality: these are the beginning and the end of a career that abides both for Swift and for his critic. The career is a literary one whose record exists in works that ought to have become political history but which linger on, like the Struldbruggs, as ineffectual remnants. "On Poetry" derives its strength not only from the vehemence of its attack on debased poetry, but also from a despair that this debasement after all is what poetry now really is. Is it not an unhappy fact that Swift's instructions—here and in the *Directions to Servants* (1745), *The Polite Conversation*, and so on—were always manuals of bad work elaborately described? What could be described then was what was accessible to written language, and both subject and medium were infected substitutes for the realities that remained outside their field. The productive force of Swift's energy as a writer need not be portrayed as emanating from a vision we create of him as an Anglican divine whose life can be described as a sequence of events over a period of time. On the contrary, we do him a greater service if we accept the discontinuities he experienced in the way he experienced them: as either actual or imminent losses of tradition, heritage, position, history, losses located at the center of his disjointed verbal production. And this acceptance is not so much a psychological interpretation as it is a set of conditions that makes the whole range of Swift's psychology possible, from a concern with "fair liberty" to an excremental fixation.

To Swift, then, modern literature was the displacement of older literature; this observation, of course, is made to work throughout *A Tale of Tub*. A modern author writes *during* the loss of a tradition. He is present because of the absence of the ancient authors who were being crowded out by a fading memory of the classics. Frances Yates's book *The Art of Memory* sheds important light on the demotion of traditional mnemonic remembrance in the later seventeenth century: this change was there for Swift to witness. Thus the private inner light that the Quakers or Presbyterians claim for their guides replaces the common heritage, and it is this dislodgement that *A Tale of a Tub* enacts. Moreover, the orderly sequence of historical progress had, for Swift, been dismantled by the Puritan revolution and regicide. As the vagaries of his own history attested, continuity was largely a matter arranged between interested parties, but not a *given* in which everyone could be located securely. *The Sentiments of a Church of England Man* (1711) and the ill-fated *History of the Four Last Years of Queen Anne* (1712–13) were two of Swift's attempts to correct the unreliable opinions upon which the nation's sense of its history and meaning depended. Those works were his rather more problematic, earth-bound versions of Pope's deism and cosmic toryism.

It was in Ireland during the 1730s, however, that Swift more deliberately than before began to provide the stabler framework in which he wished the future to regard him. An incorrigible revisionist, a habitual keeper of accounts whom Taine characterized as the businessman of English letters, and a man with what Nigel Dennis has described as a schoolmaster's attitude to life, it befitted Swift to make sure that the last things to be said about him should be controlled by him. For the last memory he left behind would necessarily be the first to which the future would turn, and in the "Verses on the Death of Dr. Swift" (1731) that he constructed the continuity he wished to perpetuate. In that magnificent poem he chooses courageously, even arrogantly, to see himself in the entirely negative aspect of his own death, at once a loss to the world and a gain for history—but in either case an exemplary *subject.* This summational fiction of his own death is made to take place in the course of the poem as fragmentary responses to a loss being transformed into an event. Thus Swift could become a part of history and a master of it despite the misfortunes attributed by him to language.

The last point needs special emphasis. Whatever else he may have been, Swift realized that so far as posterity was concerned he was primarily a man committed to (that is, both involved in and imprisoned by) language. After he died he would be received by future generations as what they read: he would no longer be seen or heard. What survived of him therefore would be a verbal protrusion into the future, provided he could arrange for that in some way. Yet he would be working against himself. During most of his life he had relied confidently on his personality and on the ubiquitous personality—rather than the undoubted authorship—of his writing. No matter what he did, the supervening fact of his presence overcame the dispersion of his efforts and the variety of his disguises on behalf of the church, the state, Ireland, traditional learning, and morality. If, as I suggested above, those institutions were felt to be in imminent danger of disappearing, then he took his task to be one of assuring their continued presence. The cast of his mind, however, made him undertake these assurances in the form of written imitations of the enemy, imitations that went the opposition several times further in imagination, fantasy, and ostensible disorganization. His element was language, as was the enemy's, but far more than anyone he was able to exploit the negative aspects of the medium: its airiness, its impermanence, its potential for solipsistic debasement. Coleridge, for one, saw this as Swift's tremendous gift. What, to the enemy he attacked, had been an inevitable consequence of flawed thought was for him the willed function of his orderly self-defeating logical and virtuosic analysis. This was Swift's style.

The threat to his posthumous reputation is obvious. Today, for example, we still approach him on the basis of some coherence imputed to his work, which we consider connected to him filiatively as the product of his labor. But it is precisely this connection that so much of his writing denies. "A Modest Proposal" announces itself as the thought of everyone but Swift, yet it is indubitably by Swift. Thus, as Joyce says in *Ulysses,* absence is the highest form of presence. And this insight is above all true of language, which exists in its written form as a substitute for the presence of its author. Any substitute for the real thing is ruled by transience, and by a law of endless substitution. It was fear of this fate that Swift reckoned with in the "Verses" by allowing himself to die at cards, at Walpole's levee, in the booksellers' shops. The event of his death, "news [which] thro' half the town has run," is a loss welcomed—according to La Rochefoucauld's cynical law—as one "no more easy to supply." Yet with the dissipation of all the news' energy, paralleled by the quickness of shifting scenes in the poem exhausted by the passing of time, Swift's death is transformed from a variety of gossipy stories into an event on which a dispassionate, anonymous voice can pass true judgment.

The poem is governed by a series of elaborate paradoxes that are not merely rhetorical: hence, to my mind, the poem's special place as a point of departure for any reading of Swift and any ascertainment of his text. These paradoxes are all consequences of the untenable structure that holds human existence together. This is the opposition between the absolutes of life (birth, death, individuality, community, in short, Nature) and particular manifestations of them that relativize and distort them. The strength and fruitfulness of this opposition is that the absolutes never really appear in the poem because the particulars dominate them so fully. Yet so thorough is the competence with which Swift illustrates this that, by the time we chafe at how impoverished the world has become, we begin to be impressed at the supreme art with which the impoverished has been rendered. This is very similar to the achievement of "On Poetry."

The proverb by La Rochefoucauld initiates us immediately into a world drawn from Nature, but since the maxim's import is mankind's fault it implicates La Rochefoucauld as well.

> In all Distresses of our Friends
> We first consult our private Ends,
> While Nature kindly bent to ease us,
> Points out some Circumstance to please us.

The poem is therefore shut off from any recourse outside it, and to this somber imprisonment the narrator quickly assents, asking, however, "for one Inch at most" in which to illustrate his desire, thoroughly congruent with the world's way, to rise above his equals. For the writer this means literally that his verbal composition will occupy a space he denies others, and Swift proceeds without delay to show the validity of La Rochefoucauld's observation. Yet we must note how the examples Swift gives are what he called raillery, for what he begrudges friends like Pope and Gay is their talent; this is a negative way of praising them. When at lines 60 and 61, he accuses "them" of having driven him "out of date," a shift in tone has occurred: raillery at friends gives way to a serious indictment of the times, now the property of ministers of state who can (and did) maul him, because *his* time and good fortune—the heyday of Tory power—displeased them. La Rochefoucauld is a double-edged blade.

From this point on, the poem is dominated by the inevitable temporal order that leads every man to his death. And this order is large enough to contain not only the trivial pastimes of the idle but the transcendent judgment of history. The focal point in time is the event of Swift's death and it is set, like a fixed node, amid three movements that emanate from it and surround it. First of all, there is the movement of dispersion by which the news of Swift's death is spread through town. Second, and less apparent, is an objective chronology that carries us forward into a future considerably beyond Swift's death. Third, there is the poem's movement itself, an inch that spreads out into a powerful verbal structure. The poem's purpose is to let dispersion occur. The Dean begins to die, "he hardly breathes," then he dies—and "what is Trumps?" What is dispersed and lost is a negligible part of the Dean, the part of him possessed by other people. The ingenuity of dispersion is exhausted, not because, as was the case with Swift's political pamphlets, history has absorbed it but rather because the source of its energy is gossipy meanness, a form of polite conversation that has no real duration or status. Above all, this conversation belongs neither to the public nor to the private world, but to an entirely independent verbal order that obliterates every worthwhile distinction. It is a social version of the same order that overcomes the world at the end of *The Dunciad*.

Swift's death, it needs to be said, occurs in conversation, in language—nowhere else. Neither the reader nor the poet can penetrate beyond the verbal dimension, which is the imposition of a human standard upon nature ("a world drawn from nature"). Thus even so serious and natural a subject as death cannot be treated except as a function of language: hence the unashamed artificiality of the poet's stage directions and shifting of scene by which the death is literally arranged. It becomes Swift's problem then to show language as the arena in which fictions battle each other until only the most worthy remain. What remains of Swift can only be described, a long time later, by an impartial, anonymous voice that—and this is a sign of Swift's extraordinarily proleptic sense of himself as a problem for the future—understands Swift as a man who was *too much* for his own time.

The setting of the poem's final scene is one of the most carefully engineered things Swift ever did.

> Suppose me dead; and then suppose
> A Club assembled at the Rose;
> Where from Discourse of this and that,
> I grow the Subject of their Chat:
> And, while they toss my Name about,
> With Favour some, and some without;
> One quite indiff'rent in the Cause,
> My Character impartial draws. (*Poetical Works*, 506)

We watch discourse of this and that exhausting itself, whereas Swift the subject, that is, the topic of history, grows: not the personality whose human situation had likewise aged and been exhausted by the common human time, but an impartial character that emerges to fuller and fuller presence. Such a character can persist in history as a supplement to the specific time he outlived because of his having been too much for it: "Had he but spar'd his Tongue and Pen,/ He might have rose like other men." He does rise now, not as a man but as a subject. The terms of description are almost uniformly those of excess, of incongruence with the manners and habits of his time, so much so that sovereign and state cannot contain him.

> With Princes kept a due Decorum,
> But never stood in Awe before 'em:
> And to her Majesty, God bless her,
> Would speak as free as to her Dresser,
> She thought it his peculiar Whim,
> Nor took it ill as come from him.
> He follow'd David's Lesson just,
> In Princes never put thy Trust.
> And, would you make him truly sower;
> Provoke him with a slave in Power:
> The Irish Senate, if you nam'd,
> With what Impatience he declaim'd!
> Fair Liberty was all his Cry;
> For her he stood prepar'd to die;
> For her he boldly stood alone;
> For her he oft expos'd his own.
> Two Kingdoms, just as Faction led,
> Had set a Price upon his Head;
> But, not a Traytor cou'd be found,
> To sell him for Six Hundred Pound.   (*Poetical Works*, 507)

His innocence defended by Heaven (1. 429), Swift achieves his own sovereignty by transgressing the ordinary limits, symbolized by queens and princes, with "due decorum." Here then Swift portrays himself in a state that is properly his own, the unity between decorum and liberty—a state that recalls Blackmur's phrase "tory anarchy." Paulson calls this the merging of "Swift's satiric exploitation of his situation and his serious reflections on it."[5] I think, however, that the explicitly satiric portion of the poem is reserved by Swift deliberately until the very end, where it becomes apparent that rather than being a technique or a genre (which is Paulson's argument), satire for Swift was the mode of his sovereignty and transgression and indeed, finally, of his intelligible existence. In fine, satire was the name of his excess and, as his legacy to Ireland proves, the objective structure of his negative duration in history.

Perhaps I may allow, the Dean
Had too much Satyr in his Vein;
And seem'd determin'd not to starve it,
Because no age could more deserve it.
Yet, Malice never was his Aim;
He lash'd the vice but Spar'd the Name.
No individual could resent,
Where Thousands equally were meant.
His Satyr points at no Defect,
But what all Mortals may correct. . . .
"He gave the little Wealth he had,
To build a House for Fools and Mad:
And Shew'd by one satyric Touch,
No Nation wanted it so much:
That Kingdom he hath left his Debtor,
I wish it soon may have a Better."
        (*Poetical Works*, 512–513)

The "Verses" deliver Swift to history at the poem's end. A real event is projected into the fictive element of language and submitted bravely to the chaos of gossip and transience, until what must be lost cedes to the assertion of posterity's "impartial" gain. In the process Swift the man, of course, dies, buried in the trivia of an age that neither could nor would let him live. This must be the source of the persistent legend of his madness—his alienation from the prescriptive canons of decency that he himself yearned for but which the unendurable honesty of his last years forced him to believe were lost. So he believed himself to have lived and died in that loss. Yet the poem demonstrates how his Irish exile is reinstated as a subject of discourse, but not at all as a personality, nor as a body of works, but rather as a presence *for* those who can simultaneously accept, as he did, waste and power. It is in that condition, between the world and the archive, sharing both, that Swift lasts. His imagination was the transactor of that difficult business, and an extraordinarily difficult challenge for the twentieth-century reader.

3
Swift as Intellectual

FOR reasons having to do both with contemporary critics and with what the great Augustan writers present to them, the early eighteenth century in England has not been particularly responded to by the major contemporary literary theorists. If we compare the kind of use made by the modern critical sensibility of figures like Dr. Johnson, Sterne, Gibbon, and Richardson with what has been made of Pope and Swift, the contrast will be stark. Another way of understanding what I mean is to note the extent to which the study of Gibbon and Johnson, say, is felt to be of interest to nonspecialists in the eighteenth century. Walter Jackson Bate's Johnson biography or the 1976 *Dedalus* symposium on Gibbon have a way of attracting general attention, as much for their subjects' intrinsic merit as for the interest a literate reader might take in the way they are approached. Such an interest has simply not been the case with recent work on Swift. There have been works by well-known critics such as Irvin Ehrenpreis and Denis Donoghue, and there remains the formidable fact of Swift's untarnished, undiminished reputation as a classic. Why then this vacancy, this ominous gap between Swift's potential as an author of extraordinary power for modern critics and the disappointing critical performance outside the professional guild of eighteenth-century scholarship?

It is perfectly possible that what we might call advanced contemporary criticism has not come round to Swift as the result of simple accident. After all, it is true that Norman O. Brown did study Swift very appreciatively twenty-odd years ago, and since his *Life Against Death* was a vanguard work then, there is a good possibility that Swift will again become the exemplary author for vanguard contem-

porary criticism. In other words we might stipulate that the time has
not yet occurred, but it will.

Yet this is an argument that refuses to take seriously the intellectual and cultural circumstances that, throughout human history, have
made the avoidance of or the attention to certain texts matters of deliberate will and conscious choice, not of raw accident. As for Swift's
threadbare case before the contemporary critical jury, there are
ample grounds for judging that case to be the result of certain very
concrete determinations.

In the first place I think it must be said that Swift, along with contemporaries of his like Dryden and Pope, to say nothing of Steele,
Addison and Bolingbroke, has been the beneficiary in the main of a
certain kind of scholarship. I do not mean to be sarcastic when I say
that so formidable are the scholars who maintain the Swift canon,
who uphold his textual orthodoxy—a very important thing, after
all—that approaching him has become a daunting prospect. In
Swift's case there are such facts to be reckoned with as the great
Harold Williams and Herbert Davis editions. So high is the standard
of work that such labors have upheld, so focused and so scrupulous
their attention to strict factuality (which is what one must have from
good editors), that Swift seems even more like the rather dry and
abrasive Anglican divine he must have been at least some of the time
in real life. It is not that Swift scholarship has restricted Swift's appeal, but that with so many of the textual problems having been so
spendidly solved, scholars seem to have felt a certain unwillingness to
venture beyond that realm. And indeed that realm has come to resemble the ambiance of a club, which is not so surprising perhaps if
we remember that Swift's circle during his London days was called a
club.

An important aspect of the club for modern readers seems to have
been determined by what, some years ago, Louis Bredvold called the
gloom of the Tory satirists. This view of Swift, Pope, and Arbuthnot
is, I believe, a natural intellectual concomitant of the textual scholarship I spoke of a moment ago. It is a view with which most readers of
Swift and Pope must concur because it is true and it is persuasive. So
far as human nature was concerned, Swift was a pessimist, and
whether in the final analysis we belong to the "hard" or "soft" school
of interpreters of *Gulliver's Travels* we must say that taken in isolation the Yahoos represent an idea of human nature that is uncomfort-
ably close to being misanthropic. That this view further corresponds
to Swift's own is something that most readers are prepared to allow,

so ingrained in the cultural consciousness is the idea of Swift's generalized *saeva indignatio*.

The trouble with these readings of Swift is that their currency and
authority have confined him either to a circle of like-minded associates ("the Tory satirists") or to a set of beliefs that is not at all difficult to ferret out from his writing. With the possible exception of *A
Tale of a Tub*, whose unrestrained exuberance seems to have amazed
its own author later in life, all of Swift's work does in fact support a
fairly strict, not to say uninteresting, conservative philosophy. Man is
either unimprovable or predisposed to nastiness, corruption, or petti-
ness; the body is naturally disgusting; enthusiasm, like schemes of
conquest or of pseudo-scientific projection, is dangerous and threat-
ens the polity; the Church of England, the classics, and the monarch
(those three institutions Swift believed were fully comprised in the
right-minded sentiments of a Church of England man) together
formed the pillars and the legacy of moral and physical health—this
is not an unfair summary of Swift's doctrine. There are several other
regretably pathological traits that, when they are put next to the
barely controlled violence of Swift's imagination, present us with a
man whose outlook is narrow, constricted, even sadistic.

No one would argue then that Swift is a canonical or classic author
because, like Johnson for example, he offers the reader vitality of
mind in alliance with sanity of perspective. He is *not* like Johnson,
the movement of whose writing is to open things out; Swift's shuts
things down. Even if we agree with Herbert Read, that Swift is the
greatest prose stylist in English, we are likely to feel his effects as essentially unyielding, hard, tight. He belongs to an important and se-
lect group—the Shakespeare of *Troilus and Cressida*, Milton at
times, Gerard Manley Hopkins—for whom language can scarcely
bear the weight of some urgency or other and thereby becomes at
once, and with equal force, afflicted and afflicting. In Swift's intense
and yet highly polished fury of language, there is little room for what
Wordsworth called the still sad music of humanity. We find ourselves
dealing with contortions of the mind, acrobatics of spirit that intrigue
and debate with us but that tend to refuse us in the end, since so often
Swift impersonates people we would not like to resemble. The questions we ask when we read Swift are usually of the "what is going on"
or "how does it work" sort. Not illogically such questions arise precisely because of Swift's incredible economy of line, which is the
essence of Swift's description of the style, "proper words in proper
places," a description to which we might only add "with a ven-
geance."

It is worth going a bit further in stressing the limitations that seem to have removed Swift as a candidate for interesting critical attention. One of the most consistent themes in Swift's work is loss, and even above its lithe power his writing frequently sets about to communicate a literal sense of loss. Therefore one misses in Swift the very dimension of amplitude and sanity which, in the course of his writing, we can see being pushed out of sight. The human body, for example, is exhibited (as in the *Tale* or *Gulliver*) only to be flayed or abused with so intense a microscopic attention as to transmute it into a disgusting object. The poignancy of such deliberate impoverishments is that the writer seems to know this, and even to record the loss with self-mocking revelry in technique that has the uniquely corruscating accuracy we call "Swiftian." The objects of Swift's attention—ideas, people, events—are stripped of real power or life and left, in his prose, as remnants, exhibits that shock, amuse, or fascinate. When we think of the human "content" of Swift's work, and think of it suspended in the plain style, we realize with some discomfort that we have before us a show of freaks and horrors: a mad writer, an astrologer being murdered, an absurd and impossible war, a disjointed political writer (Steele), a gallery of raving freethinkers, men burrowing in dung, and so on. The violent images of war, disease, madness, and depravity, to say nothing of the consequences of dwarfism and giantism offered us by *Gulliver's Travels*, are of a piece with the general loss of normality he seems attracted to. We would not be wrong in saying that a significant aspect of Swift's coherence as a writer is the intellectual and spiritual feat that sustained such a style as his, performing so drastic a transmutation of reality with such forceful negativity for such regrettably narrow ends.

I would not have succeeded in describing the case for Swift the limited, deeply flawed writer if I do not clinch it now with some reference to George Orwell's essay "Politics vs. Literature: An Examination of *Gulliver's Travels*," which was originally published in a late 1946 issue of *Polemic*. Again, my reason for doing so is that I take seriously the fact that Swift has not had his due from contemporary criticism, a failure I ascribe in large measure to certain influential aspects of the general kind of critical attention that Swift *has* had. My point, of course, is that even though Swift must be admitted to be a problematic and in many ways a limited and humanly unattractive figure, these admissions need not prevent him from becoming the object of really fruitful contemporary criticism—but more about that later.

Orwell's essay belongs to the period of his growing disenchantment with modern politics. He tells us that Swift has meant a great deal to him ever since his eighth birthday, when he was given a copy of *Gulliver's Travels*. Orwell's argument is familiar enough and, so far as it goes, one we can recognize from reading Lukacs on Balzac or, more recently, Fredric Jameson on Wyndham Lewis (in *Fables of Aggression*). The general line is that, despite a writer's expressed ideological commitment to right-wing views, his great literary gifts give him special value. Unlike Lukacs and Jameson, Orwell does not try to prove that by virtue of style or technique the author is really progressive. Quite the contrary, Orwell insists that "in a political and moral sense" he is against Swift even though "curiously enough he is one of the writers I admire with least reserve." Thus Orwell's liking for Swift is built around an attempt at finding a great deal to admire in Swift even though he was reactionary, nihilistic, and diseased, words that Orwell uses more than once in this context. In addition he suggests that Swift is one of those writers whose enjoyment can, for his reader, overwhelm disapproval. According to Orwell, "In his endless harping on disease, dirt and deformity, Swift is not actually inventing anything, he is merely leaving something out. Human behaviour, too, especially politics, is as he describes it, although it contains other more important factors which he refuses to admit … Swift did not possess ordinary wisdom, but he did possess a terrible intensity of vision, capable of picking out a single hidden truth and then magnifying and distorting it. The durability of *Gulliver's Travels* goes to show that, if the force of belief is behind it, a world-view which only just passes the test of sanity is sufficient to produce a great work of art."[1]

This is a fair summary of Orwell's judgment on Swift, except that it leaves out a very interesting observation, which I shall come back to later, on what he calls Swift's "irresponsible violence of the powerless." In the meantime, we can safely say that like most scholarly authorities Orwell finds Swift to be admirable over and above whatever he says about life, politics, and mankind. In other words, Swift's views are so compellingly unpleasant in their anarchism, in their illiberal attacks on all society and the human race, as to leave the modern reader with very little either to approve or to respect.

Let me state my own position at last. Orwell, to begin with, is not so much wrong as characteristically partial, insufficient, not really political enough in his verdict. Reading his assessment of Swift one would not know that *Gulliver's Travels* is a late book, or that during most of his earlier life Swift was an active, perhaps even an opportunistic political pamphleteer and polemicist. It is perfectly fair for Orwell to read *Gulliver's Travels* alone and then derive Swift's political views from that isolated reading; it is distorted, however, to make *Gulliver* stand for everything about Swift. Orwell's analogies between Swift and Alan Herbert, G. M. Young, and Ronald Knox, "the innumerable silly-clever Conservatives of our own day," are silly-clever analogies themselves, and rigidly close-minded to boot. To say of Swift that "he did not like democracy" is to say something of great irrelevance to the context of the time, since not even Swift's enemies of the "progressive party," to which Orwell alludes quickly in passing, could be described as believers in democracy. Can one seriously believe that Godolphin or the Duke of Marlborough, both of whom are Whigs that Swift attacked mercilessly, believed in democracy? When Orwell gives Swift credit for being astonishingly prescient about "what would now be called totalitarianism"—spy trials, informers, police plots, and so on—he does so only to be able to damn him in the next breath for not thinking "better of the common people than of their rulers, or to be in favour of increased social equality, or to be enthusiastic about representative institutions." Orwell seems unable to realize that one can be steadfastly opposed to tyranny, as Swift was all his life, and not have a well-developed position on "representative institutions."

What Orwell takes no account of then is ideological consciousness, that aspect of an individual's thought which is ultimately linked to sociopolitical and economic realities. Swift is very much a part of his time: there is no point therefore in expecting him to think and act like a prototype of George Orwell since the cultural options, the social possibilities, the political activities offered Swift in his time were more likely to produce a Swift than an Orwell.

As for the canonical view of Swift as a Tory satirist, it too diminishes Swift the activist and promotes Swift the producer of teleological images. My impression is that too many claims are made for Swift as a moralist and thinker who peddled one or another final view of human nature, whereas not enough claims are made for Swift as a kind of local activist, a columnist, a pamphleteer, a caricaturist. Even the useful analyses of Swift's satiric methods, his use or personae for example, are sometimes vitiated by this prejudice. It is as if critics assume that Swift really wanted to be a John Locke or a Thomas Hobbes, but somehow couldn't: therefore it becomes a critic's job to help Swift fulfill his ambition, turning him from a kind of marginal, sporty political fighter into a pipesmoking armchair philosopher.

Swift is, I think, preeminently a *reactive* writer. Nearly everything he wrote was occasional, and we must quickly add that he responded to, but did not create, the occasions. There are doubtless evident economic reasons for this: Swift, after all, was a minor cleric most of his life and needed the opportunities given him by wealthier patrons, from Temple to Harley to, finally, the Irish polity, on whose behalf he spoke in *The Drapier's Letters*. His originality therefore was in answering, reacting to situations he tried to influence or change. Something he says in the Apology to *A Tale of a Tub* gives a very marked emphasis to his self-consciousness about this: "to answer a Book effectively, requires more Pain and Skill, more Wit, Learning, and Judgement than were employed in creating the situations in the first place." His contribution almost always overturned whatever he discussed by creating new situations, persons, or books in his writing. Hence the new creation, which his polemical methods invariably engendered, and with that a release of energy far in excess of the amount presented to him at the outset, plus a great deal of irony.

Orwell is absolutely correct to say that in *Gulliver's Travels* Swift attacks that aspect of totalitarianism which makes people "less conscious" in general. I would go further and put the matter in positive terms. Swift's aim is to make people more conscious than they would otherwise be of what is being put before them. As Wilde said, "no class is ever really conscious of its own suffering. They have to be told of it by other people, and they often entirely disbelieve them . . . Agitators are a set of interfering, meddling people, who come down to some perfectly contented class of the community and sow the seeds of discontent among them. That is the reason why agitators are so completely necessary."[2] Swift's interfering and meddling agitational method is always to blow up or draw out the implications of a book, a position, or a situation, all of which are otherwise likely to be digested mindlessly by people. Thus he induces consciousness and awareness, he activates recognition. But what has made his later readers (and perhaps even his contemporaries) uncomfortable about his writing is that it has seemed so parasitic on what it responds to. In other words, Swift's impersonations have either seemed too close to what they caricature or too unforgiving about what they propose as an alternative: his portrait of the deranged hack in *A Tale* is an instance of the former, the Yahoos and Houyhnhnms examples of the latter. Swift's severity has then had to be tempered with references to a Tory ethos, to which he belonged, or to some derangement or misanthropic craziness that gave him no choice. No wonder that

Coleridge spoke about Swift as the spirit of Rabelais in a dry place—*anima Rabelaisii in sicco.*

I should like to suggest, however, that if we restrict ourselves to seeing Swift not as a philosopher or as a madman or even as a canonically "creative" writer, but rather as an intellectual, his dryness, severity, and intensity will seem a great deal more systematic and modern. No doubt Swift wanted more out of life than to be Dean of St. Patrick's, or that he hoped Harley and St. John would some day make him a minister, or that he would acquire more wealth and position than his modest station allowed him initially. But these ambitions, however much their frustration angered him, did not prevent him from being energetic, powerful, and effective when he did his writing. In other words there is enough going on, and more than enough to engage the contemporary critic's attention, in Swift's actual, his *local*, performances.

It is probable that the notion of an *intellectual* is not usually associated with any period before the late nineteenth century, just as the role of intellectuals in society is not often studied in periods that antedate the French Revolution. Lewis Coser's *Men of Ideas*, which is one of the best historical surveys of the modern Occidental intellectual, confines its account of eighteenth-century England to half a dozen pages on the London coffeehouses, for which it relies on Harold Rossitt's chapter on Addison and Steele in the 1912 *Cambridge History of English Literature.* Coser is right to say that the coffeehouses leveled class ranks, "bred a new respect and tolerance for the idea of others," encouraged "sociability," and led to "new forms of integration" based on conversational exchange.[3] But he is quite wrong to exclude from investigation the spirited intellectual activity carried on in print during the period. Still Coser's two conditions for "the intellectual vocation to become socially feasible and socially recognized" can usefully be mentioned here:

First, intellectuals need an audience, a circle of people to whom they can address themselves and who can bestow recognition. Such an audience will also, as a rule, provide economic rewards, but the prestige or esteem accorded to the intellectual by his public, his psychic income, may often be more important to him than his economic return. Second, intellectuals require regular contact with their fellow intellectuals, for only through such communication can they evolve common standards of method and excellence, common norms to guide their conduct. Despite popular myth to the contrary, most intellectuals cannot produce their work in solitude, but need the give and take of debate and discussion with their peers in order to develop their ideas. Not all intellectuals are gregarious, but most of them need to test their own ideas in exchange with those they deem their equals.[4]

This is roughly true of Swift, except that it needs to be qualified on one or two points. Swift needed the approbation of his peers, it is true, but it is also the case that he aimed for and generally got a wider audience beyond them. *The Conduct of the Allies* was by any standard a best-selling pamphlet not because it accidentally became one, but because Swift himself deliberately wrote it for a very large audience. Similarly, Swift wrote for *The Examiner* in a remarkably adroit and canny way, even to the extent of using journalistic tricks to encourage the paper's extensive distribution. But, after all is said and done, we should probably not underestimate the importance Swift attached to the good opinion his peers had of him. This is as true during his London days with Arbuthnot and Gay as it is of later Dublin friends like Delaney and Sheridan.

Intellectuals traffic in ideas: this is a minimum kind of definition. In modern times, intellectuals are thought of as playing the important role of gaining legitimacy and currency for ideas. In addition, there is a long tradition of intellectuals being the propagators of useful knowledge and values, and in doing that they are sometimes thought of as functioning as a sort of conscience, as keepers of values, for the society in which they work. This is clearly the idea of an intellectual that Julien Benda had in mind when he published *La Trahison des clercs* in 1928. Benda's definition of the intellectual is doubtless too narrow and idealistic, but his argument on behalf of the intellectual's obligation to adhere to absolute values and to tell the truth regardless of material consequences is powerfully appealing. The duty of intellectuals, he says, "is precisely to set up a corporation whose sole cult is that of justice and of truth, in opposition to the peoples and the injustice to which they are condemned by their religions of this earth."[5] There are echoes of Benda's indictment of intellectuals who have sold out to the ruling passions of state, class, and race in what Noam Chomsky has been writing for the past decade.[6]

In addition to the thesis that the intellectual's models are to be found among such people as Voltaire, Zola, and Socrates, there is another tradition, which begins in Marx's and Engels' *The German Ideology*, where the intellectual is depicted as playing a crucial role in both the change and the preservation of civil society. To a certain extent I think it is true to say of Swift that he was an intellectual in Benda's sense of the word. He certainly thought of himself as a champion of conscience and as an enemy of oppression. Most of his earlier life, however, he was a man engaged in sociopolitical issues, and it is in this more or less partisan role that he needs to be discussed. For this role, we are in need of the critical vocabulary that derives from the broad Marxist and neo-Marxist tradition, which happens also to include a paradoxically anti-Marxist strain.

The authors of *The German Ideology* demonstrate that, far from having an autonomous and sheltered life of its own, philosophy is part of material reality. Consciousness itself is determined by economic conditions they say, and even if we wish to argue, along with Marxists like Lukacs, that Marx and Engels did not mean that consciousness was simply the result of economic conditions, it is certainly the case that *The German Ideology* argues that even such rarefied things as ideas, consciousness, and metaphysics cannot be fully understood without taking stock of politics, sociology, and economics. In any event, what concerns us here is that the intellectual—who is not named as such by Marx and Engels—is either anyone involved in propagating ideas that seem to be independent of social reality or someone (like the two of them) whose main purpose is to show the connections between ideas and social reality. The former kind is obviously a conservative, the latter a revolutionary, since, they argue, anyone who strips ideas of their transcendental aloofness is really urging a revolutionary change in the intellectual and hence the sociopolitical status quo. The struggle between the two types of intellectual is, in Marxist terms, described as taking place not only in consciousness and in society, but in a realm called the *ideological,* a realm of discourse that falsely pretends to be made up of ideas but in reality veils its complicity with and its dependence on material institutions. Thus when Bruno Bauer speaks about self-consciousness, Marx and Engels say, he is disguising the fact that self-consciousness is made possible as a subject for discussion not because it is real but because traditional philosophy, which is an ally of the church, the university, and the state, enables philosophers to speak that way and to create subjects for discussion.

None of what Marx and Engels say as revolutionary intellectuals using what Marx calls "the weapons of criticism" would have been unacceptable to nonrevolutionary intellectuals in the later nineteenth century. This may seem a paradox, but it is not when we think, say, of Matthew Arnold and Ernest Renan, whom no one ever accused of being socialists let alone Marxists. When Arnold writes *Culture and Anarchy* he, like the authors of *The German Ideology*, asserts the social function of culture and ideas; the same is just as true of Renan in his *L'Avenir de la science*. For the nineteenth-century intellectual, being an intellectual includes the ideas of a central social role in addition to furnishing the public with what we might call a critical self-consciousness; this is one reason why a celebrated study of intellectuals (Karl Mannheim's *Ideology and Utopia*) ascribes to the intellectual the role of unmasking ideas.

I want to mention only two further items of recent thinking on intellectuals, both of whom shed useful light on Swift. The first of these items comes from Antonio Gramsci, who was the first—and in my opinion the most acute—modern Marxist to make the intellectual the central point of his sociopolitical analyses. Gramsci says that intellectuals are usually of two kinds: organic intellectuals, those who appear in connection with an emergent social class and who prepare the way for that class's conquest of civil society by preparing it ideologically; and traditional intellectuals, those who seem to be unconnected with social change and who occupy positions in society designed to conserve the traditional processes by which ideas are produced—teachers, writers, artists, priests, and the like. Gramsci's thesis is that all intellectuals are really organic intellectuals to some extent; even when they seem completely disconnected with a political cause, schoolteachers, for instance, play a social role to the extent that they unconsciously legitimate the status quo they serve. Throughout his life Gramsci spent time studying Croce, whom he described in one of his prison letters as a sort of lay pope because of the philosophic hegemony he exercised over the liberal Italian society that, Gramsci believed, directly produced fascism.

Since Gramsci the discussion of intellectuals has taken center stage in analyses of the modern postindustrial state, certainly a far cry from Swift's England. But there are interesting analogies. In 1979 Alvin Gouldner wrote his *Future of the Intellectuals and the Rise of the New Class*, where he sees the new class of intellectuals as challenging the old monied class for power. Leaving aside the questionable aspects of Gouldner's thesis, he is worth soliciting on the question of what he calls the intellectual's *capital*. Earlier I said that many of Swift's critics pay too much attention to his ideas and not enough to the deployment and disposition of his energies, his local performances I called them. What such assertions do is to ally Swift too closely with the real holders of those basically reactionary values, the great landed aristocracy, the established church, the imperial monarchy. Translated into ideology this class is represented by these Tory values ascribed to Swift. Swift himself was not a propertyowner, and it is perfectly evident from his work that he had a low opinion of conquering armies, of colonial oppression, and of scientific schemes for manipulating people and opinion. In Gouldner's terminology, Swift's capital was that of the intellectual: rhetorical skill as a writer on the ideological field of battle. By the same token, then, we must look at Swift as an intellectual engaged in particular struggles of a very limited sort, not as a man who formulated, defended and owned a consistent set of ideological values, which were not his class prerogative to begin with since they quite literally belonged to the class he sometimes served.

During his lifetime Swift could fairly be described as an outsider. He was not well-born, his high-placed patrons invariably disappointed him, and he regularly angered and alienated authorities he was supposed to be serving. There is an ironic reminder of this in Gulliver's voyage to Lilliput, when in putting out the fire by urinating on it Gulliver also succeeds in offending the Queen. So far as I know, Swift had no alternative to social advancement outside the church, except through patronage, intellectual activity on behalf of partisan causes (most but not all of the time), and sheer wit (as a conversationalist and writer). He never amassed anything resembling a fortune, and he died as alienated from Ireland as he had been, over twenty years before, from England. From a class standpoint, then, Swift was a traditional intellectual—a cleric—but what makes him unique is that unlike almost any other major writer in the whole of English literature (except possibly for Steele) he was also an extraordinarily important organic intellectual because of his closeness to real political power. At certain stages in their careers Defoe and Johnson were pamphleteers and, in Johnson's case, public figures; neither of them, however, was visibly affiliated with a political formation in ascendancy as Swift was with the Tory government between 1711 and 1713. For then it was Swift's job to legitimize Harley's admittedly opportunistic politics of peace (culminating in the Peace of Utrecht) and to delegitimize the Whig politics of war. It must also be said of his later intellectual work that it was organically linked to a very different kind of nascent political power, the Irish colonial community, which Swift himself played a significant part in creating. Who except Swift could say as simply and as truthfully as he does in *The Drapier's Letters:* "By engaging in the Trade of a Writer I have drawn upon myself the Displeasure of the Government."[7]

What are the major issues—barring such teleological questions as

the nature of man and the forms of civil or ecclesiastical authority—
that Swift's work defined? Principally I would say anything connected with human aggression or organized human violence. Under
this heading Swift was able to place such disparate things as war itself (about which he never had a good word to say: a remarkable
fact), conquest, colonial oppression, religious factionalism, the manipulation of minds and bodies, schemes for projecting power on nature, on human beings, and on history, the tyranny of the majority,
monetary profit for its own sake, the victimization of the poor by a
privileged oligarchy. Each of these things can be easily documented
in at least one of Swift's works, and it should be remembered that
there are very few authors before the late nineteenth century—Blake
and Shelley being among the few—whose position on these matters
diverges so sharply from the reigning majority view. There is nothing
that so consciously and so deliberately reveals both the sheer horror
of war and the even more horrible delight and pride that men take in
it than this passage from *Gulliver:*

To confirm what I have now said, and further to shew the mis-
erable Effects of a *confined Education;* I shall here insert a Passage which will hardly obtain Belief. In hopes to ingratiate myself farther into his Majesty's Favour, I told him of an Invention
discovered between three and four hundred Years ago, to make a
certain Powder; into an heap of which the smallest Spark of Fire
falling, would kindle the whole in a Moment, although it were as
big as a Mountain; and make it all fly up in the Air together, with
a Noise and Agitation greater than Thunder. That, a proper
Quantity of this Powder rammed into an hollow Tube of Brass
or Iron or Lead with such Violence and Speed, as nothing was
able to sustain its Force. That, the largest Balls thus discharged,
would not only Destroy whole Ranks of an Army at once; but
batter the strongest Walls to the Ground; sink down Ships with
a Thousand Men in each, to the Bottom of the Sea; and when
linked together by a Chain, would cut through Masts and Rig-
ging; divide Hundreds of Bodies in the Middle, and lay all Waste
before them. That we often put this Powder into large hollow
Balls of Iron, and discharged them by an Engine into some City
we were besieging; which would rip up the Pavement, tear the
Houses to Pieces, burst and throw Splinters on every Side,
dashing out the Brains of all who came near. . . .
    The King was struck with Horror at the Description I had
given of those terrible Engines, and the Proposal I had made. He
was amazed how so impotent and groveling an Insect as I (these

were his Expressions) could entertain such inhuman Ideas, and
in so familiar a Manner as to appear wholly unmoved at all the
Scenes of Blood and Desolation, which I had painted as the
common Effects of those destructive Machines; whereof he said,
some evil Genius, Enemy to Mankind, must have been the first
Contriver. As for himself, he protested, that although few
Things delighted him so much as new Discoveries in Art or in
Nature; yet he would rather lost Half his Kingdom than be
privy to such a Secret; which he commanded me, as I valued my
Life, never to mention any more.[8]

Or there is this devastating analysis of the war of Spanish succession
in *The Conduct of the Allies:*

whether this War were prudently begun or not, it is plain, that
the true Spring or Motive of it, was the aggrandizing a particular
Family, and in Short, a War of the General and the Ministry,
and not of the Prince or People; since those very Persons were
against it, when they knew the Power, and consequently the
Profit, would be in other Hands.[9]

Here Swift speaks the truth simply; he tries neither to dress it up nor
to conceal the secrecy or greed with which profitable wars are
planned. Hence the anger Swift feels on behalf of future generations:
"it will no doubt be a mighty Comfort to our Grandchildren when
they see a few Rags hung up in Westminster Hall, which cost an hundred Millions, whereof they are paying the Arrears, and boasting, as
Beggars do, that their Grandfathers were Rich and Great."[10] And
there is no more relevant description than Swift's of the way great
powers tie themselves to allies who are supposed to be their surrogates, but become their masters (one thinks of Generals Thieu and
Ky during the Vietnamese war):

By two other Articles (beside the honour of being Convoys and
Guards in ordinary to the Portugese Ships and Coasts) we are to
guess the Enemies Thoughts, and to take the King of Portugal's
Word, whenever he has a Fancy that he shall be invaded: We are
also to furnish him with a Strength superior to what the Enemy
intends to invade any of his Dominions with, let that be what it
will: And, till we know what the Enemy's forces are, his Portugese Majesty is sole Judge what Strength is superior, and what
will be able to prevent an invasion; and may send our Fleets,
whenever he pleases, upon his Errands, to some of the Furthest
Parts of the World, or keep them attending upon his own Coasts

till he thinks fit to dismiss them. These Fleets must likewise be subject, in all things, not only to the King, but to his Viceroys, Admirals and Governors, in any of his foreign Dominions, when he is in a humour to apprehend an Invasion; which, I believe, is an indignity that was never offered before, except to a Conquered Nation.[11]

When it was assumed by his countrymen that they knew everything important about their Irish colony, it was Swift who in his letter to Lord Chancellor Middleton on October 26, 1724, described the stereotype that made it possible for England to mistreat Ireland so cavalierly (similar caricatures of African and Asian peoples exist even today):

There is a Vein of Industry and Parsimony, that runs through the whole people of England; which, added to the Easiness of their Rents, makes them rich and sturdy. As to Ireland, they know little more than they do of Mexico; further than that it is a Country subject to the King of England, full of Boggs, inhabited by wild Irish Papists; who are kept in Awe by mercenary Troops sent from thence: And their general Opinion is, that it were better for England if this whole Island were sunk into the Sea: For, they have a tradition, that every Forty Years there must be a Rebellion in Ireland. I have seen the grossest suppositions pass upon them; that the wild Irish were taken in Toyls; but that, in some time, they would grow so tame, as to eat out of your hands.[12]

We can see the unmistakable connection between this sort of thinking and the logic that gave rise to *A Modest Proposal*, for once you dehumanize people into a mere bundle of unchanging attributes it is a very short step to turning them into articles of consumption.

Despite all this, it would not be fair to Swift simply to characterize him as a courageous intellectual. What we must also be able to understand about him is that everything he did as an intellectual heightened and affected consciousness, even to the extent that he brought out his own self-conscious position in his writing. This immediately gets us to the canonical question of Swift's satire, his irony, and the use of personae.

Let me do so first by returning to what I said at the outset about modern criticism. I had made it seem then that Swift has not been favored with avant-garde critical attention because he has seemed the exclusive property of a circle of scholars, and because there is general agreement that Swift's values are, in Orwell's words, clearly reactionary. In general, contemporary criticism has been concerned with authors and texts whose formal characteristics exist in some disjunctive relationship with their ideological or thematic surface: thus the critic's job is to illuminate the disjunction by exposing, or deconstructing, the contradictions woven into the text's formal being. Moreover, the critic's position about the texts he analyzes is a marginal one; that is, the text is important whereas the critic's role is a secondary one, limited to revealing the text's conditions of being. This procedure is true, I think, of the Derridean school, the school of Marxist readers, of Foucault's disciples, the semioticians, of the so-called Yale school.

Swift resists this approach and, as I said earlier, it is his resistance that makes him so interesting and challenging a figure. My argument is that the main avenue to understanding Swift is that we take seriously the way in which he resists any kind of critical approach that does not make his existence, his functioning, and above all his self-consciousness as an intellectual—albeit an intellectual in the special historical circumstances of his cultural moment—the main avenue to approaching him.

Consider therefore three theses I want to propose. (1) Swift has no reserve capital: his writing brings to the surface all he has to say. His fictions, his personae, his self-irony turn around the scandal, first announced in *A Tale of a Tub,* that what is being said is being said at that moment, for that moment, by a creature of that moment. This is always literally true—what we can know about Swift or Gulliver or the Drapier is what is before us, and only that. The irony completes itself in the reading; there is nothing to check it against (who would consider appealing from the "modest proposal" to a real person who doesn't think that people should be eaten?) since what it says is what it means. (2) Swift is invariably attacking what he impersonates. In other words, his technique is to become the thing he attacks, which is normally not a message or a political doctrine but a style or a manner of discourse. Note how many of Swift's works are about iterative performances, activities, styles of behavior: proposal, tale, conduct, conversation, voyage, letter, argument, examination, sermon. The space between satirist and object satirized disappears, as for instance in a digression concerning digression or madness. (3) Ahead of his critics, Swift is always aware—and troubles the reader with the awareness—that what he is doing above all is *writing* in a world of power. Swift is the realist par excellence and can make, indeed embody in what he writes, distinctions between idle language and the language of authority, the language of institutions and the language of alienated or marginal individuals, the language of reason and what he called polite conversation. Thus Swift is among the most worldly of writers—perhaps the most worldly. Yet these distinctions have a habit of collapsing into one another. He will, for example, seriously propose a scheme for ascertaining, establishing, and correcting the language, then a few years later parody the scheme by writing *The Polite Conversation*, which is nothing if not a centralized, socially agreed upon scheme for all language in society.

This habit of turning something into its opposite is a corollary of Swift's vocation as a reactive writer. It is also the consequence of Swift's realization that what he is doing is merely writing, albeit on behalf of one or another cause. Yet more than anything else Swift's activity as intellectual, that is, his mission to make his reader more conscious of what a given political or moral position entails, seems always to have infected his own self-consciousness. The worm of consciousness, to borrow from Nicola Chiaromonte, infects Swift the writer. This is the source of his extraordinary self-irony. I am reminded of an observation about Wittgenstein made by Erich Heller: such self-consciousness as Wittgenstein's arrives at "the stage where every act of creation is inseparable from the critique of its medium, and every work, intensely reflecting upon itself, looks like the embodied doubt of its own possibility."[13] Surely this is the ironic consequence of *A Tale of a Tub*, which in attacking enthusiasts of all sorts turns and incriminates the author of the writing himself. Or as a wonderfully suggestive series of images seems to be saying, isn't all writing by someone like Swift just as vulnerable to criticism, irony, and answering as the things he attacks? I am thinking of Swift's images in *A Tale* for the ridiculous and shaky opportunities available if one wishes to intervene verbally into reality—the pulpit, the stage itinerant, or the ladder—and how these things, like a tract, a tale, a digression, or a pamphlet, are subject to other sorts of more worldly power, which a writer or an intellectual without really solid capital does not possess. Intellectual writing protrudes into space and time, but its occasions are in the end controlled by real power. Beyond its immediately serviceable qualities (which are in thrall to a monied or political class), all such writing has its internal ironies, which concern and delight the intellectual. Or consider the occasion in the *Travels* when Gulliver creates a space on his spread-out handkerchief for the Lilliputian cavalry and how we realize that, if the giant Gulliver withdraws, they will collapse. The power he possesses as a giant works against him in turn when as a dwarf in Broddingnag he performs on small tables for the audience.

The greatest intellectual irony, or the greatest irony of an intellectual, is to be found in the fourth voyage, that one episode in Swift's work that has haunted all his readers. We cannot easily exhaust its power or its devastating imaginative originality, nor should we try. But we can see in the Houyhnhnms and the Yahoos—with Gulliver between them—a measure of Swift's general intellectual disenchantment with society, a disenchantment that in the end presents us with minimal options for a satisfactory life. The crucial thing about the Houyhnhnms is not whether they are supposed to be an ideal, but that they are animals; as for the Yahoos, they are humans who act more like animals than men. This state of affairs is perhaps an instance of what Orwell calls "the irresponsible violence of the powerless": nothing of human life is left for Swift to take pleasure in, so he attacks it all. But what has always impressed me in the fourth voyage is that over and above its genuine disillusionment there still remains, as impressive as anything else in the tale, Gulliver himself, recording his recognitions and discoveries, still making sense, still—even in Houyhnhnmland—finding out where the occasions might exist for him to do something. That each of the voyages ends with Gulliver's banishment or escape reflects, I think, the ultimately tragic restlessness of Swift's intellectual energy, just as Gulliver's voyages to fully imagined places, where he must respond to the minute pressures of each situation, testify to Swift's energetic desire to look for concrete things in order to "answer" them.

I think finally that in a passage from *The Drapier's Letters* we can hear the accents of Swift's general intellectual alertness, and his sense of the healthy cynicism, the fragility, the marginality, but also the mastered irony of the intellectual's true situation:

I am now resolved to follow (after the usual Proceeding of Mankind, because it is too late) the Advice given me by a certain Dean. He shewed the mistake I was in, of trusting to the general good Will of the people; that I had succeeded hitherto, better than could be expected; but that some unfortunate circumstantial Lapse, would probably bring me within the reach of Power: that my good intentions would be no Security against those who watched every Motion of my Pen, in the Bitterness of my Soul.[14]

4

Conrad:
The Presentation of Narrative

BOTH in his fiction and in his autobiographical writing Conrad was trying to do something that his experience as a writer everywhere revealed to be impossible. This makes him interesting as the case of a writer whose working reality, his practical and even theoretical competence as a writer, was far in advance of what he was saying. Occurring at the time when he lived and wrote, this irony of Conrad's writing has a critical place in the history of the duplicity of language, which since Nietzsche, Marx, and Freud has made the study of the orders of language so central to the contemporary understanding. Conrad's fate was to write fiction great for its presentation, not only for what it was representing. He was misled by language even as he led language into a dramatization no other author really approached. For what Conrad discovered was that the chasm between words saying and words meaning was widened, not lessened, by a talent for words written. To have chosen to write, then, is to have chosen in a particular way neither to say directly nor to mean exactly in the way he had hoped to say or to mean. No wonder that Conrad returned to this problematic concern repeatedly, a concern that his writing dramatized continuously and imaginatively.

There is unusual attention paid to the motivation of the stories being told—evidence of a felt need to justify in some way the telling of a story. Such attention to the exact motive for telling a story conflicts with Conrad's account in *A Personal Record* of his beginning as a writer. Instead of a reasoned process by which a sailor became a writer, he says that "the conception of a planned book was entirely outside my mental range when I sat down to write." One morning he called in his landlady's daughter:

"Will you please clear away all this at once?" I addressed her in convulsive accents, being at the same time engaged in getting my pipe to draw. This, I admit, was an unusual request . . . I remember that I was perfectly calm. As a matter of fact I was not at all certain that I wanted to write, or what I meant to write, or that I had anything to write about. No, I was not impatient.

"This" is breakfast. Then *Almayer's Folly* was begun: so much for an event of "general mysteriousness."[1] Conrad's narratives deal simultaneously with actions without obvious rational motivation, such as this event in *A Personal Record*, and with such actions as the telling of a story motivated by ascertainable causes. A clear example is found in *Heart of Darkness*. Marlow's desire to visit the dark places is long-standing but really unexplained, and yet his account of the journey to a group of listeners is related exactly to an occasion that motivates it. Marlow's hankering after blank spaces doesn't have a sequential history and it doesn't develop. It is fairly constant; even in *A Personal Record*, as he describes his birth as a writer, Conrad tells the same story as this one of Marlow's:

Now when I was a little chap I had a passion for maps. I would look for hours at South America, or Africa, or Australia, and lose myself in all the glories of exploration. At that time there were many blank spaces on the earth, and when I saw one that looked particularly inviting on a map (but they all look that) I would put my finger on it and say, When I grow up I will go there. (VI, 52)

Years later one blank space

had become a place of darkness. But there was in it one river especially, a mighty big river, that you could see on the map, resembling an immense snake uncoiled, with its head in the sea, its body at rest curving afar over a vast country, and its tail lost in the depths of the land. As I looked at the map of it in a shopwindow, it fascinated me as a snake would a bird—a silly little bird. (VI, 42)

If we compare this story of stupefied fascination with the occasion that gives rise to Marlow's telling of his African adventure, we notice how, from even the tale's first paragraph, a rationale and a motive for the narration are described. The *Nellie* is forced to "wait for the turn of the tide," the five men have a common history of seafaring, the lower reaches of the Thames do not suggest a snake fascinating a

dumb bird but a thread leading back to "the great spirit of the past
. . . the dreams of men, the seed of commonwealths, the germs of empires," and then there is Marlow, with his well-known "propensity to
spin yarns." Before the narration begins (and how unlike Conrad's
inability to conceive of a planned book before he became an author)
"we knew we were fated, before the ebb began to run, to hear about
one Marlow's inconclusive experiences" (XVI, 51).

As Conrad surveyed his novels for the Author's Notes he wrote at
a late point in his career, he was often impressed with the way his
narratives seemed to emanate by chance. Frequently then he provided his reader with originating reasons for the story he had written.
More often than not these reasons were an appealing anecdote, a bit
of personal experience, a newspaper story, and so on. Norman
Sherry's labors have unearthed far more of that evidence than Conrad
revealed, not only because Conrad was forgetful and evasive but also
because he was concerned mainly with justifying what he did as
being reasonable. Conrad, I think, judged that to be more important
than supplying clues to his methods of work. Hence we ought to take
seriously his protest in the Note to *Lord Jim* that Marlow's narration
could have been spoken during an evening of swapping yarns. It is a
surprising line to take, but Conrad was addressing what was to him
always an important point, the dramatized telling of the story, how
and when it was told, for which the evidence was an integral part of
the novel as a whole.

> Men have been known, both in the tropics and the temperate
> zone, to sit up half the night "swapping yarns." This, however,
> is but one yarn, yet with interruption affording some measure of
> relief; and in regard to the listener's endurance, the postulate
> must be accepted that the story was interesting . . . That part of
> the book which is Marlow's narrative can be read through aloud,
> I should say, in less than three hours. Besides . . . we may pre-
> sume that there must have been refreshments on that night, a
> glass of mineral water of some sort to help the narrator on. (XXI,
> vii)

Quite literally, therefore, Conrad was able to see his narratives as
the place in which the motivated, the occasional, the methodical, and
the rational are brought together with the aleatory, the unpredictable,
the inexplicable. On the one hand, there are conditions presented by
which a story's telling becomes necessary; on the other hand, the essential story itself seems opposite to the conditions of its telling. The

interplay of one with the other—and Conrad's attention to the persuasively realistic setting of the tale's presentation enforces our attention to this—makes the narrative the unique thing it is.

Such an interplay of antitheses ought to be characterized as doing
for Conrad what no other activity, whether verbal, plastic, or ges-
tural, could have done for him. I attach a great importance to this observation. Too often Conrad's text is searched for supervening sub-
texts or privileged meanings of the sort that seem more important
than the book itself. Not enough care is given the near truism that,
such as it is, the text was for Conrad a produced thing, *the* produced
thing—something he returned to often as author, critic, defender,
spectator, or victim. The text was the never-ending product of a continuing process. For him, as many letters testify, the necessity of
writing, once he had become an author, was preeminently the problem; for all the general mysteriousness of the Rubicon crossed into
authorhood, he viewed his career as writer as a physical process and
as a particularly onerous task that was his fate. "La solitude me gagne;
elle m'absorbe. Je ne vois rien, je ne lis rien. C'est comme une espèce
de tombe, qui serait en même temps un enfer, où il faut écrire, écrire,
écrire."[2] Loneliness, darkness, the necessity of writing, imprisonment: these are the pressures upon the writer as he writes, and there
is scarcely any I have read who seems so profligate in his complaining. How different in tone this is from the aesthetic credo delivered
by Conrad in his 1896 Preface to *The Nigger of the 'Narcissus.'* He
speaks there of the artist's capacity for communal speech and for the
clarity of sight he affords the reader; those are achievements presumably won after much struggle with the writing itself.

> To snatch in a moment of courage, from the remorseless rush of
> time, a passing phase of life, is only the beginning of the task.
> The task approached in tenderness and faith is to hold up un-
> questioningly, without choice and without fear the rescued frag-
> ment before all eyes in the light of a sincere mood. It is to show
> its vibration, its colour, its form; and through its movement, its
> form and its colour reveal the substance of its truth—disclose its
> inspiring secret: the stress and passion within the core of each
> convincing movement. (XXIII, xiv)

Yet this is no set of euphemisms. To rescue a fragment and give it
shape and form, to make the reader see, to do this by overcoming rational choice at the outset and fear during the performance: these imperatives are much more formidable when we insist, as Conrad does a

little earlier, that the medium is words. To produce or to read words is something quite different, obviously, than the more visual and more well-known goals Conrad formulates for his work. Indeed the perceptual transformation that occurs when writing or reading results in sight is very drastic, even antithetical. So antithetical in fact that one tends to forget the whole sentence in which he formulates his primary ambition. "My task which I am trying to achieve is, by the power of the written word to make you hear, to make you feel—it is before all, to make you see." Conrad's narratives thus embody (provide a locale for) the transformation in the act of taking place. Conrad's own efforts, he says, are to employ the power of written words, with their origin in the painstaking craft of writing, in order to make his reader experience the vitality and the dynamism of seen things. Most often, however, this happens through the mediation of spoken words.

Interestingly, the dramatic protocol of much of Conrad's fiction is the swapped yarn, the historical report, the mutually exchanged legend, the musing recollection. This protocal implies (although often they are explicitly there) a speaker and a hearer and, as I said earlier, sometimes a specific enabling occasion. If we go through Conrad's major work we will find, with the notable exception of *Under Western Eyes*, that the narrative is presented as transmitted orally. Thus hearing and telling are the ground of the story, the tale's most stable sensory activities and the measure of its duration; in marked contrast, seeing is always a precarious achievement and a much less stable business. Consider Kurtz and Jim. Both are heard and spoken about more than they are seen directly in the narrative setting. When they are seen—and Jim is a particularly striking instance: "for me that white figure in the stillness of coast and sea seemed to stand at the heart of a vast enigma"—they are enigmatic and, in some curious way, grossly distorted. "Kurtz looked at least seven feet long . . . I saw him open his mouth wide—it gave him a weirdly voracious aspect, as though he had wanted to swallow all the air, all the earth, all the men before him" (XVI, 134). As Marlow speaks, furthermore, his voice remains steady as his listeners' sight of him fades. So frequent is that sort of disappearance that Conrad's stated goal in the 1896 Preface was for him a specially challenging one, since the course of narrative words seems frequently not only to run counter to vision but to protract the silence of "an impenetrable darkness," despite the insistence of words on the page or between speaker and hearer.

Perhaps it is useful to schematize some of what I have been saying.

Narratives originate in the hearing and telling presence of people. In Conrad's case this is usually true whether or not the narratives are told in the first person. Their subject is illusory or shadowy or dark: that is, whatever by nature is not easy to see. So much at least is ascertainable by the sheer telling of the tale, for what the tale usually reveals is the exact contours of this obscurity. Much of the time obscurity, regardless even of extravagant outward splendour (as with Nostromo or Jim or the Black Mate), is a function of secret shame. Paradoxically, however, the secret is all too easily prone to the wrong kind of exposure, which Conrad's notoriously circumspect methods of narrative attempt to forestall. The reflective narrator is always a narrator preventing the wrong sort of interpretation. His narrative invariably assumes the currency of a rival version. For example, the whole of *Nostromo* is built out of competing histories of Costaguana, each claiming to be a more perspicacious record of momentous events, each implicitly critical of other versions. The same is true of *Under Western Eyes, Lord Jim,* and so on.

We can conceive of Conrad's narratives abstractly as the alternation in language of presence and absence. The presence of spoken words in time mitigates, if it does not make entirely absent, their written version; a speaker takes over the narrative with his voice, and his voice overrides the fact that he is absent (or unseen) to his listeners as he speaks. Conrad's goal is to make us see, or otherwise transcend the absence of everything but words, so that we may pass into a realm of vision beyond the words. What is that realm? It is a world of such uncomplicated coincidence between intention, word, and deed that the ghost of a fact, as Lord Jim has it, can be put to rest. There, rifts in the community of man or in the damaged ego are healed, and the space separating ambition from activity is narrowed. Retrospective time and events are corrected for divergences. Or, still more radically, the writer's intention of wishing to say something very clearly is squared completely with the reader's seeing; by the labors of a solitary writer, words affixed to the page become the common unmediated property of the reader, who penetrates past the words to their author's visual intention, which is the same as his written presentation.

For Conrad the meaning produced by writing was a kind of visual outline, which written language would approach only from the outside and from a distance that seemed to remain constant. We can perhaps ascribe this peculiar limitation on words to Conrad's faith in the supremacy of the visible along with his radical doubt that written language could imitate what the eye saw. His use of such essentially retrospective and investigative narrative devices as the inquiry (*Lord Jim*), historical reporting (*Nostromo*), methodical quest (*Heart of Darkness*), the translation (*Under Western Eyes*), and the ironic investigation (*The Secret Agent*) shows him to be employing language as if the purpose of these devices is for actual vision to occur, so that then language would no longer be necessary. But these devices are themselves based on the assumption that there is a central place, a "heart of darkness" which may be somewhere in central Africa, in Central America, or central London, which is well and perhaps even centrally located for understanding some action in a past whose characteristic is to go on radiating significance from that place to other places and at later times.

To think of Conrad's fiction in such terms is to be struck by how compulsively the whole complex of ideas associated with "the center" (approach to the center, radiations away from the center) keeps appearing in his work, especially if we remember that Conrad never lets us forget that written narrative transcribes a told narrative that draws attention to itself as a process of getting closer and closer to the center. Thus in *Heart of Darkness* Marlow's voyage toward the various trading stations of the interior posits Kurtz as the ultimate goal. Kurtz is described as being at the Inner Station and is much spoken about. By reaching him Marlow hopes to put a stop to all the rumors he has heard and finally to see silently for himself what exactly Kurtz is and has done. Most of the time, though, both the reader and Marlow must be satisfied with fewer words rather than no words once the center has been reached. Hence the eerie power in Conrad of minimal but hauntingly reverberating phrases like "the horror" or "material interests": these work as a sort of still point, a verbal center glossed by the narrative and on which our attention turns and returns. See the thing they announce, and you might have no further use for words. Find their visual equivalent, and you might have a total presence that the duplicitous order of language has made absent in the narrative. Not for nothing is Conrad's first extended narrative, *Almayer's Folly*, about a structure called "the folly," designed to house the gold brought out from the interior, gold never seen, however, never brought out, only spoken about.

So irrational must the coincidence between the effacement of words and the unmediated visual presence of meaning have become by the time of *The Secret Agent* (1907, twelve years after *Almayer*) that Conrad's use of a deranged boy's habitual activity to represent the coincidence is, I think, strongly self-commenting:

innocent Stevie, seated very good and quiet at a deal table, drawing circles, circles; innumerable circles, concentric, eccentric, coruscating whirl of circles that by their tangled multitude of repeated curves, uniformity of form, and confusion of intersecting lines suggested a rendering of cosmic chaos, the symbolism of a mad art attempting the inconceivable. The artist never turned his head; and in all his soul's application to the task his back quivered, his thin neck, sunk into a deep hollow at the base of the skull, seemed ready to snap. (XII, 45–46)

Mr. Verloc merely "discloses the innocent Stevie" when he opens the kitchen door, for Stevie's autistic art intends no hearer and is unspoken. It is only a ceaseless, intense application to a repeated action whose meaning is unchanging. Conrad's choice of the word "task" here was probably an involuntary quotation from the 1896 Preface whose moral seriousness he drew upon frequently. The solitary, repetitive, uniform, and confusing nature of Stevie's art parallels Conrad's description of writing ("un enfer, òu il faut écrire, écrire, écrire"), just as the concentric, eccentric circles suggest the interplay of antithesis and the alternation in language of presence and absence. What is most remarkable is the silence of the whole scene and its general mysteriousness. Can we say that Stevie is being overlooked or overheard? For indeed it is hard to know whether Mr. Verloc's "grunt of disapproving surprise" means anything more than the merest awareness. Circles do not speak, they tell only of the inconceivable (and that by a very attenuated symbolism), and they enclose blankness even as they seem partly to be excluding it. Moreover, Stevie's circles are page-bound; they tie him to a blank white space and they exist no place else. I think it entirely likely that Conrad imagined Stevie as a kind of writer viewed *in extremis* who, in being taken for a sort of pointless idiot, is limited terribly to two poles: inscribing a page endlessly or blown to bits and without human identity. There are rough but affecting antecedents for Stevie and the Verlocs in "The Idiots," a short story completed in 1896. The story opens in much the same way as "Amy Foster" (1901), which also deals with an alienated figure who appears to be insane, with the narrator seeing the vestiges of an old story as he visits a locale new to him. The story—"at last before me, a tale formidable and simple"—is of a peasant couple who unaccountably produce four idiot children. The wife's hurt perplexity and rage drive her to kill her husband. She then kills herself by jumping off a cliff into the sea; a witness to the suicide hears "one shrill cry for help that seemed to dark upwards . . . and soar past, straight into the high and impassive heaven" (VII, 84).

Still later, the language teacher in *Under Western Eyes* (1911) comments further upon the attempt to transcend language by vision. Now, however, that "folly" has a political meaning as well, despite its formulation by him in verbal terms. "That propensity," he says, "of lifting every problem from the plane of the understandable by means of some sort of mystic expression, is very Russian" (XXII, 104). Elsewhere he remarks on what it is like to listen to Russians speaking: "The most precise of her [Natalia Haldin's] sayings seemed always to me to have enigmatical prolongations vanishing somewhere beyond my reach" (XXII, 118). The verbs of physical action and perception to describe language put to extraverbal use are thoroughly consistent with Conrad's usual practice. "Lifting" suggests the "holding up" of the 1896 Preface, but it is associated here with the derogatory "mystic expression," an unreliable instrument at best. The net effect of this kind of communication, no matter how precisely formulated, is to extend meaning so far away from the words that it disappears completely. What the old teacher constantly reiterates is that the tendency in Russian to mystic expression is a kind of ontological flaw present to a much lesser degree in Western languages. Razumov feels the flaw hysterically when Haldin throws himself upon the poor student's mercy. Order is associated with the careful study and use of language (both the teacher and Razumov are students of the word), whereas disorder, transcendence, and a kind of political aestheticism are linked to Haldin's revolutionary wish directly to see, to change, to embrace.

By the time *Chance* (1913) gave him an unexpected popularity, Conrad had determined that he was after all an English writer and neither, as some critics had alleged, a French one manqué nor a crypto-Slav. In the second, much later preface (1919) to *A Personal Record* he wrote this astonishingly "Russian" account of his use of English. I quote it at length for its passion and its determination not to press rationality too far:

The truth of the matter is that my faculty to write in English is as natural as any other aptitude with which I might have been born. I have a strange and overpowering feeling that it had always been an inherent part of myself. English was for me neither a matter of choice nor adoption. The merest idea of choice had never entered my head. And as to adoption—well, yes, there was adoption; but it was I who was adopted by the genius of the language, which directly I came out of the stammering stage made me its own so completely that its very idioms I truly believe had a direct action on my temperament and fashioned my still plastic character.

A matter of discovery and not of inheritance, that very inferiority of the title makes the faculty still more previous, lays the professor under a lifelong obligation to remain worthy of his great fortune ... All I can claim after all those years of devoted practice, with the accumulated anguish of its doubts, imperfections and falterings in my heart, is the right to be believed when I say that if I had not written in English I would not have written at all. (VI, vii–viii)

Even if this is not the most lucid treatment of the problem, at least one gets from this passage an inkling of how complex and how close to "Impossible" (the capital is Conrad's) the problems were for him as he considered the dissemination, reception, and perception of language.

His letters portray Conrad perpetually struggling with language. His narratives always dramatize how a story happens to someone else: he is either told it or, if he is the protagonist, he experiences it like Jim, with its rationale herded under the heading of Romance. "Romance had singled Jim for its own—and that was the true part of the story, which otherwise was all wrong." Written language was therefore essentially a passive, retrospective, transcription of action. As author Conrad presented his writing as methodically overshadowed by the speaking voice, the past, vision, and restful clarity. How revealing is this moan in a letter of January 4, 1900, to Cunningham Grahame: "But difficulties are as it were closing round me; an irresistible march of blackbeetles I figure it to myself. What a fate to be so ingloriously devoured."[3]

Conrad seemed to have overestimated language, or at any rate its power over him. I do not intend this as a judgment against him since from this overestimation derives the extraordinary care he took with the way his narratives are delivered. *Heart of Darkness*, for instance, is a complex structure with half a dozen "languages" in it, each with its own sphere of experience, its time, its center of consciousness. To say that Conrad wrote in English therefore is to say really that Conrad makes highly imaginative distinctions within English, distinctions no other writer before him would have thought necessary, distinctions that were his "physical recognition" of verbal sources for a story that always lay just beyond and outside him. These distinctions were Conrad's defense against the assault of language: by redisposing and redispersing, then reassembling, language into voices, he

could stage his work as a writer. The plurality of narrative components is then imagined as encircling a subject in many different ways.
The net effect, as Mallarmé says in *Crise de vers,* is finally to concede
"l'initiative aux mots, par le heurt de leur inegalités mobilisés."[4]
What gets left out of the words is that intransigent remnant of the
writer's identity that is not amenable to language. By a curious irony,
which doubtless appealed to a writer who wishes to make you see, the
excluded remnant is the actual inscribing persona himself, the author,
and yet Conrad pretended that the author was secondary. Once again
we note how voices leading to vision efface what Conrad called "the
worker in prose," whose disappearance, according to Mallarmé,
ought to yield *l'oeuvre pur.* Unlike both Mallarmé and Flaubert,
however, this does not happen in Conrad's case.

REFLECTING on Leskov's storytelling, Walter Benjamin
argues that the success of narrative art has traditionally
depended upon a sense of community between speaker and listener
and on the desire to communicate something useful. Those two conditions are interdependent. Information is useful only because it can
be put to use by others with the same set of values, and a set of values
is perpetuated only by the adherence to it of more than one individual. That this is no longer true in modern times, according to Benjamin,

> is a concomitant symptom of the secular productive forces of
> history, a concomitant that has quite gradually removed narra-
> tive from the realm of living speech and at the same time is mak-
> ing it possible to see a new beauty in what is vanishing . . . The
> storyteller takes what he tells from experience—his own or that
> reported by others. And he in turn makes it the experience of
> those who are listening to his tale. The novelist has isolated
> himself. The birthplace of the novel is the solitary individual,
> who is no longer able to express himself by giving examples of
> his most important concerns, is himself uncounseled, and cannot
> counsel others. To write a novel means to carry the incommen-
> surable to extremes in the representation of human life.[5]

Conrad's personal history made him acutely sensitive to the different
status of information in the sea life, on the one hand, and in the
writing life, on the other. In the former, a working community and a
shared sense of what is useful are essential to the enterprise; in the
latter, solitude and its uncertainties override everything. Thus

Conrad had the dubious privilege of witnessing within his own double life the change from storytelling as useful, communal art to novel writing as essentialized, solitary art.

What does the change specifically entail? First of all, since the status of information has become problematical, the medium of its delivery is given greater prominence. Second, the speaker has to vary his words and his tone enough to compensate for his doubts about the usefulness of what he is saying. James and Wilde, Conrad's contemporaries, repeatedly referred to this sort of variation as the creation of interest; interest in such an instance depends closely upon an uncertainty toward (or even an ignorance of) the usefully practical. Conrad's virtuosic skill in narrative management, which reached its apex in *Chance*, is always as important as—and usually more interesting and important—any information the tale conveys. One can say this without in any way belittling either the sea lore in Conrad's fiction or its devotees among his readers. Third, the narrative no longer merely assumes listeners. It dramatizes them as well, so that frequently even the author himself appears to be participating in the tale as an audience or, more precisely in Conrad's case, as the dramatized recipient of impressions. Fourth, narrative is presented as utterance, something in the actual process of being spoken rather than as useful information. In Conrad the refinement of information from narrative utterance, as well as the fact that his language is usually in the mode of reported speech, are signs that the content of what is said need not by definition be as important or clear as who says it, why, and how.

I think that this last change has to be considered an aspect of the general loss of faith in the mimetic powers of language to which I referred earlier. It once was possible for the writer to lose such a faith and still retain a belief in the supremacy of the visible. Writing therefore cannot represent the visible, but it can desire and, in a manner of speaking, move toward the visible without actually achieving the unambiguous directness of an object seen before one's eyes. Foucault has studied this apparent contradition in his *Les Mots et les choses* by treating it as a specific historical phase embodied variously in the work of de Sade, Mallarmé, and Nietzsche: Conrad's narratives offer particularly rich illustrations of it. Within a general perspective of the sort Foucault draws we can understand the deep necessity of Conrad's decision to ground narrative epistemologically in utterance—as speech reported or spoken during periods that were dramatized as situations of enforced calm—and not in action, community, or information.

The springs of Conrad's narrative utterances are what I shall call wanting-to-speak and the need to link a given utterance with other utterances. What makes a Conradian character a special creature comes from something he or she possesses that needs to be told about. Often there is a guilty secret; at other times the character is someone of whom other people talk obsessively. At still other times he is a taciturn man, like James Wait or Charles Gould or MacWhirr or Axel Heyst, whose entire life speaks in an exemplary way to other men. Thus Conrad's tales are about personages who are presented in the course of the tale, being taken note of. The internal continuity of each tale, however, derives from the speaker's self-consciousness as someone producing an utterance that, as I said above, stands against or among conflicting or complementary utterances. In a sense every narrative utterance in Conrad contests another one: Marlow's lie to Kurtz's intended is only the most notable instance of a common enough habit. Nostromo's great ride out of Sulaco is the subject of Mitchell's admiring reports, but these must be judged to be but a few of the reports that generally treat the *capataz de cargadores* as Sulaco's savior. Then too Decoud's notes personify the cynic's attitude, in deliberate contrast to Gould's sentimentalism. Avellanos, Emilia, Giorgio, Viola, Sotillo—each perceives and reports events in a manner turned either explicitly or implicitly toward other perceptions. In no place more than in *Chance* can the reader see Conrad make tension and conflict, and thereby a dynamic narrative texture, out of an utterance at odds with and yet ineluctably linked to other utterances.

Lord Jim is one of the first of Conrad's extended narratives to make knowledge, intelligibility, and vision into functions of utterance. The novel takes off in "the act of intelligent volition" that directs Marlow's eyes to Jim's during the inquiry. After a period of "endless converse with himself" and at a time when "speech was no use to him any longer," Jim at last meets a man whose presence loosens the tongues "of men with soft spots, with hard spots, with hidden plague spots." Marlow not only listened but is "willing to remember Jim at length, in detail and audibly." True, Jim has "influential confidences" to confess, and yet Marlow's propensity to tell and remember is just as important to the book. "With the very first word [of his narrative] Marlow's body, extended at rest in the seat, would become very still, as though his spirit had winged its way back into the lapse of time and were speaking through his lips from the past" (XXI, 33). Marlow's generosity toward Jim is rooted in precisely that same tendency to romantic projection because of which Jim so embarrassingly prefers courageous voyages in projective inspiration to voyages in actuality. Neither man, whether hearer or storyteller, truly inhabits the world of facts. First Jim and then Marlow wander off "to comprehend the Inconceivable," an activity so urgent and rarefied at the same time that it involves "a subtle and momentous quarrel as to the true essence of life." Ultimately Conrad points out that Jim does not speak to Marlow, but rather in front of him, just as Marlow cannot by definition speak to the reader but only in front of him.

What first seems like a meeting of minds turns into a set of parallel lines. Moreover Marlow explicitly says later that Jim exists for him, as if to say that Jim's confession before Marlow mattered more than *what* Jim confessed (both Marlow and Jim seem equally confused anyway). Only because of that performance—not just because of Jim's exploits in and of themselves—does Jim exist for his listener. I have already commented on Conrad's practice, which is evident in what Marlow says of Jim's enigmatic appearance and his need to talk, of alternating the visual and the oral modes: the way the narrative shows how "Romance had singled out Jim for its own" follows directly from this practice. Jim's appetite for disastrous adventure, like Marlow's narrative, like our attention to the tale, corresponds not to any communicable pattern of linear progress from, say, ambition to accomplishment, but conforms rather to a more abstract impulse. The impulse can find no expression in action, and no image, other than the vague rubric of Romance, conveys the aim of Jim's troubled quest. Forced into the duration of reported speech or utterance, the impulse's exigencies are such relatively ethereal things as pattern, rhythm, phrase, sequence.

But, we are entitled to ask, what is the pressure on Jim that makes him favor death over life, and which urges Marlow and Conrad toward "inconclusive experiences" that reveal less to the reader than any reader is prepared to expect? In all cases the dominating factor is not narrative energy but a fatalistic desire to behold the self passively as an object told about, mused on, puzzled over, marveled at fully, in utterance. That is, having everywhere conceded that one can neither completely realize one's own nor fully grasp someone else's life experience, Jim, Marlow, and Conrad are left with a desire to fashion verbally and approximately their individual experience in the terms unique to each one. Since invariably this experience is either long past or by definition almost impossible, no image can capture this, just as finally no sentence can.

Nevertheless the utterance is spoken, if not only to, then in the presence of, another. Words convey the presence to each other of speaker and hearer but not a mutual comprehension. Each sentence drives a sharper wedge between intention (wanting-to-speak) and communication. Finally wanting-to-speak, a specifically verbal intention, is forced to confront the insufficiency, and indeed the absence, of words for that intention. It is not too extreme to say that in a complex way Conrad is dramatizing the disparity between verbal intention grammatically and formally apprehendable and possible on the one hand and, on the other, verbality itself, as a way of being in the world of language with other human beings. In "Amy Foster," that most poignant of all his stories, the disparity is spelled out in particular human detail. Washed ashore in England, Yanko Goorall lives among people who cannot make him out and to whose language he is always a foreigner:

> These were the people to whom he owed allegiance, and an overwhelming loneliness seemed to fall from the leaden sky of that winter without sunshine. All the faces were sad. He could talk to no one, and had no hope of ever understanding anybody. It was as if these had been the faces of people from the other world—dead people he used to tell me years afterwards. Upon my word, I wonder he did not go mad. He didn't know where he was. Somewhere very far from his mountains—somewhere over the water. Was this America, he wondered? . . . The very grass was different, and the trees. All the trees but the three old Norway pines on the bit of lawn before Swaffer's house, and these reminded him of his country. He had been detected once, after dusk, with his forehead against the trunk of one of them, sobbing, and talking to himself. They had been like brothers to him at that time, he affirmed. Everything else was strange . . . Many times have I heard his high-pitched voice from behind the ridge of some sloping sheepwalk, a voice light and soaring, like a lark's but with a melancholy human note, over our fields that hear only the song of birds. And I would be startled myself. Ah! He was different; innocent of heart, and full of good will, which nobody wanted, this castaway, that, like a man transplanted into another planet, was separated by an immense space from his past and by an immense ignorance of the future. His quick, fervent utterance positively shocked everybody. (XX, 128, 129, 132)

Conrad's excruciatingly detailed understanding of this predicament makes this choice of utterance as his way of presenting narratives something far more urgent than a comfortable aesthetic choice. It is clear he believed that only a fully imagined scene between a speaker and a watching hearer could present—continuously, directly, and, since it occurs in story after story, repeatedly—the fundamental divorce he stood for as a writer: the rift between a fully developed but, with regard to other people, only an intentional or latent capacity for complete expression and an inescapable human community. "There are no words for the sort of things I wanted to say" (*Lord Jim*). Hence Conrad's penchant for repeating phrases like "he was one of us" together with reminders of how unique each individual and his experiences were. And the text Conrad worked at ceased simply to be a written document and became instead a distribution of utterances around both sides of the rift. They are held together by the reader's attention to both sides. In its duration for the length of *Lord Jim*, such overarching attention binds together Jim's verbal intention and Marlow's forbearance as a witness. Only in the domain of intention and fantasy to which Conrad's heroes have a fatal attraction can there be completion for schemes of the kind Jim devises for himself; but such a place is apprehendable only during the constantly progressing narrative of his doom and failure. When Marlow sees Jim for the last time, there is this passage:

Jim, at the water's edge, raised his voice. "Tell them ..." he began. I signed to the men to cease rowing, and waited in wonder. Tell who? The half-submerged sun faced him. I could see its red gleam in his eyes that looked dumbly at me ... "No—nothing," he said, and with a slight wave of his hand motioned the boat away. I did not look again at the shore till I had clambered on board the schooner ... He was white from head to foot, and remained persistently visible with the stronghold of the night at his back, the sea at his feet, the opportunity by his side—still veiled? I don't know. For me that white figure in the stillness of coast and sea seemed to stand at the heart of a vast enigma. The twilight was ebbing fast from the sky above his heat, the strip of sand had sunk already under his feet, he himself appeared no bigger than a child—then only a speck, a tiny white speck that seemed to catch all the light left in a darkened world ... And suddenly, I lost him." (XXI, 336)

Much is brought together here. Jim's terminal silence indicates that once again "a silent opportunity" takes over his life. He seems for a moment to have become the point of visual, as well as intellectual, reference for which words are both inadequate and never relinquished. Then he disappears. His life is covered over with the few suggestive traces—a letter, an incomplete narrative, a patchy oral report—that

Marlow can garner much later. But at least Jim holds the privacy of his being intact, something Axel Heyst, for example, cannot do for very long. Heyst is the last of those substantial Conradian figures to attempt a life of almost pure virtuality and, almost by definition, the last of men whose passivity is an invitation to the assaults of Romance. Yet in *Victory* (1915) Heyst's seclusion on his private island is ineffective. No man can become invisible so long as he retains even the slenderest contact with the actual. The subject of Schomberg's malicious gossip, of Ricardo's venality, of the Archipelago's speculations, Heyst cannot use his father's philosophy of detachment to much purpose. Besides, Heyst's attraction to Lena is too strong for him, just as his earlier sympathy for Morrison's plight crushes his reserve.

Of course there is an important sexual theme in *Victory*, but Conrad's deliberate juxtaposition of Morrison's boat with Lena as successive objects of Heyst's romantic intervention in the world belongs, I think, to another more strictly verbal enterprise, one found in many other places in his fiction. I have said that Conrad's primary mode, although he is a writer, is presented as the oral, and his ambition is to move toward the visual. These are the situations that employ yarns, tales, and utterance for their depiction, and which in the end present us with the disparity between intention and actuality, or in sensuous terms between wanting-to-speak and hearing, on the one hand, and seeing and comprehending on the other. In *Lord Jim* we have also seen the way all these things are at work in the text, as well as the intense attraction to each other, despite the gulf between them, of intention (not silence) and an intensive actuality.

But, it needs hardly be said, Conrad is a novelist, not a philosopher and not a psychologist. One can suppose that during the writing of his fiction an essential place in Conrad's imagination was filled by substances around which a great deal of the narrative action is organized: Lingard's gold, Kurtz's ivory, the ships of sailors, Gould's silver, the women that draw men to chance and romance. A large proportion of the tension in Conrad's fiction is therefore generated as the author, narrator, or hero tries to make us see the object that draws out the writing, the thought, the speech, on and on. I said earlier that, with telling or reporting as their basis, these activities begin to approach the condition of substantiality. But why? and why, after all, did Conrad ground all these activities, given verbal form, in the utterance or reported speech of identifiable persons, and not for example in the impersonal purity adopted by Mallarmé or Joyce?

The main interest of this question is, I think, that it distinguishes, however minimally and schematically, between Conrad's personal psychology (which is the exclusive subject of psychoanalytic studies like Bernard Meyer's biography) and the psychology of Conrad's writing. As a source of evidence for the man's psychohistory, fiction is "finished" by literary process in a way that everyday behavior, itself conditioned by culture, society, and history, is not. Moreover, as I have tried to show elsewhere,[6] so impressively particular is the psychosocial dynamic shaping a literary career and its text that neither can be read for immediate evidence of an author's actual psychology. But does this special entity called a literary career or text mean some sort of denial of the evidence that the author's psychopathology might provide? Is there any useful nontrivial way of separating, or for that matter of bringing together, "the man who suffers and the mind which creates"? To be even more specific, can there be an exact analogy between an author's personal and artistic writing, on the one hand, and on the other the same man's spoken discourse and his dreams?

Writing and dreams are subject to different sorts of control from the ones governing spoken discourse. Yet it is difficult to conceive of written work being done under conditions that resemble those of what Freud referred to as dream-work. Wakefulness, a pen or a typewriter, paper, your past writing, a plan for what is being written, a set of physical gestures, what you have consciously learned about writing: these count importantly in differentiating writing and dreaming, at least if the two activities have any status as psychoanalytic evidence. The differences become more interesting, however, when writing is denied its importance in the writer's work itself, especially by the writer like Conrad for whom it was sheer agony.

If we say, as I think we must, that in his writing Conrad is generally unhappy with the idea of writing, so much so that when he is not complaining about it he is always turning it into substitute speech, then we can go as far as saying that Conrad's writing tries overtly to negate itself as writing. Of negation Freud has said, though, that it is a way of affirming what is repressed. But then what does it mean for a writer to affirm writing that is repressed? Again Freud is helpful: "With the help of the symbol of negation, thinking frees itself from the restriction of repression and enriches itself with material that is indispensable for its proper functioning." For Conrad, writing and its negation constituted a way of permitting himself a number of things otherwise impossible. Among these things are the use of English, the use of experiences from out of his past that are reconstructed and, most of the time, deformed into "fictional" novels and stories, the use of events about which no explanation can or need be satisfactory.

Let us continue a step further with Freud's argument. Negation is the result of an intellectual judgment made on two grounds. First there is a judgment as to whether a thing has or does not have a particular property. Second, a judgment is made as to whether or not an image or presentation exists in reality. There are two possible criteria of internality "expressed in the language of the oldest—the oral—instinctual impulses . . . 'I should like to eat this' or 'I should like to spit this out,' " and two possible criteria of externality (I reject this, or, that image also has an existence in reality outside me) for making the judgment, both of them of course requiring an ego. Freud had been led to these discoveries because, he says, "in the course of analytic work we often produce a further, very important and somewhat strange variant of this situation. We succeed in conquering the negation as well, and in bringing about a full intellectual acceptance of the repressed; but the repressive process itself is not yet removed by this." Therefore, when a negative reality-judgment about an image is made, the ego may still be affirming the image's existence by repression; for so long as it is used or solicited (even if only to be denied or dismissed), an image is a rediscovery of what has already been lost. Thus only when "the symbol of negation has endowed thinking with a first measure of freedom from the consequences of repression and, with it, from the compulsion of the pleasure principle" is there a mature judgment.[7] Only some of Freud's argument is directly relevant to Conrad, which means that not everything Freud says can be expected to correspond with Conrad's practice as a writer.

Writing for Conrad was an activity that constituted negation—of itself, of what it dealt with—and was also oral and repetitive. That is, as an activity Conrad's writing negated and reconstituted itself, negated itself again, and so forth indefinitely; hence the extraordinarily patterned quality of the writing. The utterance is the oral form of the negation. As such, its function was to postpone judgment indefinitely, on itself and its subject matter: it too is repetitive and it is internalizing, for we have seen Conrad imagining narrative being uttered from one tale to the next while the reality of what Marlow calls the "life-sensation," the existential content of actual experience, remained private, undeveloped, uncommunicable except by radical qualifications that function as negations ("we live, as we dream—

alone"). But at some stage in their lives, Conrad's male characters are powerfully affected by externally real material objects: women, treasure, ships, land. Most of the time, these objects at the outset are passively as well as externally there and only gradually endowed with force. Thus Charles Gould involuntarily inherits his father's mine. Only after that does he begin to build the imperial quasi-mythological power of the San Tomé Mine. At the point in Conrad's fiction when that process of mythical building becomes apparent, an important cleavage appears between the character reported about and the report. From being a form of internal negation, the utterance becomes then the instrument of Conrad's judgment. In time and through the usually spacious structure of his fiction, writing transforms the writer from failed speaker (a speaking character or "narrating pen" who has direct, visual, and even material goals passively accepted because of heritage or convention) into the reflective writer discussing and rendering stories external to him, the author who adopts the aesthetic form of utterance habitually from novel to novel and forces it through a maximum of different and interesting developments. In each tale Conrad's autobiographical presence is distributed in numerous roles: first as the person to whom events happened, as speaker, as listener, then finally as author who at one moment presents narrative, negates it by pretending it is speech, then negates that (in letters during the throes of composition) by denouncing its difficulties, then negates even that (late in his career) by sounding like Everyone's Favorite Old Novelist. My argument in short is that Conrad's writing was a way of repeatedly confirming his authorship by refracting it in a variety of often contradictory and negative narrative and quasi-narrative contingencies, and that he did this in preference to a direct representation of his neuroses. Perhaps this was Conrad's way of escaping the debilitating consequences of repression and the compulsion of the pleasure principle.

Conrad tried to use prose negatively for the transcendence of writing and the embodiment of both direct utterance and vision. Every experience begins for him in the presence of speaker to hearer and vice versa; consequently each speaker tells of action whose goal is clarity, or realized intention. Yet in almost every case, what enables the latter fulfillment is an inert substance like silver, which has been given power over life. Such a substance is felt mistakenly to be capable of embodying the visible, the timeless, the unmediated sensory possession of all reality. But also in each case this substance turns out to embody the ego's nearly limitless capacity for extension and transformation. Surely awareness of this is what makes *Nostromo* the impressively pessimistic edifice that it is: the novel rests in a sense on the impregnation of silver with an imaginative conception of its power. The totality of this conception encompasses both life and death, and thus the Goulds, for all their pretention to humanity, are no different from the Professor in *The Secret Agent* or Kurtz in *Heart of Darkness.* "By her imaginative estimate of its power she [Amelia Gould] endowed that lump of metal with a justificative conception, as though it were not a mere fact, but something far-reaching and impalpable, like the true expression of an emotion or the emergency of a principle ... for the San Tomé mine was to become an institution, a rallying point for everything in the provinces that needed order and stability to live. Security seemed to flow upon this land from the mountain range" (IX, 107, 110).

Matter is transmuted into value as, in an ideal world, emotion can be converted into "true expression." For Conrad's heroes matter becomes a system of exchange underlying language. The self, which is the source of utterance, attempts the reconciliation of intention with actuality; words are really being bypassed as a direct embodiment in material is sought by the imagination, at the same time that the ego reports its adventures and its disappointments. If language fails ultimately to represent intention and, analogously, if the mimetic function of language is sorely inadequate to make us see, then by using substance instead of words the Conradian hero, like Conrad himself, aims to vindicate and articulate his imagination. Every reader of Conrad knows how this aim too is bound to fail. In the end, like the dying Kurtz with his hoard of ivory, the hero becomes a talking insubstantiality. For every brief discursive success like Gould or Verloc, there is a Nostromo or a Stevie whose destroyed body tells on. And for every Kurtz and Jim, there is a Marlow by whose memory a body can be recaptured in all its splendor and youth. That this takes place only in "the lapse of time" and because the speaker's words are being written does not diminish its achievement, except as words negate and diminish, without actually delivering, a man entire. Conrad is the writer whose work repeatedly embodies this rich irony.

5

On Repetition

NEAR the end of *The New Science*, after having laid forth
in detail the precise way in which human history is not
only made by men but also made by them according to cycles that
repeat themselves, Vico then proceeds to explain how these repetitions are intelligent patterns that preserve the human race. The whole
section resembles a kind of Platonic meditation upon ideal history.
But the detail of what Vico describes is not quite Platonic:

It is true that men have themselves made this world of nations
(and we took this as the first incontestable principle of our Science, since we despaired of finding it from the philosophers and
the philologists), but this world without doubt issued from a
mind often diverse, at times quite contrary, and always superior
to the particular ends that men had proposed to themselves;
which narrow ends, made means to serve wider ends, it has always employed to preserve the human race upon this earth. Men
mean to gratify their bestial lust and abandon their offspring,
and they inaugurate the chastity of marriage from which the
families arise. The fathers mean to exercise without restraint
their paternal power over their clients, and they subject them to
the civil powers from which the cities arise. The reigning orders
of nobles mean to abuse their lordly freedom over the plebeians,
and they are obliged to submit to the laws which establish popular liberty. The free peoples mean to shake off the yoke of their
laws, and they become subject to monarchs. The monarchs
mean to strengthen their own positions by debasing their subjects with all the vices of dissoluteness, and they dispose them to
endure slavery at the hands of stronger nations. The nations
mean to dissolve themselves, and their remnants flee for safety to

the wilderness, whence, like the phoenix, they rise again. That which did all this was mind, for men did it with intelligence; it was not fate, for they did it by choice; not chance, for the results of their so acting are perpetually the same.[1]

The gist of this passage is that any examination of the concrete facts of human history, which is accessible neither to a philosopher nor to a philologist, reveals a principle or force of inner discipline within an otherwise disorganized series of events. Mind is the general system of brakes that restrains the always accelerating irrationality of human behavior. Out of each instance of men's folly comes a consequence that acts against the human being's immediate intention and that seems to be dictated by mind, whose ultimate purpose is to preserve the human race. How? By making certain that human history continues by repeating itself according to a certain fixed course of events. Thus the sexual relations between men and women give rise to matrimony, the institution of matrimony gives rise to cities, the struggle of plebeians gives rise to laws; people in conflict with laws give rise to tyranny; and tyranny leads finally to capitulation to foreign powers. Out of this last debasement a new cycle will begin, arising out of man's absolute degeneration in the wilderness.

Without mind there would be no history properly speaking, and without history of course humanity is impossible. Those things that make history possible—and Vico here as elsewhere is not afraid of tautology—are human institutions like matrimony, laws, nations. These institutions manifest an ironical stubbornness, mind, determined to keep man inside history and meaning; the irony is that irresistibly men act out "the uncontrollable mystery on the bestial floor," even while, just as irresistibly, mind illuminates the darkness by giving birth to sensible patterns, endowing man with a history that his fierce lusts seem otherwise determined to expend wastefully. Instead of unlimited copulation there is matrimony, insted of uninhibited autocracy there are laws and republics, and so forth.

All this is described by Vico throughout *The New Science* as something to be understood more or less immediately, that is, without the prejudiced mediations of Cartesian philosophy or Erasmian philology. For Vico claims to be speaking exactly about the realm of unadorned fact. What human beings do is what makes them human beings; what they know is what they have done. These seminal precepts resound everywhere in *The New Science*. Human history is human actuality is human activity is human knowledge. Methodolog-

ically *The New Science* adds to the equation the scholar's contribution: the scholar, (that is, Vico) discovers all these relationships by
recognizing them or, to use a favorite Vichian term, by refinding
them (*ritrovare*). If at times we are bothered by Vico's habit of
himself repeating the essential sketch of human history from pure
bestiality, to moderate rationality, to overrefined intellectuality, to
new barbarism, to a new beginning again—and if we question the
neatness of a cycle imposed by Vico on the huge variety of human
history—then we are forced to confront precisely what the cycle itself circumvents, the predicament of infinite variety and infinite
senselessness. Take history as a reported dramatic sequence of dialectical stages, enacted and fabricated by an inconsistent but persistent humanity, Vico seems to be saying, and you will equally avoid
the despair of seeing history as gratuitous occurrence as well as the
boredom of seeing history as realizing a foreordained blueprint. And
never mind if epistemologically the status of repetition itself is un-
certain: repetition is useful as a way of showing that history and actuality are all about human persistence, and not about divine originality.

It is most nearly true to say, I think, that whatever else it is, repetition for Vico is something that takes place inside actuality, as much
inside human action in the realm of facts as inside the mind while
surveying the realm of action. Indeed repetition connects reason with
raw experience. First, on the level of meaning, experience accumu-
lates meaning as the weight of past and similar experiences returns.
Men are always afraid of their fathers; they bury their dead; they invariably worship a divinity fashioned in their image. These repetitions are what human society is based on. Second, repetition contains
experience in a way; repetition is the frame within which man represents himself to himself and for others. The primitive *pater familias*
sets himself up as Jove does, repeating his imperiousness, ruler of a
family he has created and which he must try to keep from overthrow-
ing him. Finally, repetition restores the past to the scholar, illuminating his research by an inexhaustible constancy. "In the night of thick
darkness enveloping the earliest antiquity, so remote from ourselves,
there shines the eternal and never-failing light of a truth beyond all
question: that the world of civil society has certainly been made by
men, and that its principles are therefore to be found within the modifications of our own human mind."[2] For Vico then, whether as the
beginning of sense, as representation, as archeological reconstruction,
repetition is a principle of economy, giving facts their historical factu-

ality and reality its existential sense. Certainly it is true that each repetition of a *corso* or *ricorso* is generally the same as its predecessors;
yet Vico is sensitive to the losses and gains, the differences in short,
within each repeating phase of the cycle.

Formally speaking, Vico's understanding and use of repetition
bears a resemblance to musical techniques of repetition, in particular
those of the *cantus firmus* or of the chaconne or, to cite the most developed classical instance, Bach's *Goldberg Variations.* By these devices a ground motif anchors the ornamental variations taking place
above it. Despite the proliferation of changing rhythms, patterns, and
harmonies, the ground motif recurs throughout, as if to demonstrate
its staying power and its capacity for endless elaboration. As Vico
saw the phenomenon in human history, there is in these musical
forms a tension between the contrariety or eccentricity of the variation and the constancy and asserted rationality of the *cantus firmus.*
Nothing Vico could have said about mind's triumph over irrationality can equal the quiet triumph that occurs at the end of the *Goldberg Variations,* as the theme returns in its exact first form to close
off the aberrant variations it has generated. These uses of repetition
conserve the field of activity; they give it its shape and identity, as
Vico saw repetition confirming the essential facts of what he called
gentile human history.

I use Vico's word *gentile* as a synonym for the *filiation* discussed
in the introduction to this book. What we cannot describe formally in
music, except by rather strained analogy, is Vico's notion of human
history being generated, being produced and reproduced in the very
way that men and women generate themselves by procreating and
elaborating the species. Gentile history is the history of the *gens* and
gentes who are generated naturally in time and develop there; they
are not created once and for all by a sacred power standing outside
history. All of *The New Science* concerns this gentile process, which
fills Vico's ideas about repetition. His images for historical process
are invariably biological and, more, they are invariably paternal. The
passage I quoted earlier is good evidence for the cast of Vico's imagination, which grasped the progressive movement of the *corsi* and *ri-
corsi* as the relationship between parents and offspring. Repetition
therefore is gentile because filiative and genealogical. Vico's etymo-
logical punnings on the derivatives of *gens* obviously captivated him,
since they work not only as representations of how history derives
from human fertility but also of how words repeat the process in the
production of cognates out of radicals: *gens, gentes, gentile, genialis,*

genitor, and so forth. Generally, then, Vico understands repetition as filiation, but filiation that is problematic, not mindlessly automatic. Students of Vico have not made much of the filiative obsession in his historiography, and neither have they associated Vico's genealogical investigations with efforts, roughly contemporary with his, in natural history to study generation, reproduction, and heredity. In both fields, in Vico's study of historical experience and in the work say of Maupertuis and Buffon in natural history, taxonomy was a device for identifying phases through which living beings pass and repass but, more important—as both Vico and Buffon were able to show—"life" was a category that transcended mere classification, had its own internal and self-reproducing organization, and was transferred from one generation of parents to the next. The question to answer was how life was generated and how it reproduced itself, once life was no longer considered the result of a continuing divine intervention in the affairs of nature. Repetition for Vico and the eighteenth-century naturalists is the consequence of, and indeed can be identified with, physiological reproduction, how a species perpetuates itself in historical time and space.

According to François Jacob in *La Logique du vivant*, the notion of reproduction was itself born in the early eighteenth century as naturalists took account of animal capacity for the regeneration of amputated limbs. At first it was believed that the organism reproduced both itself and its lost periphery because it was realizing a preexisting blueprint, or plan, which was an ideal model fulfilled by the whole of nature. In time this notion was given up. Instead it appeared both to Maupertuis and Buffon during the 1740s that nature repeated or reproduced itself by virtue of a sufficient internal capacity, demonstrated in the organization of organic matter into assembled elements, for generating itself from within. When it came to showing that reproduction and regeneration invariably produced similarity (that is, repetition), Buffon's explanation was that heredity, the pressure on the offspring, was guided by memory. Reproduction was the process by which organized elements from one generation were transmitted into the next generation; since this process was clearly not random, and since filition involved strong resemblance if not always actual repetition, Buffon and Maupertuis postulated a faculty, memory, whose function it was to direct the transmission of generations. Thus the repetition of features was guaranteed into the next generation.[3]

Vico employs a strikingly similar notion. History, he said, issues from the mind, and what is mind but historical memory, capable of infinite articulation, modulation, change. Fundamentally, however, memory restrains mind; memory is all about an actuality that whether for primitive men or for the most refined modern philosopher remains essentially a human actuality. However much it may seem to change, it cannot ever be more or less than human. *The New Science* studied the structures of this immemorial actuality as it is transferred from primitive to modern man or, as Vico saw in one of those startling observations that dot his work, primitive man literally fathers modern man, the latter recapitulating the former. According to Vico, history is where nothing is ever lost. In Pope's phrase, "whatever is" has for Vico both a prior and a later form, the two connected by what I called earlier a problematic filiation.

Vico's theory of repetition is more interesting than that of his contemporaries in natural history. Memory for them directed the transmission of generations, it enabled reproduction: it did not cause it, nor did memory manifest itself except in space, as a physical presence of one object standing before another. The difference between Buffon and Lamarck was that the latter introduced a temporal dimension into heredity. Time, and not a sort of vast general natural space, connected living beings to one another, a common past history with succession, duration, the possibility of perfected organization occurring through generation.[4] Heredity involved a genetic theory, not a passive memory. Generation involves struggle; this was the essence also of Vico's gentile history. With struggle, as between the generation of the fathers and of the sons, there is difference generated, as well as repetition. In other words Vico was aware that filiation from one point of view is recurrence, but from another, that of history as the form of human existence seen as a domain of its own, it is difference. The vacillation in Vico's thought about filiation between repetition or recurrence and difference was really an expression of the vacillation between an interest in the unchanging, the universal, the constant, the repeatable, on the one hand, and on the other an interest in the original, the revolutionary, the unique and contingent.

These remarks on Vico are intended to accentuate the centrality of ideas about repetition to speculations about temporal process, to the idea of human productivity, and to the thesis that time-bound human facts must in some way be regarded as repetitions of some prior presence or as differences from it. We must take note quickly here of how in recent literary critical theory this problematic of repetition and originality is treated—also genealogically—as the problem of influence between a strong paternal precursor and a filial latecomer. Naturally I refer to Harold Bloom's plot for poetic history. My interest is in maintaining that for literary theory, for Vico's gentile history, for natural history up to and including Darwin, it is natural to see the passing of time as *repeating* the very reproductive, and repetitive, course by which man engenders and reengenders himself or his offspring. According to Jacob, survival thus appears to be the survival of the best reproducers, the best repeaters. The family metaphor of filial engenderment, when it is extended throughout the whole of human activity, Vico called *poetic;* for men are men, he says, because they are makers, and what before everything else they make is themselves. Making is repeating; repeating is knowing because making. This is a genealogy of knowledge and of human presence.

I think it can be shown that narrative fiction during the European eighteenth and nineteenth centuries is based on the filial device of handing on a story through narrative telling; moreover that the generic plot situation of the novel is to repeat through variation the family scene by which human beings engender human duration in their action. If a novelistic heroine or hero has one task set above all the others it is to be different, so heavily do paternity and routine weigh upon them. To be novel is to be an original, that is, a figure not repeating what most men perforce repeat—the course of human life, father to son, generation after generation. Thus the novelistic character is conceived as a challenge to repetition, a rupture in the duty imposed on all men to breed and multiply, to create and recreate oneself unremittingly and repeatedly. In Emma Bovary's refusal to be the same kind of wife that her class and the French provinces require of her, the filiative bonds of society are challenged. She is a woman about whom it was possible for Flaubert to write because repetition, her feeling of boring, prosaic sameness, gives birth to difference, her desire to live romantically, and difference produces novelty, which is at once her distinction and affliction.

In speaking about the classical European realistic novel I find myself once again reverting to Vico's problematic citation of human history as a series of genealogical repetitive cycles. And yet both Vico and Flaubert seem to employ the generative cycle of human time because within it, located at its very core, is a basic antithesis that time exposes rather than resolves. This is what I mean: Vico's filiative sequence, fathers and mothers giving birth to offspring, thereafter engendering not only families but a struggle between the generations, produces two sorts of consequence. One is intentional: "men *mean* to justify their bestial lust and abandon their offspring." The other is involuntary: "and they inaugurate the chastity of marriage from which the families arise." Both consequences are included in the repetition of human history; yet between them, quite evidently, there is a significant rift. For intentionally, in an unmediated and wholly natural way, filiation gives rise not only to conflict but is driven by a desire to exterminate what has been engendered, the abandonment of offspring. Unintentionally, however, the opposite takes place: marriage as an institution is established, offspring and parents become bound by it. The same rift between intentional sexual desire and an unintentional thwarting of it by institutions takes place in *Madame Bovary*. History in Vico's case, the very form of the novel in Flaubert's, is on the side of institutions preserving, transmitting, confirming not only the process of filiative repetition by which human presence is repeatedly perpetuated. In addition, those same institutions—say marriage or community—protect filiation by instituting affiliation, that is, a joining together of people in a nongenealogical, nonprocreative but social unity. What is historically important about marriage to Vico is not that it enables procreation; rather, since procreation takes place naturally anyway (and wastefully, at least by intention), marriage as an institution interdicts sexual desire so that affiliations, other than purely filial ones, can take place.

The father's place therefore loses its unassailable eminence. The paternal and filial roles, necessary to each other as much in their natural concomitance as in their mutual hostility, seem to give rise to other relationships, affiliative ones, whose undoubted historical and factual presence in human society concerns the historian, philosopher, social theorist, novelist, and poet. But an additional complication has crept in. You will have noticed that in speaking of the origin of affiliative relationships I used the somewhat dodgy explanation "to give rise to." This phrase avoids more common metaphors, "to give birth to" or "the birth of," which, considering the antithesis between genealogical filiation and social affiliation I have been sketching, are metaphors I could not have used without explanation. Men and women give birth to; human beings are born. Is the same kind of description possible and does it make as much sense in discussing social or literary phenomena?[5] Moreover, and this question is the relevant one, within the framework of repeating human gentile history what methods are there for dealing with the interdiction of paternal and familial sequences, what forms, what images, if *not* the generative, procreative ones we would otherwise employ without second thought?

These are questions I should like now to investigate in some specific instances. My perspective will remain one in which repetition is an optic employed (or employable) to discuss the continuity, the perpetuity, and the recurrency of human history. Among the most interesting and effective contemporary efforts to deal with the first appearance of something, say a scientific discovery or the datable advent of an institution, are Foucault's archeological studies. The difference between what he does in *La Naissance de la clinique* and *Surveiller et punir: La Naissance de la prison* and what is done in the history of ideas is that Foucault is determined to show the accommodations of singular events to repeating epistemological structures he calls discourse and archive. He shows the triumph of regularity and recurrency over irregularity and uniqueness: in this he belongs in the tradition of Georges Canguihelm and, in this country, Thomas Kuhn. Yet as is evident by the two titles I have just cited, Foucault is attracted by the procreative metaphor without, it seems to me, adequately trying to reconcile his brilliant conceptual formulations with these metaphors of biological reproduction. Lurking behind his archeological terminology is an acceptable analogy between the engenderment of humans and of institutions. For there is an unresolved tension in what Foucault writes not only between uniqueness and repetition, but also between filiation and affiliation as instances of repetition.[6]

In Foucault's case, as in the cases of Harold Bloom, Vico, and the natural historians Maupertuis and Buffon, there is consensus of a very general sort: that from about the middle of the eighteenth century the problem of change, while customarily represented in many fields as the generation, reproduction, or transmission of life from parent to offspring, is intruded upon by forces troubling the continuity. In natural history written during the early nineteenth century— Cuvier's investigations are a case in point—such discontinuity is exemplified in the theory of geological disturbances. Similarly, theories of linguistic origin such as Herder's or Rousseau's, which depict a first parent-man uttering the first parent word and thereafter siring language as we know it, are disturbed first by the newly learned unimaginable age of non-Western and nonbiblical languages, then by the discovery that linguistic history, so far as the modern researcher is concerned, cannot be described as moving in simple genealogical succession. In still a third field, biblical hermeneutics as Hans W. Frei has described it, the congruence between the New Testament biographies of Jesus and factual recurrences in Jesus' life, a congruence heretofore imagined as genealogical, is definitely split apart by

Strauss, Bauer, and others.[7] In short, it is only as a kind of metaphorical nostalgia for early faith that the generative terms can be made to apply to the world of scientifically observable facts. The paradox is that everywhere the search for origins and genetic explanations was fueled rather than stifled by the inapplicability of these explanations, except as wish-fulfilling metaphors.

Vico's prophetic vision foresaw the paradox and adumbrated the alternatives to it. The idea of repetition increases in validity as a consequence of the divergences between genealogical metaphor and factual discovery. The repeating patterns of which human and natural existence seem to be composed gain credibility as their origin loses it. Yet at the very center of human reality stands the fact of human continuity, which, if one were to observe it as a fact of historical continuity, is yoked to human generation. How does one connect this fact of repeating generation to the compelling facts of natural, hermeneutical, and cultural dispersion, divergence, diversification? Obviously pressure is placed upon what is understood by repetition, and for the two alternatives that will culminate, on the one hand in Kierkegaard's *Repetition* and on the other in Marx's *The Eighteenth Brumaire of Louis Bonaparte*, Vico is again useful. Recall that he had envisaged one cycle ending in dissolution, from which human remnants "like the phoenix . . . rise again." Call this regeneration an act of supernatural will. It is one form of repetition. The other involves circumstances that Vico can spell out in great detail: the rise of civilization, its flourishing, debasement, final dissolution. Here we note a pattern of repeating action—human, social, and historical existence—characterized by a general debasement in the level of existence, from civility to barbarism. And this pattern, while on the surface appearing to follow a genealogical line of descent, is in fact guided by inner laws of development and regression, laws social and historical that contravene the power of direct generative continuity.

Kierkegaard's *Repetition* exploits the first view of repetition but, given the eccentricity of his genius, it does so in ways that no one, not even Vico, could have predicted. Kierkegaard's focus, here as in *Fear and Trembling*, is not on the general notion of repetition but on its infinite particularity, its exceptionality. We must remember that both the young man seeking a repetition of his first love as well as the biblical Abraham have it in common that mere filiality, and for that matter any human relation as between husband and wife or father and son, is neither ethically nor metaphysically enough. Repetition is not recollection, and it is not longing for something not there. Repetition is "*return*, conceived in a purely formal sense."[8] For the poet, as for the Knight of Faith, there is conflict between the self and the whole of existence, which is God. Such conflict is a losing one since, unable to conform, unable to speak, the lonely self is threatened with its own annihilation, even though it never relinquishes its hold on reality. For repetition involves no giving up, but a self-possession carried to the point of no return. Existence itself, represented by the beloved's marriage to another or by the sudden availability of a ram for Abraham, absolves the self "at the instant when he would as it were annihilate himself." Therefore Abraham and the poet can repossess the world, repeat the minute particulars of experience in it, return to reality with a "consciousness raised to the second power, [which] is repetition."[9] Abraham has Isaac restored to him again, and the poet in *Repetition* says: "I am again myself. This self which another world would not pick up from the road I possess again. The discord in my nature is resolved, I am again unified. The terrors which found support and nourishment in my pride no longer enter in to distract and separate."[10]

It is no surprise that such a religious result, and with it a sense "that existence which has been, now becomes," is difficult to understand. Kierkegaard opposes this type of experience to Hegelian mediation, which unlike the abruptness of detailed repetition instead winds reality in and out of categories that rob it of the very factual immediacy Kierkegaard seems anxious at all costs to preserve. Kierkegaard's own writing, especially in the forms it utilizes, attempts to compensate for the rupture between what has been and what now becomes. The book *Repetition*, for example, is constructed like a narrative by James or Conrad, complete with frames and narrators surrounding a difficult-to-grasp action. Yet so strong even in Kierkegaard is the genealogical and procreative metaphor his philosophy of repetition is designed to transcend that at the end of the treatise he describes himself, Constantine Constantius, as "a midwife in relation to the child she has brought to birth. And such in fact is my position, for I have as it were brought him to birth, and therefore as the older person I do the talking."[11] Whereas the philosophy of repetition remains affiliation, the means used to describe it are, according to Kierkegaard himself, filiative. But the tension between the two views is permissible presumably because faith enables their joint tenure. Vico could call Kierkegaard a sacred historian committed to gentile methods.

Let us now turn to the other alternative, Marx's in *The Eighteenth*

Brumaire of Louis Bonaparte. Its superb opening pages, as well as the 1869 preface supplied by Marx, announce hostility to the thesis that history takes place freely or at the whim of a self-born great man, to the emotions of confusion created by complex events, to the lack of discipline in methods of historical analysis based on superficial analogies. Everywhere Marx insists on the formula for which the work has become most famous: all world historical events recur twice, first as tragedy, then as farce. Repetition is debasement, but for Marx, unlike either Swift in *The Polite Conversation* or Flaubert in the *Dictionnaire des idées reçues*, debasement is not a function of seeing human society as a closed system of stupidly uttered clichés, but a consequence of a methodological theory of relationship between one event and another. Marx wishes to stay clear of positivism, vulgar determinism, and despondent hand-wringing or regret. If it is true that events of importance occur twice, then repetition is their spatial form; their aesthetic, political, and temporal form is different. But how is this to be demonstrated?

Standing behind Louis Bonaparte is not his father but his uncle, the great emperor, just as before 1848 there is not 1847 but 1789, and before farce, tragedy, before *The Eighteenth Brumaire*'s opening not merely everyone who wrote before Marx, but Hegel and Diderot. What installs these forcibly instituted precedents, Marx tells us in the 1869 preface, is an occurrence within French literature, an occurrence little noticed outside France—and the whole of *The Eighteenth Brumaire* is a forcible repetition of this occurrence in Marx's terms—namely, a blow dealt the Napoleonic legend "by the weapons of historical research, criticism, satire and wit" (*mit den Wafen der Geschichtsforschung, der Kritik, der Satire und des Witzes*).[12] For if Napoleon III pretends that he is really Napoleon II, a direct descendant of the emperor, it is the task of the historian to see the facts as they are, that the son is really the nephew: Louis's genealogical revision is thus set right polemically by Marx's, and a French reality is universalized, Engels was later to say, for scientific socialism. The *gen* in *legend*, a word related etymologically to *legere* and *logos*, bears only a superficial and misleading relation to the *gen* either in *genitor* or in *genialis*. Marx therefore corrects the egregious error fathered by the Napoleonic legend, that a great man bears a son who in turn inherits his position. What Marx does in his own writing is to show that rewritten history can be re-rewritten, that one sort of repetition usurped by the nephew is but a parodied repetition of the filial relationship.

The importance of languge and representation to Marx's method are crucial. Not only is his exploitation of every verbal device enough to make *The Eighteenth Brumaire* a paradigm of intellectual literature; but Marx reflects in his language an understanding of the way in which language itself, while genealogically transmitted from generation to generation, is not simply a fact of biological heredity but a fact as well of acquired identity.

> The revolution of 1848 knew no better than to parody at some points 1789 and at others the revolutionary traditions of 1793–5. In the same way, the beginner who has learned a new language always retranslates it into his mother tongue: he can only be said to have appropriated the spirit of the new language and to be able to express himself in it freely when he can manipulate it without reference to the old, and when he forgets his original language while using the new one.[13]

In language as in families, Marx implies, the past weighs heavily on the present, making demands more than providing help. The direct genealogical line is parenthood and filiation which, whether in language or in the family, will produce a disguised quasi-monstrous offspring, that is farce or debased langue, rather than a handsome copy of the precursor or parent—unless the past is severely curtailed in its powers to dominate present and future. But in the case of Napoleon II Marx perceives a whole series of pressures for fraudulence at work, all of them, like a play of mirrors, blossoming out of the motif of repetition: the father or mother imposing an imprint upon the child that causes him to repeat the past; second, the nephew pretending to be a son; third, the clownish monster (referred to near the end of the tract) bursting forth untimely and unnaturally as fatherless embryo, in reality without true genealogical lineage; fourth, the representative man claiming to be of one class but actually forcing another class to accept him as its representative (as Marx says of this class of petty landowners, "they cannot represent themselves, they must be represented" [*sie können sich nicht vertreten, sie müssen vertreten werden*]); fifth, all the unproductive segments of society—the thieves, brigands, courtesans, scoundrels—begetting this creature, even as the class he claims to be representing, the landowning peasantry whose very role in society is to be productive, is in fact silenced and forever destroyed by him. Is it any wonder then that Louis Bonaparte's exploitation of his uncle's legacy centers precisely on that article in the Napoleonic Code stipulating that "la recherche de la paternité est interdite"?[14]

In other words, Louis Bonaparte legitimizes his usurpation by appeals to repetition in natural sequences. Marx, on the other hand, repeats the nephew's repetition and so deliberately goes against nature. In *The Eighteenth Brumaire* repetition is Marx's instrument for ensnaring the nephew in a manufactured world of analyzed reality. From the work's opening sentence, the celebrated citation from Hegel, Marx's method is to repeat in order to produce difference, not to validate Bonaparte's claims, and to give facts by emending their apparent direction. Just as the pretended son turns into a clearly revealed nephew, so even Hegel, who had considered the repetition of an event a strengthening and confirmation of its value, is cited and turned around. Repetition shows nature being brought down from the level of natural fact to the level of counterfeit imitation. Stature, authority, and force in the original sink through each repetition into material for the historian's scorn.

> When Cromwell dissolved the Long Parliament, he went alone into its midst, drew out his watch so that it should not exist a minute beyond the time limit he had set, and drove out the members of parliament individually with jovial and humorous invective. Napoleon, though smaller than his model, at least went to the Council of the Five Hundred on 18 Brumaire and read out its sentence of death, albeit in an uneasy voice. The second Bonaparte, who, by the way, found himself in possession of an executive power very different from that of Cromwell or Napoleon, sought his model not in the annals of world history but in the annals of the Society of 10 December, in the annals of the criminal courts.[15]

Only at the end of the work do we understand the true reversal of history nature that Bonaparte has carried out, which Marx announces near the opening: "All that exists deserves to perish"[16] To repeat a life is not to produce another life; it is to place death where life had been.

The Eighteenth Brumaire embodies the corrective transfer of vitality from the world of France in 1848, where it had been destroyed by death masking itself as life, to the pages of Marx's scientific, critical prose. Prose analysis captures and gives circumstantiality to Louis Bonaparte's masquerade as Napoleon's substitute, "als den Ersatzmann Napoleons." Marx's is neither a natural feat nor a miraculous assertion: it is an affiliative repetition made possible by critical consciousness. It portends a methodological revolution whereby, as in the natural and human sciences, the facts of nature are dissolved and then reassembled polemically, as during the nineteenth century in the museum, the laboratory, the classroom, or the library facts are dissolved and then assembled into units of didactic sense, perhaps to illustrate human power more to transform nature than to confirm it. A parallel affiliative process takes place in philology, in fiction, in psychology, where repetition turns into an aspect of analytic structural technique. Probably repetition is bound to move from *immediate* regrouping of experience to a more and more *mediated* reshaping and redisposition of it, in which the disparity between one version and its repetition increases, since repetition cannot long escape the ironies it bears within it. For even as it takes place repetition raises the question, does repetition enhance or degrade a fact? But the question brings forth consciousness of two where there had been repose in one; and such knowledge of course, like procreation, cannot really be reversed. Thereafter the problems multiply. Naturally or unnaturally, filiatively or affiliatively? That is the question.

6

On Originality

THERE are a few principal ways in which originality as a quality or an idea seems essential to the experience of literature, but what I think counts just as impressively is the sheer number of subsidiary insinuations of orginality into our thinking about literature. Not only does one speak of a book as original, of a writer as possessing greater or lesser originality than another, but also of original uses of such and such a form, type, character, structure; moreover, specialized versions of originality are found in all thinking about literary origins, novelty, radicalism, innovation, influence, tradition, conventions, and periods. There is no good reason to disagree now with Wellek and Warren: originality, they said laconically in 1948, is indeed "a fundamental problem of literary history."[1] But just how fundamental and how persistently elusive is the problem? Ought it to claim the analytic attention of the scholar, the teacher-writer, and the student of literature?

I shall argue that originality is something worth examining, especially if one takes more than casually the belief that the study of literature has a crucial but insufficiently defined intellectual and critical role to play in the contemporary world. I should say immediately that any interest in this privileged quality we associate with literature, in order for this interest to add up to more than a catalogue of examples (Marlowe is original because . . . , or Dryden has originality because . . .) can be sustained profitably only at a level of investigation not ordinarily associated with the practice of literary study, namely the theoretical. Now the going dogma is that literature is concreteness, human, social, and historical, which is to say that literature affords us aesthetic instances of every variety of experience.

Theory on the other hand is associated with abstractions and ideas, or with whatever it is conceived of by the defensive literary student. This is not to say that theory has no influence among literary people, for the extent to which various theories of criticism now have power over students and teachers alike is a sign of susceptibility to theoretical devices.

It is an instructive coincidence that what I mean by the theoretical level of investigation is connected historically in the West to a notion of originality. A theme first taken up in Plato's dialogues, then again critically in Aristotle, is the relationship between the knowledge of Ideas (theory) and a man's life. Plato, Werner Jaeger says, "was the first to introduce the theoretical man as an ethical problem into philosophy and to justify and glorify his life."[2] Between Plato and the generation made up of Aristotle' students—Aristotle himself never abandoned his Platonic legacy (of a belief in the moral value of the theoretic life) "that had been so decisive for his attitude of research and his ideal of science"[3]—there occurred a fluctuation of belief that moved from the ideal of a contemplative life to arguments for an active, involved life. And Jaeger points out that stories about philosophers were used as evidence for the *originality*, the theoretically and contemplatively oriented unusual behavior, of the philosophers among men. Thus,

> at first we find Socrates and Plato linking the moral world to the philosophical knowledge of being. Then in Dicaearchus' [a student of Aristotle] practical ideal, life and ethics are entirely withdrawn again from the rule of high philosophical speculation and restored to independence, and the daring wing of speculative thought is pinioned. With it fades the power of the ideal of theoretic life. When we meet it thereafter it is always the world of "pure science" and contrasted as such with the life of practice ... Not until the destruction of scientific philosophy and metaphysics by skepticism could the theoretic life achieve renewal, now in the religious form of the contemplative life, which has been the monastic ideal since Plato's work of that name.[4]

From this debate comes the general division of work into active, on the one hand, and theoretical-contemplative on the other. In a specialized form this division persists today in literary demotic as the distinction between creative-original and critical-interpretive writing. This generates another division, symmetrical to it, that creative-original writing is primary, whereas any other kind is secondary. There is only a slight exaggeration in saying that the study of literature in the

West is conducted with these distinctions very much in mind. A *writer*-author suggests the glamor of doing, of bohemia, of originality close to the real matter of life (always we find this closeness of reality and originality); a critic/scholar-author suggests the image of drudgery, passivity, impotence, second-order material, and faded monkishness. As the parallels between original work and secondary criticism have further multiplied in time, opinion has not been kind to the critic, even if allowances have been made for what the eighteenth-century English Augustans called the true critic. Today students of literature are encouraged by the curriculum and the ideology of study to bring themselves out from the haze of criticism and nearer the firm touchstones (Arnold's critical imagery is still influential) of "creative writing": students try for the concreteness and vivacity denied them, by definition, in study. With this process so established, it perhaps seems an idle impertinence to introduce the Platonic-Aristotelian theoretic life as one worth considering, if not living.

Not if *theoria* is properly grasped. And not if the theoretical level of investigation can be shown to be capable now not only of dealing with such questions as originality, but also of being able to identify areas and methods of study less shy of the whole range of experience available for modern writing. This course constitutes relevance, but I intend a very disciplined sort that makes short work of modish and ill-defined subjects with a contemporary look. By theory and theoretical investigation applied to literature, I mean in a basic and extremely limited way an active attention paid to concerns that are irreducible, that do not belong to any but verbal experience in general and literature in particular. Only on this level can there be some hope for rigor and for the formulation of distinctive problems that are genuinely amenable to study. Most of the present courses and methods of literature are the product of a humanistic outlook no longer produced by the culture or even by the university. The study of authors and periods, occasionally of genres and themes, has always presupposed a knowledge of classical languages at least, and some sort of scholarly grounding in history, philology, and philosophy: this is no longer the case now. Therefore both the student and the teacher have one alternative in the "appreciation" of literature (for which such terms as sensibility, impressiveness, and wit serve as an intellectual scaffolding), and another in "methodologies" and "techniques" of study (for which machines erected from other systems first prepare, then deliver the text into interpretation). Theory, as I understand it, is more generous and capable of finer strictness than either alternative.

Reading and writing are activities that theoretically and actually incorporate within them most of one's needs for the production and the understanding of a text. This is a truism only for someone who will not, for example, see that writing is the complex, orderly translation of innumerable forces into decipherable script: at bottom these forces converge on a *desire to write*, which is a choice made over the desire to speak, to gesture, to dance, and so on. So far as a theoretical view is concerned, then, a first question to be answered is why was writing intended in the case of a given text and not some other activity? Why that particular kind of writing and not another? Why, with relation to other similar writing, at that moment and not at another? Implied here are sequences, constellations, complexes of rational choices made by the writer for which the evidence is a printed text. Strictly speaking, unconscious and even involuntary motivation is a boundary of sorts, but by no means—as Freud and more recently Jacques Lacan have demonstrated—a theater closed to the rational investigation of language. As for reading, there is a series of related questions: reading is always for a purpose that involves the writing in question. Why read this and not write? reading in order to do what? reading as development or reading as appropriation?

Even in formulating these questions we leave behind much of the vagueness and privacy normally associated with uses of "originality." Most of us do no more than perceive originality as a quality of our attention, which is enlivened or shocked by an experience that pushes all others either into second place or out of sight. Since this sort of displacement is relatively common, originality might just as well be a name for an endless, perhaps occasionally violent, substitution of one experience for another. But rather than leave it at that, we can study writing itself as an activity in which identifiable forces are in play, some being combined, others being displaced, still others being returned. Therefore the value of writing as an object of analysis is that it makes more precise the almost anonymous alternation of presence and absence we impressionistically and perceptually associate with originality. Presence and absence cease to be mere functions of our perception and become instead willed performances by the writer. Thus presence has to do with such matters as representation, incarnation, imitation, indication, expression, whereas absence has to do with symbolism, connotation, underlying unconscious unity, structure. Writing can be seen then also as the setting in which the interplay of presence and absence *methodologically* takes place. Rilke's description of the fundamental element of Rodin's art catches my meaning perfectly: "This differently great surface variedly accentuated, accurately measured, out of which everything must rise."[5]

All this so far leaves one crucial issue somewhat unclear. What is the *unit* of theoretical interest: that is, what—how defined and demarcated a spatial or temporal interval—does one focus upon in a theoretical examination of writing or reading? Here we must situate ourselves in our own time. If there is anything that centrally characterizes modern writing, it is a dissatisfaction with traditional units of interest like the text, the author, the period, and even the idea. These are now seen at most to do provisional service as makeshift terms in an agreed upon shorthand covering *textuality*, but in reality they are but signs themselves in need of careful demystification and analysis. As Foucault has asked, at what point does an author's text begin, and where does it end; is a postcard or a laundry list written by Nietzsche a sequence within his integral text, or not? From the standpoint of writing, who is Swift, or Shakespeare, or Marx?[6] How can one apprehend a personality supposedly contained by graphemes on a page? In short, so expanded and diverse and specialized have the levels and dimensions of verbal apprehension become, and so sustained the exploitation of these levels of modern writing—witness the overwhelming use of parallels, echoes, fragments, parodies in Eliot, Joyce, Kafka, Mann, Borges, Beckett—that a newly adequate scheme for assembling them into intelligible units has to be sought.

Such comparatively recent schema as style (or idiolect) or structure have generated extraordinarily interesting disciplines (stylistics and structural analysis respectively).[7] These are affiliated less with traditional methods like philology than with modern linguistics, which in turn is itself based upon the study of linguistic universals that enable linguistic performance. Early systematic criticism such as Northrop Frye's, resourceful though it is, also presumes a specific and innate literary faculty capable of generating a finely ordered "stubborn structure." My point here is that the kind of theoretical study I am suggesting will not, except in a very literal way, assume the universal and prior presence of imperatives pressing writers to write any more than it assumes the prior existence of units like the novel or the essay; rather what is assumed is a set of contingent and worldly circumstances or conditions from which came the decision—selected from among other courses of action—to write. The unit of study is determined by those circumstances that, for the writer in question, seem to have enabled, or generated, the *intention* to write.

The distinction I am making is well illustrated near the end of the *Phaedrus* (S.276) where Socrates marks off "an intelligent word," the living word of knowledge from words "tumbled out anywhere . . . [with] no parent to protect them." The former are words deliberately cultivated, sowed, and planted; the latter are "written in water." Socrate's many-tiered argument is centered on how it is that knowledge is formulated, disseminated, and acquired in words, a process he likens both to the slow, methodic cultivation of a garden and to the creation of a family by a solicitous father. Here again theory and originality coincide, for there can be no theoretical knowledge without a discernible origin: all true knowledge, whatever its form, exists within the domain of the knowable, which is also to say that the knowable is attained by "dialectical study," by seriousness, and above all by caring for what is the mind's "legitimate offspring." Socrates' merging of theoretical knowledge with man's most intimate production, his offspring, emphasizes what is too often forgotten, namely the proximity of a particular, concrete human function and need to an abstract, theoretical, and general intention. Actually Socrates presses the relation more closely by saying that a theoretical capacity fathers practical works: hence the appearance of filiation.

This is quite literally one of the more fertile truths available to human thought. It is to be found in Marx obviously, but also in Hegel and Kant and Freud, as well as in any writing that brings together, as in the novel, continuity and originality. Socrates is not talking simply about the intention to yoke theory to practice, as the slogan has it, but he is also validating the direct relevance of an abstracted, hence vigilant, knowledge to a practical impulse. Conversely and more interestingly, this truth presses responsibility for a theoretical extension upon the practical intention. How this has long gone neglected in literary studies is a function of what Georg Lukacs and Roland Barthes have characterized as the reification, the mythologization, of things; things seem not only present, given, natural, and unchanging, but they exclude the traces of their origin and that of any thought that might show them to have been the result of a theory, or a process designed exactly to show no theory or process at all.[8] Therefore to study literature as inertly *given* writing, canonized in texts, books, poems, works, or dramas, is to treat as natural and concrete that which derives from a desire—to write—that is ceaseless, varied, and highly unnatural and abstract, since "to write" is a function never exhausted by the completion of a piece of writing. Thus only a theoretical interest in the abstract—a general interest in what is permanently knowable, though subject to numerous contingencies—can possibly deal with so apparently limitless an original (irreducible) impulse. Indeed one could argue persuasively that contemporary writing is best seen as an outstripping of practical occasions by theoretical, impractical, even utopian desires; to write a novel or a story thus, as in the case of fabulists like Borges, Pynchon, and Garcia Marquez, is a desire to *tell* a story much more than it is one for telling a *story*.

A legitimate objection to this sort of argument is that I have confused knowledge of something like writing with the act of producing writing. After all in the *Phaedrus*, in the *Ion*, and the *Republic* and the *Laws* Plato separates the philosopher from the artist, the knower from the morally liable performer, the contemplative from the actor. Such a line of reasoning is partially true. But in the main it overlooks how urgently Socrates in the *Phaedrus* brings together the lover and the lover of knowledge, the philosopher. He carefully withholds the epithet of "wise" from them

> for that is a great name which belongs to God alone,—lovers of wisdom or philosophers is their modest and befitting title.
> *Phaedrus.* Very suitable.
> *Socrates.* And he who cannot rise above his own compilations and compositions, which he has been long patching and piercing, adding some and taking away some, may be justly called poet or speech-maker or law-maker. (S.278)

Less lyrically than Socrates perhaps, we can translate "lovers of" as "desirers of" or "seekers after" writing. Hence the critic, as much as the novelist, is a writer who seeks writing in writing. On that theoretical and practical level, the search to produce writing unites (a) originality as an irreducible intention to perform a specific activity with (b) originality as an irreplaceable action giving forth the writing. Whether one is the novelist producing a novel or the critic producing a work on that novel, in the admittedly special terms I have been using both are equally original. To ask if one is more original than the other is to risk sociological conclusions of the same order as the talk about equality in *Animal Farm*, but even that kind of conclusion requires something more like Pierre Macherey's or Lucien Goldmann's strictness than Orwell's.[9]

Two examples of criticism based on some of these premises come to mind immediately, by Lukacs and the French classicist, Jean-Pierre Vernant. *The Theory of the Novel* undertakes an investigation of what original consciousness enabled the novel, given a certain set of intellectual, psychological, and spiritual conditions. Lukacs' discipline was in defining his task as the formulation for the first time of what the novelistic impulse originally was; he could do this only because, again for the first time, the novel had reached a stage of development that permitted explicit statements about the novel in a non-novelistic form.[10] Vernant's essays on Greek tragedy are based (like Nietzsche's analyses) on a presumption that the tragedies were not substitutes for ideas, but were "things" intended originally to perform an original function; thus tragedy takes place as an invention that is something radically new in every respect. Tragedy occurs at a highly conditioned moment when the Greek city "enacts itself on the stage . . . and most important, it enacts its own problematics." Vernant determines that these problematics revolve around a difficult change in man's communal conception of himself, a change that "could be neither thought, lived, nor even expressed otherwise than through the form of tragedy . . . All the problems of responsibility, of degrees of intention, of the relationship between the human agent and his acts, the gods and the world are posed by tragedy, and it is only in the form of tragedy that they could be posed."[11]

Lukacs's Hegelianism had not yet undergone its later Marxist reworking, so that "theory" in the early phase of his thought still inhabited a largely ideal realm. Not so in Vernant's theory of tragedy's moment. For him language has a material status with carefully regulated uses in the tragic form. Yet why do both critics, one as much as the other, stress the extreme difficulty of apprehending the forms they study? Because both novel and tragedy are dated back to a pure origin, either spiritual or material, that cannot be immediately or fully grasped. Unlike Dilthey's interpretive theory, these theories do not fall back upon a sympathetic intuition that overrides the sheer age of the documents being studied. Both tragedy and the novel belong to a period forever lost. Therefore the forms' originality, in the purest sense, is a type of loss that the critic's writing attempts to convey.

Originality in one primal sense, then, has to be loss, or else it would be repetition; or we can say that, insofar as it is apprehended as such, originality is the difference between primordial vacancy and temporal, sustained repetition. Kierkegaard for one saw no contradiction (in religious experience) between repetition and originality, but generally we associate repetition either with debasement (the first time tragedy, the second farce) or with a challenging recurrence. Probably because he was a philologist, Nietzsche was obsessed with the study of genealogy in terms of different sorts of originality. Thus *Ursprung* (which corresponds with the notions I discussed above in connection with Lukacs and Vernant) is an original, pure, first, appearance; *Enstehung* signifies the historical emergence of a phenomenon, its *point de surgissement* (the type of originality analyzed by Thomas Kuhn and by Georges Canguihelm in his analyses of singularity);[12] and *Herkunft* designates the stock and the provenance from which originality arises.[13]

Yet Nietzsche, Marx, and Freud are writers in whose work there is a remarkable symmetry between attempts made to characterize originality (revolution, will to truth, the unconscious) and attempts made to regularize, pattern, and schematize the conditions of human experience. Thus for every revolution there must be a set of recurring circumstances; as Foucault says, the result is that true originality as a kind of absolute term becomes an impossibility.[14] Human singularity, and hence any originality associated with human endeavor, is a function of the transpersonal laws that make up the patterns (psychological, economic, and intellectual) we call history, which is documented in thousands of written records. Therefore written history is a countermemory, a kind of parody of Platonic recollection, that permits the discernment by contemplation of true, first, *original* things. For Nietzsche, according to Foucault, the historical sense is parodic in its opposition to recollection, it is dissociative with regard to continuity, it is destructive with regard to knowledge. Because originality becomes harder to discern, its characteristics are more and more finely defined. In the end originality has passed from being a Platonic ideal to becoming a variation within a larger, dominating pattern.

Language plays the great role in this change. Every utterance, no matter its singularity, has to be understood as part of something else; it is precisely against this order of regularity that Artaud rebelled. Nevertheless the result of understanding is that the large pattern domesticates the single act, the order of language overtakes the idiosyncrasies even of script. So close is the liaison between intelligibility and language that Freud, for example, made the verbal order the stage for his exploration of the unintelligible. To write therefore comes to mean more (Derrida's designation is *supplementarity*[15]) than to speak, for the appearance of writing alone gives assurances of regularity and meaning that the tumble and dispersion of speech denies. Writing, as Mallarmé was to discover, can even dispense with an author: "The pure work of art implies the disappearance of the poet as speaker, who thereby cedes the initiative to words and the force of their mobilized inequality."[16] The Book, an unfinished and unfinishable repository of all writing, stands above all particular books.

We return now to a question asked earlier: What is the unit of writing in which we can study the interplay of repetition and originality? It can no longer be only a work or an author, since each of these—given an integral theoretic perspective—aspires to writing beyond such purely functional limits. But since one has neither the time nor the capacity to study all writing, it becomes necessary to analyze the intention or, where it can be decoded, the stated desire from which a specifically demarcated set of writing originally derives. Here the example of modernist writing gives the theoretical critic of all other historical periods a difficult but cogent lesson, for one cannot teach or write about literature today without in some way being influenced by the contemporary literary situation. In no way does this situation have as coherent a defining characteristic as in its profound dissatisfaction with the units, the genres, the expectations of earlier times. Paradoxically, therefore, the originality of contemporary literature in its broad outlines resides in the refusal of originality, or primacy, to its forebears.

Thus the best way to consider originality is to look not for first instances of a phenomenon, but rather to see duplication, parallelism, symmetry, parody, repetition, echoes of it—the way, for example, literature has made itself into a topos of writing. What the modern or contemporary imagination thinks of is less the confining of something to a book, and more the release of something from a book in writing. This release is accomplished in many different forms: Joyce releases the *Odyssey* into Dublin, Eliot frees fragments from Virgil and Petronius into a set of jagged phrases. The writer thinks less of writing originally, and more of rewriting. The image for writing changes from *original inscription* to parallel script, from tumbled-out confidence to deliberate fathering-forth (in which Hopkins' alliteration signifies parallel), from melody to fugue. And since writers no longer inaugurate a new locale, they tend to see their time as an interregnum. Philippe Sollers puts it this way: "The life of a writer is an 'interregnum.' The ostensibly useless work he does as well as the game he seems to be playing are really both in touch with the future, which we know to be the place of all work done using symbols. Literature belongs to the future, and the future, as Mallarmé said, 'is never more than the shock of what should have been done prior to or near the origin.' "[17]

Much of what I have been saying about the transformation of the

imaginative terms by which we can now understand originality is indicated in the French critical phrase *le refus du commencement*.
Since our self-perception as writers has changed from being *lonely
begans* (Hopkins again) to being workers in the *already-begun* (the
always already), the writer can be read as an individual whose impulse historically has been always to write through one or another
given work, in order finally to achieve the independence, like Mallarmé, of writing that knows no bounds. The Book is a myth, but
scarcely ever the reality, of writing. A parallelism, say between Dublin and Attica, sustained over many pages and years leads the writer
not toward another book but rather toward "writing in progress."
Still more fascinating is the case of Thomas Mann in *Doctor Faustus*.
The technique of that novel, as many critics have shown, is the montage and the echo. Both Mann and his protagonist master the art of
doubling, inverting, imitating to infinity. Their originality is to play
this game until they achieve a state of vacancy—the destruction of
Western civilization and morals, the reversion of originality to silence
by way of repetition. Adrian Leverkuhn's pact with the devil gives
him the gift of artistic distinction over a period of years, but since his
earliest days, and since the novel's opening, both Mann and Adrian
are fascinated with parallel and parody, especially because even nature duplicates itself in the most curious way: the inorganic mimics
the organic, one form is reproduced by another, and so on. Thus the
fabric of the novel, as well as its theme, is made of rewriting, one original *cantus firmus* being imitated so many times as to lose its primacy.

   Mann's treatment of all this in a novel has a very unusual analogue
in an essay by Leo Spitzer. Given first as a lecture at Princeton in
1945, "Linguistics and Literary History" is Spitzer's professional
authobiography, his account of the development of his philological
theory and practice. He tells of a fascination he has had, since coming
to America, with the etymology of *conundrum* and *quandary*. Tracing the instability of their phonetic structure, Spitzer finds that an et-
ymological search reveals how "an agglomeration of mere sounds appears motivated." The two words derive from common French and
Latin roots, and their genealogy thus includes *calembour* (pun),
carrefour (crossroads), *quadrifurcus* (Latin for crossroads), and
calembourdaine, which in one development becomes *colundrun*,
then *concundrum*, and in another parallel development *conimbrum*,
conundrum, *quonundrum*, *quandorum*, finally *quandary*. Hence he
concludes that

The instability and disunity of the *word-family* (conundrum-quandary) is symptomatic of its position in the new environment.

But the instability apparent in our English words had already been characteristic of *calembredaine-calembour*, even in the home environment: this French word-family, as we have said, was a blend of at least two word-stems. Thus we must conclude that the instability is also connected with the semantic content: a word meaning "whim, pun" easily behaves whimsically—just as, in all languages throughout the world, the words for "butterfly" present a kaleidoscopic instability.[18]

Now any reader of *Doctor Faustus* will immediately see how suggestive for the novel this entire line of reasoning is. For not only is the mature Adrian surrounded in Munich by a parody of his original *family* in Kaisersaschern, but his interests in doing as his father did, "speculating the elements," persist. Near the beginning of the book Zeitblom describes a butterfly "of transparent nudity," *Hetera esmeralda*, whose appearance and habits, like those of the leaf butterfly, are profoundly duplicitous:

> Hetera had on her wings only a dark spot of violet and rose; one could see nothing else of her, and when she flew she was like a petal blown by the wind. Then there was the leaf butterfly, whose wings on top are a triple chord of colour, while underneath with insane exactitude they resemble a leaf, not only in shape and veining but in the minute reproduction of small imperfections, imitation drops of water, little warts and fungus growths and more of the like. When the clever creature alights among the leaves and folds its wings, it disappears by adaptation so entirely that the hungriest enemy cannot make it out . . . For one cannot ascribe the trick to its own observation and calculation. Yes, yes, Nature knows her leaf precisely: knows not only its perfection but also its small usual blunders and blemishes; mischievously or benevolently she repeats its outward appearance in another sphere, on the under side of this her butterfly, to baffle others of her creatures . . . This butterfly, then, protected itself by becoming invisible.[19]

These descriptions look ahead to Adrian's seduction by the prostitute, to a concealed motto in his music, to his pact with the devil, all ascribed generically to *Hetera esmeralda*. The butterfly's cunning is a function of nature's, and the idea of an unstable butterfly resonates through Spitzer's speculations on the nature of language. In the cases of both the philologist and the novelist there is, moreover, no attribution of the process of duplication and repetition to anything more personal than "nature." Thus we might say that originality does not reside either in language or in the elements, since both make virtually impossible any attempt to determine the true from the copy. That is a conclusion on one level. On another level, as readers we take note of Spitzer's personal intervention as a philologist, of Mann's as a novelist, of Adrian as a Faust-figure, in the workings of an unstable medium so as to clarify in it the order of cunning symmetry. Hence the wielding of individual authority transforms the elements sufficiently to implicate the individual in a career of working them: Spitzer as philologist, Adrian as demonic musician.

I have purposely left unasked the question: Did Spitzer "influence" Mann? For such a question inevitably raises the problem of originality; and indeed I seem to have been hinting that the critic has in a sense been more original than the original writer. But that is not the point. My argument is to stress the responsibility for originality in every vocation that "works" language. From my theoretical point of view, Mann and Spitzer themselves recognize no originality per se, since nature and language are orders of duplication. Perceptually, on the other hand, originality is a quality discovered in whichever author of the two we discover first, as well as in impressions of novelty and force too subjective for sustained analysis. But because of the shift from inscription to parallel script there is a more crucial theoretic shift also in the conception of originality, which now becomes a sort of faculty for combinatorial play. A writer's responsibility is to control this play, which still leaves entirely up to him or her such matters as point of departure, the center on which the writing is built, and so on. Nevertheless these responsibilities of the writer are not implicit or abstract ideas heaped upon language by a critic, but physically intrinsic to the writing itself. I mean essentially the actual sense of distance or of closeness to a "subject" imparted to the writing, and the sense writing has of being materially coextensive with what it is saying.

Traditionally the temporal convention in literary study has been retrospective. We look at writing as already completed. A critic therefore restores to a text its original meaning, one imagined to have been lost through time or technique. We are now even less likely to be interested in study that demonstrates a text's contemporary relevance except, as I said above, for modish reasons. But how much more challenging is a theoretic for study that takes writing as being produced for something formed *in the writing:* this was Mallarmé's discovery. Thus the ultimate, perhaps infinite goal of writing is a Book conceived of as a bibliosystem, a kind of activated library whose effect is to stimulte the production of forms of disciplined, gradually actualized freedom. If originality as a conception has had the power for too long of depressing time backwards into lost primacy at best, and regained utopias at worst, this is a good reason for reorienting our study systematically toward the future. As Foucault and Gilles Deleuze have said, so drastic a reversal of perspective has the effect of de-Platonizing thought.[20] For what could be more Platonic (in a debased way) than seeing literature as a copy, experience as an original, and history as a line moving from origin to the present? Once this type of linearity is revealed for the theology it really is, a secular reality for writing is enabled. Foucault's phrase for that reality is *l'ordre du discours,* but we can recognize in it the proper, formidably complex originality of writing as, in its complex affiliations with the social world, it counters nature.

7

Roads Taken and Not Taken
in Contemporary Criticism

IT is still true that the basic anthologies of modern literary theory and criticism, compiled in response to the demand for theoretical texts, enable us to surmise that a large quantity and variety of work is being done today.[1] Yet even though these anthologies are helpful as an indication of what is considered the main body of literary theory, they are not so helpful in assisting us to estimate how much better or worse literary criticism has become in general.

Not only is it difficult to know with what to compare "modern" or "contemporary" criticism (with "classical" criticism? with "traditional" criticism? with the criticism of "a generation ago"? what is "a generation" in criticism anyway?). It is next to impossible to get readers, much less professional critics, to agree about the purposes of criticism or its effectiveness. Still more problematic is the distinction often made between critical theory and practical criticism, or between the theory *of* something and criticism of or about it. Surprisingly enough, sophisticated critical polemicists are likely to be satisfied with crude national labels ("French" or "European" versus "English" or "American") in dealing with these distinctions and in letting them settle very large areas of intellectual discrimination. Names are often enough. "Frye" and "Leavis" stir up undignified passions; "Derrida" and "Leavis" might provoke more rowdy emotions still. "Good," in the sense of approved, criticism can thus be associated with Anglo-Saxon moral concern, evaluative assertion, a certain kind of attention to stylistic performance, an emphasis on concrete reading as opposed to abstract (and foreign) pseudo-philosophy or generality. Stand on the other side of the net and adjectives like "provincial," "untheoretical," "unproblematic," and "unselfconscious" will be opening shots at the opponent; after that, one can hurl "structure," "semiological," "hermeneutical," and the more or less ultimate cross-court word "deconstruction." Any reader of literary journals knows either repertoire, and probably yawns at them both, as much as he or she is also bored by any eclecticist who tries to use all the factional vocabularies to make a transcendental synthesis. But, in the manner of an impressionistic historian, one can say that there *are* things about what goes on in contemporary criticism today that are representative of the mode. What assumptions would clever anthologists make about their readers' interest in contemporary criticism, assuming that by "contemporary" they understood "criticism that one cannot afford to ignore" or "criticism that seems, by its novelty, modishness, or sheer intellectual power, to make people believe that it is the representative and perhaps even the vanguard contemporary type"?

A question of this sort does not pretend to answer some of the basic problems faced by criticism. Neither, at the outset, does it get past the level of a useful exercise, by which one delineates the critical field in order to propose changes for it or lacks in it. If these anthologies serve any real function—aside from being convenient ways for a reader to get hold of fugitive essays—it is to let one think that they make up a consensus for today's critics, an immediate background they presume to be accurate, from which they launch their own work, to which they respond, against which they define themselves, their allies, or their opponents. In accepting such a background critics also presume a background for the background and, without being too dodgy, they would say that these anthologies and what they represent aim to be different from previous anthologies and consensi, which in turn were different from previous ones, and so on. Critical change is obviously less sequential and abrupt than that. But let us grant for the moment a sense of change that these anthologies incorporate and exploit.

In a perfectly evident way, criticism in America today is more cosmopolitan than it has been since the first two decades of this century. The Macksey-Donato collection (*The Structuralist Controversy*) most authoritatively records a seemingly lasting French intervention into American critical discourse, just as the 1966 conference of which it was the published proceedings was the first important gathering of foreign critics in the United States. The French intervention additionally caused doors and windows to be opened onto the rest of Europe, first onto Romance cantons and countries (Geneva and Italy, notably), then onto areas like Germany and the Soviet Union. And indeed the new cosmopolitanism revived interest in old or native approaches—those of C. S. Peirce, *Philologen* like Auerbach, Curtius, and Spitzer, as well as the Russian Formalists—previously known mainly to specialists.

A remarkable result for the practicing critic who wrote in English and who had an interest in theoretical issues was that English studies had their centrality eroded. Richard Poirier's well-known essay in Polletta's *Issues* in 1970 spelled out the English-speaking critic's uneasiness with the position taken, from Arnold to Leavis, that "our" moral center was to be found stretched out in the English classics.[2] The touchstones were being transformed into activity, such as what Barthes called *l'activité structuraliste* and *écriture*,[3] or into a rather more generously conceived entity called modern literature. The latter is Lionel Trilling's phrase, which, when he employed it first in 1961, resonated against Arnold in particular. That Arnold's best critic, who was also the critic whose work in the United States had most assuredly placed English studies centrally on the literary agenda, spoke of a modern literature that included Diderot, Mann, Freud, Gide and Kafka was a significant announcement of how international and dialectical English-speaking criticism had become.[4]

Not only does it seem pertinent to have had sessions of the English Institute addressed in French about French authors, but an intelligent young critic will now spend a vast amount of time reading and citing Barthes, Derrida, Todorov, and Genette. A new vocabulary— call it Anglo-French—disposes terms like *découpage, décodage,* and *bricolage* with some assurance that everyone will understand them. A fortunate few will quote approvingly from Szondi, Benjamin, Adorno, Mayer, Enzensberger, Bakhtin, Eco, Lotman, and of course the ubiquitous Jakobson. So it is not exceptionable that anthologies of literary theory will draw most heavily on international, as opposed to strictly local, work. From what had seemed to be the fierce parochialism of New Criticism, for example, to the sometimes abandoned cosmopolitanism of *this* New Criticism, it has mainly been the isolated integrity of English studies—as a body of tests, a tradition, an object, a tone of voice, a coherent, well-defined discipline—that suffered in the change.

One could call the loss a loss of objectivity, in the sense of objecthood. Notions of boundary, limits, and, with those, the ideas of a national literature, a genre, a period, a confined text, an author, seem to have weakened. The ease with which one could assert that Romanticism is such and such, or that the tradition is certain works arranged in certain order, has been replaced with either a theory or a praxis of textual functions. Barthes' critical theory, with its emphases on *écriture*, a defused author (in his *Racine*), an omnicompetent text (in *S/Z*), a text as sensation (in *Le Plaisir du texte*), fairly maps the shift from a kind of objectivized historicism, with English or French studies at its center, to a kind of international critical apparatus important for its activity, not by any means for the literary material it may or may not validate. Curiously enough, a certain restraint operated on these anthologists who while excerpting Barthes and Todorov shied away from the most radical semioticians, Kristeva, Sollers, Jean-Pierre Faye, and others in the *Tel Quel* group; later of course *Tel Quel* renounced its Left past and became a disturbing reminder of how fickle intellectual fashions are.

On the one hand, there appears an international critical vocabulary aimed not at texts or traditions but at a condition of existence we may rightly call *textuality;* on the other hand, various counterorthodoxies arise to replace the old notions of author, period, work, or genre. As is always the case with criticism, certain past authors seem suddenly important. Think of Dante or Donne and the New Critics; think of Hölderlin for Heidegger; think of Rousseau, Artaud, Bataille, Saussure, Freud, and Nietzsche for the latest "new" critics. These authors are employed as principles beyond which texts as texts cannot and need not go. To return to them, as Lacan returned to Freud, is to establish them as a canon whose legitimacy is maintained with loyal devotion. An unfortunate consequence for assenting critics is that, even if they do not use Arnold's image of venerable petrification as an equivalent for high value, they are no less susceptible to the dangers of received authority from canonical works and authors. A maddening new critical shorthand is to be observed. Instead of arguing a point, there tends often to be a lackluster reference to Nietzsche or Freud or Artaud or Benjamin—as if the name alone carried enough value to override any objection or to settle any quarrel. Most of the time the citation carries with it no discrimination that such a passage in such a work may be better or more useful than others, or less so in some unintentionally comic instances; the name and the reference are enough.

A new canon means also a new past or a new history and, less happily, a new parochialism. Any reader of modern French criticism will be astounded to realize that Kenneth Burke, in whose huge output many of the issues and methods currently engaging the French were first discussed, is unknown.[5] Is this the result of ignorance, convenience, or deliberate ideological omission? Another example, for which the Europeans are not to blame of course, is the slavish attitude to them by American critics. Yet what seems especially wasteful is the way one critic elaborates on or criticizes the work of a canonical critic like Barthes or Derrida and is rarely answered or even recognized by the canon. Similarly there is a pronounced tendency to avoid historical research as something less interesting intrinsically than theoretical speculation. Derrida's essays on Rousseau and Condillac, to cite two influential examples, have spawned a whole array of imitations, all of them as historically and contextually thin as Derrida's.[6]

What then of the prevailing critical discourse itself—or, to be more exact, what does critical discourse do? I shall speak here of a majority *a priori* belief that seems to direct critics' attention to one important aspect of the literary experience: function. In most of the anthologized material, as well as the dominant critical modes these anthologies represent, we will find the critic talking about what a text does, how it works, how it has been put together in order to do certain things, how the text is a wholly integrated and equilibrated system. Much as it may seem to be an impoverishing view of literature, this particular kind of functionalism has had a salutary effect. It has done away with empty rhetorical testimonials merely proclaiming a work's greatness, humanistic worth, and such. For another, it has made it possible for critics to talk seriously and technically and precisely about the text. Academic, journalistic, or amateur criticism has usually been considered a branch of belles-lettres; until the advent of American and English New Criticism, the job of a critic was an appreciation of work as much for the general reader as for other critics. Functionalist criticism makes an extremely sharp break between the community of critics and the general public. The assumption is that to write a literary work and to write about one are specialized functions with no simple equivalent or cause in everyday human experience. Therefore critical vocabulary must emphasize the antinatural and even antihuman characteristics of verbal behavior in written language. And, since genetic theses seem particularly suspect so far as literature is concerned—writing cannot be reduced simply to a natural past or to a natural urge or to an empirically prior moment—critics will go out of their way to find a technical language with no other possible use than to describe the text's functions.

An antecedent for this decision to employ a rigorous technical vocabulary is found in I. A. Richards' criticism. Of course he did not use linguistic terminology; but what distinguished him, and Empson as well, from the American New Critics was his search for critical exactness without appeals to the prestige of literature or of everyday experience. Precision in dealing with literature was gained for him in the use of words, and words can only be made precise by a science of words, purified of inexactness, emotion, or sloppiness. Richards' subsequent attention to Basic English, as well as his continued borrowings from ordinary-language or utilitarian philosophy and empirical and behavioral psychology, set him apart from his contemporaries. What is additionally true of his work is also true of the critics I am discussing now: the temptations of a rigorous technical critical vocabulary induce occasional lapses into a sort of scientism. Reading and writing become at such moments instances of regulated, systematized production, as if the human agencies involved were irrelevant. The closer the linguistic focus (say in the criticism of Greimas or Lotman), the more formal the approach, and the more scientistic the functionalism.

Definitions, more often than not, point the reader back toward the method, since one aim of functionalism is to perfect the instrument of analysis as much as any understanding of a text's workings. Thus while an intelligent critic like Barthes will have the good taste to know the qualitative difference between Ian Fleming and Balzac, what he actually says is that the latter *works* better (is more responsive to a full-scale semiological reading by Barthes) than the former. This is almost the same as saying that you can write a good story if you know the rules of composition, which obviously guarantees no such result. For practical purposes, however, the constant peril of a functionalist bias is in giving the reader uniform, unvarying claustrophobia. Since the relationship between the work and the critic is self-sealing and self-perpetuating, and since the specialized character of the relation is exclusive and rigidly systematic, a reader can expect only to receive knowledge of a sort already confirmed and enclosed by the initial definitions. You experience the text making the critic work, and the critic in turn shows the text at work: the product of these interchanges is simply that they have taken place. Critical ingenuity is pretty much confined to transposing the work into an instance of the method.

Most great critics are methodical; this means only perhaps that they are able to articulate and rationalize their intuitive awareness of literature. But it also means that they are not afraid of making their methods and their own writing independently interesting and intellectually consistent, over and above a work or an occasion. For less great critics, such challenges are rare. They will use the work in order to make it work, which it always will. Their method will demonstrate its effectiveness, which it will always possess. And on and on, without any sense of the drama underlying method or of its fundamental ground in intellectual life.

The great virtue of Derrida's "Structure, Sign and Play in the Discourse of the Human Sciences" is that method is shown turning upon itself at the very moment of its greatest victories, in order to achieve a still more novel, more differentiated lucidity. Derrida goes on to say that "the risk of sterility and of sterilization has always been the price of lucidity,"[7] and hints with appropriate courage that he is willing to pay the price. But these are partial statements made with a full realization that contemporary methodology occurs at a particular moment in human self-consciousness, not randomly because a method was thought of and then employed at will. Such essays as Derrida's are occasionally to be found in the anthologies. Their value is to make explicit a sense of the drama of method and its underlying roots in intellectual vitality. Thereafter we can better recognize that contemporary critical discourse is fundamentally antidynastic in its attitudes—to the work, to the critic, to knowledge, to reality. Orphaned by the radical Freudian, Saussurean, and Nietzschean critique of origins, traditions, and knowledge itself, contemporary criticism has achieved its methodological independence by forfeiting an active situation in the world. It has no faith in traditional continuities (nation, family, biography, period); rather it improvises, in acts of an often inspired *bricolage*, order out of extreme discontinuity. Its culture is a negative one of absence, antirepresentation, and (as Blackmur used to put it repeatedly) ignorance.

Learned or gifted ignorance is no mean thing, however. All of the major critics now writing make themselves over into critical instruments, as if from scratch; for their presumptive ignorance makes possible the finding out of important truths about, and important methods for, the study of literature. Consider a constellation of critics that might include Auerbach, Spitzer, Blackmur, Barthes, Genette, and Benjamin; their careers span almost a century, but there is a good deal of overlap between them. All are comprised within the scope of the main anthologies. Each of them, to begin with, is a reader whose learning is *for* the text and whose method is *from* the text. The divergences between them are very wide because of the ways each doctors his ignorance. Yet no one of them cares much for tidy distinctions between bloodless theory and practice or between literary criticism and philology, philosophy, linguistics, psychology, sociology. Such as it is, their common method is incorporative; it converts what seems to be alien material, or in some cases quixotic and trivial material, into pertinent dimensions of the text.

Some of these dimensions appear eccentric, even determinedly so. But this will to eccentricity, I think, is a major project of contemporary critical discourse, Northrop Frye's included. For the critic, texts are texts not as symbols of something else but as displacements (Frye's vocabulary is useful here) of other things; texts are deviations from, exaggerations and negations of, human presence. They are at times phenomena of excess and of rupture. Style does not represent an author, any more than authors are their biography. Instead the facts of style exist together in an affiliative relation to a text, which itself is part of an affiliative structure of eccentric elements. All of this is a much noted consequence of subjectivity's weakened position with regard to a text. No longer is it commonly held that Taine's data (*race, moment, milieu*) both exhaust and define the writer as the producer of his text. Even as staunch a defender of fertile authorial consciousness as Georges Poulet accepts before anything else the eccentricity, contingency, and instability of self, its mutability and powerlessness before the text. "Reading, then, is the act in which the subjective principle which I call *I*, is modified in such a way that I no longer have the right, strictly speaking, to consider it as my *I*."[8]

What makes such statements methodologically valid, as opposed to being testimonials of effusive sympathy between critic and text, is that the critic's proper identity, the working point of departure, is neither an empirical self (the same self that eats, goes shopping, breathes, dies) nor an official persona. Instead the critical identity, the critic's *author*itative, *author*izing method of dealing with texts, is built upon a linguistic and perhaps an institutional base, not a psychological, social, or historical one. In effect this means that language is considered as a constituted community of language users, not merely as a vertical means of communication. Such a community is intersubjective of course, but it has codes that give it order, coherence, intelligibility. The critical method—Auerbach's, Spitzer's, Blackmur's, Barthes', or Poulet's—is effective because every aspect of language is significant. And the production of significance is precisely the principal capability of language. What concerns the critic is how language signifies, what it signifies, in what form.

A vast range of possibilities immediately opens out. Are these linguistic significations intentional, are they all equal, is one signification more determined historically or sociologically than another, how do they influence each other?—the list of options for critical attention can be extended to include every critical act. For critics are of course potentially intelligent readers first of all, but their role after that is nothing if not an active and dialectical one. It is their work—their existence, their role—that determines significance as a subject for study and analysis. Thus the history of literary criticism, as Hazard Adams' anthology amply demonstrates, is the history of critical mediations, which is another way of saying that it is a history of critics gaining identity by endowing certain linguistic objects with significance for the critic, and after that for other critics and readers.[9] The critical identity is the presentational device for certain, formally determined matters in language. To study the history of criticism is in reality to understand the history of literature critically. Such a history is, no less than the history of biology described by François Jacob, "to find out how certain objects became accessible to analysis, thus making it possible for new domains of research to be constituted as sciences."[10]

T HE functionalist attitude in critical discourse has some unfortunate limitations, however. A functionalist attitude pays too much attention to the text's formal operations, but far too little to its materiality. In other words, the range assumed for the text's operations tends to be either wholly internal or wholly rhetorical, with the critic serving as a sort of one-person *Rezeptionsgeschichte*. On the one hand, the text is imagined as working alone within itself, as containing a privileged, or if not privileged then unexamined and *a priori*, principle of internal coherence, *Zusammenhang*; on the other hand, the text is considered as in itself a sufficient cause for certain precise effects it has on an ideal reader. In both cases the text does not remain but is metamorphosed into what Stanley Fish has called a self-consuming artifact. A perhaps unforeseen consequence is that the text becomes idealized, essentialized, instead of remaining as the special kind of cultural object it really is, with a causation, persistence, durability, and social presence quite its own.

Some notable omissions from the anthologies indicate this prevailing idealist and antimaterialistic bias. Michel Foucault is scarcely to be found, although more recently he has become a cult figure in his own right. Auerbach and Spitzer—whose philological scholarship is mainly concerned not with reading but with describing the modes of persistence of texts—are misrepresented completely; untutored readers will assume (if they do not read the two or three essays *about* Spitzer and Auerbach) that they were rather old-fashioned versions of Brooks or Warren. Lukacs stands out as a dull polemicist for realism since the company he keeps, anthologically speaking, extols artistic isolation and the value of aesthetic rarification. The extracts from his work are uniformly the same in critical anthologies generally, and uniformly uninteresting as a result, since they are chosen simply, and uninterestingly, to prove his Marxism.[11] Even in their efforts to give some idea of how resourceful the functionalists are about style as a major instrument of the text's activity, the anthologies do not excerpt work by Michael Riffaterre, M.A.K. Halliday, or other vigorous stylisticians. Moreover, such sophisticated historical criticism as the anthologies present cannot compare in its isolation from sociocultural history with straight history-of-ideas writing, which fills the pages of the scholarly journals. This insensitivity to history spoils the very matter being anthologized; history is irrelevant. Gras's anthology of modern "European Literary Theory," is grotesquely portrayed without Ingarden, the Sartre of *What Is Literature?* and *The Critique of Dialectical Reason*, or the Heidegger of *Being and Time*.

These distortions stem in part from a peculiar disorder in modern criticism itself. As a discipline, criticism has given very little notice to its history as a discipline. One of the signs of modern criticism is a willingness to write criticism of other critics. But it is comparatively rare to find critics undertaking critical histories of criticism itself. True, there are encyclopedic efforts like those of René Wellek, but we must ask why the preference in critical history is always for the encyclopedia (handbook, anthology, casebook) and rarely for the critical critical history, of which two excellent recent examples by Frank Lentricchia (*After the New Criticism*) and Geoffrey Hartman (*Criticism in the Wilderness*) are exceptions proving the general preference. Such a history would undoubtedly entail consideration of social and political impingements on criticism; it would also require attention to the question of when criticism is a discipline and when not. In short, critical attention to criticism viewed as an intellectual phenomenon in a historical, social setting is resisted in ways exactly congruent with those I have listed for functionalist attitudes. Criticism is considered as what critics do, regardless of their archival or worldly circumstances. To produce criticism is to do what has always been done, with no change or past to speak of.

For the anthologist, a choice or exclusion is often dictated by the sheer unintelligibility of a potential choice, since excerpts are even harder to understand than a whole book. Packageability is more relevant than historical or even aesthetic accuracy. But that is not always the case. What we will detect, then, is a conscious avoidance of criticism whose focus is the text as something other, as something historically and materially more, than a critical occasion. By "material" in this case I mean the ways, for example, in which the text is a monument, a cultural object sought after, fought over, possessed, rejected, or achieved in time. The text's materiality also includes the range of its authority. Why does a text enjoy currency at one time, recurrency at others, oblivion at others?[12] By the same token, an author's *fama*, his reputation and status, is by no means a constant thing. Is an account of this inconstancy, or at least this inconsistency, within the critic's job? It is, I believe, the more so now as the possibilities of archeological historical research have been so extended and refined by Foucault.

Foucault's method is to study the text as part of an archive, which is composed of discourses, which are composed of statements. In short he deals with texts as part of a system of cultural diffusion, rigidly controlled, tightly organized, difficult to penetrate. He argues that everything stated in a field like literary discourse or medical discourse is produced only with the most selective method, with little regard for individual genius.[13] I have argued that similar things take place when "other" cultures and peoples are discussed. Each statement is therefore a material effort to incorporate a particular piece of reality as selectively as possible.

But there are other ways of dealing with the materiality of texts, and these are no less scanted by the consensus. The opposite of incorporation as discussed by Foucault, no less material, is the theme of literary influence as recently theorized first by W. J. Bate and more elaborately by Harold Bloom.[14] Here too context is of the essence, since their assumption is that every writer, but especially the romantic post-Miltonic writer, is almost bodily aware of his predecessors as occupying the poetic space he now wishes to fill with his poetry. The intertextual struggle for the poet, according to Bloom, is no charming tea party, but a fierce battle whose all-pervading jostle spills over into and becomes the topic of the new poet's verse. The text's materiality here is what the poetry *is*, and whether it can be a poetic text or not is something never taken for granted by the poet. Each line, in short, is an achievement, a space snatched out of the predecessor's clutches, filled by the poet with his words, which in time will have to be fought over by a successor. The family romance of poetry as Bloom portrays it breeds a defensive poetry, a child of limitation and defensive anxiety.

What Foucault, Bloom, and Bate have in common is that their work is about, and indeed is, the text's situation in the world. Foucault's of course is the world of culture and what he calls "discipline"; Bloom's and Bate's is the world of art. This is almost like saying that criticism always ought to be in the world, and that any world will do. But that is a sloppy notion, which I have tried earlier in this book to refine somewhat. Yet compared not only with Foucault, Bate, and Bloom, but with the unreasonably ignored work of Raymond Schwab,[15] contemporary critical discourse is worldless, in a frequently numbing way. Considering that much of the truly valuable work in literary theory and scholarship being done now in America is about Romanticism (and note, by the way, that the anthologies before us are remarkably stingy on poetics or the various theories of poetic performance), there seems to be no good reason for keeping Schwab out. His thesis in *La Renaissance orientale* is a simple one: Romanticism cannot be understood unless some account is taken of the great textual and linguistic discoveries made about the Orient during the late eighteenth and early nineteenth centuries. To be convincing, such a thesis needs to be buttressed with a tremendous amount of detail drawn from history, sociology, literature, academic Orientalism itself, philosophy, and linguistics. Schwab has the detail but, what is more to the point for a critical theorist, he organizes it superbly, not according to a reductive linear scheme but in terms of a subtle analysis of the process of gradual, then increasingly rapid, acculturation of the Orient by European society and culture. Schwab's point is that texts are the result of an encounter between familiar and novel ideas; yet such an encounter is eminently circumstantial and material, as when Anquetil-Duperron risks his life trying to get hold of the Zend-Avesta texts in Surat, texts he then translates for the benefit of European culture at large. The innumerable and sometimes minute facts of such encounters are destined by Schwab to support his view of the change in European cultural institutions as a result of their reception of the Orient. Individual texts are seen from a perspective that is able to pull in as well the salon, the museum, the laboratory, the learned academies, and even bureaucratic and governmental organizations.

I cite Schwab, Foucault, Bate, and Bloom as exemplifying a possible trend for criticism to be taken seriously only if literature is going to be studied in a more situated, circumstantial, but no less theoretically self-conscious way. There is no point in my further qualifying "situated" and "circumstantial," since it should be obvious that I mean "worldly" and "historical": literature is produced in time and in society by human beings, who are themselves agents of, as well as somewhat independent actors within, their actual history. For some reason contemporary vanguard criticism has assumed that the relations between texts and between texts and society are taken care of by the superstructure or by something called traditional scholarship. That assumption is not warranted, if one means by the relation between texts and society anything like the complexity assigned to it by Benjamin (the student of Baudelaire), the Goldmann of *Le Dieu caché*, or Lukacs. So-called traditional scholarship has rarely possessed the methodological rigor and vision of such critics. But the critics of influence have at least the great merit of believing that literature is produced because of other poets and texts, *in* their company, not despite them. Schwab and Foucault have gone very far in determining the social and external constraints upon production, as well as the discursive and cultural (that is, internal) systems that provoke and assimilate literary production.

To approve and admire such historically generous critics is by no means to overlook problems in their theory and practice. From the viewpoint of learning, however, nothing they say has that airless and technically lucid finality characterizing a structural *critifact*, to coin a neologism for what is in fact only an analytical neologism. In my opinion, though, Schwab's and Foucault's work places too great a premium on dramatic change. The same is no less true of Bate and Bloom. Literary history has been regarded by them all as a more or less steady drama, with one great age succeeded ponderously by another. History then becomes at bottom "linear succession," even though what-succeeds-what is described in very complex nonlinear detail. More recently, Foucault has tried rather programatically to understand textual history in terms of those comparative stabilities (borrowing from Braudel) he called "the slow movements of material civilization."[16] Perhaps this refocusing on how texts maintain, instead of always changing, history is a return to Foucault's early interest in Raymond Roussel: "Roussel's machinery does not fabricate being; it maintains things inside being."[17]

What is it that maintains texts inside reality? What keeps some of them current while others disappear? How do authors imagine for themselves the "archive" of their time, into which they propose to put their text? What are the centers of diffusion by which texts circulate? For example, what equivalents in early nineteenth-century English culture are there for the French academies and the literary-scientific Parisian salons as agents of cultural dispersion and organization? Goldmann's theory of homologous structures, while it anticipates some of these questions, does not go far enough in beginning to answer them. Moreover, we need to understand with precision what role critical scholarship plays in the production of "literary" works, a question raised seriously by both Wilde and Nietzsche. How, for example, are the great philological discoveries contemporary with the European Romantic movement influential in poetry, remembering that Coleridge, the Schlegels, Holderlin, Chateaubriand, and others were writers with a deep interest in those discoveries? What method do we have for methodically assimilating such verbal institutions in a given social era to narrative, philology, or history? In what way are etymology in philology and plot succession in the novel related? To call them all textual phenomena is hardly a satisfying answer, but so far this is the only answer we get. Of what moment to literary history are the rifts in relations between language and philosophy and religion, which had been aligned at the end of the eighteenth century, and the new rapprochement between language and natural science (comparative anatomy in particular) by the first third of the nineteenth century? Think of the closeness between Locke and Sterne; then think of how Balzac and Cuvier or Geoffrey-de-Sainte Hilaire come together a generation later. Here there is no question of derived ideas but of their inherent currency, or recurrency if we prefer.

Any attention to these and similar questions must draw critics deep into the rationale of their work. One of the unfortunate losses in contemporary critical discourse is that sense critics once had of their work as an intellectual adventure. An earlier tradition, which lasted until the middle of the eighteenth century, was for scholars or critics to consider their life as having exemplary value; scholarly biography was a recognized genre. In both instances what critics did, how they went from work to work, how they formulated their projects, were treated as meaningful parts of the methodological experience, not simply as anecdotal tidbits. I draw notice to these historical aspects of critical practice in order to approve their value for the future of critical discourse. Pedagogically, there is every good reason for regarding the choice of a subject and its formulation as being not only the beginning of a critical project but also the critical project itself. If we could have accounts by critics of what led them to a given project, why and how they fashioned the project, how they undertook its completion and in what context, we would have opportunities for future study of a very important sort. Not only would it be possible to understand once and for all that criticism creates its subject matter—there are no problems simply lying about to be dealt with—but also young critics would understand criticism to be an activity whose main purposes are the enablement of learning and the multiplication of critical discourse, from restriction to comparative freedom. If critics today feel that they are paralyzed by the sheer difficulty of finding a subject about which to write, it is because they have not realized the part of independent creation in criticism.

Critical discourse is still ensnared by a simplistic opposition between originality and repetition, in which all literary texts worth studying are given the former classification, the latter being logically confined mainly to criticism and to what isn't worth studying. Such schema are hopelessly paralyzing, as I have argued. They mistake the regularity of most literary production for originality, while insisting that the relationship between "literature" and criticism is one of original to secondary; moreover, they overlook in both traditional and modern literature, the profoundly important constitutive use of repetition—as motif, device, epistemology, and ontology. Perhaps it is not until the nineteenth century that such a view of repetition becomes explicit (in Kierkegaard, Marx, and Nietzsche, for instance), though Curtius and Auerbach have taught us that that is not really the case. From its earliest beginnings, narrative fiction, to take a further example, has been built around the tantalizing figure of the family, in which its recurring circumstantial perpetuity is tampered with by the upstart "original" hero. Why this modal constancy if not to preserve, maintain, *repeat,* the form of fiction within the "slow movements of material civilization"?

As for the relationships in value between originality and ideas of novelty, of primacy, or of "the first"—this is a crucial matter. All critics take for granted that there is some connection between a great work and its priority. Bloom's theory of influence is built around this notion, that a great work has power because it was first, that it came before and preempted others. Now such ideas also carry with them an extremely crude understanding of what it means to be first or to have come first. The necessity of such biological crudeness—it is biological, since in context "first" means "father" and "second" means "son"—for Bloom is unquestioned; he uses it, and it is by no means incidental to his poetics of misreading. But for other critics priority is associated rather lackadaisically with novelty, with coming or happening first, with simple precedence, as if history were like a series of children being born one after the other from past to present *ad infinitum*. An irreducibly serial, filiative conception of sociohistorical time such as this totally obscures the interesting problem of emergence, in which cultural phenomena are not simply ascribed priority or a miraculous birth, but are treated as a family of ideas emerging "permanently in discourse."[18] Cultural events are not best understood as if they were human beings born on a certain day; the past is not a set of such births, and time does not move like a clock, in discrete moments. If the history of science has learned to deal with the emergence problem, why not literary theory? What are the limits to employing the human life cycle as a model of literary history? How really useful is a critical approach based on anthropomorphic units of originality like "work," "author," or "generation"? so forth? What vocabulary can we employ that deals with human agency as well as the impersonal repeating discourse of literary structure?

These are difficult questions to answer, but they are indispensable to the development of a critical discourse that will be intellectually serious and socially responsive in the largest humane sense. Only if the development occurs will it be possible dialectically to assess the genuine force, in literary history and institutions, of threats to coherence or order. There is no way to grasp these threats so long as cultural history is viewed as a lazy series of births and deaths. If culture is maintained materially, then it cannot be dependent on events but on institutions constructed by men and women, these institutions also having an independent history of their own.

The dialectical opposite of the repeating material civilization to which I have been referring is an allied set of forces—Blackmur called them collectively the Moha[19]—whose presence in human life disturbs, wastes, the noumenal coercion of culture. One of the signal achievements of psychoanalytic criticism has been the attempt to deal with the Moha. Yet too often symptology, or the mere willingness to consider this force as culturally deviant (whereafter it is confined to the neurotic weaknesses of the artist), has resulted. Recently the attention in France to Nietzsche and Freud has remedied the situation, but we need a more situated account of the Moha *getting in* to literature. This is a current of critical analysis begun effectively by Georges Bataille in 1933 with "La Notion de dépense."[20] To date the challenge has not been taken up except in Morse Peckham's *Man's Rage for Chaos* and in Richard Poirier's *The Performing Self*.[21]

The interplay of order and disorder frames the essentially dispersed sense of the literary text. Within that frame, however, there is an entire order of genetic questions, neglected since the 1944–45 Wimsatt-Beardsley attack on intention, an attack continued in Wimsatt's forceful "Genesis: A Fallacy Revisited."[22] Certainly one must feel that the irreducible dualities—subjective/objective, inside/outside, author/poem, and so on—held on to by Wimsatt and others extort too high a cost in understanding and discrimination. Furthermore, there is a large body of modern literature beseeching readers to make intentional leaps into the author's psyche and into their own (see Trilling's "On the Teaching of Modern Literature" or Blackmur's *Anni Mirabiles*).[23] Strict boundaries between self and object or ego and world encourage a useful, yet preliminary, pedagogical discipline; nevertheless they do not describe anything more than an analytic reality. "Every manifestation [of intellectual and artistic phenomena] is the work of its individual author and expresses his thought and his way of feeling, but these ways of thinking and feelings are not independent entities with respect to the actions and behavior of other men. They exist and may be understood only in terms of their inter-subjective relations which give them their whole tenor and richness."[24] If we assume this, with Goldmann, our responsibility is to venture beyond the rudimentary demarcations.

I see no particular use in insisting that a poem is a solitary object existing independent of any context: for clearly it is not. Each poem or poet is involuntarily the expression of collectivities. What becomes an interesting theoretical problem for criticism is to determine how, or when, or where, the poet or poem can be said to be a voluntary (personal and intentional) expression of difference and of community. Here genesis is not a simple empirical idea like birthdate, which has no special genetic power of explanation, but a conceptual test of critical interpretation. To admit that we now have only a few genetic theses about literary production is quite another thing from saying categorically that there can never be a satisfactory genetic thesis. A Luddite approach to what after all is in the critic's possession as a sentient historical being—the capacity to make genetic hypotheses—is a violent denial of some portion of his or her humanity. For genetic hypotheses, such as how or why such and such a work came to be written, are not one-way referrals of "a" work back to "a" biography or society or whatever, just as iconic or textual studies need not always exclude the historical context surrounding the text. A genetic hypothesis admits the notion of human agency into the work—not a daring idea in itself. But the obligation to rational interpretation along these lines goes further to include as part of the dialectic the critic's own shaping awareness of what he or she is doing. This awareness obviously increases and is refined in the very act of making a critical way.

Perhaps one way of imagining the critical issue of aesthetic genesis is to view the text as a dynamic field, rather than as a static block, of words. This field has a certain range of reference, a system of tentacles (which I have been calling affiliative) partly potential, partly actual: to the author, to the reader, to a historical situation, to other texts, to the past and present. In one sense no text is finished, since its potential range is always being extended by every additional reader. Now the critic's task is obviously first to understand (in this case understanding is an imaginative act) how the text was and is made. No details are too trivial, provided one's study is directed carefully toward the text as a vital aesthetic and cultural whole. The critic therefore mimes or repeats the text in its extension from beginning to whole, not unlike Pierre Menard. Or like Proust in his pastiches of Flaubert, Balzac, Renan, and the Goncourts. In making over the authors he imitated, Proust set himself the aim of producing them from the opening to the conclusion of a passage. Only by reproducing can we know what was produced and what the meaning is of verbal production for a human being: this is the quintessential Vichian maxim. And it is no less valid for the literary critic for whom the genesis of a human work is as relevantly interesting as its being.

8

Reflections on American "Left" Literary Criticism

NEVER before in the history of American literary culture has there been such widespread and such serious, sometimes technical, and frequently contentious discussion of issues in literary criticism. Every critic or teacher of literature is affected by the discussion. Still, there is no automatic agreement on what the main or even the important issues are in the critical hurly-burly. It is probably true, for example, that even though many of the critical schools (among others, semiotics, hermeneutics, Marxism, deconstruction) continue to have their strict apostles, the critical atmosphere is a mixed one, with everyone more or less in touch with most of the reigning methods, schools, and disciplines. Nevertheless it is almost certain that no one underestimates the sociological as well as the intellectual importance of the large division separating adherents of what may be called new New Criticism from those of the old or traditional criticism. Not all critics are polarized by this often invidious division. But what is remarkable, I think, is that in debates between the sides there is a marked willingness to take positions simplifying and exaggerating not only one's opponent but one's own team, so to speak. A deconstructionist speaking *sub specie aeternitatis* for vanguard criticism makes us feel that a challenge to Western thought itself is being portended when he or she analyzes some lines by Rousseau, Freud, or Pater; conversely, critics who believe themselves to be pronouncing in the name of sanity, decency, and the family when they discuss the ideas of what humanism is all about denigrate even their own work unintentionally by appearing to simplify the formidable codes of academic scholarship that make intelligible what they do as scholars.

Without thinking through all of the aspects of this large opposition, we cannot properly hope to know in detail what really goes on in literary criticism and theory today, although we can speak accurately of certain patterns common both to criticism and to the history, society, and culture that produced it. One of my points will be that if the fierce polemics between, say, M. H. Abrams and J. Hillis Miller, or between Gerald Graff and the so-called Yale School, or between *Boundary 2, Glyph,* and *Diacritics* and other little magazines, seem to present clear theoretical demarcations between old or right-wing positions and new or left-wing positions, the divergence on both sides of the controversy between the rhetoric of theory and the actualities of practice is very nearly the same. This is of course always true in polemics: we argue in theory for what in practice we never do, and we do the same kind of thing with regard to what we oppose. Nonetheless we find that a new criticism adopting a position of opposition to what is considered to be established or conservative academic scholarship consciously takes on the function of the left wing in politics and argues *as if* for the radicalization of thought, practice, and perhaps even of society by means not so much of what it does and produces, but by means of what it says about itself and its opponents. True, there are important actual achievements to which it can point with pride. There are genuinely original, even revolutionary works of critical theory and interpretation, and these have been surrounded by a whole rhetorical armor of apology, attack, and extended programmatic elaboration: Harold Bloom's work and the repeated arguments about it come immediately to mind. But in the main Bloom's work and what it has produced in the way of anger and praise on theoretical grounds remain solidly within the tradition of academic criticism. The texts, authors, and periods have stayed inside a recognizable and commonly agreed-upon canon, even if the words and phrases used to describe them vary considerably depending on whether you are for or against Bloom.

To such a thesis there is first the response that I, in my own turn, am being a reductionist and, second, that criticism is perforce restricted to the academy and banned—not only by virtue of its own politeness—from the street. Both objections are justified in part. But what I am trying to say (with almost embarrassing generality) is that the oppositional manner of new New Criticism does not accurately represent its ideas and practice, which, after all is said and done, further solidify and guarantee the social structure and the culture that produced them. Deconstruction, for example, is practiced as if West-

ern culture were being dismantled; semiotic analysis argues that its
work amounts to a scientific and hence social revolution in the sciences of man. The examples can be multiplied, but I think what I am
saying will be readily understood. There is oppositional debate without real opposition. In this setting, even Marxism has often been accommodated to the wild exigencies of rhetoric while surrendering its
true radical prerogatives.

   All of this is a long way of explaining why in my title the word
Left is enclosed in skeptical quotation marks. Also, I find the transition from the notion of the Left in politics to the Left in literary criticism a difficult one to make. Of course there is opposition between
Abrams and Derrida or Miller, but can we say with assurance that
what is at stake, which seems at most to be a question of whose su-
perstructural visions are better, matches the apparent violence of the
disagreement? Both new and old critics have been content to confine
themselves to the academic matter of literature, to the existing institutions for teaching and employing students of literature, to the often
ridiculous and always self-flattering notion that their debates have a
supremely important bearing upon crucial interests affecting human-
kind. In accepting these confinements the putative Left, no less than
the Right, is very far from playing a genuinely political role. Indeed,
what distinguishes the present situation is, on the one hand, a greater
isolation than ever before in recent American cultural history of the
literary critics from the major intellectual, political, moral, and ethical
issues of the day and, on the other hand, a rhetoric, a pose, a posture
(let us at last be candid) claiming not so much to represent as *to be*
the afflictions entailed by true adversarial politics. A visitor from another world would surely be perplexed were he to overhear a so-
called old critic calling the new critics dangerous. What, this visitor
would ask, are they dangers to? The state? The mind? Authority?

   A quick glance at recent intellectual history reveals the story pretty
well. No one would have any trouble finding a Left in American culture between the twenties and the fifties, as Daniel Aaron's book
Writers on the Left will immediately testify. Certainly it is true that
during those decades intellectual debate in this country was preeminently conducted in political language having a direct connection
with actual politics. The careers of such men as Randolph Bourne
and Joseph Freeman, for instance, are inextricable from the problems
of war or nonintervention, class conflict, Stalinism or Trotskyism. If
we feel that what these writers wrote lacked the sophistication of the
criticism of their contemporaries—Eliot, Valéry, Richards, Emp-

son—we also feel that their awareness of literature as literature (that is, literature as something more than ideological construct) was impressively strong. In the work of the best of them, say the Edmund Wilson of *To the Finland Station*, there is a fairly high order of intellect and scholarship, as well as considerable political sophistication and historical engagement, neither of which rarely comes through as untreated propaganda or as what we have come to call vulgar Marxism. When, in this rather large and amorphous period that I designate simply as "recent cultural history," a major critic in the academy would seek to place her- or himself responsibly in the world, we might get an essay such as F. O. Matthiessen's "The Responsibilities of the Critic," originally written in 1949. Matthiessen makes no pretense at being a Marxist, but he does make it very clear that the critic of literature must be concerned with the material with which Marxism deals along with "the works of art of our own time." The essay's controlling metaphor is an horticultural one: criticism can become "a kind of closed garden" unless the critic realizes "that the land beyond the garden's walls is more fertile, and that the responsibilities of the critic lie in making renewed contact with the soil." Not only does this mean that critics are to acquaint themselves with "the economic foundations underlying any cultural superstructure." It means

> that we in the universities cannot afford to turn our backs . . .
> upon the world . . . The proper place for the thinker, as William
> James conceived it, was at the central point where a battle is
> being fought. It is impossible for us to take that metaphor with
> the lightness that he could. Everywhere we turn in these few
> fateful years since the first atom bomb dropped on Hiroshima
> we seem menaced by such vast forces that we may well feel that
> we advance at our peril. But even greater peril would threaten us
> if those whose prime responsibility as critics is to keep open the
> life-giving communications between art and society should
> waver in their obligations to provide ever fresh thought for our
> own society.[1]

There is an unmistakable implication in these remarks that the vast menacing forces of post-Hiroshima history can be kept at bay and comprehended by the critic's "fresh thought." We might easily smile at Matthiessen's naiveté here, since today very few critics consider their work to be pitted directly against these or any other brute historical forces. Moreover, as any reader of Paul de Man can tell you, the language of crisis is endemic to criticism, but, he would warn, unless language in such situations turns back upon itself, there is more likely to be mystification and falseness than knowledge or real criticism. To Matthiessen, then, literature and criticism are nourished by the very same experiences out of which economics, material history, and social conflict are generated. Such a proposition, in all its seemingly unproblematic ontological simplicity, is most unlikely to reappear today, when what de Man calls "the fallen world of our facticity" is considered to be matched ironically by a literature whose language "is the only form of language free from the fallacy of unmediated expression." And yet Matthiessen's achievement as a critic was a considerable one; books such as his *American Renaissance* reveal neither a deluded *schone Seele* nor a crude sociologist of knowledge. The problem is to see how he spoke so passionately and politically of the critic's responsibilities and why, twenty-odd years later, critics like de Man (whose current influence is very estimable) direct their attention to the impossibility of political and social responsibility.

For de Man, "philosophical knowledge can only come into being when it is turned back upon itself." This is another way of saying that anyone using language as a means for communicating knowledge is liable to fall into the trap of believing that his or her authority as possessor and communicator of knowledge is not bound by language, which in fact is only language and not immediate facticity. Literature, on the other hand, is basically about demystification and, according to de Man, "poetic language names this void [the presence of nothingness, supposedly denoted by the words of a literary composition whose essential task is to refer only to itself and to be ironically aware of so doing] with ever-renewed understanding and, like Rousseau's longing, it never tires of naming it again." Such an insight allows de Man to assert that in its endless naming and renaming of the void, literature is most emphatically itself, never more strongly than when literature seems to be suppressed in order that mere knowledge might be allowed to appear. Thus:

> When modern critics think they are demystifying literature, they are in fact being demystified by it, but since this necessarily occurs in the form of a crisis, they are blind to what takes place within themselves. At the moment that they claim to do away with literature, literature is everywhere; what they call anthropology, linguistics, psychoanalysis is nothing but literature reappearing, like Hydra's head, in the very spot where it had supposedly been suppressed. The human mind will go through amazing feats of distortion to avoid facing "the nothingness of human matters."[2]

Unlike Derrida, for whose work he was later to show considerable affinity, de Man is less interested in the force and productivity of human distortion (what Derrida calls *l'impensé*) than he is in its continuing and repeated performance, its insistence as insistence so to speak. This is why corrosive irony is really de Man's central concern as a critic: he is always interested in showing that when critics or poets believe themselves to be stating something, they are really revealing—critics unwittingly, poets wittingly—the impossible premises of stating anything at all, the so-called aporias of thought to which de Man believes all great literature always returns. Yet these intellectual hobbles on the possibility of statement have not inhibited de Man from stating and restating them on the numerous occasions when, more ably than most other critics, he analyzes a piece of literature. I would hesitate to call de Man a polemicist, but insofar as he exhorts critics to do one thing rather than another, I would say that he tells them to avoid talking as if historical scholarship, for example, could ever get beyond and talk seriously about literature. Why? Because if great literature is already demystified, scholarship could never tell us anything essential about it that the literature itself had not previously predicted. The most that can happen is that the critic is demystified, which amounts to saying that he acknowledges literature's prior demystification of itself.

I have no wish to use de Man as a general representative of what is being done these days in literary criticism: his work is too important, his talents too extraordinary for merely representative status. But I think that he can be regarded as exemplifying an intellectual current opposing, in no very explicit way, what customarily is the norm in academic literary studies. The literary work for him stands in a position of almost unconditional superiority over historical facticity not by virtue of its power but by virtue of its admitted powerlessness; its originality resides in the premise that it has disarmed itself "from the start," as if by having said in advance that it had no illusions about itself and its fictions it directly accedes to the realm of acceptable form. These ideas of course express a major tendency in all symbolist art, a tendency made considerably interesting by every variety of twentieth-century critical formalism: to paraphrase a famous remark by Mallarmé, underlying it is the notion that, if the world exists at all, it must have ended up in or as a book, and once in a book then the world is left behind forever. Literature, in short, expresses only itself (this is a maximalist position; the minimalist view is that literature is "about" nothing): its world is a formal one, and its relationship to quotidian reality can only be understood, as de Man implies, by means either of negation or of a radically ironic theory, as severe as it is consistent, whose workings depend on the opposite propositions that, if the world is not a book, then too the book is not the world. These are perhaps not as unexceptionable as they may seem, especially if we remember the extent to which most criticism since Aristotle has admitted of a certain amount of an often surreptitious and unadmitted mimetic bias.

But de Man's criticism garners some of its justified authority because de Man has been a pioneer of European "metaphysical criticism," as some people like to call it. Here we rush headlong into the sociological and historical actuality that contemporary "left" or oppositional criticism in America is heavily influenced by European, especially French, criticism. One could give a number of reasons for the dramatic change in language and tone that came over the American critical scene during the late 1960s, and I do not intend here to spend much time doing so. But it is fair to say that among the effects of European criticism on our critical vocabulary and positions was a sense that the primacy of "English studies" in the literary field had come to an end. Most of the literary criticism dominating the academy, indeed even the world of journalism, was based on the achievements of British and American modernist writers, and a feeling too that assumptions of national primacy—in all senses of that phrase— ought to dominate criticism. The believers in this area include Arnold at the beginning, later Leavis, Empson, Richards, and most of the southern New Critics. I do not mean to say that these were provincial or local-minded men, but that for them everything outside the Anglo-Saxon world had to bend around to Anglo-Saxon ends. Even T. S. Eliot, much the most international critic of the period until the early 1960s, saw in European poets like Dante, Virgil, and Goethe the vindication of such Anglo-Saxon values as monarchy, an unbroken nonrevolutionary tradition, and the idea of a national religion. Thus the intellectual hegemony of Eliot, Leavis, Richards, and the New Critics coincides not only with the work of masters like Joyce, Eliot himself, Stevens, and Lawrence, but also with the serious and autonomous development of literary studies in the university, a development that in time became synonymous with "English" as subject, languge, and attitude.

At its very best "English" had Lionel Trilling, W. A. Wimsatt, Reuben Brower, and a small handful of others as its prominent, deeply intelligent and humane, and very diverse defenders. But it was challenged—well before the French efflorescence—in two ways, one internal to it, the other external. Internally "English" produced only an implicit ideology, and no easily communicable methods. There are complex reasons for this, and anyone attempting to describe the situation that prevailed would have to go into such matters as the revulsion from Stalinism, the Cold War, the circumvention of theory, and the paradoxical unmediated, ahistorical association of values, commitment, and even ideas with "style." What I am most interested in here is what, generally speaking, they produced intellectually: a type of criticism based principally on endless refinement. In the sudden mood of competition and expansion that followed Sputnik, there were the various national-security language programs funded by NDEA, and then there was "English," which refined, without essentially adding to, our "strength" as a nation. The dissertation model was not the carefully researched historical monograph but the sensitive essay; students of English became adjuncts to, and felt themselves, at a very far point away from what was important. The role of English was at best an instrumental one (this clearly was what Richard Ohmann and Louis Kampf were reacting to in the late sixties), although its practitioners like Trilling, Abrams, and Wimsatt were looked to as nonideological reassurances that style, humanism, and values really mattered. The net result of all this was an endemic flaccidity in English studies, for how far could one go in these circumstances along the road of mere refinement?

As an instance of how brilliant and resourceful literary refinement could become there was Northrop Frye, whose meteoric theoretical ascendancy over the whole field of English studies in the fifties and sixties can partly be accounted for by the climate of refinement (which he dignified and intensified in his *Anatomy*) and the prevailing historical-theoretical vacuum. As an instance of how dull and enervating it all was, there was a huge agglomeration of various literary industries (Joyce, Conrad, Pound, Eliot) that had never even pretended to be a coherent part of the general march toward knowledge. In a unique and perhaps puzzling way then, literary modernity was associated first not with the present but with an immediate past, which was endlessly validated and revalidated; second, with the production of a virtually unassimilable secondary elaboration of a body of writings universally accepted as primary. The point to be made is that this body of secondary elaborations—like de Man's literary texts—was demystified from the start. It too pretended to no illusion about itself; it was secondary, harmless, and ideologically neutral, ex-

cept within the internal confines of the more and more profession-
alized profession.

The second challenge to "English" was external. Here I have found
it useful to employ the concept, seriously alluded to first by George
Steiner, of extraterritoriality. Again there are many things to be
mentioned in this connection, and again I must be summary and selective. There was the greatly expanded paperback book market and
with it the dramatic increase in the number of translations from foreign languages; there was the gradual impression upon "English" of
such outside fields as psychoanalysis, sociology, and anthropology;
there was the decentering effect (under NDEA auspices by the way)
of comparative literature and with it the weighty prestige of genuinely extraterritorial critics like Auerbach, Curtius, and Spitzer; and
finally there was what now seems to have been a genuinely fortuitous
intervention in our literary scene of ongoing European criticism, first
through residents like de Man and Georges Poulet, then through
more and more frequent visitors from abroad. It is important to mention at this juncture that Marxism became an intellectual presence to
be reckoned with in this context of external challenge of importation
from abroad. So far as I have been able to tell, the kind of Marxism
practiced or announced in university literary departments owes very
little to the American radical movement that ended with the
McCarthy period. The new Marxism came to this country partly as a
result of the interest in French criticism and later the Frankfurt
School, partly because of the general wave of antiwar agitation on the
campuses. It did so in the form of sudden discovery and just as sudden application to literary problems. Its main weaknesses were the
comparative absence of a continuous native Marxist theoretical tradition or culture to back it up and its relative isolation from any concrete political struggle.

Between them, the internal and external challenges to English
studies were decisive—but only in very limited ways. This is a crucial thing to understand. During the great upheavals of the sixties the
academic literary establishment, which had for years been accustomed to being a factory for turning out refined minds and essays,
responded to the times with a demand for instant relevance. In fact
this meant only that the teaching and scholarship of literature should
occasionally show us how literary masterpieces were relevant to contemporary reality, that in reading Swift or Shakespeare we could
"understand" man's inhumanity to man or how evil apartheid is. I
have little hesitation in saying that the much-vaunted Modern Lan-

guage Association revolution brought only cosmetic changes, and these changes testified not to the will for change in various well-intentioned scholars, but rather to the depth and resilience of an ideology of refinement that had effectively absorbed even this new and potentially violent challenge. True, there was an extraordinary, not to say alarming, tendency to overkill in the oppositional rhetoric of the late sixties and early seventies. The vocabulary became suddenly more "technical" and self-consciously "difficult"; the Barthes-Piccard controversy was relived and even reproduced in many journals, congresses, and departments; and it became *de rigeur*—indeed profitable for many of us—to aspire to the condition of "literary theorists," a position in departmental rosters virtually unthinkable a scant ten years before. There was a peculiar search for interdisciplinary projects, programs, "minds," and gimmicks, all of this accentuating the extent to which one could not discuss a Donne poem without also referring to Jakobson, perhaps even to European Latinity, and at least to metaphor and metonymy. On the one hand, therefore, you had the appearance of a genuine new subculture of theoretical opposition to the old nationalist literary traditions institutionalized in the academy, and, on the other, you had those old traditions fighting back with appeals to humanism, tact, good sense, and the like. The question is whether in these instances Tweedledum and Tweedledee were really all that different from each other, and whether either had produced work that justified both the oppositional rhetoric of the one or the strong moral defensiveness of the other.

I am only concerned, however, with the "Left" side of the controversy, and my real beginning point is a pair of observations about what the Left has not produced. Consider, first, that in American literary studies there has not in the past quarter century been enough work of major historical scholarship that can be called "revisionist." I use this last adjective to indicate some parallel with what has gone on in American historical studies, in the work of Williams, Alperovitz, Kolko, and many others. For there to be effective interpretation in what is, after all is said and done, a historical discipline, there must also be effective history, effective archival work, effective involvement in the actual material of history. Certainly the individual work of literature exists to a considerable extent by virtue of its formal structures, and it articulates itself by means of a formal energy, intention, capacity, or will. But it does not exist only by those, nor can it be apprehended and understood only formally. And yet for the most part literary studies have been dominated, even in their Marxist variety, by a relative absence of the historical dimension. Historical research on the Left has been neutralized by the notion that interpretation is based ultimately on method or rhetoric, as if either of those two defined the separate competency and dignity of the literary theorist. Moreover, the whole concern with oppositional knowledge (that is, a knowledge that exists essentially to challenge and change received ideas, entrenched institutions, questionable values) has succumbed to the passivity of ahistorical refinement upon what is already given, acceptable, and above all already defined. One looks everywhere and finds few alternatives to the attitude that argues how, for instance, *Our Mutual Friend* can be understood better and better the more you see it in itself as more and more of a novel, which is the more you study it as a finer and finer illustration of a precisely reticulated theory of narrative fiction, whose conditions of readability and whose force depend on formal grammars, generative abstractions, and innate structures. There is a certain element of parody in my description, but some accuracy too.

The second observation is the other side of the coin, that literary studies on the Left, far from producing work to challenge or revise prevailing values, institutions, and definitions, have in fact gone too long a way in confirming them. In many ways this is a more serious matter.

No society known to human history has ever existed which has not been governed by power and authority, and, as Gramsci says repeatedly, every society can be divided into interlocking classes of rulers and ruled. There is nothing static about these basic conceptions, since if we consider society to be a dynamic distribution of power and positions we will also be able to regard the categories of rulers and ruled as a highly complex and highly changeable pair of categories. To use only Gramsci's terminology for the moment, we can divide society into emergent and traditional classes, into civil and political sectors, into subaltern and dominant, hegemonic and authoritative powers. Yet standing over and above all this activity is at least an idea, or set of ideas, and at most a group of agencies of authority, which gain their power from the State. The central reality of power and authority in Western history, at least since the period from the end of feudalism on, is the presence of the State, and I think we would have to say that to understand not only power but authority—which is a more interesting and various idea than power—we must also understand the way in which any authority in modern society is derived to some degree from the presence of the State.

To a great extent culture, cultural formations, and intellectuals exist by virtue of a very interesting network of relationships with the State's almost absolute power. About this set of relationships I must say immediately that all contemporary Left criticism of the sort I have been discussing is for the most part stunningly silent. There are a few exceptions to this. Foucault is one, and Ohmann, and Poulantzas; one is hard put to name others whose criticism is directly concerned with the matter. Quite the contrary, nearly everyone producing literary or cultural studies makes no allowance for the truth that all intellectual or cultural work occurs somewhere, at some time, on some very precisely mapped-out and permissible terrain, which is ultimately contained by the State. Feminist critics have opened this question part of the way, but they have not gone the whole distance. If it is true that, according to an art-for-art's-sake theory, the world of culture and aesthetic production subsists on its own, away from the encroachments of the State and authority, then we must still be prepared to show that independence was gained and, more important, how it is maintained. In other words, the relationship between aesthetics and state authority obtains in the case both of direct dependence and of the much less likely one of complete independence.

The sense I now have of taking on far too huge an area of historical experience is intensified by the realization that cultural, theoretical, or critical discourse today provides me with no vocabulary, no conceptual or documentary language, much less a concrete body of specific analyses, to make myself clear. For the most part our critical ethos is formed by a pernicious analytic of blind demarcation by which, for example, imagination is separated from thought, culture from power, history from form, texts from everything that is *hors texte*, and so forth. In addition we misuse the idea of what method is, and we have fallen into the trap of believing that method is sovereign and can be systematic without also acknowledging that method is always part of some larger ensemble of relationships headed and moved by authority and power. For if the body of objects we study—the corpus formed by works of literature—belongs to, gains coherence from, and in a sense emanates out of the concepts of nation, nationality, and even of race, there is very little in contemporary critical discourse making these actualities possible as subjects of discussion. I do not intend to advocate a kind of reductive critical language whose bottom-line rationale is the endlessly affirmed thesis that "it's all political," whatever in that context one means by *it, all,* or *political.* Rather what I have in mind is the kind of analytic pluralism proposed by Gramsci for dealing with historical-cultural blocks, for seeing culture and art as belonging not to some free-floating ether or to some rigidly governed domain or iron determinism, but to some large intellectual endeavor—systems and currents of thought—connected in complex ways to doing things, to accomplishing certain things, to force, to social class and economic production, to diffusing ideas, values, and world pictures. If we agree with Gramsci that one cannot freely reduce religion, culture, or art to unity and coherence, then we will go along with the following theses for humanistic research and study:

> What must . . . be explained is how it happens that in all periods there co-exist many systems and currents of philosophic thought, how these currents are born, how they are diffused, and why in the process of diffusion they fracture along certain lines and in certain directions. The fact of this process goes to show how necessary it is to order in a systematic, coherent and critical fashion one's own intuitions of life and the world, and to determine exactly what is to be understood by the word "systematic," so that it is not taken in the pedantic and academic sense. But this elaboration must be, and can only be, performed in the context of the history of philosophy, for it is this history which shows how thought has been elaborated over the centuries and what a collective effort has gone into the present method of thought which has subsumed and absorbed all this past history, including all its follies and mistakes. Nor should those mistakes themselves be neglected, for, although made in the past and since corrected, one cannot be sure that they will not be reproduced in the present and once again require correcting.[3]

I have quoted the last sentence not because I agree with it, but because it expresses the didactic seriousness with which Gramsci believed all historical research should be conducted. But this main point of course is the suggestive insight that thought is produced so that actions can be accomplished, that it is diffused in order to be effective, persuasive, forceful, and that a great deal of thought elaborates on what is a relatively small number of principal, directive ideas. The concept of elaboration is crucial here. By elaboration Gramsci means two seemingly contradictory but actually complementary things. First, to elaborate means to refine, to work out (*e-laborare*) some prior or more powerful idea, to perpetuate a world view. Second, to elaborate means something more qualitatively positive, the proposition that culture itself or thought or art is a highly complex and quasi-autonomous extension of political reality and, given the extraordinary importance attached by Gramsci to intellectuals, culture, and philosophy, it has a density, complexity, and historical-semantic value that is so strong as to make politics possible. Elaboration is the ensemble of patterns making it feasible for society to maintain itself. Far from denigrating elaboration to the status of ornament, Gramsci makes it the very reason for the strength of what he calls civil society, which in the industrial West plays a role no less important than that of political society. Thus elaboration is the central cultural activity and, whethher or not one views it as little more than intellectual propaganda for ruling-class interests, it is the material making a society a society. In other words, elaboration is a great part of the social web of which George Eliot spoke in her late novels. Gramsci's insight is to have recognized that subordination, fracturing, diffusing, reproducing, as much as producing, creating, forcing, guiding, are all necessary aspects of elaboration.

One could even go so far to say that culture—elaboration—is what gives the State something to govern and yet, as Gramsci is everywhere careful to note, cultural activity is neither uniform nor mindlessly homogenous. The real depth in the strength of the modern Western State is the strength and depth of its culture, and culture's strength is its variety, its heterogenous plurality. This view distinguishes Gramsci from nearly every other important Marxist thinker of his period. He loses sight neither of the great central facts of power, and how they flow through a whole network of agencies operating by rational consent, nor of the detail—diffuse, quotidian, unsystematic, thick—from which inevitably power draws its sustenance, on which power depends for its daily bread. Well before Foucault, Gramsci had grasped the idea that culture serves authority, and ultimately the national State, not because it represses and coerces but because it is affirmative, positive, and persuasive. Culture is productive, Gramsci says, and this—much more than the monopoly of coercion held by the State—is what makes a national Western society strong, difficult for the revolutionary to conquer. Consequently the intellectual is not really analogous to the police force, nor is the artist merely a propagandist for wealthy factory owners. Culture is a separately capitalized endeavor, which is really to say that its relationship to authority and power is far from nonexistent. For we must be able to see culture as historical force possessing its own configurations, ones that intertwine with those in the socioeconomic sphere and that finally bear on the State as a State. Thus elaboration's meaning is not only that it is there, furnishing the material out of which society makes itself a going enterprise, but that like everything else in the world of nations, elaboration aspires to the condition of hegemony, with intellectuals playing the role of what Gramsci calls "experts in legitimation."

Because I consider them essential, I have pulled these ideas out of Gramsci to serve as a point of comparison with the historical and political ideas now propagated by oppositional or avant-garde literary theory. What I have been calling contemporary "Left" criticism is vitally concerned with various problems stemming from authority: such problematics as that of the return to Marx, Freud, and Saussure, the issue of influence and intertextuality, the questions of *l'impensé* and the undecideable in deconstructive criticism, ideology as a factor in literary creation and dissemination. Yet hardly anywhere in all this does one encounter a serious study of what authority is, either with reference to the way authority is carried historically and circumstantially from the State down into a society saturated with authority or with reference to the actual workings of culture, the role of intellectuals, institutions, and establishments. Furthermore, if the language of magazines like *Critical Inquiry, Glyph,* and *Diacritics* is brimming with sentiments of depth, radicality, and insight, there is rarely a paragraph expended on what in the way of ideas, values, and engagement is being urged. Nor, for that matter, does one often stumble on a serious attempt made to characterize what historically (and not rhetorically) it is that advanced critics are supposed to be opposing. Our impression is that the young critic has a well-developed political sense; yet close examination of this sense reveals a haphazard anecdotal content enriched neither by much knowledge of what politics and political issues are all about nor by any very developed awareness that politics is something more than liking or disliking some intellectual orthodoxy now holding sway over a department of literature.

Considering its potential, oppositional Left criticism contributes very little to intellectual debate in the culture today. Our bankruptcy on the once glamorous question of human rights alone is enough to strip us of our title to humanism, and as for dealing with the subtle distinction between authoritarianism and totalitarianism, we are not even willing to analyze these terms semantically, much less politically. Yet I do not wish to downgrade the period of almost Renaissance brilliance through which technical criticism has passed in the last few decades. We can gratefully acknowledge that and at the same time add that it has been a period characterized by a willingness to accept the isolation of literature and literary studies away from the world. It has also been a period during which very few of us have examined the reasons for this confinement, even while most of us have tacitly accepted, even celebrated, the State and its silent rule over culture—without so much, during the Vietnam and post-Vietnam period, as a polite murmur.

My disappointment at this stems from a conviction that it is our technical skill as critics and intellectuals that the culture has wanted to neutralize, and if we have cooperated in this project, perhaps unconsciously, it is because that is where the money has been. In our rhetorical enthusiasm for buzz words like scandal, rupture, transgression, and discontinuity, it has not occurred to us to be concerned with the relations of power at work in history and society, even as we have assumed that a text's textuality is a matter endlessly to be explored as something concerning other texts, vaguely denoted conspiracies, fraudulent genealogies entirely made up of books stripped of their history and force. The underlying assumption is that texts are radically homogeneous, the converse of which is the extraordinarily Laputan idea that to a certain extent everything can be regarded as a text. The result so far as critical practice is concerned is that rhetorical individualism in criticism and in the texts studied by the critic is cultivated for its own sake, with the further result that writing is seen as deliberately aiming for alienation—the critic from other critics, from readers, from the work studied.

The compelling irony of this depressing isolation, given the way we (as part of the secular priesthood of what Bakunin called "the era of scientific intelligence") are viewed by our political leaders, is almost staggering. A 1975 Trilateral Commission publication, *The Crisis of Democracy*, surveyed the post-1960s era with some degree of concern over the masses' sense of their political demands and aspirations; this has produced a problem of what the authors call "governability," since it is clear that the population at large is no longer so docile as it once was.[4] To this situation, then, the class of intellectuals contributes two things that derive directly from the two kinds of intellectuals contemporary democratic societies now produce. On the one hand are technocratic and policy-oriented, so-called responsible intellectuals; on the other, politically dangerous, value-oriented "traditional" intellectuals. The second group is where, by any reasonable standard, we are supposed to be, for it is the members of this group that supposedly "devote themselves to the derogation of leadership, the challenging of authority, and the unmasking and delegitimation of established institutions." The irony is, however, that literary critics, by virtue of their studious indifference to the world they live in and to the values by which their work engages history, do not see themselves as a threat to anything, except possibly to each other. Certainly they are as governable as they have always been since state worship became fashionable, and certainly their passive devotion to masterpieces, culture, texts, and structures posited simply in their own "texts" as functioning yet finished enterprises, poses no threat to authority or to values kept in circulation and managed by the technocratic managers.

But in more specific terms, what actually is the role of modern critical consciousness, of oppositional criticism? The relevant background, in very schematic terms, is as follows. As Raymond Williams has shown, words like *culture* and *society* acquire a concrete, explicit significance only in the period after the French Revolution. Before that, European culture as a whole identified itself positively as being different from non-European regions and cultures, which for the most part were given a negative value. Yet during the nineteenth century the idea of culture acquired an affirmatively nationalist cast, with the result that figures like Matthew Arnold make an active identification between culture and the state. It is the case with cultural or aesthetic activity that the possibilities and circumstances of its production get their authority by virtue of what I have called affiliation, that implicit network of peculiarly cultural associations between forms, statements, and other aesthetic elaborations on the one hand and, on the other, institutions, agencies, classes, and amorphous social forces. Affiliation is a loose enough word both to suggest the kinds of cultural ensembles Gramsci discusses in the passage I quoted earlier, as well as to allow us to retain the essential concept of *hegemony* guiding cultural and broadly intellectual activity, or elaboration, as a whole.

Let me try to suggest the general importance of this notion to contemporary critical activity. In the first place, as a general interpretive principle affiliation mitigates somewhat the facile theories of homology and filiation, which have created the homogeneously utopian domain of texts connected serially, seamlessly, and immediately only with other texts. By contrast affiliation is what enables a text to maintain itself as a text, and this is covered by a range of circumstances: status of the author, historical moment, conditions of publication, diffusion and reception, values drawn upon, values and ideas assumed, a framework of consensually held tacit assumptions, presumed background, and so on and on. In the second place, to study affiliation is to study and to recreate the bonds between texts and the world, bonds that specialization and the institutions of literature have all but completely effaced. Every text is an act of will to some extent, but what has not been very much studied is the degree to which texts are made permissible. To recreate the affiliative network is therefore to make visible, to give materiality back to, the strands holding the text to society, author, and culture. In the third place, affiliation releases a text from its isolation and imposes upon the scholar or critic the presentational problem of historically recreating or reconstructing the possibilities from which the text arose. Here is the place for intentional analysis and for the effort to place a text in homological, dialogical, or antithetical relationships with other texts, classes, and institutions.

None of this interest in affiliation—both as a principle of critical research and as an aspect of cultural process itself—is worth very much unless, first, it is actively generated out of genuine historical research (and I mean that critics are to feel themselves making discoveries, making unknown things known) and, second, it is ultimately fixed for its goals upon understanding, analyzing, and contending with the management of power and authority within the culture. Let me put it this way: we are humanists because there is something called humanism, legitimated by the culture, given a positive value by it. What we must be interested in directly is the historical process by which the central core of humanist ideology has produced literary specialists, who have construed their domain as restricted to something called literature whose components (including "literarity") have been given epistemological, moral, and ontological priority. In acting entirely with this domain, then, the literary critic effectively confirms the culture and the society enforcing those restrictions; this confirmation acts to strengthen the civil and political societies whose fabric is the culture itself. What is created as a result is what can reasonably be called a liberal consensus: the formal, restricted analysis of literary-aesthetic works validates the culture, the culture validates the humanist, the humanist the critic, and the whole enterprise the State. Thus authority is maintained by virtue of the cultural process, and anything more than refining power is denied the refining critic. By the same token, it has been true that "literature" as a cultural agency has become more and more blind to its actual complicities with power. That is the situation we need to comprehend.

Consider how this situation was formed during the nineteenth century by cultural discourse: one things immediately of people like Arnold, Mill, Newman, Carlyle, Ruskin. The very possibility of culture is based on the notion of refinement. Arnold's thesis that culture is the best that is thought or said gives this notion its most compact form. Culture is an instrument for identifying, selecting, and affirming certain "good" things, forms, practices, or ideas over others and in so doing culture transmits, diffuses, partitions, teaches, presents, propagates, persuades, and above all it creates and recreates itself as specialized apparatus for doing all those things. Most interestingly, I think, culture becomes the opportunity for a refracted verbal enterprise whose relationship to the State is always understated and, if the solecism is permitted, *under*stood. The realistic novel plays a major role in this enterprise, for it is the novel—as it becomes ever more "novel" in the work of James, Hardy, and Joyce—that organizes reality and knowledge in such a way as to make them susceptible to systematic verbal reincarnation. The novel's realistic bodying forth of a world is to provide representational or representative norms selected from among many possibilities. Thus the novel acts to include, state, affirm, normalize, and naturalize some things, values, and ideas, but not others. Yet none of these can be seen, directly perceived, in the novel itself, and it has been the singular mission of most contemporary formalist critics today to make sure that the novel's remarkably precise articulation of its own selectivity appears simply either as a fact of nature or as a given ontological formalism, and not as the result of sociocultural process. For to see the novel as cooperating with society in order to reject, what Gareth Steadman Jones has called outcast populations, is also to see how the great aesthetic achievements of the novel—in Dickens, Eliot, Hardy—result from a technique for representing and appropriating objects, people, settings, and values in affiliation with specific historical and social norms of knowledge, behavior, and physical beauty.

In the widest perspective, the novel, and with it dominant currents in modern Occidental culture, is not only selective and affirmative but centralizing and powerful. Apologists for the novel continue to assert the novel's accuracy, freedom of representation, and such; the implication of this is that the culture's opportunities for expression are unlimited. What such ideas mask, mystify, is precisely the network binding writers to the State and to a world-wide "metropolitan" imperialism that, at the moment they were writing, furnished them in the novelistic techniques of narration and description with implicit models of accumulation, discipline, and normalization. What we must ask is why so few "great" novelists deal directly with the major social and economic outside facts of their existence—colonialism and imperialism—and why, too, critics of the novel have continued to honor this remarkable silence. With what is the novel, and for that matter most modern cultural discourse, affiliated, whether in the language of affirmation or in the structure of accumulation, denial, repression, and mediation that characterizes major aesthetic form? How is the cultural edifice constructed so as to limit the imagination in some ways, enlarge it in others? How is imagination connected with the dreams, constructions, and ambitions of official knowledge, with executive knowledge, with administrative knowledge? What is the community of interests that produces Conrad and C. L. Temple's *The Native Races and Their Rulers?* To what degree has culture collaborated in the worst excesses of the State, from its imperial wars and colonial settlements to its self-justifying institutions of antihuman repression, racial hatred, economic and behavioral manipulation?

Nothing in what I have been trying to say rapidly here implies mediating or reducing the specific density of individual cultural artifacts to the impersonal forces supposedly responsible for producing them. The study of cultural affiliation necessitates an acute understanding of the specificity of objects and, even more important, of their intentional roles, neither of which can be given their proper due by reductionism or by positivistic refinement. I would guess that Williams' term *cultural materialism* suits the methodological attitude I am trying to describe. In the main American literary criticism can afford to shed its partly self-imposed and socially legislated isolation, at least with reference to history and society. There is a whole world manipulated not only by so-called reasons of state but by every variety of ahistorical consumerism, whose ethnocentrism and mendacity promise the impoverishment and oppression of most of the globe. What is lacking in contemporary oppositional criticism is not only the kind of perspective found in Joseph Needham's civilizational approach to culture and society, but some sense of involvement in the affiliative processes that go on, whether we acknowledge them or not, all around us. But, as I have been saying over and over, these are matters to do with knowledge, not refinement. I suspect that the most urgent question to be asked now is if we still have the luxury of choice between the two.

9
Criticism Between Culture and System

BETWEEN one form of interpretation, say the strict kind performed by a linguist reconstructing the rules of a dead language, and another more obviously inventive kind, say one involving speculations about the character of Dickens as a Victorian middle-class writer, there are more similarities than there are differences. These similarities derive from the inevitable contamination of what is supposedly solid positive knowledge by human interpretation, vagaries, willfulness, biases, grounding in personality, radically human circumstantiality, worldliness. It appeared to Nietzsche, Marx, and Freud each in his own way that such apparently safe steps in the production of knowledge as the collecting and disposing of evidence, or the reading and understanding of a text, all involve a very high degree of interpretative leeway, subject not so much to rationality and scientific control as to the assertion of will, arbitrary speculation, repressive (and repressing) judgment. It was then a short step for critics to argue that the previously simple question of what a text itself was had become a complex one. Michel Foucault puts these questions about how we can actually see this complexity in the form of a series of bewildering choices, upon which epistemological decisions must be made:

> at first sight [the question of trying to decide what an author's oeuvre is] what could be more simple? A collection of texts that can be designated by the sign of a proper name. But this designation (even leaving to one side problems of attribution) is not a homogenous function: does the name of an author designate in the same way a text he has published under his name, a text that

he has presented under a pseudonym, another found after his death in the form of an unfinished draft, and another that is merely a collection of jottings, a notebook? The establishment of a complete *oeuvre* presupposes a number of choices that are difficult to justify or even to formulate: is it enough to add to the texts published by the author those that he intended for publication but which remained unfinished by the time of his death? Should one also include all his sketches and first drafts, with all their corrections and crossings out? Should one add sketches that he himself abandoned? And what status should be given to letters, notes, reported conversation, transcriptions of what he said made by those present at the time, in short, to that vast mass of verbal traces left by an individual at his death, and which speak in an endless confusion so many different languages? . . . In fact, if one speaks so undiscriminately and unreflectingly of an author's *oeuvre*, it is because one imagines it to be defined by a certain expressive function . . . But it is at once apparent that such a unity, far from being given immediately, is the result of an operation; that this operation is interpretive (since it deciphers, in the text, the transcription of something that it both conceals and manifests).[1]

Nor is this all. There is a prior series of questions asked by Foucault which he thinks ought to trouble anyone who believes that oeuvres are constructed out of, or on, "the material individualization of the book." For even the material unity of a book is an interpretive matter:

Is this the same in the case of an anthology of poems, a collection of posthumous fragments, Desargues' *Traité des Coniques*, or a volume of Michelet's *Histoire de France*. Is it the same in the case of Mallarmé's *Un Coup de dés*, the trial of Gilles de Rais, Butor's *San Marco*, or a Catholic missal? In other words, is not the material unity of the volume a weak, accessory unity in relation to the discursive unity of which it is the support? But is this discursive unity itself homogenous and uniformly applicable? A novel by Stendhal and a novel by Dostoievski do not have the same relation of individuality as that between two novels belonging to Balzac's cycle *La Comédie humaine* . . . The frontiers of a book are never clear-cut; beyond the title, the first lines, and the last full-stop, beyond its internal configuration and its autonomous form, it is caught up in a system of references to other books, other texts, other sentences: it is a node within a network.

And this network of references is not the same in the case of a mathematical treatise, a textual commentary, a historical account, and an episode in a novel cycle; the unity of the book, even in the case of a group of relations, cannot be regarded as identical in each case. The book is not simply the object that one holds in one's hands; and it cannot remain within the little parallet pipe that contains it: its unity is variable and relative. As soon as one questions that unity, it loses its self-evidence; it indicates itself, constructs, only on the basis of a complex field of discourse.[2]

Few scholars in the human sciences trouble themselves seriously with these questions, not so much because they are lazy or stupid but because—as Foucault's own work goes very far to show—their work is conducted as on-going activity within an already constituted field of discourse. Most of today's literary scholars, for example, are not concerned with the epistemological status of the texts or even the authors they write about. Nor perhaps should they be, since libraries, journals, easily available copies of books, institutions, students, pedagogical practice, and, most of all, other scholars assume the over-all stability of such authors and oeuvres as "Shakespeare," the Waverley novels, or the *Four Quartets.* This is not a trivial point. A complex discourse, of which one example is what I have called literary scholarship, assumes consensus on a few fundamental points, as a matter of both economy and convenience. To study Swift, as I said earlier in this book, it cannot be necessary each time he is written about to re-examine the provenance of everything known about his biography or to revise the concept organizing his oeuvre. It is assumed that there is an author called Swift, whose works comprise *A Tale of a Tub, Gulliver's Travels, A Modest Proposal,* that he lived during the early eighteenth century, and so forth. These are what we may call primitive threshold notions before which Swift experts do not feel themselves obligated to go. The threshold is implied, although rarely formulated except in ways I shall be discussing, as a result of many factors: the consensus of experts in a field, the mass of previous writing, the administration of teaching and research, conventions about what an author or a text is, and so on.

Because in the human sciences such thresholds exist (even though the vast multipication of journals and books seems to testify to the absence of all limits), this does not mean that they can easily be specified. One reason is obvious. We generally assume that knowledge about human beings is inexhaustible and cumulative, and so it must be possible to say new things. And if that is possible, then the thresholds or limits that give a field of specialization its outline are very loose, if not fictitious. Anyone who thinks seriously about this proposition will see that it is utopian, if only because what defines something as new is something defining everything else as not-new, and in neither case is one individual capable of making such judgments; therefore everyone working in a field, by a process of acculturation and professionalization, accepts certain guild standards by which the new and not-new are recognizable. These standards are far from absolute of course, just as they are far from being fully conscious. They can be very harshly applied nevertheless, particularly when the guild's corporate sense feels itself under attack.

As I said in discussing the notion of originality, new and not-new are highly relative terms. In the context of literary studies the terms will refer either to innovations associated with the originality or novelty of a "creative" writer (Dickens was the first novelist to do X or Y) or to the interpretations of critics who seem in one of many ways to be original or novel. Yet in discussing the achievements of a creative writer or those of a critic, the categories of newness or derivativeness depend for their force very much on persuasiveness—a certain rhetorical skill in convincing an audience of this originality—as well as on good sense.[3] Everyone may think that the statement "Ronald Firbank is a greater writer than Jane Austen" is outrageous; yet it might be possible to get away with the remark that Scott is a more original writer than Austen.

Such easy generalizations are less bland than they appear. Behind and around as well as inside them, so to speak, is an entire complex of partly articulated, partly inarticulable constraints, and these act on not only what I have already said but on what any scholar writes or says. Principal among these constraints is the sheer fact that no one makes statements about a body of texts on an empty field; there is an already inscribed terrain presented to scholars, and what they can do is to inscribe their own work (just as for a novelist many other novels are somehow involved in what he does) on that far from virgin field. Therefore, in order to specify the possibilities for genuine knowledge in a field, we must be able to specify not only what that knowledge is or might be but where it might be inscribed, what it might do with reference to everything that has preceded it (revise it, confirm it, modify it), what is contemporary with it, what is related to it in other fields, what its relationship would be to what comes after it (will it enable further discovery, inhibit it, close the field down, create a new field?), how it will be transmitted or preserved, how it will be taught, how institutions will accept or reject it: these are a few of the questions that propose themselves. The immediate question, though, is slightly different. What is the role of what I have been calling the critical consciousness in these matters? Is the critical consciousness or criticism (I shall use the terms interchangeably) principally to deliver insights about writers and texts, to describe writers and texts (in critical biographies, commentaries, explications, specialized scholarly monographs), to teach and disseminate information about the monuments of culture? Or—and this is what I believe to be the task—is it to occupy itself with the intrinsic conditions on which knowledge is made possible? For in order to see what it is that we can know as students of texts, we must be able to understand the units of knowledge as functions of textuality, which itself must be describable in terms dealing with not only the agencies of culture in their ideological, political, institutional, and historical forms but also the requirements of intelligible method and the material form of knowledge which, if it is not of divine or supernatural provenance, is produced in the secular world.

All this will seem hopelessly large and ambitious as a critical project. What is worse, it may also seem impertinent to what a literary scholar or critic has traditionally done. My own point of departure is the common and to my mind exemplary sense of distance that some critics have felt vis-à-vis the stable conventions of literary and generally intellectual work. In modern culture crisis is congenital, since criticism is an art as well as a topic of crisis. Yet in the acutely contemporary form of crisis and response to crisis that I am considering here, it has been the problem of knowledge, of *how* we know what we know, that has been central.

I want now to consider what I take to be two of the most powerful alternative responses to the crisis. These two formulations are those associated with the names of Jacques Derrida and Michel Foucault. I shall discuss them in analytic and critical detail as illustrations of the attempt to turn the textual problems of the human sciences into descriptions of the processes of textual knowledge. In addition I shall argue that Derrida and Foucault propose not only to describe but to produce knowledge of the sort that will fall neither into the prepared molds provided by the dominant culture nor into the wholly predictive forms manufactured by a quasi-scientific method. In both cases, dramatically different though each may be from the other, there is a conscious effort to release a very specialized sort of textual *discovery* from the mass of material, habits, conventions, and institutions constituting an immediate historical pressure. Yet what is of special interest to me is how both Derrida and Foucault situate their work within boundaries defined by that history. Thus their originality will not be seen as residing in the outlandishness of their vocabulary or techniques but in their rethinking of those techniques.

Now it is true that, in reading criticism by people like Foucault and Derrida, one will be struck by the fact that criticism of this sort is not a branch of belles-lettres. It is much too difficult to be that, or even to be an elevated form of explication. At its best the work of R. P. Blackmur, a great representative of classical New Criticism, was not that either, but we tend to forget that. The obscurity, technical demands, and ellipses of this criticism do not make it a new "school" philosophy, although it can become a kind of orthodoxy. Yet in principle this claims to be antiorthodox criticism, despite the lamentable proliferation of epigones and fellow travelers who have given it the worst aspects of unquestioning orthodoxy. Thus, potentially at least, contemporary criticism exists to confront problems of the sort abandoned by philosophy when it became as insular and scholastic as it became in the Anglo-American tradition. The problem of language and of its unique and difficult being is central to this criticism, which has taken on the task of producing a type of thought that, as Foucault says, "in the density of its workings, should be both knowledge and a modification of what it knows, reflection and a transformation of the mode of being of that on which it reflects."[4]

L ET me start by indicating a highly schematic divergence, dramatized by the polemical conflict between Derrida and Foucault. Their critical attitudes are opposed on a number of grounds. The one specially singled out in Foucault's attack on Derrida seems appropriate to consider first: that Derrida is concerned only with reading a text, and that a text is nothing more than what is in it for the reader.[5] For if the text is important to Derrida because its real situation is literally a textual element with no ground in actuality—this is the *écriture en abîme* with which, he says in "La Double séance," criticism has so far been unable to deal—then for Foucault the text is important because it inhabits an element of power (*pouvoir*) with a decisive claim on actuality, even though that power is invisible or implied. Derrida's criticism moves us *into* the text, Foucault's *in* and *out*.

Yet neither Foucault and Derrida would deny that what unites them, more even than the avowedly revisionist and revolutionary character of their criticism, is their attempt to make visible what is customarily invisible in a text, namely the various mysteries, rules, and play of its textuality. Except for one word, Foucault would not, I think, disagree with the rather abrupt definition of textuality advanced by Derrida at the opening of "La Pharmacie de Platon": "A text is not a text unless it hides from the first comer, from the first glance, the law of its composition and the rules of its game. A text remains, moreover, forever imperceptible. Its law and its rules are not, however, harbored in the inaccessibility of a secret; it is simply that they can never be booked, in the *present*, into anything that could rigorously be called a perception."[6] The probably troublesome word is "never," although it is so trickily qualified by Derrida as partly to lose its interdictory force. So I shall ignore the qualifiers and retain the obvious assertiveness of the statement. To say that the text's intention and integrity are invisible is to say that the text hides something, which also means that the text implies, perhaps also states, embodies, represents, but does not immediately disclose something. At bottom, this is a gnostic doctrine of the text, to which in quite different ways Foucault and Derrida assent.

But Foucault's whole enterprise has, he has argued retrospectively, taken it for a fact that if the text hides something, or if something about the text is invisible, these things can be revealed and stated, albeit in some other form, mainly because the text is part of a network of power whose textual form is a purposeful obscuring of power beneath textuality and knowledge (*savoir*). Therefore, the countervailing power of criticism is to bring the text back to a certain visibility. More: if some texts, particularly those in the later phases of a discursive development, assume their textuality because their sources in power have either been incorporated into the text's authority as text or obliterated, it is the archeologist's task to serve as a counter-memory for the text, putting the network around, and finally, before the text, where it can be seen. Derrida works more in the spirit of a kind of negative theology.[7] The more he grasps textuality for itself, the greater the detail of what is not there for him—since I consider his key terms *dissémination, supplément, pharmakos, trace, marque,* and the like, to be not only terms describing "la dissimulation de la texture" but also quasi-theological terms ruling and operating the textual domain his work has opened.

In both cases, nevertheless, the critic challenges the culture and its apparently sovereign powers of intellectual activity, which we may call "method," when in dealing with texts these powers aspire to the condition of science. The challenge is delivered in characteristically large gestures of differentiation. Derrida refers everywhere to Western metaphysics and thought, Foucault in his earlier work to various periods, epochs, *epistemes*, those totalities building the dominant culture into its controlling institutions. Each way, Foucault's and Derrida's, attempts not only to define these challenged entities but also in some persistent fashion to de-define them, to attack the stability and power of their rule, to dissolve them if at all possible. For both writers, their work is meant to replace the tyranny and the fiction of direct reference—to what Derrida calls *presence*, or the transcendental signified—with the rigor and practice of textuality mastered on its own highly eccentric ground and, in Foucault's case, *in* its highly protracted persistence. Dedefinition and antireferentiality are the common response to the *positivist* ethos that both Derrida and Foucault abhor. Yet there has been in their work a constant appeal to empiricism and to the nuanced perspectivism both seem to derive from Nietzsche.

There is some irony in the fact that both Derrida and Foucault are solicited nowadays for literary criticism, whereas neither of them is in fact a literary critic. One is a philosopher, the other a philosophic historian. Their material, on the other hand, is generically hybrid: quasi-philosophical, quasi-literary, quasi-scientific, quasi-historical. Similarly, their positions in the academic or university world are anomalous. I suppose that what I am drawing attention to is a fundamental uncertainty in their work as to what it is doing, theorizing over the problem of textuality or—and this is egregiously obvious in Derrida's case, especially since *Glas*, but also noticeable in Foucault's—practicing an alternative textuality of their own. Later I propose to discuss the doctrinal and didactic aspect of their work, but now I want simply to state that, at least since *De la grammatologie*, Derrida has attempted what he has called a form of *écriture double*, one half of which provokes an inversion of the cultural domination Derrida everywhere identifies with metaphysics and its hierarchies, the other half of which "allows the detonation of writing in the very interior of the word, thus disrupting the entire given order and taking over the field."[8] This unbalanced and unbalancing (*decalée et decalante*) writing is intended by Derrida to mark the admittedly uneven and undecideable fold (*pil*) in his work between the description of a text, which he deconstructs, and the enactment of a new one, with which his reader must now reckon. Similarly in Foucault's case, there is a "double writing" (which is not the name he gives it), intended first to describe (by representing) the texts he studies, as discourse, archive, statements, and the rest, then later to present a new text, his own, doing and saying what those other invisible texts have repressed, doing and saying what no one else will say and do.

This simultaneous, intertextual before and after in their writing is designed by both Derrida and Foucault to dramatize the differences between what they do and what they describe, between the logocentric and discursive worlds, on the one hand, and the Derridean and Foucaldian critique on the other. In both cases there is a postulated and repeatedly proved culture against which their dedefinitions are directed. Their characterizations of the culture are ample of course, but so far as I am concerned one aspect of these characterizations is extremely problematic.

First Foucault. As he outlines it in *The Archeology of Knowledge* and *The Discourse on Language*, the archeological method is supposed to reveal how discourse—impersonal, systematic, highly regulated by enunciative formations—overrides society and governs the production of culture. Foucault's thesis is that individual statements, or the chances that individual authors *can* make individual statements, are not really likely. Over and above every opportunity for saying something, there stands a regularizing collectivity that Foucault has called a discourse, itself governed by the archive. Thus his studies of delinquency, the penal system, and sexual repression are studies of a certain anonymity during and because of which, Foucault says in *Discipline and Punish*, "the human body was entering a machinery of power that explores it, breaks it down and rearranges it." The responsibility for this *machinerie* is a discipline, a turn taken by discourse when it enters the ranks of administrative justice; but here too Foucault dissolves individual responsibility in the interests not so much of collective responsibility as of institutional will. "These methods, which made possible the meticulous control of the operating of the body, which assured the constant subjection of its forces and imposed upon them a relation of docility—utility, might be called 'disciplines.' "[9]

In a variety of ways therefore Foucault is concerned with *assujetissement*, the subjugation of individuals in society to some suprapersonal disciplines or authority. Though obviously anxious to avoid vulgar determinism in explaining the workings of the social order, he pretty much ignores the whole category of intention. Foucault is conscious of this difficulty, I think, and his account of something called a will to knowledge and power—*la volonté de savoir*—attempts in some way to redress the assymmetry in his work between the blindly anonymous and the intentional. Yet the problem of the relationship between individual subject and collective force (which reflects also the problem of the dialectic between voluntary intention and determined movement) is still an explicit difficulty, and it is acknowledged by Foucault as follows:

> Can one speak of science and its history (and therefore of its conditions of existence, its changes, the errors it has perpetrated, the sudden advances that have sent it off on a new course) without reference to the scientist himself—and I am speaking not merely of the concrete individual represented by a proper name, but of his work and the particular form of his thought? Can a valid history of science be attempted that would retrace from beginning to end the whole spontaneous movement of an anonymous body of knowledge? Is it legitimate, is it even useful, to replace the traditional "X thought that . . ." by a "it was known that"? But this is not exactly what I set out to do. I do not wish to deny the validity of intellectual biographies, or the possibility of a history of theories, concepts, or themes. It is simply that I wonder whether such descriptions are themselves enough, whether they do justice to the immense density of scientific discourse, whether there do not exist, outside their customary boundaries, systems of regularities that have a decisive role in the history of the sciences. I should like to know whether the subjects responsible for scientific discourse are not determined in their situation, their function, their perceptive capacity, and their practical possibilities by conditions that dominate and even overwhelm them.[10]

This is shrewd, perhaps even disarming, self-criticism—but the questions have still to be answered. Certainly Foucault's work since the *Archeology* and since the two long interviews given in 1968 to *Esprit* and *Cahiers pour l'analyse*[11] has progressed in the directions suggested by his remark about individuals: "I wonder whether such descriptions are themselves enough." That is, he has provided a prodigiously detailed set of possible descriptions whose main aim is, once again, to overwhelm the individual subject or will and replace it instead with minutely responsive rules of discursive formation, rules that no one individual can either alter or circumvent. These rules exist, he argues, and they are to be complied with, mainly because

discourse is not a mere formalization of knowledge; its aim is the
control and manipulation of knowledge, the *body* politic, and ultimately (although Foucault is evasive about this) the State. Perhaps
his interest in rules is part of the reason why Foucault is unable to
deal with, or provide an account of, historical change.

Foucault's dissatisfaction with the subject as sufficient cause of a
text, and his recourse to the invisible anonymity of discursive and archival power, is curiously matched by Derrida's own brand of invol-
untarism. This is a very complex and, to me, deeply troubling aspect
of his work. On the one hand, there are Derrida's frequent references
to Western metaphysics, to a philosophy of presence and all that it
entails and explains about a wide variety of texts, from Plato through
Descartes, Hegel, Kant, Rousseau, Heidegger, and Lévi-Strauss. On
the other hand, there is Derrida's attention to the minutiae, the inadvertent elisions, confusions, and circumspections on certain key
points to be found in a number of important texts. What his readings
of a text are meant to uncover is silent complicity between the super-
structural pressures of metaphysics and an author's ambiguous innocence about a detail at base level—for example, Husserl's merely
verbal distinction between expressive and indicative signs or the vacillation (discussed in *"Ousia* et *Grammé"*) between Aristotle's *nun*
and *ama*.[12] Yet the mediating agency between base and superstructure is neither referred to nor taken into account. In some cases, including the two I have mentioned, Derrida's implication is that the
writer deliberately eluded the problems sprung on him by his own
verbal behavior, in which event we are to suppose perhaps that he is
being pressured involuntarily by the superstructure and the teleological biases of "metaphysics." In other instances, however, the writer's
own complex textual practice is divided against itself; the undecidability of a term—*pharmakos, supplément,* or *hymen*—is built into the
text and its working. Yet whether or not the writer was aware of this
undecidability is a question posed explicitly only once by Derrida,
and then dropped. Here is his rather allusive treatment of the problem in *Of Grammatology:*

> In Rousseau's text, after having indicated—by anticipation and
> as a prelude—the function of the sign "supplement," I now pre-
> pare myself to give special privilege, in a manner that some
> might consider exorbitant, to certain texts like the *Essay on the
> Origin of Languages* and other fragments on the theory of lan-
> guage and writing. By what right? And why these short texts,
> published for the most part after the author's death, difficult to
> classify, of uncertain date and inspiration?

To all these questions and within the logic of their system, there is no satisfying response. In a certain measure and in spite of the theoretical precautions that I formulate, my choice is in fact *exorbitant.*[13]

What Derrida is really asking himself is whether what he does and whether the texts he has chosen for this analysis of Rousseau have anything to do with Rousseau, what Rousseau did or intended to do. Did Rousseau value and emphasize the *Essay on the Origin of Languages* or not? Moreover, in posing the questions and then saying that there is no satisfying response, isn't Derrida himself still relying on the very notion of intention he tried to make "exorbitant" to his method? For despite his insistent criticism of such terminalistic or barrier ideas as *source* or *origin*, Derrida's own writing is full of them. His word *privilege* for what he does, like his escape at the end of the passage into *exorbitance*, does not diminish his reliance on the notion of "Rousseau" as an author having a specifiable life span, an evident canon of texts, datable and classifiable works and periods, and so forth. There is also an eighteenth century, an age of Rousseau, and a much larger closure called Western thought—all of which seem to exert some influence on what texts mean, on their *vouloir-dire*. What "Rousseau" designates in all this is something clearly more than Derrida can ignore, even when he puts quotation marks around the name. To what extent is the phrase *my choice* to be understood as indicating mere intellectual willfulness, and to what extent a methodological act of philosophic liberation from "the totality of the age of logocentrism"? Is the word *supplément* emphasized before Derrida's exorbitance, and is it therefore his passage prepared for in part by Rousseau himself out of the logocentric world; or is the choice made *exorbitantly*, and hence from exteriority, in which case we must ask how (since the method is the issue) he can systematically place himself outside the logocentric world when every other writer somehow could not? And what is the context of the will enabling such a translation of verbally ensnared philosopher into a new, efficient reader?

The severity of these questions is validated by Derrida himself, who in his critique of Foucault had peppered the *Histoire de la folie* with objections to its cavalier indifference about its own discursive complicities. In accusing Foucault of not having dealt sufficiently with the philosophic and methodological problems of discussing the silence of unreason in a more or less rational language, Derrida opens up the question of Foucault's rigor. For even if Foucault claims to be himself using a language maintained in "a relativity without recourse," Derrida is entitled to ask "what, in the last resort, supports this language without recourse or support: who enunciates the possibility of nonrecourse? Who wrote and who is to understand, in what language and from what historical situation of logos, who wrote and who is to understand this history of madness?"[14] The issue here is Foucault's claim to be liberating folly from its forcible enclosure inside Western culture. To which claim Derrida's answer is: "I would be tempted to consider Foucault's book a powerful gesture of protection and internment. A Cartesian gesture for the twentieth century. A reappropriation of negativity. To all appearances, it is reason that he interns, but, like Descartes, he chooses the reason of yesterday as his target and not the possibility of meaning in general."[15] For what Derrida claims to have found Foucault doing is to have read Descartes naively, mistaking Descartes and domesticating notions of doubt, making it appear that Descartes had severed folly from reason; whereas, according to Derrida, a close reading of Descartes' texts shows the contrary, that Descartes' hyberbolic theory of doubt included the idea of "Malin Génie" whose function it was, not to banish, but to include folly as part of the originating and originary flaw undermining the order of rationality itself. It is this troubling economy between reason, madness, silence, and language that Derrida accuses Foucault of overlooking as he seems to announce the exteriority of the archeological method to the structures of imprisonment and enclosure he describes.

I have simplified a very complicated argument, and I shall not now rehearse Foucault's response to Derrida's criticism. For the moment my interest is in Derrida's positing of the metaphysical, logocentric world and in asking how the writers he examines as instances of that world become a part of it. This is a question I take very seriously. For it is never apparent how the logocentric fallacy—which takes many different forms: binary, axiological oppositions with one apparently equal term controlling the other, paternally organized hierarchies, ethnocentric valorization, phallic insemination—how the logocentric prejudice insinuates itself to begin with, or how it becomes the larger thing that is Western metaphysics. Neither is it apparent how metaphysical biases, including the neglect of the sign and the nostalgia for presence, can be ascribed, on the one hand, to the inadvertencies of a writer, his elisions, his sliding from one term to another (*dérapage*) and, on the other hand, to the clearly intentioned designs of Western metaphysics upon its adherents. For there is Derrida's vigilance in exposing the small mistakes, the significant lapses made by writers going from one thing to the next heedlessly, and then there is Derrida appealing to the influence of a philosophy of presence, which acts—it seems—as an agent of something still larger and more prevalent, called Western metaphysics.

If we are not to say that the point of a philosophy of presence is to accomplish certain things not only in the text but beyond the text, in the institutions of society for example, then are we forced to say that the accomplishments of Western metaphysics are (a) the infection of philosophic prose by certain errors of a false logic and (b) the deconstruction of Western texts by Derrida? As reader of these texts, then, Derrida's own will realizes itself, a process that is theoretically infinite because of the number of texts to be deconstructed is as large as Western culture, and hence practically infinite. Is it entirely inaccurate to say that Derrida's elimination of voluntarism and intention in the interests of what he calls infinite substitution, conceals, or perhaps smuggles in, an act of Derrida's will in which the deconstructive strategy, based on a theory of undecideability and desemanticization, provides a new semantic horizon, and hence a new interpretive opportunity associated with the name *Derrida?* To the extent that Derrida's disciples have availed themselves of this strategy and its "concepts," a kind of new orthodoxy has come into existence, no less held in by certain doctrines and ideas than "Western metaphysics." For this, of course, Derrida is not responsible.

But I am not convinced that such orthodoxies exist in any very simple, almost passive way. That is, it seems much more likely that any philosophy or critical theory exists and is maintained in order not merely to be there, passively around everyone and everything, but in order to be taught and diffused, to be absorbed decisively into the institutions of society, to be instrumental in maintaining or changing or perhaps upsetting these institutions and that society. To these latter ends Derrida and Foucault have been variously responsive—and this is what recommends them to our attention. Each in his own way has attempted to devise what is a form of critical openness and repeatedly renewed theoretical resourcefulness, designed first to provide knowledge of a very specific sort; second, to provide an opportunity for further critical work; third, to avoid if possible both the self-confirming operations of culture and the wholly predictable monotony of a disengaged critical system.

Ever since his earliest considerations of the various programs put forward by critical and philosophical methods, Derrida has stalked a certain self-serving quality in these methods. The military and hunting metaphor is apt, I think, since Derrida has spoken in such terms of what he does. I refer not only to the interviews published in *Positions* but also to his essay "Où commence et comment finit un corps enseignant" published in the collection *Politiques de la philosophie*.[16] What has attracted his aggressive intentions is the almost visual aspect of these methods, by which the text or the problem to be discussed by the method seems to be *entirely* doubled or duplicated— and hence deceptively resolved—in the text of the critic or philosopher. But this can only take place if the original text or problem is represented by the critic schematically, in order that the critical text can accommodate the problem completely, so that the critical text appears to stand alongside the original text, appearing also to account for everything in it.

Derrida's entire procedure is to show, either in the pretended rapport between critical and original texts or in the representation of a problem by a text, that far from criticism being able to account for everything by a doubling or duplicating representation, there is always something that escapes. Because writing itself is a form of escape from every scheme designed to shut it down, hold it in, frame it, parallel it perfectly, any attempt to show writing as capable in some way or the other of being *secondary* is also an attempt to prove that writing is *not original*. The military operation involved in deconstruction therefore is in part an attack on a party of colonialists who have tried to make the land and its inhabitants over into a realization of their plans, an attack in turn partly to release prisoners and partly to free land held forcibly. What Derrida shows over and over is that *écriture*—and here we must note that, whether he admits it openly or not, Derrida does introduce oppositions, themes, definitions, and hierarchies between different sorts of writing—what Derrida shows is the *écriture* is not so much only a process of production and effacement, tracing and retracing, but essentially a process of excess, overflowing, bursting through, just as his own work itself attempts to be a bursting through of various conceptual repressions.

Before I give examples of Derrida's revisionary disruption of critical duplication and containment, I should like to note one important thing in his choice of texts. Most are texts in which there is very little narrative, or texts that use narrative so as to illustrate or represent a point. And this choice of texts is similar in the work of Derrida's disciples and critical allies. In fact, illustrative narrative—for instance, as it is used by Plato or Rousseau or Lévi-Strauss—is precisely what (in the case of Lévi-Strauss) draws Derrida's suspicious attention to the author's elisions and complicities, or in its ambiguity (Rousseau's narrative of language bursting forth as a supplement to the passion of primitive man) to what the author tries to tell and obscure at the same time. Similarly, insofar as Derrida has concerned himself with openly proclaimed historical texts (the only instance is Foucault's *Histoire de la folie*), texts committed to some thesis of consequentiality internal to their structure, Derrida's attention has been taken by what seems to be a momentary lapse in description (Descartes' theory of dreams and madness).

What does this avoidance of narrative mean? Inasmuch as he has focused on the theatrical dimension of representation in his analyses, Derrida has stressed and criticized the surreptitious mixing in of hierarchies, doctrines, and unadmitted prejudices in the text. Now, unlike other texts, the realistic novel is governed by a different, a nontheatrical, mode of presentation. Though it is true of course that many novels use the same device of the storyteller recounting a story to an audience, this device is incorporated into the novel and is therefore an already admitted fiction—that is, in Derrida's terminology, a *mimique* or *supplément* or *simulacrum*. Moreover, as I have tried to show for Conrad, many modern novels often are themselves about the alternation of writing and speaking—an alternation that does not favor speech over writing—and the alternation of presence and absence. The very problematic of textuality is neither eluded nor elided, but made into an explicit intentional and constitutive aspect of the narrative. Sterne comes to mind immediately, but so do Cervantes, Proust, Conrad, and many others. The point is that these motifs, which are the very ones in a sense constructed by Derrida's criticism, already exist in narrative not as a hidden (hence inadvertent) element but as a principal one. Such texts cannot therefore be deconstructed, since their deconstruction has already been begun self-consciously by the novelist and by the novel. Thus this aspect of narrative poses the challenge, as yet not taken up, of what there is to be done *after* deconstruction is well under way, after the *idea* of deconstruction no longer represents elaborate intellectual audacity.

Moreover, in one important way the history of the novel, or the history of narrative plot in the novel, has undergone a crucial evolution: the novel exceeds, goes beyond, biography as its organizing structure. To compare Robinson Crusoe or Tom Jones with Marlow, Kurtz, or Jude is immediately to see not only the almost total attenuation in fiction of the grounding role of biography, but also to note the more and more striking emergence in narrative of writing itself as a substitute for—or supplement to—biography. The paternal motif and with it the entire edifice of filiation so central to the management of fiction, the thematics of identity, genealogy, parenthood, and marriage: all these undergo profound alteration during the course of the late nineteenth- and early twentieth-century novels. The point about these changes is not that they are in some vulgar way caused by extrinsic socioeconomic factors, but that they occur in the course of narrative's progressive secularization. Whereas the novelist had ascribed unqualified generative and godlike powers to himself and to his creation, the course of their sustained performance in real historical time, these powers submit to an acknowledgment of their mundane or worldly circumstances. And these circumstances reveal the *novelist writing*, not the god creating or the man or woman presenting. Whether he is Flaubert, Proust, Conrad, Hardy, or Joyce, the novelist is aware of the discourse of which voluntarily he is a part. In all this we have two things with which deconstruction as a general interpretive strategy, based on allegedly universal characteristics of Western thought, cannot deal: writing as a highly complex *surface* activity and formal element in narrative; two, writing that appears already differentiated from other activities not because of some preordained decision, but as the *consequence* of a historical evolution unique, and yet absolutely crucial, to the narrative form itself.

IN the *Grammatology* Derrida speaks of an "effaced and respected doubling of commentary,"[17] the idea being that traditionally a critic will read a given text respecting its supposed stability and securely reproducing that stability in a critical commentary that stands alongside the original text. Similarly, a formalist reading of a poetic text will posit the form as being principally there to receive the text's meaning. The visual equivalent of such a procedure is described brilliantly by Derrida as geometrical, one text (square, circular, or having an irregular contour) reproduced in another text whose shape corresponds exactly with the first. Between them the pair of texts presumably allows the critic to have "the tranquil assurance that leaps over the text toward its presumed content, in the direction of the pure signified."[18] The teleology of the whole business is what Derrida legitimately questions, as when he describes Jean Rousset's "teleological structuralism": "Rousset does not seem to posit . . . that every form is beautiful, but only the form that is aligned with meaning, the form that can be understood because it is,

above all, in league with meaning. Why then, once more, this geom-
eter's privilege?"[19] Such neatness as Rousset's can do nothing with
the irreducible primordial shock delivered by all writing, an initial
violence common to all *écriture.* So whether it is a critic doubling a
text, or saying about a text that its form coincides perfectly with its
content, the neatness is a repressing one, and it has been Derrida's
remarkable project everywhere to open language to its own richness,
thereby to free it from the impositions of helpful schemata.

But Derrida has been less perspicacious in lifting off the covers of a
great many assertions that, more recently in his work, he has called
thèmes or *catégorèmes*—words that claim to refer to something definite and unshakable outside themselves, for which they are supposed
to be exact duplicates. These words involve a great deal of purely linguistic maneuvering hidden behind their calm Apollonian facade.
Not for nothing was Derrida's first extended work a study of Husserl's *Logische Untersuchungen* of 1900–01 (a date with almost vulgar significance for phenomenology as a science of "pure principle"
or primordiality), a set of investigations whose stated effort was to
understand meaning and its implements more radically than ever before. Into every one of Husserl's definitions Derrida insinuates his
technique of trouble, showing generally that Husserl's denigration of
the sign, his subordination of the sign to a meaning it existed eco-
nomically to express, was an unsuccessful attempt to "eliminate signs
by making them derivative";[20] and, still more important, such an attitude to signs and to language pretended that signs were mere modifications of "a simple presence," as if, using language, presence could
never be present except as re-presence (or representation), reproduction, repetition—to all of which signs were not only inevitable
but, paradoxically, the only presence, a re-presence proclaiming the
absence of what it presented. Derrida's role is that of an investigative
reporter "attentive to the instability [and the messy quality] of all
these [philosopher's] moves, for they pass quickly and surreptitiously into one another." Far from being a set of neat radical distinctions made between one thing and another, Husserl's whole science
of origins thus turns out instead to be "a purely teleological structure" designed mainly to eliminate signs, and other trivia, and restore
"presence." And what is presence, but "an absolute will-to-hear-one-
self speak?"[21] The self-confirmation not only of philosophy but also
of a kind of lumpish, pure, and undifferentiated presence to oneself
(ontological egoism) simply ignores language that, while being used
to bring about "presence," is being denied simultaneously. Despite

Husserl's desperate scramble to keep it secondary and a serviceable double for presence, language manufactures the very meanings that philosophy desires to suppress as embarrassing, marginal, accessory. Thus for every big word like "god" or "reality" there are small words like "and" or "between" or even "is," and Derrida's philosophic position is that the big words don't mean anything outside themselves: they are significations attached for their entire sense to all the small words (the *chevilles syntaxiques* as he calls them), which in turn signify more than they can be adequately understood to be expressing.

What Derrida refers to portentously as Western metaphysics is a *magical* attitude licensed ironically by language and, so far as I know, is not necessarily a Western attitude. But perhaps that is a small point. Derrida's argument stresses the again visual thesis that the valorization of voice, presence, ontology, is a way of not looking at writing, of pretending that expression is immediate and not reliant upon the signifying visual chain, which is *écriture*. The grammatological attitude and with it the strategy of deconstruction, therefore, is a visual, theatrical one, and its consequences for intellectual production (Derrida's in particular) are quite specific and quite special.

I should like to begin this section with what may seem a somewhat irrelevant quotation from *Great Expectations*. Pip and Herbert go off to watch a performance of *Hamlet* in which Mr. Wopsle, Pip's fellow townsman, has the leading role. The performance comes before Pip finds out who his benefactor is, so the near farce of what he and Herbert see on the stage is meant to be a mocking allusion to Pip's own pretentions to be a gentleman.

> On our arrival in Denmark, we found the king and queen of that country elevated in two armchairs on a kitchen-table, holding a Court. The whole of the Danish nobility were in attendance; consisting of a noble boy in the wash-leather boots of a gigantic ancestor, a venerable Peer with a dirty face, who seemed to have risen from the people late in life, and the Danish chivalry with a comb in its hair and a pair of white silk legs, and presenting on the whole a feminine appearance. My gifted·townsman stood gloomily apart, with folded arms and I could have wished that his curls and forehead had been more probable.
> Several curious little circumstances transpired as the action proceeded. The late king of the country not only appeared to have been troubled with a cough at the time of his decease but to

have taken it with him to the tomb, and to have brought it back. The royal phantom also carried a ghostly manuscript round its truncheon, to which it had the appearance of occasionally referring, and that, too, with an air of anxiety and a tendency to lose the place of reference which were suggestive of a state of mortality. It was this, I conceive, which led to the Shade's being advised by the gallery to "turn over".—a recommendation which it took extremely ill ... The Queen of Denmark, a very buxom lady, though no doubt historically brazen, was considered by the public to have too much brass about her; her chin being attached to her diadem by a broad band of that metal (as if she had a gorgeous toothache), her waist being encircled by another, and each of her arms by another, so that she was openly mentioned as the "kettledrum" ... Lastly, Ophelia was a prey to such musical madness, that when, in course of time, she had taken off her white muslin scarf, folded it up and buried it, a sulky man who had long been cooling his impatient nose against an iron bar in the front row of the gallery, growled, "Now the baby's put to bed, let's have supper". Which, to say the least of it, was out of keeping.

Upon my unfortunate townsman all these incidents accumulated with playful effect. Whenever that undecided Prince had to ask a question or state a doubt, the public helped him out with it. As for example; on the question whether 'twas nobler in the mind to suffer, some roared yes, and some no, and some inclining to both opinions said "toss up for it": and quite a Debating Society arose. When he asked what should such fellows as he do crawling between earth and heaven, he was encouraged with loud cries of "Hear, hear" ... On his taking the recorders ... he was called upon unanimously for Rule Britannia. When he recommended the player not to saw the air thus, the sulky man said, "And don't *you* do it neither; you're a deal worse than him!"[22]

The comedy of this is immediately obvious: Dickens takes a well-known play, never mentions it by name, and proceeds to describe the somewhat demeaning incongruities that occur when it is being staged by an incompetent and ridiculous company. The technique of Dickens' description, however, bears a little more analysis. In the first place, several levels of action are formed in a scene that, because Dickens describes a staged performance at a theater, is expected to keep all those levels distinct from one another. There are Pip and Herbert; there is an audience; there are several vociferous members of the audience who stand out; there are bad actors; there is a stage setting that is supposed to be Denmark; and finally, very far away it seems, there is supposed to be a play written by Shakespeare, commanding the entire proceedings (although the actor playing the part of the ghost carries the text with him).

Now, in the second place, these levels are hardly distinct from one another during the performance, which is why the whole business is so funny. Since nothing and no one—actors, spectators, setting, Pip and Herbert—does what is expected, we come to realize without much difficulty that no one and nothing fits the part assigned. The fit between actor and role, between audience and performer, between speaker and words, between supposed setting and actual scene: all these are out of joint and behave differently than they would if, for example, actor and part were perfectly matched. In short, nothing during this hilariously inept performance perfectly represents what we expect to be represented. In our heads we have a picture telling us that Hamlet ought to look noble, that the audience ought to be quiet, that the ghost be ghostlike. The effect of these foiled expectations is a travesty of a great play that, despite its abuses, nevertheless manages to weave its way more or less into everything Dickens describes, informing the entire proceedings. Indeed it would be quite accurate to say that Shakespeare's play, its text, is there offstage, and what happens onstage is a result of the text's imperfect or insufficient power to command this particular performance. For what goes wrong is in some measure due not only to the company's and the audience's incompetence but also to the text's insufficient authority to make a representation or performance of itself work "properly."

One more thing. Not only are the levels scrambled, not only is there no correspondence between original text and its realization; there is also the fact that *Hamlet* the play is everywhere in Dickens' account of this disastrous evening. What Dickens gives us is in fact a double scene or, to use a musical analogy, a theme and variations in which one text or theme and a confused, new version of it take place simultaneously in Dickens' prose. His narrative somehow manages to portray *Hamlet* and *Hamlet* travestied, together, not so much only as montage but as criticism, opening the venerated masterpiece to its own vulnerability, letting a monument of literature accept and actually accommodate the fact of its written, and hence unprotected, consequence, which is that each time it is performed the performance is a substitute for the original, and so on to infinity, with the original becoming a more and more hypothetical "original." So at one and the same time Dickens narrates a dramatic text in the process of its performance as it intended to be performed, as well as the same text in a new configuration, as it is being performed and grossly travestied. The old and the new can cohabit this way for us only because Dickens puts the two together and lets them happen together in his text, according to a relatively strict method of comic exfoliation. If we say that *Hamlet* as Shakespeare wrote it is at the center or origin of the whole episode, then what Dickens gives us is a comically literal account of the center not only unable to hold, but *being* unable to hold, producing instead a number of new, devastatingly eccentric multiples of the play. Thus the power of the text turns out to be the exact reverse of what I said about it earlier; the text commands and indeed permits, invents, all its misinterpretations and misreadings, which are functions of the text.

From the beginning of his career Derrida has been fascinated with the possibilities of this sort of thing. Some of his philosophic ideas about presence, about the privilege given by Western metaphysics to voice over writing, about the disappearance of the idea of center or origin in modern thought, are assumed in a most unphilosophic way by Dickens, for whom the simple incontrovertible fact that Shakespeare may have been the author of a great play called *Hamlet*, but who is not around to prevent *Hamlet* from being taken over and literally redone by anyone who has a mind to do so, is an assumption resembling Derrida's notion that ideas of voice, presence, and metaphysical "origins" are simply inadequate for the performative actualities of language. The other side of this view is the paradoxical one that Shakespeare's *text* is about its travesties of course, but those have to do with the text's powers, which are tied to its written state and the exigencies of performance and not to Shakespeare's presence as a once alive human being.

The technique of showing how these myths about voice and presence persist in our thinking and in much writing (whose whole status is undermined by the idea that writing is simply a reflection for something, like thought or a voice, which it is expected to represent) is Derrida's, as much as it is Dickens' in this scene and—to mention another example—Mark Twain's in *A Connecticut Yankee in King Arthur's Court*. Derrida himself has made the point that such debunkings as his in a sense revalidate the old myths, just as Dickens' parody of *Hamlet* is an act of homage to Shakespeare. This is what Derrida means when he speaks of his philosophy as a form of *paleonymy*. For Derrida the reason for this "hold" (the word he uses in *La Voix et le phénomène* is *prise*) on us and him of the old ideas is that they have preempted our thinking almost but not quite completely, they have caused certain notions (*impensés*) to become uncritically accepted, and—this is more important—as a philosopher he has been unable to discover a new way of thinking that totally liberates us from old ideas. Derrida has been extremely scrupulous about saying that he is not attempting to replace the old ideas with new ones, since he apparently does not intend to become the promulgator of a new orthodoxy to replace the old one. Whether this new orthodoxy emerges or not in his work is an important question, I think deliberately ignored by Derrida and his disciples.

But what is Derrida's philosophic strategy of deconstruction, as he calls it, and why are its techniques helpfully illuminated by the scene in *Great Expectations?* Let us start with representation, which is one of the key problems in all criticism and philosophy. Most accounts of representation, including Plato's, involve an original and a copy or representation, the first coming first in time and higher in value, the second later and lower in time and value, the first determining the second. In principle, a representative representation is meant to be a sometimes unavoidable, sometimes merely convenient substitute for the original, which for any number of reasons cannot be present to be itself and act itself. The representative or substitute is thus qualitatively different from the original, in part because an original is itself and is not contaminated by its difference. I simplify greatly of course, but Derrida's philosophic position is that difference—as between original and representative—is not a quality merely added to a representation or secondary object, in the way language is often considered to be a substitute for the real thing (since, for example, it is commonly supposed that language represents an idea or a person not immediately present). Rather, Derrida says that difference on one level is added to objects when they are designated as representative, but on another level, the strictly verbal level of designation itself, difference is already differed and therefore cannot be thought of as a quality or an idea or a concept having originals and copies. Difference is something wholly intrinsic to language, which is diacritical and is the very activity of language itself when it is pereceived not phonetically but graphically. For this purely linguistic activity Derrida invents the word *différance*, an unnameable (or unpronounceable) name. "What is unnameable here is not some ineffable being that cannot be approached by a name; like God, for example. What is unnameable is the play that brings about the nominal effects, the relatively unitary or atomic structures we call names, or chains or substitutions for names."[23]

To name something is to specify an idea, object, or concept with some priority to the very activity of naming and to the name. Derrida wants us to see—if not to understand—that so long as we believe that language is mainly a representation of something else, we cannot see what language does; so long as we are expecting to understand language in terms of some primitive essence to which it is a functional addition, then we cannot see that any use of language means not only representation but, paradoxically, the end or permanent deferring of representation and the beginning of something else, which he calls writing. So long as we do not see that writing more accurately and materially than speaking signifies language being used not simply as a substitute for something better than itself but as an activity all its own, we cannot recognize that "something better" is a fundamental illusion (for if it could be there, it would be there). In short, we will remain in the grip of metaphysics.

Written language involves representation, just as the play that Pip sees is a representation; yet to say that language—or rather writing, since that is what Derrida is talking about always—and the performance are representations is not to say that they could be something else. They cannot be because, the play called *Hamlet* by Shakespeare is also an instance of writing, and all writing is not a replacement for anything, but an admission that there is only writing when language is to be used, at least so far as the possibility of sustained, repeatable representation is concerned. All of a sudden we see that the very notion of representation acquires a new uncertainty, just as every performance of *Hamlet*—no matter how zany—confirms the play's own verbal and even thematic instability. What we find Derrida doing is what we saw Dickens doing, allowing the very notion of representation to represent itself, on a stage (which is a profoundly apt locale, obviously) where at least two versions of a familiar text get in each other's way and on top of each other, one reversing the other, the new version supplementing the old, and the whole thing happening within Dickens' own prose, which is where and only where it can happen. Thus Derrida's endless worrying of representation involves him in a kind of permanent but highly economical tautology. He uses his own prose to represent certain ideas of presence, as well as their representations, at work in a whole series of texts from Plato to Heidegger; then in representing these texts he rereads and rewrites them, enabling us to see them not as representations of something, as references to a transcendental signified outside them, but as texts representing only themselves in, for a text, perfectly representative ways.

This is an extremely bald summary of what is by all odds one of the most sophisticated and complex theories of meaning and textuality available today. My main reason for doing the summary I did is to emphasize a small number of Derrida's ideas (by no means his system, if there is such a thing) in order to speak about them in a little more detail. These ideas have a special interest for critics today who may wish to place themselves skeptically between culture as a massive body of self-congratulating ideas and system or method, anything resembling a sovereign technique that claims to be free of history, subjectivity, or circumstance. In addition, Derrida's work has some urgency for my notion that, if it is not to be merely a form of self-validation, criticism must intend knowledge and, what is more, it must attempt to deal with, identify, and produce knowledge as having something to do with will and with reason.

Many of Derrida's essays employ not only spatial metaphors but more specifically theatrical ones. Writing, *écriture*, is seen in Freud's work, for example, to have a kind of textuality that attempts to emulate a stage setting. Derrida's two remarkable essays on Artaud in *L'Écriture et la différence* exploit Artaud's interest in an infinitely repeatable representation in order to explicate Derrida's idea about writing being an infinite substitution of one trace for another, and also to define the space of a text as being activated by play, *jeu*. Similarly Derrida shows the irreducible ambiguity in Artaud's notions of the theater, that he needed—like Derrida—to see everything in terms of a theater, although "Artaud also desired the impossibility of the theater, wanted to erase the stage, no longer wanted to see what transpires in a locality always inhabited or haunted by the father and subjected to the repetition of murder."[24] The quasi-montage technique I described earlier is characterized by Derrida as having something uniquely to do with all writing, *where* the graphological process traces, retraces, and effaces itself constantly, the old and the new combining in what he calls *la double scène*. Later, employing one of the pun series he exploits insistently, he calls what he does with it a *double science*, which itself recalls his two-part lecture on Mallarmé's writing, *la double séance*.

All this establishes a sort of perpetual interchange in Derrida's work between the page and the theater stage. Yet the locale of the interchange—itself a page and a theater—is Derrida's prose, which in his recent work attempts to work less by chronological sequence, logical order, and linear movement than by abrupt, extremely difficult-to-follow lateral and complementary movement.[25] The intention of that movement is to make Derrida's page become the apparently self-sufficient site of a critical reading, in which traditional texts, authors, problems, and themes are presented in order to be dedefined and dethematicized more or less permanently. Thus textuality is seen to be the written equivalent of a stage for which, paradoxically, there are boundaries only to be jumped over, actors only to be decomposed into numerous parts, spectators who enter and exit with impunity, and an author who cannot decide whether he writes or rewrites or reads on one side of the stage-page or the other. (The resemblances with Pirandello and Beckett here are worth remarking.)

The polemical burden of Derrida's verbal exhibitions is virtually to rethink what he considers to be the mainstays of philosophical (and even popular) thought; and of these it is, he believes, the idea of an authorizing presence as "substance/existence/essence (*ousia*)"[26] and with it the commanding fiction of such guiding notions as Platonic ideas, Hegelian synthesis, and literary critical totalizing that have now served their time and must be seen as having been valorized not by some "outside" power but by a misreading of texts. And a misreading of texts is made possible by texts themselves, for whom—in the best of them—every meaning-possibility exists in a raw unresolved state. The notion is Derrida's principal philosophic idea, out of which his announced but not practiced science, *grammatology*, is made initially possible. Yet Derrida's work also eliminates the possibility of deciding what is in a text, of being able to determine whether a critical text can so easily be detached from its parent text as critics have believed, of being able to contain the meaning of a text in the notion of meaning itself, of being able to read texts without a commanding suspicion that all texts—the greater the text, and perhaps the critic, the more skillfully—attempt to hide their almost androgynous style in a whole structure of misleading directions to the reader, fictional objects, ephemeral appeals to reality, and the like.[27] For since we have only writing to deal with writing, our traditional modes of understanding have to be altered considerably.

An important instance of Derrida's manner of muddling traditional thought beyond the possibility of its usefulness is found in this passage on the genealogy of a text:

> We know that the metaphor that would describe the genealogy of a text correctly is still *forbidden* [that is, if we try to think where a text comes from, we will be left with some outside notion like "author," and this forbids us from trying to grasp the text's specifically textual origins, an altogether different matter].

In its syntax and its lexicon, in its spacing, by its punctuation, its lacunae, its margins, the historical appurtenance of a text is never a straight line. It is neither causality by contagion, nor the simple accumulation of layers. Nor even the pure juxtaposition of borrowed pieces. And if a text always gives itself a certain representation of its own roots, those roots live only by that representation, by never touching the soil, so to speak [this is something with which it is possible to completely disagree, because Derrida goes too quickly over the way in which texts are connected to other texts, to circumstances, to reality] which undoubtedly destroys their *radical essence,* but not the necessity of their *racinating function.*[28]

The effect of such logic (the *mise en abîme*) is to reduce everything that we think of as having some extratextual leverage in the text to a textual function. What matters in a text is that its textuality transgresses even its own explicit statements about such things as its roots in, or affiliations with, reality. Rather than being mystified by the obvious analogy between the production of writing and the production of organic life (as the similarity is permitted to stand in the parallel between *seme* and *semen* for example), Derrida breaks the similarity down, reverses matters. The culturally permitted idea of the book is that of a totality—whose greatest exemplar is the encyclopedia—and the totality enables, produces, a family of ideas conceived by some single Original, which like a self-delighting pedagogue or father makes meaning cyclical, derived from and imprisoned by the one source. Every concept testifies to auto-insemination, the one confirming and reconfirming the other.[29] As against this set of concepts—the sexual language usually used to discuss meanings and texts is very much at the center of Derrida's most consistently interesting book *La Dissémination*—Derrida sets and reenacts an opposite movement (as the actors in Wopsle's *Hamlet* are set in Shakespeare's *Hamlet*). This movement he calls *dissémination,* which is not a concept at all but what he elsewhere describes as the power of textuality to burst through semantic horizons.

Dissemination does not *mean.* It does not require the notion of a return to a source of origin or father. Quite the contrary, it entails a certain figurative castration, showing the text in its writing, capable of emasculating the Platonic idea informing our views of meaning and representation, as well as the Hegelian triangle resolved in synthesis. Dissemination *maintains* the perpetual disruption of writing, maintains the fundamental undecidability of texts whose real power resides not in their polysemousness (which can after all be collected hermeneutically under the heading of several themes, the way Jean-Pierre Richard's account of Mallarmé collects all his work under the much-varied rubric of "un monde imaginaire")[30] but texts whose power is in the possibility of their infinite generality and multiplicity.

> Along with an ordered extension of the concept of text, dissemination inscribes a different law governing effects of sense or reference (the interiority of the "thing," reality, objectivity . . .), a different relation between writing, in the metaphysical sense of the word, and its "outside" . . . Dissemination *also* explains itself . . . As the heterogeneity and absolute exteriority of the seed, seminal differance does constitute itself into a program, but it is a program that cannot be formalized. For reasons that *can* be formalized. The infinity of its code, its rift, then, does not take a form saturated with self-presence in the encyclopedic circle.[31]

Every one of Derrida's extraordinarily brilliant readings since and including *De la grammatologie* therefore builds from that point in a text around which its heterodox textuality, distinct from its message or meanings, is organized, the point *toward* which the text's textuality moves in the shattering dissemination of its unorganizable energy. These points are words that are anticoncepts, bits of the text in which Derrida believes, and where he shows, the text's irreducible textuality to lie. These anticoncepts, antinames, counterideas, escape definite classification. That is why they are only textual, and why also they are heterodox. Derrida's method of deconstruction functions to release them, just as the climactic moment in each of *his* texts is a performance by these anticoncepts, these mere words. Thus what Derrida points toward is "a scene of writing within a scene of writing and so on without end, through a structural necessity that is marked in the text."[32] Only words that are *syncatégorèmes*—words having, like the copula, a syntactic function but capable of serving semantic ones too[33]— can reveal textuality in its element. These words are of an infinite, hence disseminative, pliability; they mean one thing *and* another (rather like Freud's antithetical primal words), but Derrida's interest in them is that it is they, and not the big ideas, that make a text the uniquely written phenomenon that it is, a form of supplementarity to formulable meaning. And this supplementarity is that property of the text capable of repeating itself without exhausting itself and without keeping anything (for instance, a secret hoard of meaning) in reserve. Thus Derrida's reading of the *Phaedrus* is an

explication of the word *pharmakos,* whose use for Plato is to make
him able to write in such a way as to produce a text where truth and
nontruth coexist as instances not of ideas but of textual repetition.[34]
Of these privileged words of his, these textual runes, Derrida says:

> What holds for "hymen" also holds, *mutatis mutandis,* for all
> other signs which, like *pharmakon, supplément, différence,* and
> others, have a double, contradictory, undecidable value that al-
> ways derives from their syntax, whether the latter is in a sense
> "internal," articulating and combining under the same yoke,
> *huph'hen,* two incompatible meanings, or "external," dependent
> on the code in which the word is made to function. But the syn-
> tactical composition and decomposition of a sign renders this al-
> ternative between internal and external inoperative. One is sim-
> ply dealing with greater or lesser syntactical units at work, and
> with economic differences in condensation. Without reducing all
> these to the same, quite the contrary it is possible to recognize a
> certain serial law in these points of indefinite pivoting: they mark
> the spots of what can never be mediated, mastered, sublated, or
> dialecticized through any *Erinnerung* or *Aufhebung.* Is it by
> chance that all these play effects, these "words" that escape phil-
> osophical mastery, should have, in widely differing historical
> contexts, a very singular relation to writing? These "words"
> admit into their games both contradiction and noncontradiction
> (and the contradiction and noncontradiction *between* contradic-
> tion and noncontradiction). Without any dialectical *Aufhebung,*
> without any time off, they belong in a sense both to conscious-
> ness and to the unconscious, which Freud tells us can tolerate or
> remain insensitive to contradiction. Insofar as the text depend
> upon them, *bends* to them (*s'y plie*), it thus plays a *double scene*
> upon a double stage. It operates in two absolutely different
> places at once, even if these are only separated by a veil, which is
> both traversed and not traversed, *inter*sected (*entr'ouvert*). Be-
> cause of this indecision and instability, Plato would have con-
> ferred upon the double science arising from these two theaters
> the name *doxa* rather than *epistēmē.*[35]

What all the words share is not so much a common meaning, but a
common structure very much like the word *hymen* that Derrida uses
to guide his reading of Mallarmé, or like the word *tympan* used to
open *Marges.*[36] The word's undecidable meaning—*hymen* can be decomposed by a stroke of the pen into *hymne*—is like a hypersensitive,
permeable membrane marking its different significations, different
positions, different sides (as of a folded piece of paper), but easily

penetrable by the seductive activity it gets started, attracts, and finally is compelled to release *through* it. Derrida's key words, furthermore, are unregenerate signs: he says that they cannot be made more significant than signifiers are. In some quite urgent way, then, there is something frivolous about them, as all words cannot be accommodated to a philosophy of serious need or utility are futile or unserious.[37]

Basing himself on a suggestion in Condillac, and then also on the ceaseless alternation in Nietzsche's writing between instructive philosophy and seemingly careless song, fable, aphorism, or prophetic utterance, Derrida has inaugurated a style of philosophic criticism and analysis that quite literally and self-consciously wanders (Derrida's word is *errance*, with its cognates in *erreur*) into corners neglected by supposedly serious criticism and philosophy. The form of his work, which like Lukacs' is cast in essays purposely vulnerable to the charge that they are only essays, is disseminative; and their intention is to multiply sense, not hold it down. The habitual amenities of exposition are cast aside, and the skidding from allusion to pun to neologism is sometimes impossible to follow. But in a strict sense Derrida's deconstructive technique is a form of discovery (I use Mark Schorer's famous phrase advisedly) whose material is not merely the textuality of texts, not the peculiar verbal eccentricities of a text that do not fall into categories, not even texts in whose structure there is an unresolvable uncertainty between their writing and their asserted meaning, but the opposition between diction and scription, between the absent/present word and its limitless repetition in writing. What he wants to bring to performance is "the written proposal of logocentrism; the simultaneous affirmation of the being-outside of the outside and of its injurious intrusion into the inside."[38] Invariably this conundrum will be found lodged not in a stable veridic discourse but, and here Derrida is affirmatively Nietzschean, in a discourse whose hidden instruments and agencies are the figural powers of literature. It is this latter point that Derrida emphasizes in his essay "La Mythologie blanche."[39] What each of Derrida's works tries to do is to reveal the *entame*—tear, incision—in every one of the solid structures put up by philosophy, an *entame* already inscribed in written language itself by its persistent desire to point outside itself, to declare itself incomplete and unfit without presence and voice. Voice thus appears secondary to writing, since writing's facility is precisely the facility of all fiction to authorize, even create, its opposite and then act subordinate to and become invisible to it.

The range of texts chosen by Derrida for analysis and discovery—unlike the much more restricted range of texts chosen for their analyses by his followers—is relatively wide, from Plato to Heidegger, Sollers, Blanchot, and Bataille. Insofar as his readings seek to unsettle prevalent ideas in Western culture, his texts seem to have been chosen because they embody the ideas influentially. Thus Rousseau, Plato, and Hegel are revealed to be unavoidable examples of logocentric thought enmeshed in and exemplifying its noncontradictory contradictions. More recent authors—Lévi-Strauss and Foucault, for example—are chosen with what seems to be a fairly coarse polemical goal in mind. Even a superficial reading of Derrida's work will reveal an implicit hierarchy, however, the more conventional for its not being stated than for Derrida's brilliant uncoverings of new significance in his texts. So, for Derrida, Plato, Hegel, and Rousseau either inaugurate epochs or solidify them; Mallarmé initiates a revolutionary poetic praxis; Heidegger and Bataille wrestle openly with problems they both canonize and restate. The way these figures are characterized historically would support any list compiled by a teacher of the humanities or masterpieces of Western thought. Yet there is no explanation of why the age of Rousseau should not also be known as the age of Condillac, or why Rousseau's theory of language should receive precedence over Vico's, or Sir William Jones's, or even Coleridge's. But Derrida does not go into these issues, although I think they are not problems of historical interpretation marginal to what Derrida does; on the contrary, they seem to me to lead to the major questions raised by Derrida's work.

I introduced my remarks on Derrida and Foucault by saying that, although they represent divergent views on criticism both of them consciously attempt to take revisionist positions toward a reigning cultural hegemony—and for such a position their criticism provides an account of what cultural hegemony is—and that, on the other hand, they are aware of the danger that what they do might itself turn into a critical orthodoxy, an unthinking system of thought impervious to change and insensitive to its own problems. Now Derrida's position and his entire production have been devoted to exploring both the misconceptions and the uncritically repeated notions central to Western culture. On at least one occasion he has also pointed out that a teacher of philosophy working in a state-run institution bears a special responsibility for understanding the system by which ideas get passed on mechanically from teacher to student and back again. This defines the teaching position he happens officially to occupy, to the ironies of whose name he is wryly sensitive: *agrégé-répétiteur*. In addition he also belongs to the *corps enseignant*, and to the meaning of this somewhat compromising position he is also sensitive:

> My body is glorious. All the light is concentrated on it. First the projector's light coming from above me. Then it irradiates and attracts to it the spectators' gaze. But it is also glorious insofar as it is no longer simply a body. It sublimates itself in the representation of at least one other body, the teaching body (*le corps enseignant*) of which it would have to be both a part and the whole, a member making it possible to see the whole, and this whole produces itself by effacing itself as the barely visible transparent representation of the philosophical body and of the socio-political body, the contract between both of which is never exhibited publicly.[40]

The theatrical metaphor is well employed here and elsewhere in Derrida's only explicit analysis of the institutional, historical, and political consequences and realities of being what he is, a philosopher and a teacher with a particular project of his own. Yet he has stopped the characterization of this special and privileged position rather short. Is it enough to say that the deconstructive method must not attempt to differentiate between the longer and the shorter chains of philosophical ideas, but rather to concern itself in a very general way with how "the multiple powers of the oldest machine [in this case, he refers to the whole operative structure of Western thought as exemplified in the philosophical tradition] can always be reinvested and exploited in an unedited situation"?[41] My feeling is that so long as it is referred to generally, or even if it is found concretely in individual texts, Western thought is going to remain an abstraction and as it is, not because Derrida does not oppose it—he does and does not, in some of the subtle ways I've tried to describe—but because Western thought is something more differentiated, incorporative, and, most important, institutionally representative than Derrida seems to allow.

The problem does not end here, however. To the extent that Derrida has been most careful to say that even his affirmative deconstructive technique is not a program to replace the old-style philosophic system, he has also gone to extraordinary lengths to provide his readers (and his students, in France and elsewhere) with a set of counterconcepts. The main thing claimed by the Derrideans for those words, and indeed about his deconstructive method, is that they are not reducible to a limited semantic lexicon. Neither are they supposed to be mirror opposites of the dogmas and ideas endemic to Western metaphysics that they challenge. *Différance*, for example, is first defined in 1968 as having two and perhaps three root meanings, all of them different from *différance*.[42] In 1972 he said of *différance*, however, that it resembled "a configuration of concepts that I take as systematic and irreducible, each one of which intervenes, rather takes shape, at a decisive moment in the work."[43] I think he is saying that *différance*, or some aspect of it, depends for its exact meaning on its use at a given moment in reading a text. Yet we are left wondering how something can be practical, contextual, systematic, recognizable, irreducible, and, at the same time, not really a fixed doctrine, not a concept, not an idea in the old sense of those words. Can we remain poised indefinitely between an old and a new sense? Won't this median undecidable word begin to corral more and more meanings for itself, like the old words? Similarly, if the texts he has read and organized around key words do not necessarily elevate those words into universal key words (in Raymond Williams' sense), they are not simply neutral words. *Supplément* is a perfect example, since out of the word he finds in Rousseau, Derrida has built a small repertory of words, including *supplémentarité* and the *supplément* of one thing and the other, all of which have had evident uses in the reading of other texts. More and more, a word like *supplément* gathers status and history; to leave it without some attention to its vital positional use in his work is, for Derrida, a strange negligence.

My point is that Derrida's work continues to have a cumulative effect *on him*, to say nothing of the obvious effect on his disciples and readers. I rather doubt that, in wisely attempting to avoid the compromising fall into systematic method that as a powerful philosophic teacher he is more than likely to succumb to, he has been successful in avoiding the natural consequence of accumulating a good deal that resembles a method, a message, a whole range of special words and concepts. Since it is incorrect (and even an insult) to say that Derrida's accumulation of knowledge in the course of his published work is no more than a mood or an atmosphere, we shall have to accept it as constituting a position, which is a word that he himself has used comfortably. As a position it is of course specifiable, even exportable, but Derrida's programmatic hesitation toward his historical situation, toward his work's affiliation with certain types of work and not with others: all these again programmatically deny it its own considerable position and influence. Also, the texts to which this position has been applied by Derrida have also been denied their historical density, specificity, and weight. Derrida's Plato, Rousseau, Mallarmé, and Saussure: Are all these just texts, or are they a loose order of knowledge from the point of view of a liberal believer in Western culture? How have they a professional significance for a philosopher, linguist, and literary critic, how are they events for an intellectual historian? The refinements are greatly extendable, just as the complex apparatus diffusing Plato, Rousseau, and the others, in the universities, in the technical language of various professions, in the Western and non-Western worlds, in the rhetoric of possessing minorities, in the application of power, in the creation or rupture of traditions, disciplines, and bureaucracies, is an apparatus with power and a lasting historical, actual imprint on human life. But it needs some greater degree of specification than Derrida has given it.

I will not go so far as to say that Derrida's own position amounts to a new orthodoxy. But I can say that it has not, from its unique vantage point, illuminated in sufficient detail the thing he refers to in his account of the *corps enseignant,* that is, the *contrat entre ces corps* (bodies of knowledge, institutions, power), a contract hidden because "jamais exhibé sur le devant de la scène." Much of Derrida's work has demonstrated that such a contract exists, and texts demonstrating logocentric biases are indications that the contract exists and keeps existing from period to period in Western history and culture. But it is legitimate, I think, to ask what keeps that contract together, what makes it possible for a certain system of metaphysical ideas, as well as a whole structure of concepts, praxes, and ideologies derived from it, to maintain itself from Greek antiquity through the present. What forces keeps all these ideas glued together? What forces get them into texts? How does one's thinking become infected, then taken over by those ideas? Are all these things matters of fortuitous coincidence, or is there in fact some relevant connection to be made, and seen, between the instances of logocentrism and the agencies perpetuating it in time? Borges says: "I used to marvel that the letters in a closed book did not get mixed up and lost in the course of a night." And so in reading Derrida's work we marvel at what keeps the ideas of Western metaphysics there in all the texts at night and during the day, for so long a period of time. What makes this system *Western?* Above all, what keeps the contract hidden and, more important, lets its effects appear in a highly controlled, systematized way?

The answers to these questions cannot be found by reading the texts of Western thought seriatim, no matter how complex the reading method and no matter how faithfully followed the series of texts. Certainly any reading method like Derrida's, whose main ambition is both to reveal one or another undecidable elements in a text in lieu of some simple reductive message the text is supposed to contain and, on the other hand, to shy away from making each reading of a text part of some cumulatively built explicit thesis about the historical persistence of Western metaphysical thought, certainly any method like that will finally be unable to get hold of the local material density and power of ideas as historical actuality. For not only will those ideas be left unmentioned, they cannot even be named—and this is highly consonant with the entire drift of Derrida's antinominalism, his dedefinitional philosophy, his desemanticizing of language. In other words, the search *within* a text for the conditions of textuality will falter at that very point where the text's historical presentation to the reader is put into question and made an issue for the critic.

Here the divergence between Derrida and Foucault becomes very dramatic. It is not enough to say, as I implied, that Foucault moves the text out from a consideration of internal textuality to its way of inhabiting and remaining in an extratextual reality. It would be more useful to say that Foucault's interest in texuality is to present the text stripped of its esoteric or hermetic elements, and to do this by making the text assume its affiliations with institutions, offices, agencies, classes, academies, corporations, groups, guilds, ideologically defined parties and professions. Foucault's descriptions of a text or discourse attempt by the detail and subtlety of the description to *resemanticise* and forcibly to redefine and reidentify the particular interests that all texts serve. A perfect case in point is his criticism of Derrida. Foucault is not only able convincingly to show that on one crucial point Derrida has misread Descartes by employing a French translation that adds words not present in Descartes' Latin original; he is also able apparently to prove that Derrida's whole argument about Descartes is wrong, even capricious. Why? Because true to his method and not to the text's semantic sedimentation, Derrida insists on trying to prove that Foucault's thesis about Descartes, in which Descartes separated folly from dreaming, was really not that at all but an argument about how dreams were more extravagant even than folly, folly being but a weak instance of dreaming. And that argument merely reads the text, allowing the reader's (Derrida's) opinions, uncertainties, and ignorance to override an almost invisible but present and functioning system of ideas making the text *say* specifically that madness was forcibly to be distinguished and excluded from the system of normal human activity, which included dreaming.

The trouble with this evident overriding of the text, as Foucault is at great pains to show, is that Derrida's reading of Descartes cannot read matters in the text that have the plainly intended force of active juridical and medical authority, of specific professional interests at work. Moreover, the form of Descartes' text rigorously follows the pattern of two discourses, the meditative exercise and a logical demonstration, in both of which the positional status of the objects discussed—dream and folly—as well as the positional role of the subject (the philosopher who holds and conducts both discourses in his text) constitute and even determine the text. Derrida's textualization has the effect of "reducing discursive practice to textual traces," a reduction that has given rise to a pedagogy associated with Derrida:

I would say that it is a historically well-determined little pedagogy which manifests itself here. [The phrase *une petite pedagogie* is deliberately insulting.] It is a pedagogy teaching the student that there is nothing beyond the text, but that within it, in its interstices, its blank spaces and its unsaid sounds, the origin reigns, held in reserve; that there is no need to look elsewhere but that right here, not in the positivity of words but in words as erasures, in the *grill* that they form, "the sense of being" speaks itself. This is a pedagogy that gives the voice of teachers a kind of inverse and unlimited sovereignty allowing them indefinitely to rewrite [resay] the text.[44]

This extremely bitter climax of Foucault's reply to Derrida is to some extent a way of registering anger that Derrida's pedagogy, and not so much his method, seems easily teachable, diffuseable, and, at present, perhaps even more influential than Foucault's work. The personal animus informing Foucault's judgment also supplies it with a rhetoric of furious denunciation. But isn't Foucault's intellectual point that Derrida's reading of a text does not allow for the role of information at all, that in reading a text and placing it *en abîme* in a wholly textual ether, Derrida does not seem willing to treat a text as a series of discursive events ruled not by a sovereign author but by a set of constraints imposed on the author by the kind of text he is writing, by historical conditions, and so forth? For if one believes that Descartes merely wrote his text, and that his text contains no problems raised by the fact of its textuality, then one eludes and elides those features of Descartes' text that bind it willingly to a whole body of other texts (medical, jurical, and philosophical texts) and impose upon Descartes a certain process of produced meaning which *is* his text and for which as author he accepts legal responsibility. Derrida and Foucault therefore collide on how the text is to be described, as a praxis on whose surface and in whose interstices a universal grammotological problematic is enacted, or as a praxis whose existence is a fact of highly rarefied and differentiated historical power, associated not only with the univocal authority of the author but with a discourse constituting author, text, and subject and giving them a very precise intelligibility and effectiveness. The meaning of this collision has, I think, a remarkably significant bearing for contemporary criticism.

The significance of Derrida's position is that in his work he has raised questions uniquely pertinent to writing and to textuality that tend to be ignored or sublimated in metacommentary on texts. The very elusiveness of texts, the tendency to see them homogenously either as functions of or as parasitic on some schematic philosophy or system on which they are dependent (as illustrations, exemplifications, expressions): these are the things at which Derrida's considerable dedefinitional energies are directed. In addition he has developed a particularly alert and influential reading method. Yet his work embodies an extremely pronounced self-limitation, an ascesis of a very inhibiting and crippling sort. In it Derrida has chosen the lucidity of the undecidable in a text, so to speak, over the identifiable power of a text; as he once said, to have opted for the sterile lucidity of the performative *double scène* in texts was to have neglected the implemented, effective power of textual statement.[45] Derrida's work thus has not been in a position to accommodate descriptive information of the kind giving Western metaphysics and Western culture a more than repetitively allusive meaning. Neither has it been interested in dissolving the ethnocentrism of which on occasion it has spoken with noble clarity. Neither has it demanded from its disciples any binding engagement on matters pertaining to discovery and knowledge, freedom, oppression, or injustice. If everything in a text is always open equally to suspicion and to affirmation, then the differences between one class interest and another, between oppressor and oppressed, one discourse and another, one ideology and another, are virtual in—but never crucial to making decisions about—the finally reconciling element of textuality.

If for Derrida the *impensé* in criticism that he has frequently attacked signifies a lazy understanding of signs, language, and textuality, then for Foucault the *impensé* is what at a specific time and in a specific way cannot be thought because certain other things have been imposed upon thought instead. In those two meanings of *im-*

pensé, the one passive, the other active, we can see the opposition between Derrida and Foucault—and thereafter to take our position as critics doing something it may be possible to describe and defend. For Foucault, as much as for Derrida, textuality is a more variable and interesting category than the somewhat lifeless one imposed on it by the canonizing rituals of traditional literary criticism. From the beginning of his career, Foucault has been interested in texts as an integral, and not merely accessory, part of the social processes of differentiation, exclusion, incorporation, and rule. He has said of a text, his own included, that it is an "object-event," which "recopies, fragments, repeats, simulates, and doubles itself, finally disappearing without allowing the person who produced the text to claim mastery over it." More specifically: "I would not like it for a book to give itself the status of a text that could be handled reductively as a result either of pedagogy or criticism. Instead I would prefer that a book might have the nonchalance to present itself as discourse, as simultaneously battle and arms, strategy and shock, struggle and trophy (or wound), conjuncture and vestiges, irregular encounter and repeatable scene."[46] The conflict in each text between its author and the discourse of which, for various social, epistemological, and political reasons, he is a part is central for Foucault's textual theory. Far from agreeing with Derrida's contention that Western culture has valorized speech over writing, Foucault's project is to show precisely the opposite, at least since the Renaissance, and to show also that writing is no private exercise of a free scriptive will, but rather the activation of an immensely complex tissue of forces, for which a text is a place among other places (including the body) where the strategies of control in society are conducted. Foucault's entire career from *L'Histoire de la folie* through *La Volonté de savoir* has been an attempt to describe these strategies both with greater and greater detail and with a more and more effective general theoretical apparatus of description. It is arguable, I think, that he has been more successful in the former than in the latter, and that such books as *Surveiller et punir* are of a greater intrinsic interest and power than *The Archeology of Knowledge*. But what is not arguable is Foucault's ability somehow to put aside his enormously complex theoretical apparatus (as it emerges in *The Archeology of Knowledge*) and let the material he has dug up create its own order and its own theoretical lessons. Certain basic theoretical categories, assumptions, and working principles have remained near the center of what he does, however, and I should like now to sketch them briefly.

Some of them are clearly derived from temperament. Foucault is a scholar for whom no corner is too obscure to be looked into, especially when he investigates the machinery of corporeal and mental control throughout Western history. Although it is true that he has been mainly interested in two sides of the same coin—the process of exclusion, by which cultures designate and isolate their opposites, and its obverse, the process by which cultures designate and valorize their own incorporative authority—it is now certain that Foucault's greatest intellectual contribution is to an understanding of how the will to exercise dominant control in society and history has also discovered a way to clothe, disguise, rarefy, and wrap itself systematically in the language of truth, discipline, rationality, utilitarian value, and knowledge. And this language, in its naturalness, authority, professionalism, assertiveness, and antitheoretical directness, is what Foucault has called *discourse*. The difference between discourse and such coarser yet no less significant fields of social combat as the class struggle is that discourse works its productions, discriminations, censorship, interdictions, and invalidations on the intellectual, at the level of base not of superstructure. The power of discourse is that it is at once the object of struggle and the tool by which the struggle is conducted. In penology, for example, the juridical language identifying the delinquent and the intellectual schema embodied in the prison's physical structure are instruments controlling felons as well as powers (withheld from felons obviously) to keep for oneself and deny it to others. The goal of discourse is to maintain itself and, more important, to manufacture its material continually; as Foucault has said provocatively, prisons are a factory for creating criminals. Temperamentally, and no doubt because he is an intellectual uniquely gifted to see that intellectuals are part of the system of discursive power, he has written his books in solidarity with society's silent victims, to make visible the actuality of discourse and to make audible the repressed voice of its subjects.

The master discourse of society is what Foucault in *L'Ordre du discours* has called *le discours vrai* or *le discours de verité*.[47] He has not described this even in *The Archeology of Knowledge*, but I assume he is referring to that most mysterious and general of all elements in discourse that makes its individual utterances appear to be speaking for, about, and in truth. Yet each branch of discourse, each text, each statement, has its own canons of truth, and it is these that designate such matters as relevance, propriety, regularity, conviction, and so forth. Foucault is correct to note that when one writes as a philologist, say, or philologically, what one writes, its form, its shape, its statement, is made rigorously apt by a set of enunciative possibilities unique to philology at that time and in that place. These regional but productive constraints upon the writing and subsequently the interpretation of texts make Foucault's reading of texts a very different process than Derrida's, but theoretically they also situate or locate texts and what they enact far more dramatically than is possible in Derrida's theater of representations.

Foucault's most interesting and problematic historical and philosophical thesis is that discourse, as well as the text, became invisible, that discourse began to dissemble and appear merely to be writing or texts, that discourse hid the systematic rules of its formation and its concrete affiliations with power, not at some point in time but as an event in the history of culture generally and of knowledge particularly. Here as elsewhere in his work, Foucault makes a rigorous effort to be specific even though we are not sure whether what he tries to describe is an event in the commonsense meaning of that word, or an event in a rather more special sense, or both together. My inclination is to think that Foucault is identifying a phase through which culture must have passed, at a period in time that is approximately locatable. Because this phase presumably lasted for a long time, the event then can be characterized as a gradual alteration in the essentially spatial relationship between language and representation. Once again we are in the theatrical space, although it has a considerably thicker historical dimension to it than Derrida's. In *Les Mots et les choses* (*The Order of Things*) Foucault builds his descriptions of the event around a contrast of a fairly simple and instrumental sort. At least until the end of the eighteenth century, he says, it was believed that discourse (language as representative of an order of Being) "ensured the initial, spontaneous, unconsidered deployment of representation within a table" or, we might well add, within a quasi-theatrical space. Now this at least seems to be the case before the event Foucault is about to describe, so completely and dramatically has that event altered, and made difficult even to grasp, the kind of relationship that obtained between language and reality before the event.

The change occurs when "words ceased to intersect with representations and to provide a spontaneous grid for the knowledge of things."[48] Discourse then became problematic and seemed to efface itself, since it was no longer obligated immediately to represent anything other than itself; this is the moment Foucault calls "the discovery of language," albeit a dispersed language. What he describes is something we can understand a little better in terms of the scene from *Great Expectations*. Dickens nowhere says that what he is representing is a theater, nor is *Hamlet* (Shakespeare's play, the text on which the whole performance is based) named. The comedy of the situation is that we somehow know that the characters are trying to act a play they obviously have an imperfect grasp of. But we know this because Dickens' language obliquely directs the entire scene, represents the stage and its actors, cues our responses as readers. And all this is possible because of the novelistic convention, in which a special referentiality and a quasi-realistic use of language are permissible and to which readers bring specialized expectations and responses. In other words, the theater Dickens describes exists in the language of the novel, which has absorbed and taken over reality so much as to be completely responsible for it. Novelistic convention, however, is language released from the burden of representing reality exclusively in a table, or grid; rather, the table, or in this case the theater, is one use for novelistic convention, which is obligated to perform as novels do, to refer to things novelistically, and nothing else. As for philological convention, it views words quite differently. There are therefore many kinds of language, each doing things in its own way, each requiring a different discipline to produce, transmit, or record, each existing according to rules available only after much investigation.

These special languages are the modern form of discourse:

> At the beginning of the nineteenth century, [words] . . . re-discovered their ancient, enigmatic density; though not in order to restore the curve of the word which had harbored them during the Renaissance, nor in order to mingle things in a circular system of signs. Once detached from representation, language has existed, right up to our own day, only in a dispersed way.[49]

The witnesses of this dispersion of language—who between them map the space possible for language to act in—are Nietzsche and Mallarmé, the first seeing language as wholly determined by history, by circumstance, by the individual using language at any given moment, by the terms of the speaker; the latter seeing language as pure Word, which "in its solitude, in its fragile vibration, in its nothingness, [is] the word itself—not the meaning of the word, but its enigmatic and precarious being." Therefore "the whole curiosity of our thought now resides in the question: What is language, how can we find a way around it in order to make it appear in itself, in all its plenitude?" And since language is situated between the two poles articulated by Nietzsche and Mallarmé, Foucault situates his work between them, there "to discover the vast play of of language contained once more within a single space." The imperative is to make language and if possible discourse once again appear within that field of invisible dispersion that, since the end of the classical age, language has become.

The passages I have been quoting from *The Order of Things* are, I think, typical of the earlier Foucault. To make language and discourse reappear is, we note, a task for the intellectual historian; even the disappearance of discourse is not described as anything but an archeological event so to speak. All of Foucault's work since *The Order of Things* has been a rephrasing of the question "how, when, and why did language and discourse disappear," turning it into a political and methodological question of the greatest urgency. By replying that discourse did not simply disappear but became invisible, Foucault begins his answer to the question, adding that if it disappeared it did so for political reasons, the better for it to be used to practice a more insidious form of control over its material and its subjects. Thus the very effectiveness of modern discourse is linked to its invisibility and to its rarity. Each discourse, each language—of psychiatry, penology, criticism, history—is to some degree a jargon, but it is also a language of control and a set of institutions within the culture over what it constitutes as its special domain.

The major shift that occurred in Foucault's thought in 1968—after *Les Mots* and before *L'Archéologie*—is the one reconceiving the problem of language not in an ontological but in a political or ethical framework, the Nietzschean framework. Thus we can best understand language by making discourse visible not as a historical task but as a political one. The model ought then to be strategic and not finally a linguistic one.

The longer I continue, the more it seems to me that the formation of discourses and the genealogy of knowledge need to be analysed, not in terms of types of consciousness, modes of perception and forms of ideology, but in terms of tactics and strategies of power. Tactics and strategies deployed through implantations, distributions, demarcations, control of territories and organisations of domains which could well make up a sort of geopolitics where my preoccupations would link up with your methods. One theme I would like to study in the next few years is that of the army as a matrix of organisation and knowledge;

one would need to study the history of the fortress, the "campaign," the "movement," the colony, the territory. Geography must indeed necessarily lie at the heart of my concerns.[50]

Between the power of the dominant culture, on the one hand, and the impersonal system of disciplines and methods (*savoir*), on the other, stands the critic. We are back now to my first formulation and, I hope, to a greater awareness of what such a *geopolitical* position as Foucault's might mean. Whereas Derrida's theory of textuality brings criticism to bear on a signifier freed from any obligation to a transcendental signified, Foucault's theories move criticism from a consideration of the signifier to a description of the signifier's place, a place rarely innocent, dimensionless, or without the affirmative authority of discursive discipline. In other words, Foucault is concerned with describing the force by which the signifier occupies a place, so that in *Discipline and Punish* he can show how penal discourse in its turn was able to assign felons to their places in the structural, administrative, psychological, and moral economy of the prison's panoptic architecture. Yet Foucault does not seem interested in investigating why this development took place.

Now the value of such a strictly and perhaps even deterministically historical view of the signifier in the text is not only that it is historical. Its greatest value is that it awakens criticism to the recognition that a signifier occupying a place, signifying in a place, is—rather than represents—an act of will with ascertainable political and intellectual consequences, and an act fulfilling a strategic desire to administer and comprehend a vast and detailed field of material. The nonrecognition of this act of will is what one finds the deconstructor not recognizing, thereby denying or overlooking it. Thus by virtue of Foucault's criticism we were able to understand culture as a body of disciplines having the effective force of knowledge linked systematically, but by no means immediately or even intentionally, to power. Foucault's lesson is that, while in one sense he complements Derrida's work, in another he takes a step in a new direction. The vision of history he has been propounding takes as its starting point the great, largely unexplained shift in knowledge at the end of the eighteenth century, from a despotic to a strategic articulation of power and knowledge. The range of specialized disciplines that arose in the nineteenth century were disciplines of detail by which the human subject was first collapsed into swarming detail, then accummulated and assimilated by sciences designed to make the detail functional as well as docile. From that evolved a diffuse administrative apparatus for maintaining order and opportunities for study. Thus what Foucault proposes is, I think, a criticism potentially as catholic and detailed in its descriptions as the knowledge it seems to understand. For Foucault, where there is knowledge and discourse, there must criticism also be, to reveal the exact places—and displacements—of the text, thereby to see the text as a process signifying an effective historical will to be present, an effective desire to be a text and to be a position taken.

Though severed consciously from cultural hegemony, this sort of criticism is a meaningful activity within the culture. It releases critics from the barriers imposed formalistically on them by departments, disciplines, moribund traditions of scholarship, and opens up the possibility of an aggressive study of the realities of discourse, which at least since the eighteenth century has ruled the production of texts. Yet despite the extraordinary worldliness of this work, Foucault takes a curiously passive and sterile view not so much of the uses of power, but of how and why power is gained, used, and held onto. This is the most dangerous consequence of his disagreement with Marxism, and its result is the least convincing aspect of his work. Even if one fully agrees with his view that what he calls the microphysics of power "is exercised rather than possessed, that it is not the 'privilege', acquired or preserved, of the dominant class, but the overall effect of its strategic positions,"[51] the notions of class struggle and of class itself cannot therefore be reduced—along with the forcible taking of state power, economic domination, imperialist war, dependency relationships, resistances to power—to the status of superannuated nineteenth-century conceptions of political economy. However else power may be a kind of indirect bureaucratic discipline and control, there are ascertainable changes stemming from who holds power and who dominates whom.

In short, power can be made analogous neither to a spider's web without the spider nor to a smoothly functioning flow diagram; a great deal of power remains in such coarse items as the relationships and tensions between rulers and ruled, wealth and privilege, monopolies of coercion, and the central state apparatus. In understandably wishing to avoid the crude notion that power is unmediated domination, Foucault more or less eliminates the central dialectic of opposed forces that still underlies modern society, despite the apparently perfected methods of "technotronic" control and seemingly nonideological efficiency that seem to govern everything. What one misses in

Foucault is something resembling Gramsci's analyses of hegemony, historical blocks, ensembles of relationship done from the perspective of an engaged political worker for whom the fascinated description of exercised power is never a substitute for trying to change power relationships within society.

To a great extent, Foucault's flawed attitude to power derives from his insufficiently developed attention to the problem of historical change. Though he is right in believing that history cannot be studied exclusively as a series of violent discontinuities (produced by wars, revolutions, great men), he surely underestimates such motive forces in history as profit, ambition, ideas, the sheer love of power, and he does not seem interested in the fact that history is not a homogenous French-speaking territory but a complex interaction between uneven economies, societies, and ideologies. Much of what he has studied in his work makes greatest sense not as an ethnocentric model of how power is exercised in modern society, but as part of a much larger picture involving, for example, the relationship between Europe and the rest of the world. He seems unaware of the extent to which the ideas of discourse and discipline are assertively European and how, along with the use of discipline to employ masses of detail (and human beings), discipline was used also to administer, study, and reconstruct—then subsequently to occupy, rule, and exploit—almost the whole of the non-European world.

The simple fact is that between 1815, when European powers were in occupation of approximately 35 percent of the earth's surface, and 1918, when that occupation had extended to 85 percent of the earth's surface, discursive power increased accordingly. One can very well ask what makes it possible for Marx, Carlyle, Disraeli, Flaubert, Nerval, Renan, Quinet, Schlegel, Hugo, Rückert, Cuvier, and Bopp all to employ the word "Oriental" in order to designate essentially the same corporate phenomenon, despite the enormous ideological and political differences between them.[52] The principal reason for this was the constitution of a geographical entity called the Orient, and its study called Orientalism, that realized a very important component of the European will to domination over the non-European world, and made it possible to create not only an orderly discipline of study but a set of institutions, a latent vocabulary (or a set of enunciative possibilities), a subject matter, and finally—as it emerges in Hobson's and Cromer's writing at the end of the nineteenth century—subject races. The parallel between Foucault's carceral system and Orientalism is striking. For as a discourse Orientalism, like all discourses, is "composed of signs; but what they [discourses] do is more than use these signs to designate things. It is this 'more' that renders them irreducible to the language and to speech. It is this 'more' that we must reveal and describe."[53]

In the discourse and discipline of Orientalism, this "more" is the power to make philological distinctions between "our" Indo-European languages and "their" Semitic languages—with a clear evaluation of one over the other expressed in the distinction—and the institutional force to make statements about the Oriental mentality, the inscrutable Oriental, the unreliable and degenerate Oriental, and so forth. Moreover, the enormous growth in Oriental professorships all across Europe, the mushrooming of books on the Orient (for the Near East alone, estimated at 60,000 books between 1850 and 1950), the springing up of Oriental societies, Oriental exploration funds, geographical societies, and finally the creation of a vast colonial bureaucracy, government departments, and research facilities—all this is far "more" than the Orient to which the sign "Orient" seems innocently to refer. Above all, Orientalism had the epistemological and ontological power virtually of life and death, or presence and absence, over everything and everybody designated as "Oriental." In 1833 Lamartine visited the Orient and wrote his experiences in his *Voyage en Orient*, which contains the record of many discussions with natives, of visits to their villages, of meals taken with them. Yet how is one to explain his statement in the "Résumé politique" attached to the *Voyage* that the Orient is a territory without inhabitants, real citizens, or frontiers—except by the force of Orientalist discourse assigning Europeans and Orientals to ontologically different categories of existence and nonexistence. Like all discourses, Orientalism is correlated with juridical discourse—say Emer de Vattel's theory about legally inhabited territories and the right of Europeans to expropriate and render useful territory that had no real inhabitants. Orientalism is correlated with biological discourse, not only Cuvier's typology of races but Geoffroy de Saint Hilaire's teratology of the study of deviant, monstrous types; with pedagogical discipline, of the sort expressed in Macaulay's 1835 minute on Indian education.

Most of all it is as a discipline of detail, and indeed as a theory of Oriental detail by which every minute aspect of Oriental life testified to an Oriental essence it expressed, that Orientalism had the eminence, the power, and the affirmative authority over the Orient that it had. In Orientalism the accumulation of texts, by which enormous caches of Oriental manuscripts were transported westward to be made the subject of remarkably detailed study, and more and more during the nineteenth century the accumulation of human bodies, by which the Oriental races and their territories were acquired for European suzerainty: these two went hand in hand, as did the discipline of their management. If we believe that Kipling's jingoistic White Man was simply an aberration, then we cannot see the extent to which the White Man was merely one expression of a science—like that of penal discipline—whose goal was to understand and to confine non-Whites in their status as non-Whites, in order to make the notion of Whiteness clearer, purer, and stronger. If we cannot see this, then we will be seeing a good deal less than every major European intellectual and cultural figure of the nineteenth century saw, from Chateaubriand, Hugo, and the other early romantics, to Arnold, Newman, Mill, T. E. Lawrence, Forster, Barrés, William Robertson Smith, Valéry, and countless others. What they saw was the necessary, valuable connection between the affirmative powers of European discourse—the European signifier, if you like—and constant exercises of strength with everything designated as non-European, or non-White. I am referring of course to the hegemony of an imperialistic culture. But what is alarming is the extent to which much contemporary criticism that is lost in the "abyssmal" element of textuality seems utterly blind to the impressive constitutive authority in textuality of such power as that of a broadly based *cultural* discipline, in Foucault's sense of the word.

I can conclude on a more positive note. I have been implying that criticism is or ought to be a cognitive activity and that it is a form of knowledge. I now find myself saying that if, as Foucault has tried to show, all knowledge is contentious, then criticism, as activity and knowledge, ought to be openly contentious too. My interest is to reinvest critical discourse with something more than contemplative effort or an appreciative technical reading method for texts as undecidable objects. There is obviously no substitute for reading well, and that of course criticism, in one of the branches exemplified by Derrida, does try to do and does try to teach. My sense of the contemporary critical consciousness as represented by Derrida and Foucault is that, having initially detached itself from the dominant culture, having thereafter adopted a situation and responsible adversary position for itself, this consciousness should begin its meaningful cognitive activity in attempting to account for, and rationally to discover and know, the force of statements in texts: statements and texts, that is, as doing something more or less effective, with consequences that criticism should make it its business to reveal. For if texts are a form of impressive human activity, they must be correlated with (not reduced to) other forms of impressive, perhaps even repressive, and displacing forms of human activity.

Criticism cannot assume that its province is merely the text, not even the great literary text. It must see itself, with other discourse, inhabiting a much contested cultural space, in which what has counted in the continuity and transmission of knowledge has been the signifier, as an event that has left lasting traces upon the human subject. Once we take that view, then literature as an isolated paddock in the oroad cultural field disappears, and with it too the harmless rhetoric of self-delighting humanism. Instead we will be able, I think, to read and write with a sense of the greater stake in historical and political effectiveness that literary as well as all other texts have had.

10

Traveling Theory

L IKE people and schools of criticism, ideas and theories travel—from person to person, from situation to situation, from one period to another. Cultural and intellectual life are usually nourished and often sustained by this circulation of ideas, and whether it takes the form of acknowledged or unconscious influence, creative borrowing, or wholesale appropriation, the movement of ideas and theories from one place to another is both a fact of life and a usefully enabling condition of intellectual activity. Having said that, however, one should go on to specify the kinds of movement that are possible, in order to ask whether by virtue of having moved from one place and time to another an idea or a theory gains or loses in strength, and whether a theory in one historical period and national culture becomes altogether different for another period or situation. There are particularly interesting cases of ideas and theories that move from one culture to another, as when so-called Eastern ideas about transcendence were imported into Europe during the early nineteenth century, or when certain European ideas about society were translated into traditional Eastern societies during the later nineteenth century. Such movement into a new environment is never unimpeded. It necessarily involves processes of representation and institutionalization different from those at the point of origin. This complicates any account of the transplantation, transference, circulation, and commerce of theories and ideas.

There is, however, a discernible and recurrent pattern to the movement itself, three or four stages common to the way any theory or idea travels.

First, there is a point of origin, or what seems like one, a set of initial circumstances in which the idea came to birth or entered discourse. Second, there is a distance transversed, a passage through the pressure of various contexts as the idea moves from an earlier point to another time and place where it will come into a new prominence. Third, there is a set of conditions—call them conditions of acceptance or, as an inevitable part of acceptance, resistances—which then confronts the transplanted theory or idea, making possible its introduction or toleration, however alien it might appear to be. Fourth, the now full (or partly) accommodated (or incorporated) idea is to some extent transformed by its new uses, its new position in a new time and place.

It is obvious that any satisfactorily full account of these stages would be an enormous task. But though I have neither the intention nor the capacity to undertake it, it seemed worthwhile to describe the problem in a sketchy and general way so that I might at length and in detail address a particularly topical, highly limited aspect of it. Of course the discrepancy between the general problem and any particular analysis is itself deserving of comment. To prefer a local, detailed analysis of how one theory travels from one situation to another is also to betray some fundamental uncertainty about specifying or delimiting the field to which any one theory or idea might belong. Notice, for example, that when professional students of literature now use words like "theory" and "criticism" it is not assumed that they must or should confine their interests to literary theory or literary criticism. The distinction between one discipline and another has been blurred precisely because fields like literature and literary study are no longer considered to be as all-encompassing or as synoptic as, until recently, they once were. Although some polemical scholars of literature can still, nonetheless, attack others for not being literary enough, or for not understanding (as who should not?) that literature, unlike other forms of writing, is essentially mimetic, essentially moral, and essentially humanistic, the resultant controversies are themselves evidence of the fact that no consensus exists on how the outer limits of the word "literature" or the word "criticism" are to be determined. Several decades ago, literary history and systematic theory, of the kind pioneered by Northrop Frye, promised an orderly, inhabitable, and hospitable structure in which, for instance, it might be demonstrated that the mythos of summer could be transformed definably into the mythos of autumn. "The primal human act in Frye's system," writes Frank Lentricchia in *After the New Criticism*, quoting Frye's *The Educated Imagination*, "and a model for all human acts, is an 'informative,' creative act which transforms a world that is merely objective, set over against us, in which we 'feel lonely and frightened and unwanted' into a home."[1] But most literary scholars find themselves now, once again, out in the cold. Similarly, the history of ideas and comparative literature, two disciplines closely associated with the study of literature and literary criticism, do not routinely authorize in their practitioners quite the same Goethean sense of a concert of all literatures and ideas.

In all these instances the specific situation or locality of a particular intellectual task seems uneasily distant from, and only rhetorically assisted by, the legendary wholeness, coherence, and integrity of the general field to which one professionally belongs. There seem to be too many interruptions, too many distractions, too many irregularities interfering with the homogeneous space supposedly holding scholars together. The division of intellectual labor, which has meant increasing specialization, further erodes any direct apprehension one might have of a whole field of literature and literary study; conversely, the invasion of literary discourse by the *outré* jargons of semiotics, post-structuralism, and Lacanian psychoanalysis has distended the literary critical universe almost beyond recognition. In short, there seems nothing inherently literary about the study of what have traditionally been considered literary texts, no literariness that might prevent a contemporary literary critic from having recourse to psychoanalysis, sociology, or linguistics. Convention, historical custom, and appeals to the protocols of humanism and traditional scholarship are of course regularly introduced as evidence of the field's enduring integrity, but more and more these seem to be rhetorical strategies in a debate about what literature and literary criticism ought to be rather than convincing definitions of what in fact they are.

Geoffrey Hartman has nicely dramatized the predicament by analyzing the tensions and vacillations governing contemporary critical activity. Today's criticism, he says, is radically revisionist. "Freed from a neoclassical decorum that, over the space of three centuries, created an enlightened but also over-accommodated prose," criticism is undergoing what he calls "an *extraordinary language* movement."[2] At times this language movement is so eccentric as to approach, even challenge, literature itself; at others it obsesses the critics who are borne along its currents toward the ideal of a completely "pure" language. At still others, the critic discovers that "writing is a labyrinth, a topological puzzle and textual crossword; the reader, for his part, must lose himself for a while in a hermeneutic 'infinitizing' that makes all rules of closure appear arbitrary."[3] Whether these alternatives for critical discourse are called terrorist or "a new type of sublimity or an emerging transcendentalism,"[4] there remains the need for the humanist critic both to define more clearly "the special province of the humanities" and to materialize (rather than spiritualize) the culture in which we live.[5] Nevertheless, Hartman concludes, we are in transition, which is perhaps another way of saying (as he does in his title *Criticism in the Wilderness*) that criticism today is alone, at loose ends, unlucky, pathetic, and playful because its realm defies closure and certainty.

Hartman's exuberance—for his attitude is at bottom exuberant—ought to be qualified by Richard Ohmann's devastating observation in *English in America* that English departments represent "a moderately successful effort by professors to obtain some benefits of capitalism while avoiding its risks and, yet, a reluctance to acknowledge any link between how we do our work and the way the larger society is run."[6] This is not to say that literary academics present a united ideological front, even though Ohmann is right *grosso modo*. The divisions within cannot be reduced simply to a conflict between old and new critics or to a monolithically dominant antimimetic ideology, as Gerald Graff very misleadingly argues. Consider that, if we restrict the number of debated issues to four, many of those in the vanguard on one issue are very conservative on another:

(1) Criticism as scholarship, humanism, a "servant" to the text, mimetic in its bias, versus criticism as revisionism and as itself a form of literature.

(2) The role of critic as teacher and good reader: safeguarding the canon versus subverting it or creating a new one. Most Yale critics are revisionist with respect to (1), conservative with respect to (2).

(3) Criticism as detached from the political/social world versus criticism as a form of philosophical metaphysics, psychoanalysis, linguistics, or any of these, versus criticism as actually having to do with such "contaminated" fields of history, the media, and economic systems. Here the distributional spread is much wider than in (1) or (2).

(4) Criticism as a criticism of language (language as negative theology, as private dogma, as ahistorical metaphysics) versus criticism as an analysis of the language of institutions versus criticism as a study of relationships between language and nonlinguistic things.

In the absence of an enclosing domain called literature, with clear outer boundaries, there is no longer an authorized or official position for the literary critic. But neither is there some new sovereign method, some new critical technology compelling allegiance and intellectual loyalty. Instead there is a babel of arguments for the limitlessness of all interpretation; of ideologies that proclaim the eternal yet determinate value of literature or "the humanities"; for all systems that in asserting their capacity to perform essentially self-confirming tasks allow for no counterfactual evidence. You can call such a situation pluralistic if you like or, if you have a taste for the melodramatic, you can call it desperate. For my part, I prefer to see it as an opportunity for remaining skeptical and critical, succumbing neither to dogmatism nor to sulky gloom.

Hence the specific problem of what happens to a theory when it moves from one place to another proposes itself as an interesting topic of investigation. For if fields like literature or the history of ideas have no intrinsically enclosing limits, and if, conversely, no one methodology is imposable upon what is an essentially heterogeneous and open area of activity—the writing and interpretation of texts—it is wise to raise the questions of theory and of criticism in ways suitable to the situation in which we find ourselves. At the outset, this means an historical approach. Assume therefore that, as a result of specific historical circumstances, a theory or idea pertaining to those circumstances arises. What happens to it when, in different circumstances and for new reasons, it is used again and, in still more different circumstances, again? What can this tell us about theory itself—its limits, its possibilities, its inherent problems—and what can it suggest to us about the relationship between theory and criticism, on the one hand, and society and culture on the other? The pertinence of these questions will be apparent at a time when theoretical activity seems both intense and eclectic, when the relationship between social reality and a dominant yet hermetic critical discourse seems hard to determine, and when, for all of these reasons and some of the ones I have just referred to, it is futile to prescribe theoretical programs for contemporary criticism.

Lukacs' *History and Class Consciousness* (1923) is justly famous for its analysis of the phenomenon of reification, a universal fate afflicting all aspects of life in an era dominated by commodity fetishism. Since, as Lukacs argues, capitalism is the most articulated and quantitatively detailed of all economic systems, what it imposes upon human life and labor under its rule has the consequence of radically transforming everything human, flowing, processual, organic, and connected into disconnected and "alienated" objects, items, lifeless atoms. In such a situation, then, time sheds its qualitative, variable, flowing nature; it freezes into an exactly delimited, quantifiable continuum filled with quantifiable "things" (the reified, mechanically objectified "performance" of the worker, wholly separated from his total human personality): in short, it becomes space. In this environment where time is transformed into abstract, exactly measurable, physical space, an environment at once the cause and effect of the scientifically and mechanically fragmented and specialised production of the object of labour, the subjects of labour must likewise be rationally fragmented. On the one hand, the objectification of their labor-power into something opposed to their total personality (a process already accomplished with the sale of that labour-power as a commodity) is now made into the permanent ineluctable reality of their daily life. Here, too, the personality can do no more than look on helplessly while its own existence is reduced to an isolated particle and fed into an alien system. On the other hand, the mechanical disintegration of the process of production into its components also destroys those bonds that had bound individuals to a community in the days when production was still "organic." In this respect, too, mechanization makes of them isolated abstract atoms whose work no longer brings them together directly and organically; it becomes mediated to an increasing extent exclusively by the abstract laws of the mechanism which imprisons them.[7] If this picture of the public world is bleak, it is matched by Lukacs' description of what happens to intellect, "the subject" as he calls it. After an astonishingly brilliant account of the antinomies of classical philosophy from Descartes to Kant to Fichte, Hegel, and Marx, in which he shows the increasing retreat of the subject into passive, privatized contemplation, gradually more and more divorced from the overwhelmingly fragmented realities of modern industrial life, Lukacs then depicts modern bourgeois thought as being at an impasse, transfixed and paralyzed into terminal passivity. The science that it produces is based on mere fact gathering; the rational forms of understanding therefore cannot cope with the irrationality of physical *données*, and when efforts are made to compel "the facts" to submit to "system," their fragmentation and endlessly atomized *thereness* either destroy the system or turn the mind into a passive register of discrete objects.

There is, however, one form of experience that concretely represents the essence of reification as well as its limitation: crisis. If capitalism is the embodiment in economic terms of reification, then everything, including human beings, ought to be quantified and given a market value. This of course is what Lukacs means when he speaks of articulation under capitalism, which he sometimes characterizes as if it were a gigantic itemized list. In principle nothing—no object, person, place, or time—is left out, since everything can be calculated. But there are moments when "the qualitative existence of the 'things' that lead their lives beyond the purview of economics as misunderstood and neglected things-in-themselves, as use-values [Lukacs here refers to such "irrational" things as sentiment, passion, chance] suddenly becomes the decisive factor (suddenly, that is, for reified, rational thought). Or rather: these 'laws' fail to function and the reified mind is unable to perceive a pattern in this 'chaos.' "[8] At such a moment, then, mind or "subject" has its one opportunity to escape reification: by thinking through what it is that causes reality to appear to be only a collection of objects and economic *données.* And the very act of looking for process behind what appears to be eternally given and objectified, makes it possible for the mind to know itself as subject and not as a lifeless object, then to go beyond empirical reality into a putative realm of possibility. When instead of inexplicable shortage of bread you can imagine the human work and, subsequently, the human beings who produced the bread but are no longer doing so because there is a bakers' strike, you are well on your way to knowing that crisis is comprehensible because process is comprehensible; and if process is comprehensible, so too is some sense of the social whole created by human labor. Crisis, in short, is converted into criticism of the status quo: the bakers are on strike for a reason, the crisis can be explained, the system does not work infallibly, the subject has just demonstrated its victory over ossified objective forms.

Lukacs puts all of this in terms of the subject-object relationship, and proper justice to his argument requires that it be followed to the point where he shows that reconciliation between subject and object will be possible. Yet even he admits that such an eventuality is very far into the future. Nevertheless, he is certain that no such future is attainable without the transformation of passive, contemplative consciousness into active, critical consciousness. In positing a world of human agency outside the reach of reification, the critical consciousness (the consciousness that is given rise to by crisis) becomes genuinely aware of its power "unceasingly to overthrow the objective forms that shape the life of man."[9] Consciousness goes beyond empirical givens and comprehends, without actually experiencing, history, totality, and society as a whole—precisely those unities that reification had both concealed and denied. At bottom, class consciousness is thought thinking its way through fragmentation to unity; it is also thought aware of its own subjectivity as something active, energetic, and, in a profound sense, poetic. (Here we should note that several years before *History and Class Consciousness* Lukacs had argued that only in the realm of the aesthetic could the limitations of pure theory and of pure ethics be overcome; by the former he meant a scientific theory whose very objectivity symbolized its own reification, its thralldom to objects, by the latter a Kantian subjectivity out of touch with everything except its own selfhood. Only the Aesthetic rendered the meaning of experience as lived experience—*der Sinn des Erlebnisses*—in an autonomous form: subject and object are thereby made one.[10])

Now because it rises above objects, consciousness enters a realm of potentiality, that is, of theoretical possibility. The special urgency of Lukacs' account of this is that he is describing something rather far from a mere escape into fantasy. Consciousness attaining self-consciousness is no Emma Bovary pretending to be a lady in Yonville. The direct pressures of capitalist quantification, that relentless cataloguing of everything on earth, continue to be felt, according to Lukacs; the only thing that changes is that the mind recognizes a class of beings like itself who have the power to think generally, to take in facts but to organize them in groups, to recognize processes and tendencies where reification only allows evidence of lifeless atoms. Class consciousness therefore begins in critical consciousness. Classes are not real the way trees and houses are real; they are imputable by consciousness, using its powers to posit ideal types in which with other beings it finds itself. Classes are the result of an insurrectionary act by which consciousness refuses to be confined to the world of objects, which is where it had been confined in the capitalist scheme of things.

Consciousness has moved from the world of objects into the world of theory. Although Lukacs describes it as only a young German philosopher could describe it—in language bristling with more metaphysics and abstractions than even I have been using—we must not forget that he is performing an act of political insurgency. To attain to theory is to threaten reification, as well as the entire bourgeois system on which reification depends, with destruction. But, he assures his readers, this destruction "is no single unrepeatable tearing of the veil that masks the process [of reification] but the unbroken alternation of ossification, contradiction and movement."[11] Theory, in fine, is won as the result of a process that begins when consciousness first experiences its own terrible ossification in the general reification of all things under capitalism; then when consciousness generalizes (or classes) itself as something opposed to other objects, and feels itself as a contradiction to (or crisis within) objectification, there emerges a consciousness of change in the status quo; finally, moving toward freedom and fulfillment, consciousness looks ahead to complete self-realization, which is of course the revolutionary process stretching forward in time, perceivable now only as theory or projection.

This is very heady stuff indeed. I have summarized it in order to set down some small indication of how powerfully responsive Lukacs' ideas about theory were to the political order he described with such formidable gravity and dread. Theory for him was what consciousness produced, not as an avoidance of reality but as a revolutionary will completely committed to worldliness and change. According to Lukacs, the proletariat's consciousness represented the theoretical antithesis to capitalism; as Merleau-Ponty and others have said, Lukacs' proletariat can by no means be identified with a ragged collection of grimy-faced Hungarian laborers. The proletariat was his figure for consciousness defying reification, mind asserting its powers over mere matter, consciousness claiming its theoretical right to posit a better world outside the world of simple objects. And since class consciousness derives from workers working and being aware of themselves that way, theory must never lose touch with its origins in politics, society, and economics.

This, then, is Lukacs describing his ideas about theory—and of course his theory of sociohistorical change—in the early twenties. Consider now Lukacs' disciple and student, Lucien Goldmann, whose *Le Dieu caché* (1955) was one of the first and certainly among the most impressive attempts to put Lukacs' theories to practical scholarly use. In Goldmann's study of Pascal and Racine, class consciousness has been changed to "vision du monde," something that is not an immediate, but a collective consciousness expressed in the work of certain highly gifted writers.[12] But this is not all. Goldmann says that these writers derive their world vision from determinate political and economic circumstances common to members of their group; yet the world vision itself is premised not so much on empirical detail as on a human faith that a reality exists "which goes beyond them as individuals and finds its expression in their work."[13] Writing as a politically committed scholar (and not like Lukacs as a directly involved militant), Goldmann then argues that because Pascal and Racine were privileged writers, their work can be constituted into a significant whole by a process of dialectical theorizing, in which part is related to assumed whole, assumed whole verified empirically by empirical evidence. Thus individual texts are seen to express a world vision; second, the world vision constitutes the whole intellectual and social life of the group (the Port-Royal Jansenists); third, the thoughts and feelings of the group are an expression of their economic and social life.[14] In all this—and Goldmann argues with exemplary brilliance and subtlety—the theoretical enterprise, an interpretive circle, is a demonstration of coherence: between part and whole, between world vision and texts in their smallest detail, between a determinate social reality and the writings of particularly gifted members of a group. In other words, theory is the researcher's domain, the place in which disparate, apparently disconnected things are brought together in perfect correspondence: economics, political process, the individual writer, a series of texts.

Goldmann's indebtedness to Lukacs is clear, although it has not been noted that what in Lukacs is an ironic discrepancy between theoretical consciousness and reified reality is transformed and localized by Goldmann into a tragic correspondence between world vision and the unfortunate class situation of the *noblesse de robe* in late seventeenth-century France. Whereas Lukacs' class consciousness defies, indeed is an insurgent against, the capitalist order, Goldmann's tragic vision is perfectly, absolutely expressed by the works of Pascal and Racine. True, the tragic vision is not directly expressed by those writers, and true also that it requires an extraordinarily complex dialectical style of research for the modern researcher to draw forth the correspondence between world vision and empirical detail; the fact nevertheless is that Goldmann's adaptation of Lukacs removes from theory its insurrectionary role. The sheer existence of class, or theoretical, consciousness for Lukacs is enough to suggest to him the projected overthrow of objective forms. For Goldmann an awareness of class or group consciousness is first of all a scholarly imperative, and then—in the works of highly privileged writers—the expression of a tragically limited social situation. Lukacs' *zugerechnetes Bewusstsein* (imputed consciousness) is an unverifiable, yet absolutely prior theoretical necessity if one is to effect a change in social reality; in Goldmann's version of it, admittedly limited to an acutely circumscribed situation, theory and consciousness are expressed in the Pascalian wager upon an unseen and silent god, the *deus absconditus;* they are also expressed for Goldmann the scientific researcher, as he calls himself, in the theoretical correspondence between text and political reality. Or to put the matter in another way, for Lukacs theory originates as a kind of irreducible dissonance between mind and object, whereas for Goldmann theory is the homological relationship that can be seen to exist between individual part and coherent whole.

The difference between the two versions of Lukacs' theory of theory is evident enough: Lukacs writes as a participant in a struggle (the Hungarian Soviet Republic of 1919), Goldmann as an expatriate historian at the Sorbonne. From one point of view we can say that Goldmann's adaptation of Lukacs degrades theory, lowers it in importance, domesticates it somewhat to the exigencies of a doctoral dissertation in Paris. I do not think, however, that degradation here has a moral implication, but rather (as one of its secondary meanings suggests) that degradation conveys the lowering of color, the greater degree of distance, the loss of immediate force that occurs when Goldmann's notions of consciousness and theory are compared with the meaning and role intended by Lukacs for theory. Nor do I want to suggest that there is something inherently wrong about Goldmann's conversion of insurrectionary, radically adversarial consciousness into an accommodating consciousness of correspondence and homology. It is just that the situation has changed sufficiently for the degradation to have occurred, although there is no doubt that Goldmann's reading of Lukacs mutes the latter's almost apocalyptic version of consciousness.

We have become so accustomed to hearing that all borrowings, readings, and interpretations are misreadings and misinterpretations that we are likely to consider the Lukacs-Goldmann episode as just another bit of evidence that everyone, even Marxists, misreads and misinterprets. I find such a conclusion completely unsatisfying. It implies, first of all, that the only possible alternative to slavish copying is creative misreading and that no intermediate possibility exists. Second, when it is elevated to a general principle, the idea that all reading is misreading is fundamentally an abrogation of the critic's responsibility. It is never enough for a critic taking the idea of criticism seriously simply to say that interpretation is misinterpretation or that borrowings inevitably involve misreadings. Quite the contrary: it seems to me perfectly possible to judge misreadings (as they occur) as part of a historical transfer of ideas and theories from one setting to another. Lukacs wrote *for* as well as *in* a situation that produced ideas about consciousness and theory that are very different from the ideas produced by Goldmann in his situation. To call Goldmann's work a misreading of Lukacs', and then to go on immediately to relate that misreading to a general theory of interpretation as misinterpretation, is to pay no critical attention to history and to situation, both of which play an important determining role in changing Lukacs' ideas into Goldmann's. The Hungary of 1919 and post–World War II Paris are two quite different environments. To the degree that Lukacs and Goldmann are read carefully, then to that precise degree we can understand the critical change—in time and in place—that occurs between one writer and another, both of whom depend on theory to accomplish a particular job of intellectual work. I see no need here to resort to the theory of limitless intertextuality as an Archimedean point outside the two situations. The particular voyage from Hungary to Paris, with all that entails, seems compelling enough, adequate enough for critical scrutiny, unless we want to give up critical consciousness for critical hermeticism.

In measuring Lukacs and Goldmann against each other, then, we are also recognizing the extent to which theory is a response to a specific social and historical situation of which an intellectual occasion is a part. Thus what is insurrectionary consciousness in one instance becomes tragic vision in another, for reasons that are elucidated when the situations in Budapest and Paris are seriously compared. I do not wish to suggest that Budapest and Paris determined the kinds of theories produced by Lukacs and Goldmann. I do mean that "Budapest" and "Paris" are irreducibly first conditions, and they provide limits and apply pressures to which each writer, given his own gifts, predilections, and interests, responds.

Let us now take Lukacs, or rather Lukacs as used by Goldmann, a step further: the use made of Goldmann by Raymond Williams. Brought up in the tradition of Cambridge English studies, trained in the techniques of Leavis and Richards, Williams was formed as a literary scholar who had no use whatever for theory. He speaks rather poignantly of how intellectuals educated as he was could use "a separate and self-defining language" that made a fetish of minute, concrete particulars; this meant that the intellectuals could approach power but speak antiseptically only of microcosm, profess not to understand reification, and to speak instead of the objective correlative, not to know mediation although they knew catharsis.[15] Williams tells us that Goldmann came to Cambridge in 1970 and gave two lectures there. This visit, according to Williams in the moving commemorative essay he wrote about Goldmann after his death, was a major event. It introduced Cambridge to theory, Williams claims, understood and employed as it had been by thinkers trained in the major

Continental tradition. Goldmann induced in Williams an appreciation of Lukacs' contribution to our understanding of how, in an era of
"the dominance of economic activity over all other forms of human
activity," reification was both a false objectivity so far as knowledge
was concerned and a deformation thoroughly penetrating life and
consciousness more than any other form. Williams continues:

> The idea of totality was then a critical weapon against this pre-
> cise deformation; indeed, against capitalism itself. And yet this
> was not idealism—an assertion of the primacy of other values.
> On the contrary, just as the deformation could be understood, at
> its roots, only by historical analysis of a particular kind of econ-
> omy, so the attempt to overcome and surpass it lay not in iso-
> lated witness or in separated activity but in practical work to
> find, assert and to establish more human social ends in more
> human and political and economic means.[16]

Once again Lukacs' thought—in this instance the avowedly revolutionary idea of totality—has been tamed somewhat. Without wishing
in any way to belittle the importance of what Lukacs' ideas (via
Goldmann) did for the moribund state of English studies in late
twentieth-century Cambridge, I think it needs to be said that those
ideas were originally formulated in order to do more than shake up a
few professors of literature. This is an obvious, not to say easy, point.
What is more interesting, however, is that because Cambridge is not
revolutionary Budapest, because Williams is not the militant Lukacs,
because Williams is a reflective critic—this is crucial—rather than a
committed revolutionary, he can see the limits of a theory that begins
as a liberating idea but can become a trap of its own.

> At the most practical level it was easy for me to agree [with
> Lukacs' theory of totality as a response to reification]. But then
> the whole point of thinking in terms of a totality is the realiza-
> tion that we are part of it; that our own consciousness, our work,
> our methods, are then critically at stake. And in the particular
> field of literary analysis there was this obvious difficulty: that
> most of the work we had to look at was the product of just this
> work of reified consciousness, so that *what looked like the meth-
> odological breakthrough might become, quite quickly, the meth-
> odological trap.* I cannot yet say this finally about Lukacs, since
> I still don't have access to all his work; but in some of it, at least,
> *the major insights of History and Class-Consciousness,* which
> he has now partly disavowed, *do not get translated into critical
> practice* [Williams refers here to Lukacs' later, much cruder

work on European realism] and certain cruder operations—essentially still those of base and superstructure—keep reappearing. *I still read Goldmann collaboratively and critically asking the same question,* for I am sure the practice of totality is still for any of us, at any time, profoundly and even obviously difficult.[17]

This is an admirable passage. Even though Williams says nothing about the lamentable repetitiveness of Goldmann's later work, it is important that as a critic who has learned from someone else's theory he should be able to see the theory's limitations, especially the fact that a breakthrough can become a trap, if it is used uncritically, repetitively, limitlessly. What he means, I think, is that once an idea gains currency because it is clearly effective and powerful, there is every likelihood that during its peregrinations it will be reduced, codified, and institutionalized. Lukacs' remarkably complex exposition of the phenomenon of reification indeed did turn into a simple reflection theory; to a degree of course, and Williams is too decently elegaic to say it about a recently dead old friend, it did become this sort of idea in Goldmann's hands. Homology is, after all, a refined version of the old Second International base-and-superstructure model.

Beyond the specific reminder of what could happen to a vanguard theory, Williams' ruminations enable us to make another observation about theory as it develops out of a situation, begins to be used, travels, and gains wide acceptance. For if reification-and-totality (to turn Lukacs' theory now into a shorthand phrase for easy reference) can become a reductionist implement, there is no reason why it could not become too inclusive, too ceaselessly active and expanding a habit of mind. That is, if a theory can move down, so to speak, become a dogmatic reduction of its original version, it can also move up into a sort of bad infinity, which—in the case of reification-and-totality—is the direction intended by Lukacs himself. To speak of the unceasing overthrow of objective forms, and to speak as he does in the essay on class consciousness, of how the logical end of overcoming reification is the self-annihilation of the revolutionary class itself, means that Lukacs had pushed his theory farther forward and upward, unacceptably (in my opinion). The contradiction inherent in this theory—and perhaps in most theories that develop as responses to the need for movement and change—is that it risks becoming a theoretical overstatement, a theoretical parody of the situation it was formulated originally to remedy or overcome. To prescribe "an *unbroken* alternation of ossification, contradiction and movement" toward totality as a theoretical remedy for reification is in a sense to substitute one unchanging formula for another. To say of theory and theoretical consciousness, as Lukacs does, that they intervene in reification and introduce process is not carefully enough to calculate, and allow for, the details and the resistances offered by an intransigent, reified reality to theoretical consciousness. For all the brilliance of his account of reification, for all the care he takes with it, Lukacs is unable to see how even under capitalism reification itself cannot be totally dominant—unless, of course, he is prepared to allow something that theoretical totality (his insurrectional instrument for overcoming reification) says is impossible, namely, that totality in the form of totally dominant reification is theoretically possible under capitalism. For if reification is totally dominant, how then can Lukacs explain his own work as an alternative form of thought under the sway of reification?

Perhaps all this is too fussy and hermetic. Nevertheless, it seems to me that however far away in time and place Williams may be from the fiery rebelliousness of the early Lukacs, there is an extraordinary virtue to the distance, even the coldness of his critical reflections on Lukacs and Goldmann, to both of whom he is otherwise so intellectually cordial. He takes from both men a sophisticated theoretical awareness of the issues involved in connecting literature to society, as he puts it in his best single theoretical essay, "Base and Superstructure in Marxist Cultural Theory." The terminology provided by Marxist aesthetic theory for mapping the peculiarly uneven and complicated field lying between base and superstructure is generally inadequate, and then Williams goes on to do work that embodies *his* critical version of the original theory. He puts this version very well, I think, in *Politics and Letters:* "however dominant a social system may be, the very meaning of its domination involves a limitation or selection of the activities it covers, so that by definition it cannot exhaust all social experience, which therefore always potentially contains space for alternative acts and alternative intentions which are not yet articulated as a social institution or even project."[18] *The Country and the City* records both the limits and the reactive alternatives to dominance, as in the case of John Clare, whose work "marks the end of pastoral poetry [as a systematic convention for describing the English countryside] in the very shock of its collision with actual country experience." Clare's very existence as a poet was threatened by the removal of an acceptable social order from the customary landscape idealized by Jonson and Thomson; hence Clare's turning—as an alternative not yet fully realized and not yet completely subdued by the inhuman relaionships that obtained under the system of market exploitation—to "the green language of the new Nature," that is, the Nature to be celebrated in a new way by the great Romantics.[19]

There is no minimizing the fact that Williams is an important critic because of his gifts and his insights. But I am convinced it would be wrong to underestimate the role in his mature writings played by what I have been alluding to as borrowed, or traveling, theory. For borrow we certainly must if we are to elude the constraints of our immediate intellectual environment. Theory we certainly need, for all sorts of reasons that would be too tedious to rehearse here. What we also need over and above theory, however, is the critical recognition that there is no theory capable of covering, closing off, predicting all the situations in which it might be useful. This is another way of saying, as Williams does, that no social or intellectual system can be so dominant as to be unlimited in its strength. Williams therefore has the critical recognition, and uses it consciously to qualify, shape, and refine his borrowings from Lukacs and Goldmann, although we should hasten to add that it does not make him infallible or any less liable to exaggeration and error for having it. But unless theory is unanswerable, either through its successes or its failures, to the essential untidiness, the essential unmasterable presence that constitutes a large part of historical and social situations (and this applies equally to theory that derives from somewhere else or theory that is "original"), then theory becomes an ideological trap. It transfixes both its users and what it is used on. Criticism would no longer be possible.

Theory, in short, can never be complete, just as one's interest in everyday life is never exhausted by simulacra, models, or theoretical abstracts of it. Of course one derives pleasure from actually making evidence fit or work in a theoretical scheme, and of course it is ridiculously foolish to aruge that "the facts" or "the great texts" do not require any theoretical framework or methodology to be appreciated or read properly. No reading is neutral or innocent, and by the same token every text and every reader is to some extent the product of a theoretical standpoint, however implicit or unconscious such a standpoint may be. I am arguing, however, that we distinguish theory from critical consciousness by saying that the latter is a sort of spatial sense, a sort of measuring faculty for locating or situating theory, and this means that theory has to be grasped in the place and the time out of which it emerges as a part of that time, working in and for it, responding to it; then, consequently, that first place can be measured against subsequent places where the theory turns up for use. The critical consciousness is awareness of the differences between situations, awareness too of the fact that no system or theory exhausts the situation out of which it emerges or to which it is transported. And, above all, critical consciousness is awareness of the resistances to theory, reactions to it elicited by those concrete experiences or interpretations with which it is in conflict. Indeed I would go as far as saying that it is the critic's job to provide resistances to theory, to open it up toward historical reality, toward society, toward human needs and interests, to point up those concrete instances drawn from everyday reality that lie outside or just beyond the interpretive area necessarily designated in advance and thereafter circumscribed by every theory.

Much of this is illustrated if we compare Lukacs and Williams on the one hand with Goldmann on the other. I have already said that Williams is conscious of what he calls a methodological trap. Lukacs, for his part, shows in his career as a theorist (if not in the fully fledged theory itself) a profound awareness of the necessity to move from hermetic aestheticism (*Die Seele und die Formen, Die Theorie des Romans*) toward the actual world of power and institutions. By contrast, Goldmann is enmeshed in the homological finality that his writing, brilliantly and persuasively in the case of *Le Dieu caché*, demonstrates. Theoretical closure, like social convention or cultural dogma, is anathema to critical consciousness, which loses its profession when it loses its active sense of an open world in which its faculties must be exercised. One of the best lessons of that is to be found in Lentricchia's powerful *After the New Criticism*, a wholly persuasive account of what he calls "the currently paralyzed debates" of contemporary literary theory.[20] In instance after instance he demonstrates the impoverishment and rarefication that overtake any theory relatively untested by and unexposed to the complex enfolding of the social world, which is never a merely complaisant context to be used for the enactment of theoretical situations. (As an antidote to the bareness afflicting the American situation, there is in Fredric Jameson's *The Political Unconscious* an extremely useful account of three "semantic horizons" to be figured in dialectically by the interpreter as parts of the decoding process, which he also calls "the cultural mode of production."[21])

Yet we must be aware that the social reality I have been alluding to is no less susceptible to theoretical overtotalization, even when, as I shall be showing in the case of Foucault, extremely powerful historical scholarship moves itself out from the archive toward the world of power and institutions, toward precisely those resistances to theory ignored and elided by most formalistic theory—deconstruction, semiotics, Lacanian psychoanalysis, the Althusserian Marxism attacked by E. P. Thompson.[22] Foucault's work is most challenging because he is rightly considered to be an exemplary opponent of ahistorical, asocial formalism. But he too, I believe, falls victim to the systematic degradation of theory in ways that his newest disciples consider to be evidence that he has not succumbed to hermeticism.

Foucault is a paradox. His career presents his contemporary audience with an extraordinarily compelling trajectory whose culmination, most recently, has been the announcement made by him, and on his behalf by his disciples, that his real theme is the relationship between knowledge and power. Thanks to the brilliance of his theoretical and practical performances, *pouvoir* and *savoir* have provided his readers (it would be churlish not to mention myself; but see also Jacques Donzelot's *La Police des familles*) with a conceptual apparatus for the analysis of instrumental discourses that stands in stark contrast to the fairly arid metaphysics produced habitually by the students of his major philosophical competitors. Yet Foucault's earliest work was in many ways remarkably unconscious of its own theoretical force. Reread *Histoire de la folie* after *Surveiller et punir* and you will be struck with how uncannily prescient the early work is of the later; and yet you will also be struck that even when Foucault deals with *renfermement* (confinement), his obsessive theme, in discussing asylums and hospitals, power is never referred to explicitly. Neither for that matter is *volonté*, will. *Les Mots et les choses* might be excused for the same neglect of power, on the grounds that the subject of Foucault's inquiry was intellectual, not institutional history. In *The Archeology of Knowledge* there are intimations here and there that Foucault is beginning to approach power through a number of abstractions, surrogates for it: thus he refers to such things as acceptability, accumulation, preservation, and formation that are ascribed to the making and the functioning of statements, discourses, and archives; yet he does so without spending any time on what might be the common source of their strength within institutions or fields of knowledge or society itself.

Foucault's theory of power—to which I shall restrict myself here—derives from his attempt to analyze working systems of confinement from the inside, systems whose functioning depends equally on the continuity of institutions as on the proliferation of justifying technical ideologies for the institutions. These ideologies are his discourses and disciplines. In his concrete presentation of local situations in which such power and such knowledge are deployed, Foucault has no peer, and what he has done is remarkably interesting by any standard. As he says in *Surveiller et punir*, for power to work it must be able to manage, control, and even create detail: the more detail, the more real power, management breeding manageable units, which in turn breed a more detailed, a more finely controlling knowledge. Prisons, he says in that memorable passage, are factories for producing delinquency, and delinquency is the raw material for disciplinary discourses.

With descriptions and particularized observations of this sort I have no trouble. It is when Foucault's own language becomes general (when he moves his analyses of power from the detail to society as a whole) that the methodological breakthrough becomes the theoretical trap. Interestingly, this is slightly more evident when Foucault's theory is transported from France and planted in the work of his overseas disciples. Recently, for example, he has been celebrated by Ian Hacking as a kind of hard-headed alternative to the too backward and forward-looking "Romantic" Marxists (which Marxists? all Marxists?), and as a ruthlessly anarchistic opponent of Noam Chomsky, who is described inappropriately as "a marvelously sane liberal reformer."[23] Other writers, who quite rightly see Foucault's discussions of power as a refreshing window opened on to the real world of politics and society, uncritically misread his pronouncements as the latest thing about social reality.[24] There is no doubt that Foucault's work is indeed an important alternative to the ahistorical formalism with which he has been conducting an implicit debate, and there is great merit to his view that as a specialized intellectual (as opposed to a universal intellectual)[25] he and others like him can wage small-scale guerrilla warfare against some repressive institutions, and against "silence" and "secrecy."

But all that is quite another thing from accepting Foucault's view in *History of Sexuality* that "power is everywhere" along with all that such a vastly simplified view entails.[26] For one, as I have said, Foucault's eagerness not to fall into Marxist economism causes him to obliterate the role of classes, the role of economics, the role of insurgency and rebellion in the societies he discusses. Let us suppose that prisons, schools, armies, and factories were, as he says, disciplinary factories in nineteenth-century France (since he talks almost exclusively about France), and that panoptic rule dominated them all.

What resistances were there to the disciplinary order and why, as Nicos Poulantzas has so trenchantly argued in *State, Power, Social-ism,* does Foucault never discuss the resistances that always end up dominated by the system he describes? The facts are more compli-cated of course, as any good historian of the rise of the modern state can demonstrate. Moreover, Poulantzas continues, even if we accept the view that power is essentially rational, that it is not held by any-one but is strategic, dispositional, effective, that, as *Discipline and Punish* claims, it invests all areas of society, is it correct to conclude, as Foucault does, that power is exhausted in its use?[27] Is it not simply wrong, Poulantzas asks, to say that power is not *based* anywhere and that struggles and exploitation—both terms left out of Foucault's analyses—do not occur?[28] The problem is that Foucault's use of the term *pouvoir* moves around too much, swallowing up every obstacle in its path (resistances to it, the class and economic bases that refresh and fuel it, the reserves it builds up), obliterating change and mysti-fying its microphysical sovereignty.[29] A symptom of how overblown Foucault's conception of power can become when it travels too far is Hacking's statement that "nobody knows this knowledge; no one yields this power." Surely this is going to extremes in order to prove that Foucault is not a simple-minded follower of Marx.

In fact, Foucault's theory of power is a Spinozist conception, which has captivated not only Foucault himself but many of his read-ers who wish to go beyond Left optimism and Right pessimism so as to justify political quietism with sophisticated intellectualism, at the same time wishing to appear realistic, in touch with the world of power and reality, as well as historical and antiformalistic in their bias. The trouble is that Foucault's theory has drawn a circle around itself, constituting a unique territory in which Foucault has impri-soned himself and others with him. It is certainly wrong to say, with Hacking, that hope, optimism, and pessimism are shown by Foucault to be mere satellites of the idea of a transcendental, enduring subject, since empirically we experience and act according to those things daily without reference to any such irrelevant "subject." There is after all a sensible difference between Hope and hope, just as there is between the Logos and words: we must not let Foucault get away with confusing them with each other, nor with letting us forget that history does not get made without work, intention, resistance, effort, or conflict, and that none of these things is silently absorbable into micronetworks of power.

There is a more important criticism to be made of Foucault's theory of power, and it has been made most tellingly by Chomsky. Unfortunately most of Foucault's new readers in the United States seem not to know of the exchange that took place between them several years ago on Dutch television[30], nor of Chomsky's succinct critique of Foucault contained in *Language and Responsibility*. Both men agreed on the necessity of opposing repression, a position Foucault has since found it more difficult to take unequivocally. Yet for Chomsky the sociopolitical battle had to be waged with two tasks in mind: one, "to imagine a future society that conforms to the exigencies of human nature as best we understand them; the other to analyze the nature of power and oppression in our present societies."[31] Foucault assented to the second without in any way accepting the first. According to him, any future societies that we might imagine now "are only the inventions of our civilization and result from our class system." Not only would imagining a future society ruled according to justice be limited by false consciousness, it would also be too utopian to project for anyone like Foucault who believes that "the idea of justice in itself is an idea which in effect has been invented and put to work in different societies as an instrument of a certain political and economic power or as a weapon against that power."[32] This is a perfect instance of Foucault's unwillingness to take seriously his own ideas about resistances to power. If power oppresses and controls and manipulates, then everything that resists it is not morally equal to power, is not neutrally and simply a weapon against that power. Resistance cannot equally be an adversarial alternative to power and a dependent function of it, except in some metaphysical, ultimately trivial sense. Even if the distinction is hard to draw, there is a distinction to be made—as, for example, Chomsky does when he says that he would give his support to an oppressed proletariat if as a class it made justice the goal of its struggle.

The disturbing circularity of Foucault's theory of power is a form of theoretical overtotalization superficially more difficult to resist because, unlike many others, it is formulated, reformulated, and borrowed for use in what seem to be historically documented situations. But note that Foucault's history is ultimately textual, or rather textualized; its mode is one for which Borges would have an affinity. Gramsci, on the other hand, would find it uncongenial. He would certainly appreciate the fineness of Foucault's archeologies, but would find it odd that they make not even a nominal allowance for emergent movements, and none for revolutions, counterhegemony, or historical blocks. In human history there is always something beyond the reach of dominating systems, no matter how deeply they saturate society, and this is obviously what makes change possible, limits power in Foucault's sense, and hobbles the theory of that power. One could not imagine Foucault undertaking a sustained analysis of powerfully contested political issues, nor, like Chomsky himself and writers like John Berger, would Foucault commit himself to descriptions of power and oppression with some intention of alleviating human suffering, pain, or betrayed hope.

It may seem an abrupt conclusion to reach, but the kinds of theory I have been discussing can quite easily become cultural dogma. Appropriated to schools or institutions, they quickly acquire the status of authority within the cultural group, guild, or affiliative family. Though of course they are to be distinguished from grosser forms of cultural dogma like racism and nationalism, they are insidious in that their original provenance—their history of adversarial, oppositional derivation—dulls the critical consciousness, convincing it that a once insurgent theory is still insurgent, lively, responsive to history. Left to its own specialists and acolytes, so to speak, theory tends to have walls erected around itself, but this does not mean that critics should either ignore theory or look despairingly around for newer varieties. To measure the distance between theory then and now, there and here, to record the encounter of theory with resistances to it, to move skeptically in the broader political world where such things as the humanities or the great classics ought to be seen as small provinces of the human venture, to map the territory covered by all the techniques of dissemination, communication, and interpretation, to preserve some modest (perhaps shrinking) belief in noncoercive human community: if these are not imperatives, they do at least seem to be attractive alternatives. And what is critical consciousness at bottom if not an unstoppable predilection for alternatives?

11

Raymond Schwab and the
Romance of Ideas

POET, biographer, man of letters, novelist, editor, translator, and scholar, Raymond Schwab is not known (to most
of the standard Anglo-American authorities on the Romantic movement, for example), and none of his works has been translated into
English. For a man whose interests observed no national boundaries
and whose capacities were deeply transnational, this is a depressing
irony. He was born in Nancy in 1884 and died in Paris in 1956. The
little that is easily discovered about his life and personality comes
from three issues of *Mercure de France*, where some of his hitherto
unpublished poetry and his memoirs appeared, along with reminis-
cences written by his friends.[1] He seems to have been a quiet and
rather modest man who spent most of his life in the service of letters.
For a few years (1936–1940), he edited with Guy Lavaud a journal
devoted to poetry, which was called *Yggdrasill;* its catholicity of interests and openness to currents in poetry other than those either European or fashionable were noteworthy. Schwab leaves behind the
impression that he had the tastes of a fastidious man and that he was
intensely meditative by nature and withdrawn in his habits, with a
kind of powerful, yet muted, religious sense that would cause him to
translate the Psalms or write an epic poem on Nimrod without his
necessarily having been committed to an organized faith.

In many ways Schwab resembles Borges, if not also a character in
one of Borges' *Ficciones.* When he dealt with literature, he would
produce books about little-known figures such as Elémir Bourges;
when asked to write a preface to a French translation of the *Thousand and One Nights,* he would write instead a three-hundred-page
work on Antoine Galland, a late seventeenth-century personality

who was the *Nights'* first French translator. We are reminded of Borges' interest in such odd figures as John Wilkins and G. K. Chesterton, who benefited from the rather surprising seriousness displayed in his studies of them, since unknown books and shadowy writers do not often command this kind of attention. Both Schwab and Borges reveal a fundamental personal reticence married to an almost Mallarmean idea of The Book—the quest for it, its life, the gentleness and calm heroism to be found in it despite the almost unthinkable effort expended on its behalf. One always has a sense in Schwab, as of course in Borges, of a sort of library of humanity slowly being discovered, walked into, and described, but valued less for its ponderous classics than for its surprising eccentrics.

Endless detail is the mark of Schwab's major scholarly work, of which *La Renaissance orientale* is the greatest achievement.[2] The underlying theme of this work is the European experience of the Orient, which is in turn based on the human need for absorbing the "foreign" and "different." To his description of this experience, Schwab brings a rare gift for dealing with very concentrated and meticulously gathered detail. In Schwab's view, the Orient, however *outré* it may at first seem, is a complement to the Occident, and vice-versa. The vision, as one admirer of Schwab has put it, is that of an integral humanism.[3] Its style—its verbal idiom as well as its angle of vision—is both subtle and difficult, since Schwab manages always to depict a phenomenon as it is in itself and as something that affected many lives over a long period of time. He is up to the painstaking effort required to document the cultural interchanges between Orient and Occident. But he can also create fascinating nooks, sheltered from the broad outline of his large theme, in which new, often intimate spaces appear.

Two examples will suffice here. First, in describing the complex series of events just prior to Galland's leaving Paris for Turkey, Schwab also manages to reveal how these events are alluded to by Molière in *Le Bourgeois gentilhomme.*[4] Then, in *La Renaissance orientale*, Schwab demonstrates not only the curious symbiosis between the biological sciences and Indo-European linguistics but also the interplay of these forces in Cuvier's work, as well as its social effect in Parisian salons of the period. Whether it is a batch of seemingly transparent phrases spoken by M. Jourdain or Cuvier's presence in salons frequented by Balzac, Schwab unlocks an impressive range of allusions proving, for example, that parvenu chitchat conceals references to a crisis in relations between Louis XIV and the Turkish court, or that Balzac's understanding of Cuvier's scientific achievements was an aspect of cultural diffusion peculiar to Paris in the 1820s.

The detail in such instances is the detail of influence—how one writer or event bears on another. Like Erich Auerbach, however, Schwab is stingy about giving a theoretical explanation for what he does; like Auerbach discussing in *Mimesis* the classical notion of high and low literary styles, he is content to take on an almost ingenuously obvious motif, the influence of the Orient in the West, and to let the imprints of that motif appear in myriad places in a vast body of later literature. Indeed, the analogy with Auerbach and an even more compelling one with Ernst Robert Curtius press home Schwab's *philological* learning, especially its capacity for revealing how enormous unities (the Latin cultural *imperium*, the Orient) inform, live, and take textual body in consequent ages and cultures. For to a very great extent Schwab, like Auerbach, Curtius, and Borges, is possessed by the image of the text as a locus of human effort, a "text-ile" fertility gathering in cultural identity, disseminating human life everywhere in time and space as a result. The importance to Schwab of the Oriental Renaissance (the phrase is taken from Edgar Quinet's neglected work of 1832, *Le Génie des réligions*) is that, whereas the classical Renaissance immured European man within the confines of a self-sufficient Greco-Latin terrain, this later Renaissance deposited the whole world before him. The second Renaissance, as Schwab puts it in one of the compact generalities with which his work abounds, combined India and the Middle Ages and thereby displaced the centuries of Augustus and Louis XIV. The job of displacement was apportioned to the great capitals: Calcutta provided, London distributed, Paris filtered and generalized.

So profound and beneficent is Schwab's view of the Orient that one is doubtless more accurate in describing him as an *orienteur* rather than an *orientaliste*, a man more interested in a generous awareness than in detached classification.[5] Insofar as European awareness of the Orient can be said to have had an effect, Schwab believes it was a productive one, since Oriental influences in pre-Romantic and Romantic cultures are everywhere to be found. Yet two recent scholars of the Romantic period, Harold Bloom and W. J. Bate, have advanced the opposite thesis that all influence produced anxiety and a sense of inferiority and belatedness in the writers of the time for whom an uninfluenced originality was the highest (and least possible) goal. Schwab takes the position that Romanticism welcomed the Orient as an influence benefiting poetry, prose, science, and philosophy. So here already is one major theoretical and scholarly contribution of Schwab's work: influence in Romantic literature as enrichment and useful persistence rather than as diminishment and worrying presence. But again it is detail that Schwab plentifully sees and provides to back up the generalization. He seems to be saying that if so much work—which he chronicles with vertiginous minuteness—went willingly and consciously into the discovery of the Orient, then we must regard influence finally as supplying something that would otherwise be felt as burdensome absence. What results is not that violent contest among writers for time and space sketched by Bloom with such urgency, but rather an endless accommodation similar to the one Schwab sees in the Asian temperament, which does not contrast novelty with latecoming but instead sees all time as the poet's possession: "He repeats the same interwoven patterns endlessly, not to save time, but, on the contrary, precisely because he has so much time at his disposal that there is no danger of his using it up in necessarily transient little details."[6]

Schwab's, then, is a criticism of sympathetic cast. Dualities, opposition, polarities—as between Orient and Occident, one writer and another, one time and another—are converted in his writing into lines that are crisscrossing, it is true, but also drawing a vast human portrait. A year before his death, he mused that what was needed was a "History of Universal Poetry," but unfortunately he had not written it. For his part, he had attempted a physiognomy of literature as a step in that direction.[7] Always the human image dominates in Schwab's criticism, but what provokes its interest for us is that, when we perceive it, such an image is the writer's achievement, never his given. There are the details of human effort, then their organization, finally their total portrayal. In its attempt to appropriate and reproduce the subject of its study, Schwab's criticism belongs with that of Georges Poulet, Albert Beguin, Albert Thibaudet, Jean Starobinski, and others like them, whose patient and engaged imagination dominates the business of industrious fact gathering. Unlike all of them, however (except perhaps the Starobinski of *L'Invention de la liberté*), Schwab is continually guided by events, privileged historical moments, and large movements of ideas. For him, consciousness is a cultural affair, heavily laden with empirical experience in and of the world. Whether he is describing the rise of linguistics attendant upon the numerous discoveries made in Zend, Sanskrit, Semitic, or Indo-European, or the fabulously rich interlacing of Oriental themes in

English, French, German, and American writing, or even the precise data involved in scientific or artistic activity during the years between 1771 and roughly 1860, his work is always literally a treasure of insight and information. Most of all, it deepens our appreciation for a particular and extremely rare type of unhurried scholarship, whose role, I feel, is too infrequently examined by theorists of either criticism or literature.

Appearances notwithstanding, Schwab is no Taine or Lanson. Historical criticism for him is not science, even though facts must of course command respect. But man's history gets its impulses from the desire for truth, not simply from its establishment: History "teaches us that establishing truth is less important than making a particular truth desirable. What great inventor has ever found a new truth without first looking for it in the wrong place?"[8] Schwab wrote this about the early Orientalists, but it applies as well to his own work. The tremendous cultural drama with which all his scholarship was concerned is the struggle between either acquired or felt certainties (and not facts) that takes place both within a culture and between cultures. Reinforced by his own background, Schwab sees the Judeo-Christian component in Western culture as being forced to submit to the discovery of an earlier civilization; thus Indo-European linguistics rival the primacy of Hebraic society in the European mind. Later that mind will accommodate the discovery, making the world into a whole again. But the gripping drama of Orientalism, as Schwab puts it in the superb first thirty pages of *La Renaissance orientale,* is the debate it initiates about the meaning of "the primitive," how different worlds are seen as claimants to originality and genius, how the notions of civilization and savagery, beginning and end, ontology and teleology, undergo marked transformation in the years between 1770 and 1850: "At precisely the time when a craving for disagreement spread throughout Europe in a single crisis that arose from the wave of political revolutions, those countless Orientalisms that made up the fundamental dissonance in the West burst upon the scene (31)." His task therefore is to study the progress by which the West's image of the Orient passes from primitive to actual, that is, from disruptive *éblouissment incrédule* to *vénération condescendante.* There is a saddening impoverishment, obviously, from one image to the other. Yet so judicious and modulated is the rendering and so encyclopedic the scale that we feel the impoverishment less as sentiment than as a law of cultural change. From being a *bibliothèque ... privé de départements* (30), the Orient becomes a scholarly or ideological province: *les révélations glissent à la specialité* (131). Before 1800, Europe possessed *le monde du classé*, with Homer its first and final classical perfection; after 1800, a new secular world intrudes, the "dissident." Gone is the dependence on fables, traditions, and classics. Instead texts, sources, and sciences resting on difficult, tiring, and troublesome work thrust a strange new reality on the mind. Schwab's concern is how this occurs and how quickly even the novelty is transformed into orthodoxy.

A peculiar feature of Schwab's scholarship, however, is that he does not take explicit note of the sheer folly and derangement stirred up by the Orient in Europe. For, as a subject, the Oriental Renaissance is no less bizarre a current in the Romantic imagination than those currents documented by Mario Praz, and Schwab is no less equipped than Praz to comment on them. Yet he does not, even when he is recording in detail—for instance, the madness of Anquetil-Duperron's life, as he trekked through steamy jungles, enduring impossible physical hardships, unrecognized even as a scholar until his very last years. An "abnégation des érudits" is only partly useful as explanation for such men. What they saw and felt about the Orient in many cases literally took their minds, but Schwab is too concerned with demonstrating the humanistic symmetry between this Renaissance and the earlier one to care much for the crazy enthusiasms that could produce Beckford, Anquetil, Renan, or Rückert. Conversely, Schwab's Oriental Renaissance, while it avoids the disorienting aspects of the European experience in the East, also shuns the other great Romantic appetites for nature, the macabre, heightened consciousness, folk culture.

La Renaissance orientale is in fact the apogee of Schwab's scholarly career, although chronologically it stands more or less at its center. Just as its subject matter is the preparation for, the encounter with, then the absorption of the Orient by the West, so too it is already suggested by Schwab's earlier work as well as assumed by his later. I shall speak briefly here of a circle of historical and scholarly books and monographs surrounding *La Renaissance orientale*, a circle that must exclude the substantial body of his poetry, fiction, and translation. Schwab's alternation between linear, or genealogical, fidelity to his subject and his encompassing structural ambitions to show prefiguration, latency, refraction, metalepsis despite linear history—in short, the alternation in his method between filiation and affiliation as modes of perceiving and conducting cultural history.

Schwab's first book was the *Vie d'Anquetil-Duperron* (1934), a biography of the French scholar, theoretician of egalitarianism, and ecumenist of beliefs (Jansenist, Catholic, and Brahman), who between 1759 and 1761 transcribed and later translated the *Zend Evesta* while in Surat. This event for Schwab prefigures the spate of translated documents that would appear in the West during the Oriental Renaissance. Aside from an uncritical analysis of Anquetil's strange follies and enthusiasms, we find in the book an adumbration of most of Schwab's later motifs. First among them is "abnégation des érudits," selflessness during the quest for a manuscript, total commitment to the cause of learning: "What we would regard as calamities were in his eyes just one more chance to learn something."[9] Second is Schwab's penchant for telling detail, as when he describes the real conditions of shipboard life in the eighteenth century or when he chronicles Anquetil's relations with Grimm, Diderot, William Jones, and Herder. Third is Schwab's attention to the contest in the European mind between Oriental priority and biblical "history." Both Anquetil and Voltaire were interested in India and the Bible, but "the one to make the Bible more indisputable, the other to make it more unbelievable."[10] Schwab's epigrammatic flair will strengthen in his later work into passages of extraordinary poetic beauty.

Yet the motif to which Schwab's imagination is mostly dedicated is the life of images and forms in the human consciousness, which is always located existentially in a specific historical context and is never left to float freely here and there. Cultural history is drama because the ideas that derive from archetypal images, on the one hand, cause men to struggle in their behalf and, on the other, induce in men a kind of entranced passivity or even, as in Anquetil's case, a disconcerting appetite for all ideas or faiths, regardless of contradiction. Images are historical, quasi-natural artifacts created out of the interaction of *nous à tous*. Moreover, they are limited in number, so economic is the imagination and so powerful their range: Orient, Occident, community, the human, the Origin, the divine. Among themselves they form a matrix that generates cultural romance and adventure, expressed as ideas in conflict or in concert with each other. Although idea and image seem to move freely, they are first the product of men and the texts men make, then they become the focal points of institutions, societies, periods, and cultures. For images are constants in human experience; the ideas they legitimate take different forms and varying values. Here, in a passage from the *Vie*, Schwab illustrates the interplay that will dominate his writing: "He goes to find in Asia a scientific proof for the primacy of the Chosen People and for the genealogies of the Bible: instead it happened that his investigations soon led to criticism of the very texts which had hitherto been considered as revealed, a process Assyriology would subsequently prove irreversible."[11]

These ideas of necessity have a physical dimension, which conveys not only the alternation in culture between the limited and the limitless (as when Schwab talks of pre-Anquetil Orientalism: "l'exotisme sort du bibelot"[12]) but also the metamorphoses of notions of distance, time, relationship, memory, society, language, and individual effort:

> In 1759 Anquetil finished his translation of the *Avesta* at Surat; in 1786 that of the *Upanishads* in Paris—he had dug a channel between the hemispheres of human genius, freeing the old humanism of the Mediterranean basin. Less than fifty years earlier, his compatriots were asking how one could be Persian, when he taught them how to compare the monuments of the Persians to those of the Greeks. Before him, one looked for information on the remote past of our planet exclusively among the great Latin, Greek, Jewish, and Arabic writers. The Bible was regarded as a lonely rock, an aerolite. A universe in writing was available, but scarcely anyone seemed to suspect the immensity of these unknown lands. The realization began with his translation of the *Avesta*, and reached dizzying heights owing to the exploration in Central Asia of the languages that multiplied after Babel. Into our schools, up to that time limited to the narrow Greco-Latin heritage of the Renaissance, he interjected a vision of innumerable civilizations from ages past, of an infinity of literatures; moreover, the few European provinces were not the only places to have left their mark in history, "the right direction of the universe" ceased to be "fixed between northern Spain and northern Denmark in one direction and England and the borders of western Turkey in the other."[13]

Schwab's portrait of Anquetil goes very far in attempting to dispel "the obscurity that always hides the beginnings of discoveries."[14] Ultimately Schwab locates the beginning in a change of focus generated by a mysterious fragment of *Zend* that appears in Oxford; whereas "the scholars looked at the famous fragment of Oxford and then returned to their studies; Anquetil looked, and went to India."[15]

Although in the end Schwab was to voice some misgivings about the fetishized Western biographical mode, his next work, *La Vie d'Elémir Bourges*, is governed by the life-and-works framework. Bourges' dates are 1852 to 1925, and even though he was admired by a number of authors—among them Edmond Jaloux and Henri de Regnier—he will probably remain an obscure and minor writer.[16] The book on Bourges is the least distinguished of Schwab's output; one wonders why—except for the undeveloped personal connections hinted at between Bourges and Schwab—he took on this particular chore for his complementary thesis at the Sorbonne. Occasionally we get glimpses of the authentic Schwab, notably in his analyses of Bourges' eclecticism, as well as in his capacity for spiritual renovation within an otherwise episodic life. Nor should we overlook the fact that Schwab was in his early sixties when he undertook formal petitioning for the doctorate; like the subject of one of his own studies, he transformed himself from a man of letters into an academic scholar. The *méandre* of Schwab's work—that attractive expanding sweep within which occurred the very alchemy of ideas he was so expert at describing—allowed him the maximum of self-transformation with the maximum of coherence and intelligibility. So it is hard to believe that the inward-tending intensity of Bourges' life is not really Schwab's own, rendered wth comradely loyalty by Schwab as belonging to Bourges.

The contrast with *La Renaissance orientale*, which was to follow two years later in 1950, is immediately obvious. Its itemized subtitle reads like an encyclopedia, if not also like a doctoral program in East-West literatures (incidentally, the book was the principal thesis for Schwab's doctorate): "La decouverte du sanscrit—le siècle des écritures déchiffrées—l'avènement de l'humanisme intégral—grandes figures d'orientalistes—philosophies de l'histoire et des religions—sciences linguistiques et biologiques—l'hypothèse aryenne—l'inde dans la littérature occidentale—l'asie et le romantisme—Hindouisme et Christianité." This was followed in turn by two works, both of them logical outcomes. One, a two-hundred-page portion of the *Pléiade Histoire des Littératures,* was entitled "Domaine Oriental" and modestly subtitled "Le Porche oriental." Schwab here turned his attention to all that material whose effects he had so assiduously recorded earlier. It was as if Mallarmé had finally decided to write about the object whose absence had previously engaged him (for of course *La Renaissance orientale* is a work of scholarship written from a symbolic standpoint). Then posthumously, in 1964, the *Vie d'Antoine Galland* appeared. A less exciting work than the Anquetil-Duperron, it nevertheless complemented the earlier book, as well as rounding out Schwab's career, by treating the phenomenon of pre-Orientalism as style and literature at the moment before the Orient succumbed to Western science.[17]

A principal feature of all of Schwab's mature work is his interest in what he calls *le secondaire*, the smaller figures—the translators, the compilers, the scholars, whose unflagging effort make possible the major work of the Goethes, Hugos, and Schopenhauers. Thus the major cultural renaissance called "Oriental" by Schwab is inaugurated by the translations made by two practically forgotten men, Anquetil and Galland—the one opening the road to linguistic and scientific revolution in Europe, the other initiating the stylistic literary exoticism associated in Europe with Orientalism.[18] What clearly fascinates Schwab in such men is that they have none of the finish of the major literary or cultural figures, no easily discernible shape to their careers, no fully appreciated role in the larger movements of ideas they serve. Rather they are like fragments contributing, Schwab once said, to an imaginary manuscript whose will they obey[19] and whose totality resembles what Foucault would call the archive of a particular period. Moreover, their abnegation exerts a sort of inverse reaction in the conemporary scholar, who will not allow their modesty to disappear behind the major works or figures to which they have so obviously contributed. One of Schwab's successful restorations of justice occurs when he demonstrates how Galland's style, more than being a straight transcription of an Arabic original, in fact creates the ambiance within which the achievements of the *Princesse de Clèves* are made.

There is another aspect to Schwab's interest in the secondary: his appreciation, evident throughout the "Domaine Orientale," for the anonymity of Asiatic literature and the comparative disregard for strong ego-individuality it displays. How much this appreciation derives from Schwab's impressions of the literature he discusses and how much it is a real factor in it (since one is disappointed to discover that Schwab knows Oriental literature mainly through translation), I cannot tell. I suspect, though, that as he grew older he was searching for—and in his own way finding—other means of communicating cultural history, new unities sought by the exacting and original scholar, more effective generalizations. For his work starts the process that will bridge the gap between the polymathic historians—formalists all of them—such as Élie Faure, Henri Foçillon, and André Malraux and, to their left, the systematic verbal and institutional materialism of Foucault's archeological investigations. There is, of course, a political meaning to this kind of work, although Schwab himself rarely makes it explicit. Early in the "Domaine Orientale" he does say, however, that Europe, or Western culture, needs to be reminded that it, its achievements, and its heroes are at most a particular case in the transcendental generality of human culture at large.[20]

The avoidance of ethno- and anthropocentric attitudes dictates an interest in Oriental literature for its own sake. And the "Domaine Oriental," within the limits indicated above, is a marvelous prose-poetical meditation. At times the difficulty of Schwab's autumnal style is as demanding as R. P. Blackmur's. An example:

> De même que l'intarissable des rapsodes necessite des accommodements avec la cheville et le bouche-trou, le fulgurant des moralistes a pour posterité le formel des verroteries. C'est que les routines qui vont venir trouvent des lits tout faits dans ces gaines indéformables dont nous faisons honneur aux bonnes mnémo-techniques: car, par sa force même, cette rigide armature deviendra une cause d'affaisement et d'avilissement; la mémoire encourage l'imagination au moindre effort, les vertues de la répétition aboutissent à des excès: littératures de centons et de marqueteries dans l'Indes, en Perse, en Arabie; littératures de citations, d'allusions, d'anthologie, en Chine, au Japon, en Judée.
> [Just as the endlessness of the rhapsodes required compromises with useless words and stop-gap aids, so the fulminations of the moralists appear to posterity as partly worthless. This is because those things that become tradition are found in rigid forms which we then honor by turning into mnemotechnical devices; then by its very strength, this rigid armature becomes a source of weakness and degradation; memory discourages imagination, the virtues of repetition result in excess: the literature of the centos and the miscellanies in India, Persia, Arabia; the literature of citations, allusions, anthologies in China, Japan, Judea.][21]

A much worked-over prose such as this moves from large generalizations about Asiatic literature to nuanced instances of its variety. And, indeed, one of that literature's characteristics continuously asserted by Schwab is its exemplification of unity combined with infinite variations. The Bachelardian side of the "Domaine Oriental" demonstrates, for instance, how certain figures—shepherds, laborers, trees, voyagers, riders, walkers—give Asiatic literature its strong anchor in actuality. But it is in his consideration of aesthetic and verbal means that Schwab is most impressive. Starting from the notion that Oriental literatures view historical reality as something to be transformed into "mythical parabolas" by transgression, he investigates the predominance of the nominative mode in Oriental artistic grammar, the typology of rhythmic accent, the poetics of length, time as a meditative category, the use of *mot-germes* in the structure of rhythmically obsessive poetry, the interplay between infinite particularity and infinite generality, and the frequently employed festival mood in what he calls Oriental oceanic epics. All this, with a wide range of illustration, is subordinated to the proposition that Western literature attempts to turn all the means at its disposal into verbality and articulation, whereas Oriental literature seeks to transform everything, including words, into musicality.

The comparative rarefaction of the "Domaine Oriental" is a function of limitations imposed on Schwab by the collective general work to which he was contributing and by the unimaginable scope of the subject he was attempting to treat. No such limitations exist for him, however, in *La Renaissance orientale*. There he disposes of enormous amounts of detailed information, all of which is obviously treated at first hand. Read both as a prefiguration of and as an important complement to Foucault's *Les Mots et les choses*, the book is of great importance for the understanding of the great transformation in culture and learning that took place at the end of the eighteenth century and the beginning of the nineteenth. But where Foucault is rather ambiguous, that is, in assigning a particular set of causes to the change, Schwab is uncompromising and more unstinting with information supporting his case for the Orient-as-cause. Yet both men see how it was that the acquisition of knowledge, its institutions, and its currency determine not only cultural praxis generally but aesthetic praxis as well. For neither of these scholars is the hagiolatrous view of the "poet" sufficient for understanding literary production; nor is it their view that literary works can be studied in unheeding isolation from those conditions of verbal production and textual revolution that were more or less commanding all types of verbal activity during a given period. Schwab gives flesh to such of Foucault's statements as are unquestionably true—for instance, that near the beginning of the nineteenth century we have a period in which philology as well as biology was invented. Still more, Schwab demonstrates with inexhaustible patience what it means in Foucault's sense (formulated nineteen years after *La Renaissance orientale* in *The Archeology of Knowledge*) literally for an archive to be formed.

The agents and the heroes of cultural change and formation are scholars, according to Schwab, since cultural transformations take place because of men's appetites first to know and then to organize new things. The formula is perhaps simple, but it encompasses in *La Renaissance orientale* the reeducation of one continent by another. The work is divided into six main sections with dozens of smaller subdivisions and a conclusion. Just as its subject matter seems to have operated by dilation and contraction, so too does *La Renaissance orientale*. Book One identifies and asserts the phenomenon of the European awareness of the Orient—how geographical discovery, the prestige of Egyptology, and the various colonial missions to India fortified the Oriental challenge and the predisposition for dealing with it systematically in European society. Book Two details the movement of integration by which Europe received the Orient into the body of its scientific, institutional, and imaginative structures. This section includes the wave of Sanskrit studies that swept the Continent, with a base in Paris primarily, and the enthusiasm that, in Schwab's happy phrase, multiplied the world. In Book Three Schwab doubles back over the first two sections in order to show the active changes that take place in knowledge of the Orient. Central here is the metamorphosis in knowledge about language from being a religious issue to being a linguistic, scientific, and even a racial one. Accompanying this change is the one by which India acquired a whole figurative dimension in Western literature, from the pre-Orientalism of Milton and Dryden through the Lake Poets to Emerson, Whitman, the Transcendentalists, Richter, Novalis, Schelling, Rückert, Heine, Goethe, and of course Friedrich Schlegel.

Book Four is an elaborately constructed mosaic of "case histories," items of personal witness to Oriental effect drawn from forty or so lives. Schwab's interest is to give an intimate as well as a panoramic vision of reorientations in the work of scholars, scientists, critics, philosophers, and historians. Each portrait multiplies the complexity of Orientalism as a phenomenon of reception and transmission. The treatment of subject matter is scenic, which is to say that whether he examines Balzac, Cuvier, Jules Mohl, Sylvestre de Sacy, Ampère, Ozanam, or Fauriel, Schwab also represents the changing conceptions of time and space brought forward by each. Concurrently Schwab's antennae sort out shifts both in informal relations among people affected by the Orient (salons, paraoccult leagues, gossip factories) and among disciplines (linguistics, geology, biology). His investigations of discursive formations can show, for example, that the library, the museum, and the laboratory underwent internal modifications of paramount importance. Dotting Schwab's web are countless dates, names, journals, works, exhibitions, and events (for instance, the Nineveh exposition of 1846 in Paris) that give his narrative its gripping immediacy.

Books Five and Six lift all the myriad details of Orientalism from the plane of schools, scholars, academies, sciences, salons, and ideologies into the more discriminating dramas enacted within the careers of major imaginative writers. Book Five concerns French writers wrestling with the travail of creation as erudition impinges upon it: Lamartine, Hugo, Vigny, Michelet, Leconte de Lisle, Baudelaire. In addition, there is a section on what Schwab calls the "external Orient," the exotic East so influential in the work of Nerval, Gautier, and Flaubert. There are some especially fine comments on Flaubert's *roman archéologique,* whose matter is adopted from Quinet but whose tone flatly contradicts him. Book Six, "Detournements et Prolongements," focuses for the most part on German (among them Nietzsche, Wagner, and Schopenhauer) and Russian writers later in the century. Gobineau is to be found in these pages, along with his doctrine of the inequality of races. For, as his study nears its end, Schwab attends to the often pernicious divisions (Iran versus India, Aryans versus Semites, East versus West) that filter through the gigantic cultural mass created, during almost a century of "comparatism," by the Orientalist consciousness. These divisions are all traceable to the two *techniques spirituelles* facing each other from West to East. Thus:

> In the course of the nineteenth and twentieth centuries, three divergent tendencies developed: the strict school of the technicians—the philologists and philosophers—pursued their rigorous definitions and this served to eliminate the amateurs; the circle of ideologists and initiates grafted foreign influences onto local experience; and among the theologians the old missionary zeal reappeared, resulting in conflicting doubts between science and conscience. These three considerations explain the numerous and incessant contacts that grew up as never before among the different cultures. (475)

A concluding section, written in a complex and compact style, affirms that the Oriental Renaissance was fundamentally a phenomenon of difference, generating comparative techniques, whereas the first Renaissance was essentially assimilative in that it flattered Europe without disturbing Europe's self-affirming cultural centrality. Thus the second Renaissance multiplied, rather than decreased, the points of comparison and the techniques available to Western culture and its "invisible interlocutor," the more so because the later Renaissance was a verbal event, not a verbal and plastic one as the earlier one was. Orientalism made possible a "premier tour du monde parlé," which in turn initiated a linguistic theory of constantly receding and impossible origins. Standing between history and faith, such a theory was an event

> of consequence: the linguists believed they had found the answer to Babel, the poets expected the return of Eden; a passion for origins rose up in the hearts of men with each new archeological excavation, a little as if, with each new formula produced by a chemist, came the illusion that he had created new life: the postulate of a mother tongue produced linguistics by parthenogenesis. But the notion of the primitive could be confirmed only by distorting it; it could no longer be regarded as the starting point of history, but only as an increasingly lower point on its scale. It was movable and it therefore brought into play notions about change; history no longer provided a bulwark for all time, and certainly it could not provide a foundation. At the same time, both aesthetic canons and scientific theories renounced their claims to permanence; each worker in what had been the ancient verities felt that he had been betrayed if he pursued or acquired anything durable. The Romantic aesthetic movement, the biological dogma of evolution, the imperialism of language in the intellectual empires, these were now the new and important things that one could agree upon. In our day, the heirs of the poets of instability, the metaphysicians of the unconscious, and the doctors of myth, the most revolutionary manipulators of language and literature, speak of "free words" as of a "spiritual experience"—they are confirming without knowing it Burnouf's formula: *Nomina numina.* (497–498)

The coincidence of the advent of Romanticism and Orientalism in the West, as Schwab so carefully portrays it, gave the former its complex dimensions and led it to the reformulation of human limits—indeed, to that frontier where the unconscious and even the monstrous can claim the title of natural. Governing the coincidence are two laws: the "chance des époques" and the "mission des générations"(502). Therefore Schwab's conception of cultural history in *La Renaissance orientale* is cosmological because he sees himself as mediating between the two laws and their claims on cultural understanding.

In part systolic, in part diastolic (the images are Schwab's), *La Renaissance orientale* is a virtual education in the meaning of intellectual adventure, a species of vital detective work that neglects neither the material clues nor the higher speculations involved in formulating general observations. Schwab's monumentality lies in never letting us doubt that philology, as he uses it in the large Nietzschean sense and studies it in the history of philological archeology through which Oriental texts were brought into European knowledge and consciousness, is the study of texts as constantly worked-upon monuments, arranging and rearranging the culture's sense of its identity. Recent studies of Romantic literature—such as the work of Abrams, Bloom, Hartman, de Man—would find their inescapable underpinning in Schwab; for, as Romantic writing seems best understood as a prolonged investigation of language and poetic form constructing and deconstructing planes of meaning, Schwab's textual odyssey furnishes the necessary first material. If, after reading Schwab, there is not always an orderly path to be seen from words to forms, or from linguistic discovery to linguistic and aesthetic performance, the difficulty is that as students of literature we have not yet mastered the relationship between language in history and as art. Schwab argues that the relationship is crucial, but his method rests on the dramatization, presented complexly and encyclopedically, of a cultural encounter, one whose driving force originates in the love of words, the web of textuality, the society of learning and cultural appropriation. Thus, rather than reading Schwab as a failed theorist, one would do best, I think, to appreciate his great scholarly achievement as providing an occasion for theoretical orientation and self-examination.

Except allusively, what Schwab seems uninterested in are the economic, social, and political forces at work during the periods he studies. He is an expert at giving us the circumstances of the period, and these may include economic and social details. But the circumstantiality of his details is far from adding up to a dynamics of shaping forces acting within history. Thus he mentions that the first British Orientalists were medical men with a religious-missionary vocation. In addition, they were associated with commercial enterprise in the Indian colonies. Yet nowhere does he try to fuse these disparate circumstances into a political interpretation of British Orientalism. Similarly, he remarks here and there that the great Sanskrit wave and the epidemic of Sanskrit professorships throughout Europe were connected to a rapidly developing colonial trade and that the privileged status of Egyptology was derived from the Napoleonic adventure in the Middle East. Never does he coherently put forward a thesis about Orientalism as a science, attitude, or institution for the European military, political, and economic control of Eastern colonies.

The disparity that exists between what Schwab knows in the way in awesome detail and what he concludes from that detail is striking. It is not only that there are political conclusions he will not draw about the European ravaging of the Orient, but also that he chooses to see the East-West relationship as basically an equal one—whereas in fact of course it was no such thing. Sanskrit was a language that stood for a very high cultural value in Europe, but it was a dead language, far removed from the backwardness of modern Indians. The romantic imagination of European writers and scholars was saturated with Orientalism, but their Orientalism was gained at the expense of any sympathy they might have felt for the benighted natives they ruled. One of the faint lines of thought running through early nineteenth-century Orientalist scholarship—in the work of Abel Remusat, for example—is that Orientalist enthusiasm is often fueled by apathetic ignorance not only of the ancient Orient but especially of the modern Oriental. Read Schwab and you will not remember that Conrad's Kurtz is one of the chief products of Orientalism, or that race theory, scholarly antisemitism, and proto-Fascism are literal products of nineteenth-century Oriental philology. At the same time that Friedrich Schlegel, Wilhelm von Humboldt, and Ernest Renan were making their distinction between organic, lively, wonderful Indo-European and inorganic, agglutinative, uninteresting Semitic, they were also constructing the doxology of twentieth-century anti-Arab and anti-Jewish Orientalist scholarship. And all this was possible not because, as Schwab seems to have it, of a desire to know but because of a desire to possess and control.

That this is not merely an academic issue can be proved easily enough in the case of a topical instance. The contemporary academic Orientalist is the direct heir of the nineteenth-century Oriental philologist. On questions of immediate political moment he is looked to for perspective, information, and help as United States policy, say toward the Middle East, is being formulated. Yet because Orientalism is a political phenomenon that cannot be dissociated from European (white and male) colonialism, its modern progeny bear that ugly past on their back and in their work: they take the Oriental to be an essentially backward, primitive human in need of civilizing control. Their views as Orientalists, no matter how sophisticated the form in which they are put, are debased in the extreme. The October 1973 war in particular produced a whole mass of analyses, having for their background some almost incredibly atavistic pieties about the Arab mind, the Islamic mentality, and Arab society, all of them resting upon a wickedly simplified colonial view—openly racist in its more honest expressions—of the Oriental personality.

We should, then, not simply say that what is missing in Schwab is Foucault's sense of the material and political control exemplified in such systems of discourse as Orientalism; nor should we say exclusively that Schwab fails to take into account the sociopolitical aspect of ethnocentrism as it is represented by Orientalism. Rather we should draw attention to the problem of any encyclopedically conceived work like *La Renaissance orientale* whose virtues of scope and its author's devotion to circumstantial detail make it shy of tendentious political generalities. What Schwab's ambition principally entailed was the wish to assert the presence and importance of an Oriental Renaissance, and to do so with as much fidelity to the inner dynamics of the movement as possible. Despite Schwab's dialectic reconciliation of states through which the movement passed, he seems unwilling to have admitted that Orientalism had a problematic that everywhere touched strictly and systematically upon sociopolitical attitudes and actualities. Thus he raises in our minds the question of how one can write the best sort of scholarly cultural history and at the same time take account of power, money, and colonial conquest. Clearly neither a vulgar teleology nor a vulgar theory of immediate reflection answers the question. Too carefully engineered an avoidance, however, will not do either.

It seems often to be believed of rigorous scholarship in the humanities generally, and literature particularly, that scope and detail are achieved by staying clear of *Tendenz*-mongering. The converse is no less true: that brilliant theorizing comes without heed for circumstance, depth of knowledge, or range of concrete illustration. Perhaps it is in the nature of scholarship and of contemporary intellectual discipline to imagine work as doing one kind of specialized thing or another, to see a rational task as involving the circumstances either of the theorist or of the scholar or—to cite a modern case—of the popular journalist. The theorist sees himself as answering to his own circumstances: as Marxist, as structuralist, as New Critic, as phenomenologist. For the historian, what matters is the past "as it really was," in detail and in depth. One will object and say that no intellectual still works according to such unsubtle schema, but in practice the distinctions rigidly obtain. There is very little thought or time given understanding the dialectics of pressure and response in intellectual work, to impinging circumstantiality as it bears on the production of the critical or theoretical or historical work, or, finally, to the way in which one might manage to write accurately while also writing with some sense of the acute political matters that, as is the case with Orientalism, are relevant.

This is not the place to deal with these issues. Schwab's scholarship, by virtue of its excellence and interest, brings them to mind, as it does also the predicament of any scholar who does not feel it imperative to take an explicit political position toward what work he or she does or toward things in general. But then we come to the difficult problem of deciding what scholarly or even theoretical subject matter does or does not require an explicit political attitude or position in order for the subject to be dealt with fairly and accurately. Orientalism as a subject fairly screams out for an open understanding of its unpleasant ethnocentric and colonialist background. Yet I must say that I would prefer Schwab's apolitical scholarship to a noisy and correct but less historically thorough analysis of Orientalism—but obviously that is not the only alternative. Probably it is true to say that in work like Schwab's, aside from its documentary richness, one can at least point to and perhaps later supply the aspects of reality that are missing; in less impressive scholarship there are mainly attitudes (often dissolving history) that one can support or attack and little else.

But I am trying to be precise about how some scholarship, even as it excludes material, demonstrates the complexity both of what it includes and of what it does not include. There is no surgical way of prescribing just how much complexity and richness will suffice. Exemplary instances help, such as *La Renaissance orientale*, although they cannot be used as originals to be copied slavishly. We return, then, to such matters as patience, affection, enthusiasm; they seem to express themselves infectiously and implicitly in a scholar's work, however much his learning is formidable and impartial. If one sometimes chafes at the overwhelming simplicity in such phrases as "the Asiatic mind" (in "Domaine Oriental"), one is nonetheless always aware that Schwab's intention in generalizing is sympathetic, not aggressive or hostile. In short, Schwab's work, as much in its subject matter as in its methods, multiplies the opportunities for study and learning; it does not restrict them, even though Schwab's political quietism prevents him from making a stern judgment of Orientalism's cultural rapacity. That we can thereafter study Romanticism, or investigate the influence of academies upon nineteenth-century intellectual life, or analyze the relationship between philology and ideology—or all of those things and then many more—is why Schwab's romance of ideas itself deserves serious attention. And there is the sheer pleasure of its learning.

But "pleasure" used so blithely to characterize "learning" does not imply idle enjoyment. In Schwab there is never art analyzed or intellectual achievement limned without some corresponding sense of actual involvement in the world. Thus what his historical research discovers for him, and causes his readers actively to enjoy, is the real underpinning of cultural life, which is that a culture is not mere collection, or incorporation, by triumphant egos here and there, but rather that it is work performed by human agents—of society, social bonds, generational place, history. Here I employ the vocabulary used by Quentin Anderson to contrast two opposing views of literary culture and literary study.[22] Schwab is no believer in the efficacy of imperial selves. The point to make about him is that, for all the aesthetic, civilizing, transforming import of the cultural event he describes, and for all its political thinness as he renders it, he never assumes work to be the result of an individual's linear appetite to remake the world as simply as one makes a bookshelf. Culture for Schwab is less a pantheon than a lyceum, and a bustling one at that. To the contemporary critic, still uselessly transfixed by pure form and often gullibly enraptured with an uncircumstanced structural poetics, Schwab must be the antidote. He urges the network over the isolated cell. By no other perspective can cultures be understood as the systems they really are, systems over whose activity the individual critical historian holds the bridle of a vigilant historical understanding and a moral judgment.

12

Islam, Philology, and French Culture: Renan and Massignon

READERS of Matthew Arnold may recall the exasperated and embarrassed way in which his catalogues of English provincialism in culture are compared with the maturity and finish of either French or German culture. A marvelous passage of classical English by Addison quickly reveals its triteness of thought to Arnold when he compares it with Joubert; and the orotund periods of Jeremy Taylor seem by the same token awkward when put alongside the simple grandeur of Bossuet's sentences. England never had a literary academy to watch over cultural effort, Arnold says, and this has been a blessing for the freedom of atmosphere it produced in English intellectual life, but also a drawback because it could not prevent vulgarity and triteness.[1]

A particularly striking point is made by Arnold in this connection during a discussion of what he calls English "habits of wilfulness and eccentricity." His instance is John William Donaldson, a philologist who in 1854 attempted to argue that the scriptures really derived from a mysterious book called *Jashar*. Arnold says, "I, who am not an Orientalist, do not pretend to judge *Jashar*: but let the reader observe the form which a foreign Orientalist's judgement of it naturally takes. M. Renan calls it a *tentative malheureuse*, a failure in short; this it may or may not be; I am no judge. But he goes on: 'It is astonishing that a recent article . . . should have brought forward . . . a work like this, composed by a doctor of the University of Cambridge, and universally condemned by German critics.'" Arnold goes on to quote Renan again—this time on Charles Forster's *Mahometanism Unveiled* (1829), "which enchanted the English *révérends* to make out that Mahomet was the little horn of the he-goat that figures in the eighth chapter of Daniel, and that the Pope was the great horn." Arnold interprets Renan as also saying that since it is an Englishman who has written such things, one should not be surprised at any extravagance. Such assessments come "from a grave Orientalist, on his own subject, and they point to a real fact;—the absence, in this country, of any force of educated literary and scientific opinion, making aberrations . . . out of the question."[2]

The least provincial of nineteenth-century English writers himself, Arnold envied French culture for the opportunities it presented to learned people for making statements that were authoritative and central at the same time. About the two fields on which Arnold deferred to Renan, Oriental studies and philology, he had an especially good point. Even if according to Madame de Staël (in *De l'Allemagne*) France was very far behind Germany in wealth of academic institutions and methods of instruction, France was still considerably ahead of England. In his book *The Study of Language in England, 1780–1860* Hans van Aarsleff chronicles the extraordinary slowness with which England acquired the New Philology, a science that reigned unchallenged intellectually in France and Germany from the beginnings of the century. England was not only kept behind because of Horne Tooke's great influence, but the universities themselves provided no serious possibility for instruction in philology until well into the century. The result was that in England philology was confined to "dilettantes, mere antiquaries, and amateurs."[3] When Bopp's *Conjugationssystem* was reviewed in the *London Magazine* in 1820, the writer noted that "England, with all her peculiar advantages, has [not] done so much as was to be anticipated of her in this way." Any scholar seriously interested in philology seemed likely to have been more engaged in very peculiar research than in fulfilling a major national project of the sort represented by Renan in France, Rask in Denmark, Bopp in Germany. Aarsleff says that even as competent a philologist as Friedrich August Rosen—he had studied under Sacy in Paris and with Bopp in Berlin—could not have a proper career in England, where he had "to eke out an existence by writing articles on philology for the *Penny Cyclopedia.*"[4]

This state of affairs was roughly the same in specialized Oriental studies, which for its European success and prestige depended greatly on the systematic and organized advance of the New Philology. People like Donaldson and Forster seem interchangeable with fictional characters like George Eliot's Mr. Casaubon, who is engaged in the hopeless task of trying to compile a Key to all Mythology—in unconcerned ignorance of the latest in continental scholarship. And indeed it is worth remarking that when the Orient appears significantly in English literature of the early Victorian period it is usually as something eccentric and outré, never as important and central to organized European culture. Edward William Lane of course is the exception, but his work belonged at first not to the world of high but to the world of useful culture. If in 1856 George Eliot could say that all "our" civilization (in a very general sense) came from the East,[5] it is important to remember not only that Quinet in France had spoken of an Oriental Renaissance twenty-five years earlier and that Friedrich Schlegel had said much the same thing in Germany in 1800, but that for both of them their respective culture's access to the Orient was preeminently and strictly through the discipline of philology. Even Hugo in the preface to the *Orientales* in 1828 had intimated something of the sort.

Still, if we assume that Macaulay's famous 1835 denigration of literature in the Sanskrit and Arabic languages can be regarded as expressing a general European view of modern Oriental inferiority, it is nevertheless strikingly true that for the most part the Orient—in this case the Islamic Orient—was more regularly associated in England either with the problems of empire or with the corruptions of fancy than it was with the prestige of high culture, systematic learning, and philological discipline. Clearly Arnold implies this and of course regrets it, just as much as he also regrets what accompanies it, the general English failure to appreciate France, which in its turn seems often associated with frivolity and a corresponding lack of moral seriousness.

I can't resist mentioning a wonderfully neat and amusing example of this attitude, toward France and the Orient, that appears in Thackeray's *Vanity Fair*. Becky Sharp is half-French, a fact that stamps her in English society as being somewhat suspicious and definitely not in the best of taste. Her adventures are too well-known to require any summary here, but one scene in particular is telling for its way of indicating how far toward a thoroughly bad end her Frenchness, her social climbing, and her questionable taste are probably going to take her. This is the scene in Gaunt House when, still married to Rawdon Crawley, Becky takes part in charades organized around the theme of "Eastern revels." The climax of the charades is Becky's third-act appearance as Clytemnestra (a part that is socially inappropriate for her, to say nothing of its idiotic, untidy melodrama). Her appearance is prepared for by the following caricature of an Oriental fantasy:

> The second part of the charade takes place. It is still an Eastern scene. Hassan, in another dress, is in an attitude of Zuleikah, who is perfectly reconciled to him. The Kislar Aga has become a peaceful black slave. It is sunrise on the desert, and the Turks turn their heads eastward and bow to the sand. As there are no dromedaries at hand, the band facetiously plays "The Camels are coming." An enormous Egyptian head figures in the scene. It is a musical one, and, to the surprise of the Oriental travelers, sings a comic song, composed by Mr. Wagg. The Eastern voyagers go off dancing, like Papageno and the Moorish King, in the Magic Flute.[6]

It is immediately after this that Becky flounces on stage as Clytemnestra "in a Grecian tent," a scene in which her extravagant costume and behavior compel her husband's relatives to condemn her "improper exhibitions." As if to take the point as far as it can go, Thackeray later arranges for Amelia's reunion with William Dobbin to be celebrated in Pumpernickel, a German town where this proper and finally united couple watches a performance not of Eastern charades but of Beethoven's *Fidelio*. And it is in Pumpernickel—according to Thackeray's completely detailed description—that there stands a bridge built by Victor Aurelius XIV, "on which his own statue rises, surrounded by water nymphs and emblems of victory, peace, and plenty; he has his foot on the neck of a prostrate Turk."[7]

Thackeray is no exception to what is a rather impressive view held by novelists and poets about the Islamic East. The Arabian Nights, for example, are regularly associated with the fantasies of childhood, beneficent fantasies, it is true, but ones occurring in a sense so that they may be left behind. Think of Wordsworth's account of this in *The Prelude*. Or consider Newman's evocation of his adolescent admiration for the Arabian tales, which in his case have the additional virtue of helping to prepare for his subsequent belief in miracles. Or then again take Jane Eyre, for whom the splendors and impossible romance of the Arabian Nights are her escape from the grimness of her early life in the Reed household and a little later during her ordeal at Lowood School. Even Arnold, whose own rather grave Oriental poems show that he took the material more seriously than others, was on occasion given to connecting aesthetic or stylistic excess with Oriental things in general, more particularly with immaturity and a

shoddy lack of urbanity. The wittiest point about the Orient is made
digressively by Byron in *Beppo:*

> On that I had the art of easy writing
> What should be the easy reading! could I scale
> Parnassus, where the Muses sit inditing
> Those pretty poems never known to fail,
> How quickly would I print (the world delighting)
> A Grecian, Syrian, or Assyrian tale:
> And sell you, mix'd with western sentimentalism,
> Some sample of the finest Orientalism![8]

In such a context Lane's philological efforts appear more prodi-
gious and lonely than ever. For his compatriots the Orient was only a
place where one worked, traveled, or fantasized. No less and no more
than general philology, Oriental philology was in England a subject
of eminently marginal interest. I suppose it would be true also to say
that, for the cultivated Englishman, Islam and Arabian lore generally
represented values, experiences, mores, and tendencies that were altogether too easily acquired, too quickly assimilable to a feverish imagination or by a capacity for elaborate fantasy, to be estimable. No
special prestige was gained by Oriental knowledge in England until
later in the century, and certainly much later than in France, not because no one knew anything about the Orient but because, unlike
France, England's cultural formations drew less from the metropolis
and the academy than they did from private scholarship, individual
effort, and personal illumination. It is no accident that the origins of
the modern English tradition of Arabic and Islamic scholarship
should be found in so relatively unacademic and unmetropolitan an
intellectual as Lane, whereas in France the tradition was not only
begun but embodied in so institutional, literally monarchical, and
central a figure as Silvestre de Sacy. The Duc de Broglie said about
Sacy that "Ses grands ouvrages, ce sont les orientalistes qui se sont
partagés, sous les yeux, l'Asie tout entière, et qu'il n'a cessé d'animer,
en quelque sorte, du geste et de la voix."[9]

Let me try to suggest two or three hypotheses to explain this difference between France and Britain. One is that in postrevolutionary
France the intellectuals were organized imperially, radiating out from
and commanded almost entirely by Paris, based for the most part exclusively in state institutions whose purpose was to make knowledge
depend upon officially certified sciences, scientific bodies, orthodox
canons. Arnold makes a similar but much smaller-scaled observation.

In England, on the other hand, "the new social grouping that grew up on the basis of modern industrialism shows a remarkable economic-corporate development but advances only gropingly in the intellectual-political field."[10] What this means is that intellectual progress in England was not centralized, but took place in organic association with developments in the sociopolitical sphere (hence the prestige and authority of political economy); elsewhere in the culture the values of a traditional landowning class prevailed, which in such fields as philology and biblical studies meant the hegemony of traditional views unaffected (until at least the late 1830s) by revolutionary European developments.

Another hypothesis is one I have suggested elsewhere in connection with the difference between British and French Oriental studies: the British empire was an older and more extended one than the French, and its place in English cultural life as a fact and as a source or subject of knowledge was based on its difference and its distance from, as well as its moral use to, the home society.[11] Think again of *Vanity Fair* or *Jane Eyre* and you will see what I am trying to suggest: how, for example, Josiah Sedley is always affiliated with India and later of course with Becky, as if, despite Sedley's colonial wealth, Thackeray wished to underline his moral and social unacceptability in polite English society. Rochester's wife, Bertha Morris, is a West Indian, a fact by no means incidental to her bestiality; yet she must be exorcised (or controlled) before Rochester can marry Jane. This is Brontë's way of telling us that denizens of the outlying Empire are useful as a source of wealth or as a moral ordeal for English men and women to experience, but never are they people to be accepted into the heart of metropolitan society. The pattern is repeated frequently in British writing. I do not mean to say, however, that French culture took a more charitable view of its imperial domains: rather it was a matter of approaching them differently.

My last hypothesis, which may be the most important of the three, is the most tenuous and the most tentatively proposed. It seems to me that in England the challenge of the New Philology to religion was not felt until at least after the middle of the century, that is, until roughly the appearance of *Essays and Reviews* in 1860. The English attitude to language, mainly among philologists and poets, was pretty much a religious or philosophical one. There did not yet occur that decisive rupture between the linguistic phenomenon and the Judeo-Christian theses about the origins of things (or for that matter between language and a philosophical theory of mind) that was the hallmark of European New Philology. Coleridge and Shelley, for example, understood the sheer workings of language as well as anyone in Europe, yet neither of them went beyond ideas about language that were common knowledge to Condillac, Herder, or Rousseau, a generation earlier; neither of them, in other words, had been able to separate language from mentalism or from religion. Neither of them, and certainly not English philology as a field, seems to have understood language in the secular, purely linguistic terms proposed by the New Philology.

I have proposed these cultural propositions as an introduction to my main subject, which is not only the work of Renan and Massignon but how their Orientalism had the central cultural authority that it did in France, and how their work was better known and accepted by the French literate public than the work of comparable figures was known in England. What I want to show is that Renan and Massignon were so integral a part of the French culture of their ephochs—Renan from 1850 to 1900, Massignon from 1900 to 1960—as to give their work on Islam and even Islam itself a far greater status and authority for the non-Orientalist cultural public than could have happened in England and perhaps elsewhere in the West. In other words, allowing even for their unique gifts as great prose stylists and important Islamic scholars, it is worth while to try to understand how Renan and Massignon could have happened only in France, and not—for some of the reasons I have so far given—in England. I do not mean to be saying that in Renan or Massignon French culture produced scholars of Islam necessarily superior to those in England or elsewhere. The comparison with England is simply a useful way of showing a dramatic difference in cultural production and style.

But there is something else to be said about such differences in style and production. The study of Islam in the West has been undergoing a profound crisis. For the first time in its history Western Orientalism confronts encroachments on its privileged domains of study that come from other disciplines (the social sciences, Marxism, psychoanalysis) and from the very region being studied. The net positive effect of such encroachments is that for the first time Orientalism is being asked critically to examine not only the truth or falseness of its methodology and its investigative results, but its relationship both to the culture from which it is derived and the historical period in which its main ideas were advanced. And this leads to the question: How capable is Orientalism of asking itself these critical questions, given the constitution of Orientalism as a field with a recognizable domain, traditions, and praxis? I think it is true to say that in France, where the study of Islam played a far more central role for its own sake than anywhere else in Europe, the links between Orientalism broadly considered, the culture, and contemporary history are more articulated, more visible, more important to the discipline of Orientalism than elsewhere.

There is an enormous value therefore to studying such exemplary and inherently interesting figures as Renan and Massignon for what such a study might tell us about the visible cooperation between their work and their culture: by such historical and critical studies Orientalists, cultural and intellectual historians, and Third World critics of conventional Orientalism can better judge the less visible character of "area studies" like Orientalism in cultures (this one, for instance) whose claims for studying other societies are based on neither sympathy nor cultural prestige but on scientific objectivity and an impartial intellectual curiosity. My point will be that even if each in his own way Massignon and Renan was a genius very much at home in and acknowledged by the culture he addressed, neither man was able critically to examine the assumptions and principles on which his work depended. I shall argue implicitly that humanistic fields sustaining their coherence not by criticism or by intellectual discipline, but by the unexamined prestige of culture (as in France) or by science (as in the Anglo-Saxon world), eliminate the possibility of a valuable kind of radical self-criticism, which in the case of Orientalism has meant eliminating completely any possibility of admitting that the "Orient" as such is a constituted object, or by being willing to allow for the role of power in the production of knowledge. The result in the case of Orientalism has been a self-validating, hermetic occultation, with the chances of a humane understanding of other cultures, or of culture itself, considerably reduced.

Renan and Massignon, on the other hand, enable us to know a great deal about them not only as men who had erudite things to say about Islam, but as men who reveal the processes by which knowledge gets made. What is particularly interesting is that their personal problems, concerns, and predilections are very much a part of their public work and position as Orientalists. Not only will we see that the private man does not interfere with the scholar; on the contrary, French Orientalism culturally supported personality, not because the personality was easy to support but because its relation to culture was so significant.[12]

So we must read in Massignon and Renan an account of the relationship between knowledge and the cultural, the personal, and certainly the historical circumstances in which it is produced—and it is no accident that both Renan and Massignon were especially sensitive to the problem, although they addressed it in quite different ways. Both men employ a special sort of comparative cultural anthropology, rather more than less nuanced and interesting, although in Renan's case the hierarchy he depends on for comparisons is much closer to the surface, and therefore more pronounced and unyielding, than in Massignon. Yet we shall note that exactly where they grasp Islam, they also lose it. One scholar understands the religion in secular terms but misses what in Islam still gives its adherents genuine nourishment. The other sees it in religious terms but largely ignores the secular differences that exist within the variegated Islamic world. In both instances, then, Orientalism perceives and is blinded by what it perceives.

ONE of the things that surely must have attracted Matthew Arnold to Ernest Renan is not only that Renan's writing is saturated with the experience of latecoming but that Renan gives every indication of having successfully surmounted it. For Arnold, however, latecoming means a deep sadness at living in an age neither like Periclean Athens nor like Elizabethan England, and this feeling runs everywhere through his prose. In poems like "Dover Beach," "Rugby Chapel," and the "Memorial Verses" of 1850, feelings of regret and gentle melancholy are additionally informed by the forlornness of having in the present age lost a great reassuring figure—his father, Wordsworth, Goethe. The modern predicament for Arnold is in having been born after the disappearance either of a major creative age or of a major creative moral personality.

For Renan there is a similar predicament, except that for him the potential acuteness of loss is transmuted quickly from what could be a crippling personal blow to a general, principally cultural access of power, happiness, and confidence. The *Souvenirs d'enfance et de jeunesse* tell simultaneously of the loss of his religious orthodoxy and of its happy replacement by philology, reason, and "la science critique." There is little morbid introspection in Renan—none of Arnold's insensate dialogue of the mind with itself—even when he speaks of himself in the *Souvenirs* as at war with himself, a romantic against romanticism, a tissue of contradictions, like the *hircocerf*

spoken by the scholastics. Without the slightest twinge of embarrass-
ment Renan said of himself that he thought like a man, felt like a
woman, acted like a child; such a modus vivendi he says with no little
vanity brought him the keenest possible "jouissances intellec-
tuelles."[13] Theological disputation in the young seminarian took a
very concrete textual form and, thanks to Le Hir, his extraordinary
teacher, Renan was helped to read the sacred texts in the original. "M.
Le Hir fixed my life; I was a philologist by instinct. Everything that I
am as a scholar, I am because of M. Le Hir."[14] This also happened to
include the fact, according to Renan himself, that both men were
arabisants médiocres.

The intellectual pattern that Renan always seems to transcribe is
one that makes it possible for him to admit: "In effect, I have changed
very little throughout my life; destiny has after its fashion riveted me
since my childhood to the role and function which I would have to
accomplish."[15] To express what it means to live after a unitary religious faith has given way to the many inroads made on it by rationalism—this is Renan's professed vocation. But there is more to the
vocation than that, as an attentive reading soon reveals. A great deal
of what Renan wrote and researched is organized around a rather
special temporal and psychological problematic. Like Vico and Rousseau, Renan accepted the idea that the origins of language and religion were inspired moments resembling a poetic, perhaps religious
raptus, but unlike either of his predecessors Renan makes no real effort to reconstruct or even to understand what those moments were
in terms of an outside cause. Revelation is something Renan repeatedly associates with an occurrence that took place once and for all in
an inaccessible realm, a realm fundamentally both earlier and outside
his own. When he came to tackle the origin of language in 1848
Renan was perfectly willing to grant that God may have started
everything "in the sense in which God, having placed in man everything which is necessary for the invention of language, could be
called the author of language." But to talk about God, Renan continues, is in this context to use "une expression detournée et singu-
lière," especially when there are more natural and philosophical expressions to do the job.[16]

Revelation may or may not have occurred; in any case it is not
what Renan tries to recapture. What he always assumes is that he is
on earth to show how other things can replace the primitive excitement of original revelation—so much so that for him history itself
became entirely equivalent, interchangeable with, his writing of his-

tory. Renan's vocation is to say: you cannot reexperience the past; you cannot risk losing yourself in lamenting the loss of a primitive world of Edenic plenitude and revelation; don't view what in fact you have lost as a loss; take it instead as the virtue of encountering me, and my writing.

Rarely, however, is this general claim made to depend on Renan's mere person as a writer or scientist. For his writing is part of a transpersonal enterprise, which he calls "la science" or "la science critique" most of the time, whose reason for being is not only that it replaces revelation and the individuals who claim to have revelation, but that it has reorganized existence and any perception of existence in such a way as to make religious revelation unnecessary. Renan's confidence in what he does and his unhappiness about his vocation come not only from the vocation itself but also from its being mediated and legitimized by a great person or institution. What Renan very shrewdly and, I think, accurately saw was the extent to which such things as genius, inspiration, or revelation depended upon the vagaries or the innate gifts or the personal devotions of the individual. Unlike Arnold's scholar-gypsy who was waiting pointlessly for the spark from heaven to fall, Renan premised his serious activity as a scientist generally, and as a philologist particularly, on the notion that if there were a heaven or a spark, he would not be the one to benefit. His time was not the past—which is where one would locate the *sève originale* he referred to in speaking about the early days of revealed religion—but the present and, if he was careful, the future. Therefore it was necessary to invest in disciplines like philology that moved history away from the existential problems of revealed religion and toward what it was possible to study, toward those real things that mankind still had to worry about long after primitive excitement (or revelation for that matter) was definitely over. One's career took shape inside this accessible reality, which is modern culture of course as Renan defined it, and under the auspices of teachers like Le Hir who confirmed the young man's specifically cultural instincts.

But philology does not simply displace religion or the religious attitude as one goes about studying language. Rather, Renan says in *De l'origine du language*, philology shifts one's attention away from the possibility that language was the result of some prior, exterior cause (such as God) to the certainty that language was "un tout organique, doué d'une vie propre," and hence to be studied by "une science de la vie."[17] Thus philology takes the linguistic phenomenon and redis-

poses it from the past to the present, reorganizes it within its "verita-
ble terrain," that is, *la conscience créatrice* that functions in the present and also in the future. The philologist's job must be to connect
that postlapsarian moment just after language's birth with the present, then to show how the dense web of relationships between language users is a secular reality from which the future will emerge. To
this project Renan remained extraordinarily faithful: all of his major
religious and philological studies dealt with what we can call *the aftermath*, a postprimitive state whose sole form of existence, for the
philologist, is not a believer's faith, or an apostolic succession, or a
living community, but a set of texts permitting a clever philologist to
discern in them all those faults and virtues hidden behind the protes-
tations of devotion, the proclamations of faith, the sufferings of martyrs. Renan did his work with modern investigative instruments, and
his standpoint was that of a secular professional whose judgments
were based on the incontrovertible, largely ironic truth that, in spite
of revelation, culture was moved forward by science, which left religion further and further behind. This view is specifically responsible
for Renan's radically uncompromising view of Islam. But before I
discuss that, I must say a few more things about Renan's views of
culture and science.

The crucial text here is *L'Avenir de la science*, published in 1890
but originally written in 1848. I must confess at the outset that the
book's rambunctious confidence and its air of self-esteem are somewhat repellent. But be that as it may, it is a very important book for
Renan. In it he clearly means to be situating himself at the heart of
modern culture—which he says is philological in spirit—and therefore speaking as much for that culture as about it. The title makes the
point that science is the future; more, that science will change human
life so much as even to reorganize God himself. "Organiser scienti-
fiquement l'humanité tel est donc le dernier mot de la science mo-
derne . . . et après avoir organiser l'humanité, organisera Dieu."[18] The
interesting thing is that Renan sees this happening as a result of a
change of perspective caused by modern scientific discovery. Thus
whereas the ancient (by which he meant the religious) world was
closed and narrow, the new scientific world created by Humboldt is
open, full of potentiality, rich. Here the past has been superseded entirely, transvaluated into what only a rationalistically investigative
and daring mind can exploit, revel in, feel creative about.[19] Though
he does not say it outright, Renan clearly implies that the modern
philological culture of which he is the accredited representative rules

over the rational domain that emerged as a result of modern scientific discovery. Three concentric positions are thus legitimized. At the outer rim is the physical envelope whose earliest boundaries define the place from which the open postprimitive world springs; inside that is culture itself, historical, philological, dealing with all the products of human history; and inside that, at the center, is the philologist whose activity carries human history forward. Each of these positions and each of these places enforces the other; each makes all the others possible. "Moi étant là au centre, humant le parfum de toute chose, jugeant et comparant, combinant et induisant, j'arriverais au système des choses."[20] Although that imperious "moi" seems lonely, it is in fact supported by all sorts of institutions and figures giving it authority and gravity: not only Humboldt, but Cousin, Burnouf, Le Hir, Cuvier, St. Hilaire—like Renan, central to the main activities of modern life.

A quick contrast with Arnold is instructive here. In *Culture and Anarchy* Arnold had said of the critic that if he is not to fall prey either to narrow class interests (Barbarians, Philistines, or Populace) and if he is to be truly a disinterested critic, he must belong to a small intrepid band formed by men of culture. These creatures are what we might call declassé intellectuals, and that is what Renan eminently is not. Everything about him exudes the authority of massive centralized institutions like schools, disciplines, missions, teams of cooperating but hierarchically arranged scientific workers. Far from such a smoothly running apparatus being merely what Arnold called machinery, it is for Renan the true plenitude of postlapsarian existence. Far from treating all this as a mere adjunct to the poverty of living without revelation, Renan judges the whole dense undertaking to be modern life itself, at its finest.

No wonder then that Islam comes off so badly. For Islam, as Renan said on so many occasions, is a religion whose founder never even pretended to divinity, much less to true originality. If Renan could treat organized religions like Judaism and Christianity as coming after their founders' encounter with the divine, how else could he treat Mohammed except as the latecomers' latecomer? No mystery, no miracles, no divinity, not even, he says in a remarkable passage near the end of "Mahomet et les origines de l'islamisme," women.[21] Islam in other words is opened entirely onto the present, and it will not survive into the future; it offers nothing of interest to anyone trying to resurrect a distant, vaguely religious past. It is barren, incapable of truly regenerating itself, and it will disappear entirely under the influence of modern Occidental science.

To a certain extent, Islam's disappearance is what Renan undertook to hasten. And he did it with a consistency to his views about culture and science that is positively chilling. In 1883 he gave a speech at the Sorbonne entitled "L'Islamisme et la science" which serves as the opposing pendant to *L'Avenir de la Science:* Islam in this instance is the very opposite of science and of the future. The most telling thing about the speech is Renan's insistence that Islamic culture properly speaking is neither science nor philosophy (as his book on Averroes had already asserted), but only language (his authority here is Abul-Faraj). Yet shorn of its roots in a past revelation, or even in an intimate relationship with divinity, Islam's language is not fit for science to nurture. On the contrary, Islam and its Arabic language represent hatred to reason, the end of rational philosophy, unremitting enmity to progress. Thus "pour la raison humaine, l'islamisme n'a été que nuisible."[22] Why exactly? Because it made of the countries over which it ruled "un champ fermé." In other words Islam returned one to the closed world of the primitives and away from the open world of modern science. Because it came so long after Judaism and Christianity, however, Islam pertained exclusively to an earlier age of aborted, failed human effort with no memory of vivacious revelation to guide it. Its main service to the practitioner of modern European culture was as a negative demonstration of the law of progress.

The paradox at the heart of Renan's view of Islam is resolved only when we understand him to be keeping Islam alive so that, in his philological writing, he might set about destroying it, treating it as a religion only to show the fundamental aridity of its religious spirit, reminding us that, even if all religions are essentially postscripts to permanently disappeared revelations, Islam was interesting to a philologist as the postscript to a postscript, the trace of a trace. As such it was a challenge to the philologist who, speaking for European culture, affirmed modern secularity in the space opened up not by the loss of religion, as Renan believed, but by the religious spirit itself in its continuing indifference to mere science and culture, a spirit to which he unwittingly returned in book after book, and left completely untouched.

Renan never really dealt with the secular fact of the enduring presence of religions like Islam, religions that could still exist and be powerful even in an age that culturally could prove beyond a shadow of a doubt that religion was a thing of the past. This is Renan's cultural predicament and its blind spot, however much he believed himself to have transcended religion.

L OUIS Massignon's whole massive work turns exactly on this issue, the survival of religion; he illuminates it, relives it, cherishes it, writes and rewrites it with unparalleled genius and insight. This is another way of saying that in Massignon the philological vocation adumbrated at the heart of French culture is transformed entirely. We are now dealing with a mind altogether of another sort of magnitude, with an experience so intense and remarkable that its only decent cultural analogies and supports are aesthetic and psychological, not, as in Renan's case, institutional and academic. To understand Massignon we would almost do better, that is, to read Mallarmé and Rimbaud than Sylvain Lévi. Yet no less than Renan, Massignon must be seen within the great structure of French cultural, political, and colonial domination of the Muslim world. Each of them, in very different ways, takes for granted that there is a peculiarly French mission to and in the Muslim world, in Renan's case to judge and finally to annihilate it, in Massignon's to understand and feel compassion for it, then finally to exist in harmony with its anguish, its needs, its divine dilemmas. Renan's epistemological attitude toward Islam, therefore, is one of divestiture and judgment, Massignon's of sympathetic assumption and rapprochement. Neither man doubts that Islam can in fact be an object of study for the European scholar, since both assume that scholarship dissolves all obstacles, makes all things acquirable, can represent anything, Renan by critical judgment and rejection, Massignon by sympathetic compassion.

What is most relevant for anyone trying critically to understand the nature of modern Orientalism is that in reading Renan one encounters a subtle mind, capable of making all sorts of fine distinctions, whose main project is to shut down Islam. In the end of course it is Renan, not Islam, who leaves one with the impression of something limited, superficial, and unenthusiastic. The reverse is true of Massignon, and in the rest of this essay I shall try to suggest some of the ways in which this great scholar defies routine analysis, but can still be apprehended as part of Orientalism. In his work, which spans roughly the first sixty years of this century, a reader finds embodied not only a daunting panorama of French intellectual culture (in its high Catholic variety), but also the great civilizational and political problems of colonialism and decolonization. In addition Massignon treats such complex things as the reform movement in Islam, the relationship between Islam and Christianity, science confronting revelation, linguistics, anthropology, and psychoanalysis encountering philology, religion, and faith, and above all the struggles of one extremely powerful and refined mind to deal with most of the institutions of faith, and modern as well as traditional culture, in the midst of undiminishing activity in government, academy, and church.

Massignon is Renan's exact opposite on the matter of revelation. Whereas Renan speaks and writes *after* having already decided that revelation is no longer apposite to modernity, Massignon's entire career springs out of one moment of revelation in 1907. Here is how he describes it in quaint, incorrect, but somehow very moving English:

> Studying, after Sanskrit (and the inscriptions of Angkor), Arabic and the Moslem countries, travelling during years on the boundaries of the Arab desert in Africa and Asia, warrying [*sic*] many manlike struggles, I was suddenly struck by the lightning of revelation; disguised, taken prisoner on the frontier of the desert and the rice-fields, in Irak, I could not get rid of this midday sunstroke as I had done with the reflected dawn light-glances of ancestral folktales. Furthermore, these folk-tales were reanimated in my memory, when I discovered in Islam religious symbols akin to the traditional culture of peasantry. Specially in the Islam of monsoon countries, from the Frankincense Arabia to the Spicy Indonesia.[23]

This is written in 1959, three years before his death. Massignon connects the experience with his father's sudden veneration for Japanese art in 1890, after which he felt a form of reverence for the very paper on which the images were printed. What paper was for the father, language became for the son. "La parole humaine . . . c'est un appel personnel poignant destiné à nous faire sortir de nous-mêmes, de notre pays, de notre parenté, à tout dépasser vers l'Amour."[24] There is a kind of parallel for both aspects of this experience in Marcel's rediscovery of George Sand's *François le Champi* in the Guermantes library, near the end of Proust's *Le Temps retrouvé.* An involuntary conflation of two separate situations seems momentarily to eradicate the anguish of distance, of time, of identity. What the elder Massignon understands is the material identity of his work and Japanese art; he is a sculptor. What the son is given in revelation comes directly from the spoken word; since he is a philologist, his task is to see how texts in a foreign language contain, bear witness to, the divine Presence that in each utterance this language represents.

But Massignon is not interesting to a modern intellectual simply because he had a revelation and then recalled it in his work.

Paraphrasing Sartre on Valéry, we can say that Massignon was a man who had a rich spiritual life, but not everyone who has a rich spiritual life is a Massignon. The question of what gives his career its sustained power and its unmistakable identity from beginning to end can be answered in intellectual terms. Without reducing or simplifying Massignon we can say that if, for Renan, language and culture were to be treated by philology in a temporal perspective, as aspects of a typology of historical periods, in Massignon the problems of language and of the philological vocation are considered within a *spatial* perspective, as aspects of a topography of distances, of geographical differentiation, of spirits of place separated from each other by a territory whose function for the scholar is that it must be charted as exactly as possible, and then in one way or another overcome. The underlying economy of Massignon's sprawling work is the ubiquitous fact of distance, the fact of how separate identities exist, even in a moment of revelation. At bottom, in other words, Massignon tries to experience the distance between Islam and Christianity, as a variant on the distance between man and God or between the word and spirit.

Thus he examined Islam not simply as a thing in itself, but as a differential phenomenon, as something felt in Arabia, Indonesia, and Morocco but not, say, in France or England. In much the same way, Mallarmé tried to understand language as the interplay of black and white, and Proust tried to devise a method for reducing the distance between past and present, having fully experienced the space between them and preserving the identity of both. Massignon's method derives not only from a Christian habit of witness and compassion, but from the aesthetics of late nineteenth-century *symbolisme*, in which an object is coexistent in language with its absence, in which the placing and displacing of things—their play of substitutions—are what language embodies.

There are numerous examples of this in Massignon's work; even a quick rehearsal of some gives a perfect idea of his procedures. His interest in al-Hallaj is surely one of the most obvious, since al-Hallaj is so powerfully the master figure of Massignon's oeuvre, Mansur al-Hallaj was a tenth-century Baghdad Muslim saint who was martyred because he dared not only to approach God directly but also to speak of himself as the truth, as a sort of pan-Christian incarnation. Not only did al-Hallaj himself represent an example of the substitution of one thing for another in the same man (the human and the divine, al-Hallaj's *ana'l haqq*); but al-Hallaj's Muslim experiences, although

they occur at a great distance from them, correspond with the effu-
sions of European Christian mystics. In this connection there is
"L'Experience mystique et les modes de stylisation littéraire"
(1927), where Massignon compares the verbal techniques of European writers like Eckhart, John of the Cross, and Claudel with those
of Muslim devotional poets. The point about these comparisons is not
only that they demonstrate similarities in expression, but that they
are precise despite the "differential" geographical circumstances separating them. But even in his analyses of European and Oriental
mystical encounters with the divine, Massignon preserves what I
have called his topographical problematic: he is less interested in
man's complete identification with God than with the mystical struggle between man and God, and man and man, in which what man
risks is the loss of his identity to God.

History, Massignon says, is made up of chains of individual witnesses, scattered throughout Europe and the Orient, interceding with
and substituting for one another. Substitution implies an endless
chain of resubstitutions, in which there is a ceaseless movement of
one thing always replacing another. For Massignon Islam was what,
despite the occasional appearance of an al-Hallaj and despite its being
an Abrahamanic religion, could be described as an imperfect substitute in the East for Christianity. He saw Islam displacing Christianity and Christianity displacing Islam. In Massignon's view Islam's
identity is its resistance to and its final intransigence vis-à-vis the
Christian incarnation. As such, therefore, the religion attracted and
yet resisted the Christian in him, although—and here is the man's extraordinary stroke of genius—he conceived his own philological work
as a science of compassion, as providing a place for Islam and Christianity to approach and substitute for each other, yet always remaining apart, one always substituting for the other. Moreover, the particular group of worship he founded was called Badaliya Sodality whose
"texte d'engagement" noted that "*badaliya* requires a penetration in
depth, which is the result of bringing together an attentive care for
the life of families, and of past and present Muslim generations."[25]

Underlying the notion of substitution is the ever present antithesis
between the things that get substituted. Christ as sacrifice is obviously the prime substitute, since he is both sacrificial victim for all
men and the son of God. Christianity as a system of faith, as a liturgy,
as a language, is built out of that radical antithesis. The rigor of Massignon's method is to transfer this religious antithesis and substitution to the realm of languages and from there to Arabic and to Islam:

For language is both a "pilgrimage" and a "spiritual displacement," since we only elaborate language in order to be able to go
out from ourselves toward an other: and also to evoke with this
other an absent One, the third person, *al-Ghayib* as He is called
by Arab grammarians. And we do this so as to discover and
identify all these entities with each other. This makes it possible
to render our witness to Him, because He is the truth when we
have accepted Him by virtue of the heart's fiat, this *Kun* [be]
which is mentioned eight times in the Koran, and always for
"the Word of God, Jesus son of Mary," and the Last Judgment.[26]

Massignon goes still further, this time citing Mallarmé. In one sense,
he says, words denote an absence (*manque*); but in Arabic the importance of the spoken language is that it is testimony (*shahada*),
and carried to its ultimate grammatical form (*shahid*) it means martyr. To testify is to speak, and to speak is to move from yourself toward another, to displace self in order to accommodate another, your
opposite and your guest, and also someone absent whose absence opposes your own presence. The irony of this is that you can never
directly come together with another: your testimony can at best accommodate the other, and this of course is what language does and is,
antithetically—presence and absence, unless in the case of the *shahid*
(martyr) the self is obliterated for the sake of the other, who because
of the martyr's love is more distant, more an Other than ever. This is
the ultimate sacrifice, the ultimate grace, and of course the ultimate
antithesis: it is human scandal and divine love, the *déchirante pureté*
of Mansur al-Hallaj whose sacrilege is to have dared to reach beyond
Islam toward Christianity and God. As Père de Foucauld put it,
"When God chooses a witness, even in the humblest domains, God
transforms that witness into somebody who for others is both unrec-
ognizable and odious."[27]
. All of Massignon's writing forms a constellation of images around
these notions. Arabic is a closed world with a certain number of stars
in it; entering it, the scholar is both at home and repatriated from his
own world.[28] Thus a central pair of images is that of the guest and
host. Note how there is always an antithesis to be confronted whose
poles allow one to traverse the distance from language to religion and
back again: from Arabic to French, from Islam to Christianity, then
back again. And within each pole of the antithesis there are further
antitheses—in Arabic, for example, there are differences expressed,
and they accentuate separation. Massignon's characterization of Arabic, that it is essentially a language of compression and disjuction, in

which consonants on the line are the body, vocalizations above or below the line its spirit, is part of the same thematic antithesis between alternating absence and presence. The religious experiences and rituals he was especially interested in (for example, the *mubhala*) also repeat the ritual of substitution and opposition. Similarly Massignon's style, as much as its subject matter, is a discontinuous, abrupt style—certainly one of the great French styles of the century—as if it wishes constantly to embody distance and the alternation of presence and absence, the paradox of sympathy and alienation, the motif of inclusion and exclusion, grace and disgrace, apotropaic prayer and compassionate love. Above all, we find in Massignon the continual alternation of distance and closeness between Islam and Christianity that always embodied in his work the basic idea of substitution, of attraction and repulsion itself. To the form of apotropaic prayer, therefore, Massignon assimilated in his philosophical work the notion of compassionate, substitutive sacrificial suffering, whose principle Christian form is of course the passion of Christ, whose early Greek form is the *pharmakos*, and whose Muslim form is the *abdal*.

It is probable that Massignon's ideas about sacrifice came to him from Joseph de Maistre and Alfred Loisy; yet he gave those ideas his own distinctive form. If a word is at once a presence and an absence, then one can say too that the person who suffers for the community, whose suffering is caused by what Massignon calls "le transfert de la douleur par la compassion," is at once all evil and all good, victim and hero, alien and citizen, outcast, guest, and accepted host, presence and absence. Throughout his career Massignon was actively involved not only with Islam but also with sufferers, martyrs, refugees, convicts, and expatriate workers in France, even as he remained a very great scholar of language, a great reader of difficult texts, a great interpreter of other religions, and a much-honored public figure. Together Islam and Arabic invoke in him Christian compassion which, unlike any other Orientalist of the century, he tried to convert into a meticulous understanding of both. He said on one occasion that most nineteenth-century philologists ended up by disliking the languages they studied. *His* philological vocation, unlike Renan's, was premised on the wish not to repeat that dislike, but to transform alienation into love.

Still there is something odd about so heady a mixture in the man of an exraordinarily luxuriant, often overpowering mental fertility, fixated on martyrdom, on stigmatas, on gratuitous suffering, on hopeless pilgrimages, on death, on deserts, caves, prisons, on asceticism, on absence and night. The legacy of Huysmans, Massignon's godfather, is perhaps too obtrusive in him. Jacques Berque is right to say that Massignon took Orientalism as far as it could go, the way Hegel took philosophy to its absolute limits, and right also to suggest that Massignon's attachment to Abraham as ur-Semite ought to be counterbalanced by a strong dose of Heraclitus.[29] Massignon himself was quite conscious of opening Orientalism out from the binds imposed on it by Renan. He made frequent reference to Renan's strictures, stated his disagreement with the man's hard-eyed ethnocentrism and rationalism, even carrying his antipathy as far as befriending Renan's grandson, Ernest Psichari, a mystic and an anti-Renanian.

R ENAN and Massignon are polar opposites within Orientalism: Renan is the philologist as judge, the French scholar surveying lesser religions like Islam with disdain, speaking with the authority not only of a scientific European but of a great cultural institution; Massignon is the philologist as guest, as spiritual traveler extraordinary, as—to use Gerard Manley Hopkins' words for Duns Scotus—the rarest-veined unraveler of Islamic civilization the West has produced.

One last critical point must be made. Is it too much to say that as Orientalists Renan and Massignon, opposites and opponents in a way, can also be taken as substitutes for each other? The keynote to Renan's work is, of course, difference—Renan's differences with religion and with the Orient. The keynote of Massignon's work is also difference, but he added compassion to it—his Christian compassion for Islam which, Foucauld told him in 1915, came about "in confrontation with these Moslems toward whom God has given both of us special duties."[30] But insofar as both men accept the barrier between East and West upon which Orientalism as a learned discipline is constructed, they can be considered as substitutes, *abdal*, different sides of the same coin. Both of them do their work within the edifice we call Oriental studies, which both men assumed that Franco-European culture had given them and which their work reinforced. The question raised by a juxtaposition of their works is the very question that Orientalism itself cannot really pose, much less answer—the question of the Orient. Its overwhelming reality for both Renan and Massignon was the source of one man's rejection and the other's ceaseless attempts to save Islam from itself. In neither case could the Orientalist be truly critical of himself or see his discipline critically and in a wholly secular perspective, where the other important questions—of human labor, of power, of men and women in society—might be posed and attended to.

To the situation of Massignon's and Renan's Orientalism as critical science, it is useful to apply Lukacs' ironic description: both are in "the situation of that legendary 'critic' in India who was confronted with the ancient story according to which the world rests on an elephant. He unleashed the 'critical' question: on what does the elephant rest? On receiving the answer that the elephant stands on a tortoise 'criticism' declares itself satisfied. It is obvious that even if he had continued to press apparently 'critical' questions he could only have elicited a third miraculous animal. He would not have been able to discover the solution to the real question."[31]

Conclusion:
Religious Criticism

THE idea of the Orient, very much like the idea of the West that is its polar opposite, has functioned as an inhibition on what I have been calling secular criticism. Orientalism is the discourse derived from and dependent on "the Orient." To say of such grand ideas and their discourse that they have something in common with religious discourse is to say that each serves as an agent of closure, shutting off human investigation, criticism, and effort in deference to the authority of the more-than-human, the supernatural, the other-worldly. Like culture, religion therefore furnishes us with systems of authority and with canons of order whose regular effect is either to compel subservience or to gain adherents. This in turn gives rise to organized collective passions whose social and intellectual results are often disastrous. The persistence of these and other religious-cultural effects testifies amply to what seem to be necessary features of human life, the need for certainty, group solidarity, and a sense of communal belonging. Sometimes of course these things are beneficial. Still it is also true that what a secular attitude enables—a sense of history and of human production, along with a healthy skepticism about the various official idols venerated by culture and by system—is diminished, if not eliminated, by appeals to what cannot be thought through and explained, except by consensus and appeals to authority.

There is a great difference between what in *The New Science* Vico described as the complex, heterogenous, and "gentile" world of nations and what in contrast he designated as the domain of sacred history. The essence of that difference is that the former comes into being, develops in various directions, moves toward a number of culminations, collapses, and then begins again—all in ways that can be investigated because historians, or new scientists, are human and can know history on the grounds that it was made by men and women. Knowing is making, Vico said, and what human beings can know is only what they have made, that is, the historical, social, and secular. As for sacred history, it is made by God and hence cannot really be known, although Vico understood perfectly well that in a priest-ridden age such as his, God had to be respected and loudly celebrated.

In our time there has been a curious transmutation by which the secular world—in particular, the human effort that goes into the production of literary texts—reveals itself as neither fully human nor fully apprehensible in human terms. It is not simply that this change is the result of irrationalism (though there has been plenty of that) and of radical simplification, for a purely secular view of reality is certainly no guarantee against either one or the other. What is more to the point is a dramatic increase in the number of appeals to the extrahuman, the vague abstraction, the divine, the esoteric and secret. As I have said, impossibly huge generalizations like the Orient, Islam, Communism, or Terrorism play a significantly increased role in the contemporary Manichean theologizing of "the Other," and this increase is a sign of how strongly religious discourse has affected discourse pertaining to the secular, historical world.

But religion has returned in other ways, most explicitly in the works of formerly militant secularists (such as Daniel Bell and William Barrett) for whom it now seems that the historical-social world of real men and women is in need of religious assuagement. This new mood superficially resembles, but is very unlike, the utopianism of Ernst Bloch, whose work was an attempt to metamorphize the social enthusiasm of millenarianism into everyday reality. What one discerns today is religion as the result of exhaustion, consolation, disappointment: its forms in both the theory and practice of criticism are varieties of unthinkability, undecidability, and paradox together with a remarkable consistency of appeals to magic, divine ordinance, or sacred texts.

When you see influential critics publishing major books with titles like *The Genesis of Secrecy, The Great Code, Kabbalah and Criticism, Violence and the Sacred, Deconstruction and Theology,* you know you are in the presence of a significant trend. The number of prevalent critical ideas whose essence is some version of theory liberated from the human and the circumstantial further attests to this trend. Even the revisionist readings of past critics and critical theories—say the current vogue for Walter Benjamin not as a Marxist but as a crypto-mystic, or those versions of such actively radical positions as Marxism, feminism, or psychoanalysis that stress the private and hermetic over the public and social—must also be viewed as being part of the same curious veering toward the religious. Marshall McLuhan's vision of a technological utopia, and the "retribalization" he says goes with it, is a significant foreshadowing of this basically uncritical religiosity. All of it, I think, expresses an ultimate preference for the secure protection of systems of belief (however peculiar those may be) and not for critical activity or consciousness.

The cost of this shift, which began four decades ago in the ahistorical, manifestly religious aestheticism of the New Criticism, is unpleasant to contemplate. There is an increase in the number of fixed special languages, many of them impenetrable, deliberately obscure, willfully illogical. Few people using these languages today would find themselves capable of agreeing with Roland Barthes that the system of a special language often slips toward "a kind of reductionism and disapproval": certainly there is that tendency in the discourse of Orientalism, but it exists in deconstruction and semiotics too. Instead of discrimination and evaluation, we have an intensified division of intellectual labor; objects of study both dehumanized and exorbitant have taken over the critics' attention, while intellectual debate increasingly resembles high-pitched monologue in narrow corridors. Most distressing of all is the growing resemblance between professed political neoconservatives and the religiously inclined critics, for both of whom the privatized condition of social life and cultural discourse are made possible by a belief in the benign quasi-divine marketplace. Folding back upon itself, criticism has therefore refused to see its affiliations with the political world it serves, perhaps unwittingly, perhaps not. Once an intellectual, the modern critic has become a cleric in the worst sense of the word. How their discourse can once again collectively become a truly secular enterprise is, it seems to me, the most serious question critics can be asking one another.

Notes

Index

Notes

Unless otherwise indicated, translations are my own.

Introduction: Secular Criticism

1. There is a good graphic account of the problem in Noam Chomsky, *Language and Responsibility* (New York: Pantheon, 1977), p. 6. See also Edward W. Said, *Covering Islam* (New York: Pantheon, 1981), pp. 147–164.

2. The example of the Nazi who read Rilke and then wrote out genocidal orders to his concentration-camp underlings had not yet become well known. Perhaps then the Durrell–Secretary of Defense anecdote might not have seemed so useful to my enthusiastic friend.

3. See Hayden White, *Metahistory: The Historical Imagination in Nineteenth Century Europe* (Baltimore: Johns Hopkins University Press, 1973), and his *Tropics of Discourse: Essays in Cultural Criticism* (Baltimore: Johns Hopkins University Press, 1978).

4. See my article "Opponents, Audiences, Constituencies, and Community," forthcoming in *Critical Inquiry* (Fall 1982), for an analysis of the liaison between the cult of textuality and the ascendancy of Reaganism.

5. Erich Auerbach, *Mimesis: The Representation of Reality in Western Literature*, trans. Willard Trask (1953; rprt. Princeton: Princeton University Press, 1968), p. 557.

6. See the evidence in Samuel C. Chew, *The Crescent and the Rose: Islam and England During the Renaissance* (New York: Oxford University Press, 1937).

7. Auerbach, "Philology and *Weltliteratur*," trans. M. and E. W. Said, *Centennial Review*, 13 (Winter 1969), p. 17.

8. Hugo of St. Victor, *Didascalicon*, trans. Jerome Taylor (New York: Columbia University Press, 1961), p. 101.

9. See my *Orientalism* (New York: Pantheon, 1978), esp. chap. 1.

10. A. L. Kroeber and Clyde Kluckhohn, *Culture: A Critical Review of Concepts and Definitions* (1952; rprt. New York: Vintage Books, 1963).

11. Matthew Arnold, *Culture and Anarchy*, ed. J. Dover Wilson (1869; rprt. Cambridge: Cambridge University Press, 1969), p. 70.

12. Ibid., p. 204.

13. Lionel Trilling, *Beyond Culture: Essays on Learning and Literature* (New York: Viking Press, 1965), p. 175.

14. Quoted in Philip D. Curtin, ed., *Imperialism* (New York: Walker and Company, 1971), p. 182.

15. Eric Stokes, *The English Utilitarians and India* (Oxford: Clarendon Press, 1959), p. 298.

16. See *Orientalism*, pp. 153–156; also the important study by Bryan Turner, *Marx and the End of Orientalism* (London: Allen and Unwin, 1978).

17. See my *Beginnings: Intention and Method* (New York: Basic Books, 1975), pp. 81–88 and passim.

18. The information is usefully provided by Lyndall Gordon, *Eliot's Early Years* (Oxford and New York: Oxford University Press, 1977).

19. T. S. Eliot, *Selected Essays* (1932; rprt. London: Faber and Faber, 1953), pp. 343–344.

20. Georg Simmel, *The Conflict in Modern Culture and Other Essays*, trans. and ed. K. Peter Etzkorn (New York: Teachers College Press, 1968), p. 12.

21. Ian Watt, *Conrad in the Nineteenth Century* (Berkeley: University of California Press, 1979), p. 32.

22. John Fekete, *The Critical Twilight: Explorations in the Ideology of Anglo-American Literary Theory from Eliot to McLuhan* (London: Routledge and Kegan Paul, 1977), pp. 193–194.

23. For an extended analysis of the role of interpretive communities, see Stanley Fish, *Is There a Text in This Class?* (Cambridge: Harvard University Press, 1980).

24. Raymond Williams, *Politics and Letters: Interviews with New Left Review* (London: New Left Books, 1979), p. 252.

1. The World, the Text, and the Critic

1. Paul Ricoeur, "What Is a Text? Explanation and Interpretation," in David Rasmussen, *Mythic-Symbolic Language and Philosophical Anthropology: A Constructive Interpretation of the Thought of Paul Ricoeur* (The Hague: Nijhoff, 1971), p. 138. For a more interesting distinction between oeuvre and text, see Roland Barthes, "De l'Oeuvre au texte," *Revue d'esthethique*, 3 (1971), 225–232.

2. I have discussed this in chap. 4 of *Beginnings: Intention and Method* (New York: Basic Books, 1975).

3. Riffaterre, "The Self-Sufficient Text," *Diacritics* (Fall 1973), p. 40.

4. This is the main polemical point in this tract *Ar-rad'ala'l nuhat*, ed. Shawki Daif (Cairo, 1947). The text dates from 1180.

5. Roger Arnaldez, *Grammaire et théologies chez Ibn Hazm de Cordoue* (Paris: J. Vrin, 1956), pp. 12 and passim. There is a clear, somewhat schematic account of Ibn Ginni, Ibn Mada, and others in Anis Fraiha, *Nathariyat fil Lugha* (Beirut: Al-Maktaba al Jam'iya, 1973).

6. Arnaldez, *Grammaire et théologie,* p. 12.

7. Ibid., p. 69.

8. Ibid., p. 77.

9. *The Journals and Papers of Gerard Manley Hopkins,* ed. Humphry House and Graham Storey (London: Oxford University Press, 1959), p. 195.

10. Ibid., p. 129.

11. *The Poems of Gerard Manley Hopkins,* ed. W. H. Gardner and N. H. Mackenzie (London: Oxford University Press, 1967), p. 90.

12. *The Letters of Gerard Manley Hopkins to Robert Bridges,* ed. Claude Colleer Abbott (Oxford: Oxford University Press, 1955), pp. 51–52.

13. Quoted in Anthony Bisshof, S.J., "Hopkins' Letters to his Brother," *Times Literary Supplement,* December 8, 1972, p. 1511.

14. *Poems of Hopkins,* p. 108.

15. *The Artist as Critic: Critical Writings of Oscar Wilde,* ed. Richard Ellmann (New York: Vintage, 1970), p. 386.

16. *Complete Works of Oscar Wilde,* ed. J. B. Foreman (London: Collins, 1971), p. 335.

17. Oscar Wilde, *De Profundis* (New York: Vintage, 1964), p. 18.

18. Ibid., p. 80, 61.

19. Ibid., pp. 34–35.

20. *Middlemarch,* ed. Gordon S. Haight (Boston: Houghton Mifflin, 1956), p. 302.

21. *Lord Jim* (Boston: Houghton Miffling, 1958), p. 161.

22. Ibid., p. 161.

23. Karl Marx, *Der Achtzehnte Brumaire des Louis Bonaparte,* (1852; Berlin: Dietz Verlag, 1947), p. 8.

24. Nietzsche's analyses of texts in this light are to be found everywhere in his work, but especially in *The Genealogy of Morals* and in *The Will to Power.*

25. See in particular Ernst Renan, *Histoire générale et système comparé des langues sémitiques,* in *Oeuvres complètes,* ed. Henriette Psichari (Paris: Calmann-Lévy, 1947–1961), VIII, 147–157.

26. Michel Foucault, "The Discourse on Language," in *The Archeology of Knowledge,* trans. A. M. Sheridan Smith (New York: Pantheon, 1972), p. 216.

27. *A Portrait of the Artist as a Young Man* (New York: Viking Press, 1964), p. 189.

28. Fanon, *The Wretched of the Earth,* trans. Constance Farrington (New York: Grove Press, 1964), pp. 31–32.

29. Jacques Derrida, "La Pharmacie de Platon" in *La Dissémination* (Paris: Seuil, 1972), pp. 145 and passim.

30. Georg Lukacs, *Die Seele und die Formen* (1911; rprt. Berlin: Luchterhand, 1971), p. 25.

31. Wilde, *The Artist as Critic*, p. 367.

32. Lukacs, *Die Seele und die Formen*, p. 29.

33. See Lukacs, *History and Class Consciousness: Studies in Marxist Dialectics*, trans. Rodney Livingstone (London: Merlin Press, 1971), pp. 178–209.

34. See the discussion of this point in Richard Poirier, *The Performing Self: Compositions and Decompositions in the Languages of Everyday Life* (New York: Oxford University Press, 1971).

2. Swift's Tory Anarchy

1. R. P. Blackmur, *A Primer of Ignorance* (New York: Harcourt, Brace and World, 1967), p. 13.

2. For an interesting discussion of the general problem of the eighteenth-century writer in society and the consequences of this for literary history, see Bertrand H. Bronson, "The Writer," in *Man Versus Society*, ed. James L. Clifford (Cambridge: Cambridge University Press, 1968).

3. *Prose Works of Jonathan Swift*, 14 vols., ed. Herbert Davis (1939; rprt. Oxford: Basil Blackwell, 1964–1968), IV, 87. Hereafter all citations from the *Prose Works* are included in parentheses after the quotation. Quotations from Swift's poetry, identified in the same way, are taken from *Poetical Works*, ed. Herbert Davis (London: Oxford University Press, 1967).

4. Some of these points are examined with great perspicacity by Ronald Paulson, *The Fictions of Satire* (Baltimore: Johns Hopkins University Press, 1968), pp. 129–222.

5. Ibid., p. 199.

3. Swift as Intellectual

1. George Orwell, *In Front of Your Nose, 1945–1950*, ed. Sonia Orwell and Ian Angus, vol. 4 of *The Collected Essays, Journalism and Letters of George Orwell* (New York: Harcourt Brace Jovanovich, 1968), pp. 222–223. See also the comments on Swift's reactionary versus progressive political positions in (for the former) Perry Anderson, *Arguments Within English Marxism* (London: New Left Books, 1980), pp. 83–88, and (for the latter) E. P. Thompson, *The Poverty of Theory and Other Essays* (London: Merlin Press, 1978), p. 234.

2. Oscar Wilde, "The Soul of Man Under Socialism," in *The Artist as Critic: Critical Writings of Oscar Wilde*, ed. Richard Ellmann (1969; rprt. New York: Vintage, 1970), p. 259.

3. Lewis Coser, *Men of Ideas: A Sociologist's View* (New York: Free Press, 1970), pp. 20–21.

4. Ibid., p. 3.

5. Julien Benda, *The Treason of the Intellectuals*, trans. Richard Aldington (1928; rprt. New York: Norton, 1969), p. 57.

6. See, most recently, Noam Chomsky, "Intellectuals and the State," in *Towards A New Cold War: Essays on the Current Crisis and How We Got There* (New York: Pantheon, 1982).

7. Jonathan Swift, *The Drapier's Letters*, in *Prose Works*, ed. Herbert Davis (1939; rprt. Oxford: Basil Blackwell, 1964–1968), X, 81.

8. Swift, *Gulliver's Travels*, in *Prose Works*, XI, 134.

9. Swift, *The Conduct of the Allies*, in *Prose Works*, VI, 41.

10. Ibid., 55–56.

11. Ibid., 25.

12. Ibid., 103.

13. Erich Heller, *The Artist's Journey into the Interior and Other Essays* (New York: Random House, 1965).

14. Swift, *Drapier's Letters*, p. 89.

4. Conrad: The Presentation of Narrative

1. Joseph Conrad, *Complete Works*, 26 vols. (Garden City, N.Y.: Doubleday, Page, 1925), VI, 70.

2. *Lettres françaises* (Paris: Gallimard, 1930), p. 50.

3. *Joseph Conrad: Letters to Cunningham Grahame*, ed. C. T. Watts (Cambridge: Cambridge University Press, 1969), p. 129.

4. Stephen Mallarmé, *Oeuvres complètes* (Paris: Gallimard, 1945), p. 366.

5. Walter Benjamin, *Illuminations*, ed. Hannah Arendt, trans. H. Zohn (New York: Harcourt, Brace, 1966), p. 87.

6. Said, "Beginning with a Text," in *Beginnings*, pp. 191–275.

7. Sigmund Freud, *Collected Papers*, vol. 5, trans. Joan Riviere (New York: Basic Books, 1959), pp. 236, 237, 182.

5. On Repetition

1. *The New Science of Giambattista Vico*, trans. Thomas Goddard Bergin and Max Harold Fisch (Ithaca: Cornell University Press, 1968), p. 425.

2. Ibid., p. 96.

3. François Jacob, *La Logique du vivant: Une Histoire de l'hérédité* (Paris Gallimard, 1970), pp. 84–86.

4. Ibid., pp. 158–159.

5. Historians of science have evolved sophisticated techniques for reducing their dependence on the biological model; what they mean by "nascent moments" and "emergence phenomena" is highly special. See, for ex-

ample, Gerald Holton, *Thematic Origins of Modern Thought: Kepler to Einstein* (Cambridge: Harvard University Press, 1975), and Ian Hacking, *The Emergence of Probability: A Philosophical Study of Early Ideas About Probability, Induction and Statistical Inference* (London: Cambridge University Press, 1975).

6. In Michel Foucault's *Discipline and Punish: The Birth of the Prison*, trans. Alan Sheridan (New York: Pantheon, 1977), there is a quite remarkable account of the connection between ideas about discipline (taken from the army, schools, and the monastic orders) and the rise of the modern penal institution in early nineteenth-century Europe. As an idea penality is viewed as a correction of delinquency; punishment comes to be considered a naturalization of the physical brutality formerly administered to criminals. Prison society emerges then as a mock-family, uniformly celibate and disciplined of course. Curiously, however, Foucault never remarks on the resemblance, just as he seems undecided as to whether the prison is a new institution or a redeployment of old or analogous elements.

7. Hans W. Frei, *The Eclipse of Biblical Narrative: A Study in Eighteenth and Nineteenth Century Hermeneutics* (New Haven: Yale University Press, 1974).

8. Soren Kierkegaard, *Repetition: An Essay in Experimental Psychology*, trans. Walter Lowrie (1941; rprt. New York: Harper and Row, 1964), pp. 88–89.

9. Ibid., p. 135.

10. Ibid., p. 125.

11. Ibid., p. 136.

12. Marx, *Der Achtzehnt Brumaire des Louis Bonaparte* (Berlin: Dietz Verlag, 1947), p. 8. I have used the excellent translation by Ben Fowkes in Marx, *Surveys from Exile*, ed. David Fernbach (London: Pelican Books, 1973); the passage quoted from the German above appears in the Fowkes translation on p. 144. Henceforth two page references, the English first, will be given.

13. Ibid., p. 147/p. 15.

14. Ibid., p. 239/p. 117.

15. Ibid., p. 232/p. 117.

16. Ibid., p. 152/p. 20. There are some perceptive observations on Marx and Kierkegaard scattered through Gilles Deleuze, *Différence et répétition* (Paris: Presses Universitaires Franąises, 1968).

6. On Originality

1. René Wellek and Austin Warren, *Theory of Literature* (1949; rprt. New York: Harcourt, Brace and World, 1968), p. 258.

2. Werner Jaeger, "On the Origin and Cycle of the Philosophic Ideal of Life," in *Aristotle: Fundamentals of the History of His Development*, trans. Richard Robinson (1934; rprt. Oxford: Oxford University Press, 1962), p. 429.

3. Ibid., p. 444.

4. Ibid., p. 461.

5. Rainer Maria Rilke, *Rodin*, trans. Jessie Lamont and Hans Trausil (New York: Fine Editions Press, 1945), p. 11.

6. Michel Foucault, "What Is an Author?" in *Language, Counter-Memory, Practice: Selected Essays and Interviews by Michel Foucault*, ed. and trans. Donald Bouchard with Sherry Simon (Ithaca: Cornell University Press, 1977), p. 118.

7. A celebrated example of structural analysis is to be found in Claude Lévi-Strauss, *Mythologiques*, 4 vols. (Paris: Plon, 1964, 1966, 1968, 1972). The best work in stylistics, using "the history of words" as an anlytic universal, is by Michael Riffaterre, *Essais de stylistique structurale* (Paris: Flammarion, 1971).

8. Lukacs, "Reification and the Consciousness of the Proletariat" in *History and Class Consciousness*, trans. Rodney Livingstone (Cambridge: MIT Press, 1971); Barthes, "Myth Today," in *Mythologies*, trans. Annette Lavers (New York: Hill and Wang, 1972).

9. Macherey, *Pour une théorie de la production littéraire* (Paris: Maspero, 1966); Goldmann, *Le Dieu caché* (Paris: Gallimard, 1955).

10. For an interesting essay developing this point, see Paul de Man, *Blindness and Insight* (New York: Oxford University Press, 1971), pp. 51–59.

11. Vernant, "Greek Tragedy: Problems of Interpretation," in *The Languages of Criticism and the Sciences of Man*, ed. Richard Macksey and Eugenio Donato (Baltimore: Johns Hopkins University Press, 1970), pp. 278–279, 284–285.

12. Thomas S. Kuhn, *The Structure of Scientific Revolutions*, 2nd ed. (Chicago: University of Chicago Press, 1970); Georges Canguihelm, *Etudes d'histoire et de philosophie des sciences* (Paris: Librairie Philosophique, J. Vrin, 1968).

13. Foucault, "Nietzsche, Genealogy, History" in *Language, Counter-Memory, Practice*, pp. 139–164.

14. Foucault, "Nietzsche, Marx, Freud," in *Nietzsche, Colloque de Royaumont* (Paris: Editions de Minuit, 1967), pp. 184–185.

15. Jacques Derrida, *De la grammatologie* (Paris: Editions de Minuit, 1967), pp. 203–234.

16. Stephane Mallarmé, *Oeuvres complètes* (Paris: Gallimard, 1945), p. 366.

17. Sollers, *Logiques* (Paris: Seuil, 1968), p. 117.

18. Spitzer, *Linguistics and Literary History: Essays in Stylistics* (Princeton: Princeton University Press, 1948), p. 7.

19. Mann, *Doctor Faustus*, trans. H. T. Lowe-Porter (New York: Knopf, 1948), pp. 14–15.

20. Foucault, "Theatrum Philosophicum," in *Language, Counter-Memory, Practice*, pp. 165–196; Deleuze, *Logique de sens* (Paris: Editions de Minuit, 1969), pp. 292–306.

7. Roads Taken and Not Taken in Contemporary Criticism

1. *European Literary Theory and Practice: From Existential Phenomenology to Structuralism*, ed. Vernon W. Gras (New York: Dell, 1973); *Issues in Contemporary Literary Criticism*, ed. Gregory Polletta (Boston: Little, Brown, 1973); *Modern French Criticism: From Proust to Valéry*, ed., John K. Simon (Chicago: University of Chicago Press, 1972); *The Structuralist Controversy: The Languages of Criticism and the Sciences of Man*, ed. Richard Macksey and Eugenio Donato (Baltimore: Johns Hopkins University Press, 2nd ed., 1970); *Velocities of Change: Critical Essays from MLN*, ed. Richard Macksey (Baltimore: Johns Hopkins University Press, 1974).

2. Richard Poirier, "What Is English Studies, and If You Know What That Is, What Is English Literature?", in *Issues*, ed. Polleta, pp. 557–571.

3. See Barthes, *Critical Essays*, trans. Richard Howard (Evanston: Northwestern University Press, 1972), pp. 213–20; also his *Le Degré zéro de l'écriture suivi de nouveaux essais critiques* (Paris: Seuil, 1972).

4. Lionel Trilling, "On the Teaching of Modern Literature," in *Issues*, ed., Polletta, pp. 539–556.

5. Ignorance of Burke and of Peirce, Dewey, Kroeber, Lowie, Sapir, Sullivan, and Mead is mentioned by Macksey in *The Structuralist Controversy*, p. 320.

6. Jacques Derrida, *De la grammatologie* (Paris: Editions de Minuit, 1967), and his long introduction "L'Archéologie du frivole" to Condillac's *Essai sur l'origne des connaissances humaines* (Paris: Galilee, 1973).

7. Derrida, "Structure, Sign and Play in the Discourse of the Human Sciences," in *The Structuralist Controversy*, p. 271.

8. Georges Poulet, "Phenomenology of Reading," in *Issues*, ed. Polletta, p. 107, The essay was first contained in *The Structuralist Controversy*.

9. *Critical Theory Since Plato*, ed. Hazard Adams (New York: Harcourt, Brace, Jovanovich, 1971), p. 19.

10. François Jacob, *La Logique du vivant: Une Histoire de l'hérédité* (Paris: Gallimard, 1970), p. 19.

11. The other Lukacs, by no means inconsistent with the assertively Marxist Lukacs, is to be found in *Soul and Form, The Theory of the Novel, Die Eigenart das Ästhetischen*, and variously in his *Schriften zur Ideologie* and *Literatursoziologie*.

12. For analyses of these problems, see my "An Ethics of Language," *Diacritics*, 4 (Summer 1974), 28–35; *Beginnings: Intention and Method* (New York: Basic Books, 1975), pp. 191–275; and Chapter 1 above.

13. See Foucault's *The Archaeology of Knowledge*, trans. A. M. Sheridan Smith (New York: Pantheon, 1972), pp. 79–131.

14. See W. J. Bate, *The Burden of the Past and the English Poet* (Cambridge: Harvard University Press, 1970), and Harold Bloom, *The Anxiety of Influence: A Theory of Poetry* (New York: Oxford University

Press, 1973), as well as his *A Map of Misreading* (New York: Oxford University Press, 1975).

15. In particular Schwab's *La Renaissance orientale* (Paris: Payot, 1950), but also his *Vie d'Anquetil-Duperron* (Paris: Ernest Leroux, 1934); and Chapter 11 above.

16. Foucault, *The Archaeology of Knowledge*, p. 3.

17. Foucault, *Raymond Roussel* (Paris: Gallimard, 1963), p. 96.

18. Ian Hacking, *The Emergence of Probability: A Philosophical Study of Early Ideas About Probability, Induction and Statistical Inference* (London: Cambridge University Press, 1975), p. 17.

19. R. P. Backmur, *The Lion and the Honeycomb: Essays in Solicitude and Critique* (New York: Harcourt Brace, 1955), pp. 289–309.

20. Bataille, "La Notion de dépense," in *La Part maudite* (Paris: Editions de Minuit, 1967).

21. Peckham, *Man's Rage for Chaos: Biology, Behavior and the Arts* (Philadelphia: Chilton Books, 1965); Poirier, *The Performing Self: Compositions and Decompositions in the Languages of Everyday Life* (New York: Oxford University Press, 1971).

22. Wimsatt, "Genesis: A Fallacy Revisited," reprinted in *Issues*, ed. Polletta, pp. 255–276.

23. See Blackmur's four essays, *A Primer of Ignorance*, ed. Joseph Frank (New York: Harcourt, Brace & World, 1967), pp. 3–80.

24. Lucien Goldmann, *The Human Sciences and Philosophy*, trans. Hayden White and Robert Anchor (London: Jonathan Cape, 1969), p. 128.

8. Reflections on American "Left" Literary Criticism

1. *The Responsibilities of the Critic: Essays and Reviews by F. O. Matthiessen*, selected by John Rackliffe (New York: Oxford University Press, 1952), p. 9.

2. Paul de Man, *Blindness and Insight: Essays in the Rhetoric of Contemporary Civilization* (New York: Oxford University Press, 1971), p. 18.

3. Antonio Gramsci, *The Prison Notebooks: Selections*, trans. and ed. Quintin Hoare and Geoffrey Nowell Smith (New York: International Publishers, 1971), p. 327.

4. M. J. Crozier, S. P. Huntington, and J. Watanuki, *The Crisis of Democracy: Report on the Governability of Democracies to the Trilateral Commission* (New York: New York University Press, 1975).

9. Criticism Between Culture and System

1. Michel Foucault, *The Archaeology of Knowledge*, trans. A. M. Sheridan Smith (New York: Pantheon, 1972), pp. 23–24.

2. Ibid.

3. Stanley Fish, *Is There a Text in This Class?* (Cambridge: Harvard University Press, 1980).

4. Foucault, *The Order of Things: An Archeology of the Human Sciences* (New York: Pantheon, 1970), p. 327.

5. Foucault's criticism of Derrida is to be found in an appendix to the later version of *Histoire de la folie à l'age classique* (Paris: Gallimard, 1972), pp. 583–603.

6. Derrida, *Dissemination,* trans. Barbara Johnson (Chicago: University of Chicago Press, 1981), p. 63.

7. One should cite, as an instance of negative theology, the powerfully moving early chapters of *De la grammatologie* (Paris: Editions de Minuit, 1967).

8. Derrida, *Positions: Entretiens avec Henri Ronse, Julia Kristeva, Jean-Louis Houdebine, Guy Scarpetta* (Paris: Editions de Minuit, 1972), pp. 57–58.

9. Foucault, *Discipline and Punish* (New York: Pantheon, 1977), pp. 137, 138.

10. Foucault, *The order of Things,* pp. xiii–xiv.

11. "Réponse à une question," *Esprit,* 5 (May 1968), 850–874; "Réponse au Cercle d'épistémologie," *Cahiers pour l'analyse,* 9 (Summer 1968), 9–40.

12. Derrida, *Marges de la philosophie* (Paris: Minuit, 1972), pp. 31–78.

13. Derrida, *Of Grammatology,* trans. Gayatri Chakravorty Spivak (Baltimore: Johns Hopkins University Press, 1976), p. 161.

14. Derrida, "Cogito and the History of Madness," *Writing and Difference* (Chicago: University of Chicago Press, 1978), p. 38.

15. Ibid., p. 55.

16. Derrida, *Politiques de la philosophie: Chatelet, Derrida, Foucault, Lyotard, Serres,* ed. Dominique Grison: (Paris: Bernard Grasset, 1976).

17. Derrida, *Of Grammatology,* p. 158.

18. Ibid., p. 228.

19. Derrida, "Force and Signification," *Writing and Difference,* p. 20.

20. Derrida, *Speech and Phenomena, and Other Essays on Husserl's Theory of Signs,* trans. David B. Allison (Evanston: Northwestern University Press, 1973), p. 51.

21. Ibid., pp. 101–102.

22. Dickens, *Great Expectations* (1861; rprt. Indianapolis: Bobbs-Merrill, 1964), pp. 273–274.

23. Derrida, *Speech and Phenomena,* p. 159.

24. Derrida, "The Theater of Cruelty," *Writing and Difference,* p. 249.

25. There is a very fine account of *Glas* and of Derrida's verbal bril-

liance to be found in Geoffrey Hartman's two essays on Derrida in *The Georgia Review:* "Monsieur Texte: On Jacques Derrida, His *Glas*" (Winter 1975), pp. 759–797; "Monsieur Texte II: Epiphany in Echoland," (Spring 1976), pp. 169–197.

26. Derrida, *Of Grammatology*, p. 12.

27. Derrida's most extended analysis of style and sexuality is to be found in his "La Question du style," in *Nietzsche aujourd'hui?* Paris: Editions 10/18, 1973), pp. 235–299.

28. Derrida, *Of Grammatology*, p. 101.

29. Derrida, *Dissemination*, pp. 55–61.

30. See ibid., pp. 277ff.

31. Ibid., pp. 42, 52.

32. Ibid., p. 223.

33. See Derrida, *Marges de la philosophie*, pp. 209–246 ("Le Supplement de copule").

34. Derrida, *Dissemination*, p. 134.

35. Ibid., p. 221.

36. Derrida, *Marges de la philosophie*, pp. i–xxv ("Tympan").

37. Derrida, "L'Archéologie du frivole," which is his introductory essay for Condillac, *Essai sur l'origine des connaissances humaines* (Paris: Galilée, 1973), p. 90.

38. Derrida, *Dissemination*, p. 158.

39. Derrida, *Marges de la philosophie*, pp. 247–324.

40. Derrida, "Où commence et comment finit un corps enseignant," in *Politiques de la philosophie*, pp. 87–88.

41. Ibid., p. 73.

42. In his essay "La différance," *Marges de la philosophie*, pp. 3–29.

43. Derrida, *Positions*, p. 17.

44. Foucault, *Histoire de la folie* (1972), p. 602.

45. I have referred to this citing Derrida, in "Roads Taken and Not Taken in Contemporary Literature," Chapter 7.

46. Foucault, *Histoire de la folie*, p. 8.

47. Foucault, *L'Ordre de discours* (Paris: Gallimard, 1971), p. 22 and passim.

48. Foucault, *The Order of Things*, p. 304.

49. Ibid., p. 304.

50. "Questions on Geography," 1976 interview, *Power/Knowledge* (New York: Pantheon, 1980), p. 77.

51. Foucault, *Discipline and Punish: The Birth of the Prison*, trans. Alan Sheridan (New York: Pantheon Books, 1978), p. 26.

52. See my *Orientalism* (New York: Pantheon, 1978).

53. Foucault, *Archeology of Knowledge*, p. 53.

10. Traveling Theory

1. Frank Lentricchia, *After the New Criticism* (Chicago: University of Chicago Press, 1980), p. 24.

2. Geoffrey H. Hartman, *Criticism in the Wilderness: The Study of Literature Today* (New Haven: Yale University Press, 1980), p. 85.

3. Ibid., p. 244.

4. Ibid., p. 151.

5. Ibid., p. 301.

6. Richard Ohmann, *English in America: A Radical View of the Profession* (New York and London: Oxford University Press, 1976), p. 304.

7. Georg Lukacs, *History and Class Consciousness: Studies in Marxist Dialectics*, trans. Rodney Livingstone (London: Merlin Press, 1971), p. 90.

8. Ibid., p. 105.

9. Ibid., p. 186.

10. Lukacs, "Die Subjekt-Objekt-Beziehung in der Ästhetik," originally published in *Logos*, 7 (1917–18), republished in Lukacs, *Heidelberger-Äthetik, 1916–18* (Darmstadt: Luchterhand, 1974); see pp. 96–97.

11. Lukacs, *History and Class Consciousness*, p. 199.

12. Lucien Goldmann, *The Hidden God: A Study of Tragic Vision in the "Pensées" of Pascal and the Tragedies of Racine*, trans. Philip Thody (London: Routledge and Kegan Paul, 1964), p. 15.

13. Ibid., p. 15.

14. Ibid., p. 99.

15. Raymond Wiliams, *Problems in Materialism and Culture* (London: Verso, 1980), p. 13.

16. Ibid., p. 21.

17. Ibid., p. 21; emphasis added.

18. Williams, *Politics and Letters: Interviews with New Left Review* (London: New Left Books, 1979), p. 252.

19. Williams, *The Country and the City* (1973; rprt. New York: Oxford University Press, 1975), p. 141.

20. Lentricchia, *After the New Criticism*, p. 351.

21. Fredric Jameson, *The Political Unconscious: Narrative as a Socially Symbolic Act* (Ithaca: Cornell University Press, 1981), pp. 74, 102.

22. E. P. Thompson, *The Poverty of Theory and Other Essays* (London: Merlin Press, 1978).

23. Ian Hacking, "The Archaeology of Foucault," *New York Review of Books*, 28 (May 14, 1981), p. 36.

24. There is much evidence of this in the Winter 1980 issue of *Humanities in Society*, vol. 3, entirely devoted to Foucault.

25. The distinction is made by Foucault in *Radical Philosophy*, 17 (Summer 1977).

26. Michel Foucault, *The History of Sexuality, I: An Introduction,* trans. Robert Hurley (New York: Pantheon, 1978), p. 93.

27. Foucault, *Discipline and Punish: The Birth of the Prison,* trans. Alan Sheridan (New York: Pantheon, 1977), pp. 26–27.

28. Nicos Poulantzas, *State, Power, and Socialism,* trans. Patrick Camiller (London: Verso, 1980), p. 148.

29. Ibid., pp. 150ff.

30. A transcript is to be found in *Reflexive Water: The Basic Concerns of Mankind,* ed. Fons Elders (London: Souvenir Press, 1974). The curious thing about this book and the program—"the Basic concerns of mankind"—is that "mankind" is spoken for entirely by white European-American males. No one seems bothered by the claims for universality.

31. Noam Chomsky, *Language and Responsibility* (New York: Pantheon, 1979), p. 80.

32. *Reflexive Water,* pp. 184–185.

11. Raymond Schwab and the Romance of Ideas

1. The three issues of *Mercure de France* are no. 1115 (July 1956), 560–561; no. 1120 (December 1956), 637–691 ("Hommage à Raymond Schwab"); no. 1134 (February 1958), 242–309 ("Inedits de Raymond Schwab").

2. Schwab, *La Renaissance orientale* (Paris: Payot, 1950). Hereafter quotations from this work will be identified in the text by page numbers in parentheses.

3. André Rousseaux, "Raymond Schwab et l'humanisme intégrale," *Mercure de France,* no. 1120 (December 1956), 663–671.

4. Schwab, *L'Auteur des Milles et une Nuits: Vie d'Antoine Galland* (Paris: Mercure de France, 1964), pp. 48–51.

5. Rouseaux, "Raymond Schwab et l'humanisme intégrale," p. 665.

6. Schwab, "Domaine Oriental," in *Encyclopédie de la Pleiade: Histoire des littératures.* Volume I: *Littératures anciennes, orientales, et orales,* ed. Raymond Queneau (Paris: Gallimard, 1955), p. 213.

7. Schwab, "Au moins de coincidences," *Mercure de France,* no. 1134 (February 1958), 299.

8. Schwab, *Vie d'Anquetil-Duperron suivie des Usages Civils et religieux des Parses par Anquetil-Duperron* (Paris: E. Leroux, 1934), p. 3.

9. Ibid., p. 35.

10. Ibid., p. 96.

11. Ibid., p. 4.

12. Ibid., p. 8.

13. Ibid., p. 6.

14. Ibid., p. 87.

15. Ibid., p. 10.

16. Schwab, *La Vie d'Elémir Bourges* (Paris: Stock, 1948).

17. Schwab, *L'Auteur des Milles et une Nuits*, p. 17.

18. Ibid., p. 40.

19. Schwab, "Au moins des coincidences," p. 298.

20. Schwab, "Domaine Oriental," p. 108.

21. Ibid., pp., 182-183.

22. Quentin Anderson, *The Imperial Self: An Essay in American Literacy and Culture History* (New York: Knopf, 1971).

12. Islam, Philology, and French Culture

1. Matthew Arnold, "The Literary Influence of Academies," in *Essays in Criticism* (1875; rprt. London: McMillan, 1891), pp. 42-79.

2. Ibid., pp. 58-59.

3. Hans van Aarsleff, *The Study of Language in England, 1780-1860.* (Princeton: Princeton University Press, 1967), p. 166.

4. Ibid., p. 177.

5. Eliot, *The Leader*, January 1856; quoted in Leila Ahmed, *Edward William Lane: A Study of his Life and Work and of British Ideas of the Middle East of the Nineteenth Century* (London: Longman, 1978), p. 17.

6. Thackeray, *Vanity Fair: A Novel Without a Hero* (1864; rprt. New York: Random House, 1950), p. 529.

7. Ibid., p. 661.

8. Byron, "Beppo," in *Don Juan and Other Satirical Works* (New York: Odyssey Press, 1935), p. 69.

9. Duc de Broglie, "Eloge de Silvestre de Sacy," in Sacy, *Melanges de litterature orientale* (Paris: E. Ducrocq, 1833), p. xxix.

10. Antonio Gramsci, *Prison Notebooks: Selections*, trans. and ed. Quintin Hoare and Geoffrey Nowell Smith (New York: International Publishers, 1971), p. 10.

11. *Orientalism* (New York: Pantheon, 1978), pp. 224-225.

12. For example, Jacques Berque's recent book *Arabies: Entreteins avec Mirese Akar* (Paris: Stock, 1978), could only have appeared in France.

13. Renan, *Oeuvres complètes* (Paris: Calmann-Levy, 1947-1958), II, 760.

14. Ibid., II, 864.

15. Ibid., II, 760.

16. Ibid., VIII, 45.

17. Ibid., VII, 46.

18. Ibid., III, 757.

19. Ibid., III, 805.

20. Ibid., III, 847.

21. Renan, "Mahomet et les origines de l'islamisme," in *Etudes d'histoire religieuses* (Paris: Calmann Levy, 1880), p. 285. For the response of a distinguished Muslim (al-Afghani) to Renan's views on Islam, see Nikki R. Keddie, *Sayyid Jamàl ad-Dìn "al-Afghani": A Political Biography*

(Berkeley and Los Angeles: University of California Press, 1972), pp. 189–199.

22. Renan, *Oeuvres complètes*, I, 393.

23. Louis Massignon, *Opera Minora*, ed. Y. Moubarec (Beirut: Dar el-Maaref, 1963), III, 717–718.

24. Quoted by Jacques Waardenburg in his *L'Islam dans le miroir de l'Occident* (The Hague: Mouton, 1963), p. 259.

25. Massignon, "Inédits de Massignon," in *Louis Massignon* (Paris: Editions de l'Herne, 1970), p. 516.

26. Massignon, "Valeur de la parole humaine en tant que témoignage, 1951," in *Louis Massignon*, p. 476.

27. Massignon, *Opera Minora*, III, 788.

28. Ibid., II, 619.

29. Berque, *Arabies*, p. 178.

30. Massignon, *Opera Minora*, III, p. 772.

31. Georg Lukacs, *History and Class Consciousness*, trans. Rodney Livingstone (London: Merlin Press, 1971), p. 110.

Index